# Fundamentals of Business Communication



P. D. CHATURVEDI
*Former Professor and Head*
*Department of Languages*
*Birla Institute of Technology and Science, Pilani*

MUKESH CHATURVEDI
*Professor*
*Birla Institute of Management Technology, Greater Noida*

Pearson

*Assistant Editor–Acquisitions*: Vikarn Chowdhary
*Associate Editor–Production*: Amrita Naskar



ISBN: 978-81-317-7355-0

**First Impression**

Published by Dorling Kindersley (India) Pvt. Ltd, licensees of Pearson Education in South Asia.

Head Office: 7th Floor, Knowledge Boulevard, A-8(A), Sector 62, Noida, UP 201309, India.
Registered Office: 11 Community Centre, Panchsheel Park, New Delhi 110017, India.

*Compositor*: Technophilic Solutions

*Printed in India at Repro India Limited*

*To our dear children*

*Akbar, Ritu and Milky*

# About the Authors

P. D. CHATURVEDI

Dr P. D. Chaturvedi, former Professor of English and Head of the Department of Languages at Birla Institute of Technology and Science (BITS), Pilani, is an advisor at DAV Institute of Management, Faridabad. He was the head of the English department at NAS College, Meerut, from 1952 to 1965. Between January 1981 and August 1982, he was on Government of India's Foreign Assignment Service Deputation at the University of Al-Mustansiriyah, Baghdad.

A specialist in modern literary criticism, Dr Chaturvedi has been researching on the nature and process of communication as an expression of personality for a long time. His books—*University Essays* (1949), *Principles of Applied Grammar* (1954), and *Language Through Reading* (1989)—and his numerous other contributions to national and international journals are known for their lucidity of thought and expression.

Dr Chaturvedi's name appears as Piyush Dhar Chaturvedi (1928), an academic, in *Marquis Who's Who in the World* (5th edition, 1980, and 6th edition, 1981).

MUKESH CHATURVEDI

Dr Mukesh Chaturvedi, Professor, Birla Institute of Management Technology (BIMTECH), Greater Noida, has also taught in MDI Gurgaon, XLRI Jamshedpur, and BITS, Pilani. He has been the Founder Director of the Amity Centre for CRM, Amity Business School, Noida; Director, Asia-Pacific Institute of Management, Delhi; and Acting Director, IMT Ghaziabad. Dr Chaturvedi has also been a visiting faculty at Rouen Business School, France, and IIM Ahmedabad.

Dr Chaturvedi received his MMS degree and Ph.D. from BITS, Pilani. He is also an alumnus of the prestigious International Visitor Program of USIA, Washington, D.C.

Dr Chaturvedi's areas of interest include business communication, case writing and teaching, integrated marketing communications, customer relationship, direct marketing, corporate reputation, sales management, presentation skills, and negotiation skills. He has rendered training and consulting services to a large number of MNCs and private- and public-sector companies.

Dr Chaturvedi received MDI's coveted *Award for Excellence in Teaching* in 2005. His publications include *Managing Innovation and New Product Development, Business Communication Today, Managing Global Business: A Strategic Perspective, Buying Research, New Product Development*, and *Welcome Back! Coca-Cola*. He has contributed more than 70 papers, articles, and cases to leading journals, periodicals and newspapers, and has presented papers at several international/national seminars and conferences.

# Contents

# Preface

What is communication? Communication is what it does—bringing people together. How does it do it? By establishing a "commonness" among them. The message (verbally/non-verbally developed idea), the medium (carrier of the message), and the environment (surroundings in which the communication takes place) bring about this commonness, a situational relationship for a (common) purpose. That is how the authors would like to explain *communis*, the Latin origin of the word "communication".

If, for an individual, communication is a social need, for an organization, it is the lifeblood. If we, as individuals, communicate for 70 per cent of our waking time, an organization communicates for 90 per cent of its working time. If individuals communicate for their personal purpose, communication in an organization is for business purposes. Thus, the role of communication in an organization can be seen as a job of bringing all aspects of the business together—employees, customers, suppliers, intermediaries, public, etc. That is why, we need to understand business communication at different levels—the individual level, the organizational level, etc. Therefore, this is also how a book on business communication should ideally be structured—the concepts (for a basic understanding of the fundamentals of communication by individuals), the illustrations (to provide the organizational backdrop), and the applications (for the extension of communication in a business).

This book is the result of a sum total of more than 65 years of the authors' (combined) experience of teaching, training, researching and consulting in the areas of English language, report writing, technical writing, language skills, communication skills, presentation skills, negotiation skills, personality development and marketing communication. Therefore, most of the concepts, cases and application areas presented in this book are thoroughly examined and tested with a large variety of groups of students, executives and academics.

The book includes a total of nine chapters. It deals with the concepts of communication—the definition, the nature, the process, and the barriers of communication; upward, downward and horizontal communication; and effective communication—skills, objectives, approaches and projecting. Thus, the first two chapters—'Nature, Value and Process of Communication' (Chapter 1) and 'Communication Barriers and Methods to Overcome Them' (Chapter 2)—highlight the theory and basics of communication.

The next set of chapters deal with the two different ways of communication—verbal and non-verbal. Under verbal, come oral and written; and under non-verbal, body language. Thus, the chapters included are 'Oral Communication' (Chapter 3), 'Written Communication' (Chapter 4), and 'Non-verbal Communication' (Chapter 5). Also included are chapters such as 'Listening' (Chapter 6), which emphasizes on the importance of listening in today's world, and 'Organizational Communication' (Chapter 7), which focusses on communication in an organizational setup between the superior and the subordinate and also at different levels of hierarchy.

However, the extraordinary features of the book are the chapters on applications (Chapter 8) and grammar (Chapter 9), which are becoming essential components of the business curriculum in undergraduate courses over the world.

To facilitate the modern method of teaching a course like business communication, this book has been specially designed for undergraduate teaching. The logical flow of topics and simple, interactive language should help the readers appreciate an idea, or a point, as well as the totality of the subject better.

## ACKNOWLEDGEMENTS

We express our sincere gratitude to our students, colleagues, and the executive participants of numerous management development programmes, who have helped us clarify our concepts of business communication. We are also thankful to the distinguished scholars and authors, whose works we have used over the years in our teaching, research, and training. Their works have become an unconscious part of the ideas and thoughts discussed in this book. We ap-preciate the assistance of those, without whose help, this book could never have seen the light of day—the editorial team at Pearson—Praveen Tiwari, Vikarn Chowdhary, Amrita Naskar and Abhinav Chaturvedi.

We thank our prospective readers in advance, for they would be a source of improvement and further development of this book.

**P. D. Chaturvedi**
**Mukesh Chaturvedi**

# 1 Nature, Value and Process of Communication

*Upon completion of this chapter, you should be able to:*

1 Learn the basic forms and types of communication.

2 Understand the communication process and its elements.

3 Know the nature and scope of business English as a medium of communication.

4 Analyze the essential form of two-way communication in terms of sender, receiver, and feedback.

5 Learn how communication skills help self-development as a person or as a professional.

## INTRODUCTION

The word *communication* is derived from the Latin *communis*, which means "common". It refers to a natural activity of all humans, which is to convey opinions, feelings, information, and ideas to others through words (written or spoken), body language, or signs. George Vardman defines effective communication as "purposive symbolic interchange resulting in workable understanding and agreement between the sender and the receiver".[1] This interchange of information, ideas, and thoughts may occur via different modes: words (oral and written), signs, and gestures.

The word *communication* is derived from the Latin *communis*, meaning "common". It refers to a natural activity of all humans, which is to convey opinions, feelings, information, and ideas to others through words (written or spoken), body language, or signs.

Emphasizing the processes of telling, listening, and understanding involved in the act of communicating with other people, Keith Davis[2] says that communication is "the transfer of information and understanding from one person to another person. It is a way of reaching others with facts, ideas, thoughts and values. It is a bridge of meaning among people so that they can share what they feel and know. By using this bridge, a person can cross safely the river of misunderstanding that sometimes separates people."

## BUSINESS ENGLISH AS LANGUAGE OF BUSINESS COMMUNICATION

Business English may be defined as the form of English used for the purpose of business correspondence, and writing business memos and reports. It is English used in the areas of accounting, sales, finance, export, management, manufacturing, marketing, banking and insurance, international trade, etc. for communicating with their customers and clients. And it is used also by us when we write to firms on matters of business.

### Is Business English a Different Kind of English?

First of all, remember that there is no special kind of English known as Business English or commercial English for writing business letters, etc. It is generally held that good English is good business English and good English is the standard correct English which is normally spoken and written by the educated English speaking people.

However, before we discuss the essentials of business English, it would be helpful to clear two points regarding business or commercial English having its peculiar use of expressions, not found in the ordinary writing of letters. And the other belief that every area of business has its own set of English of course, it is true that in the early twentieth century the business letters were written in an impersonal, unnatural and high flown style in which firms were referred to as "your good selves", and writers always "begged to remain your obedient servant" or "yours obediently", and the letter was itself referred to as "for the favor of your kind consideration".

However, such phrases and expressions are no more used in contemporary commercial or business English. The present day business correspondence is done in natural English and personal form and tone. We will discuss the features of natural language form and tone later.

Now, let us clarify the second impression about business English that every business has its own set-type of English.

Every language has two aspects: structure and texture. The structure is the manner in which a thing is constructed as syntax; it refers to the arrangement of the different parts that form a sentence, such as subject and predicate or sub-subject, verb and object.

The texture refers to the choice of words, specially the technical words and phrases, such as "under warranty", "invoice", "shipping cost", "Performa", etc. in business English the standard English have the same structure: S-V-O (Subject–Verb–Object). But, the texture differs from business to business and from ordinary English to technical words which belong to the specific business, words, such as "remittance", "account payee", "debited", "indemnity", and likewise, make the language of business writing sound different from normal English, and, because of the use of the same set of technical words, the letters written within the same area of business read alike.

## SCOPE OF BUSINESS ENGLISH

Broadly speaking, in business, we communicate to: (a) inform and (b) persuade. These two goals are usually present in the mind of the person initiating the communication, as is seen in sales letters and advertisements. However, he or she may at times seek only to inform—as scientific writings do. Conversely, the person initiating the communication may aim more to persuade the reader, as journalistic writings and opinion editorials do.

### Communication to Inform

Communication to inform (expository communication) is directed by the desire to expose, develop, and explain the subject. Its focus is the subject of the communication. For example, consider these short, expository pieces of writing:

1. Farming provides most of the food we eat. Our chief food crops are cereals or grains. Cereals include maize, rice, and wheat. We also grow barley and gram.
2. Flies are our deadly enemies because they feed on dirt and rubbish. When they crawl over meat, sweetmeats, and cakes with their dirty legs, they leave all kinds of germs behind and, thus, poison our food.

Clearly, in these two passages, the focus is on the subjects "our food" and "flies, our deadly enemy". The logical presentation of facts informs us about the topics being discussed, and the danger associated with flies in the second passage is clearly conveyed.

## Communication to Persuade

A communicator may seek primarily to persuade the reader or receiver of the message. In such a form of communication, the focus is on the receiver. Essentially, all communication is a deliberate and intentional act of persuasion. A persuasive communicator wants the reader to understand the message and to be influenced by it.

Consider HDFC's "Savings/Current Account" advertisement in Exhibit 1.1, which says: "Now opening a Savings/Current Account with HDFC Bank is extremely rewarding." This handbill is reader-centric. The purpose of the message is not just to inform readers about a new savings and current account, but to persuade them to open such an account with HDFC Bank. Note how different adverbs and adjectives are chosen

**Exhibit 1.1**
The HDFC Advertisement

**Journal of Indian Literature**
**Established in 1954**
Editorial Office: Centre for Language and Learning
University of Delhi
Delhi 110007

Uses style and typical format of formal letter: no date, no personal salutation (by name) — Dear JIL contributor:

Attached is a set of reprints of your contribution to the most recent issue of JIL. — Opens with a statement of the main point

Expresses gratitude and appreciation — <u>We are grateful to you for your contribution</u> and <u>look forward to more such submissions from you.</u> — Persuades for the next contribution

Urges to subscribe to JIL — If you need additional reprints or information regarding the full issue in which your contribution appeared, or <u>subscription prices</u>, please contact Ms Agatha Luiz, Managing Editor, at the editorial office, whose address is given above. — Includes contact details for action

Closes on a personal note of appreciation — Again, let me reiterate my thanks to you for your contribution.

Best wishes,

*SChatterjee*
Somnath Chatterjee
Editor

**Exhibit 1.2** A Persuasive Business Letter

Essentially, all communication is a deliberate and intentional act of persuasion. A persuasive communicator wants the reader or receiver to understand the message and to be influenced by it.

to draw the reader's attention. The adverb "now" is placed at the head (beginning) of the advertisement. This is the most important position in the structure of the sentence or paragraph. In the subject position, the adverb "now" seeks to persuade readers that until now no bank offered the convenience, benefit, and satisfaction of HDFC Bank's savings/current account. Similarly, the phrase, "extremely rewarding" aims at impressing the reader with the extraordinary operational convenience, monetary benefit, and personal satisfaction HDFC Bank offered its savings and current account holders.

As one can gather from the HDFC advertisement, business communication often needs to be persuasive. Exhibit 1.2 analyses an example of a persuasive business letter.

## BASIC FORMS AND TYPES OF COMMUNICATION

One way to classify communication is according to the number of persons who receive the message.

1 Know the principal concepts of communication.

- *Intrapersonal communication* is talking to oneself in one's own mind. Examples are soliloquies or asides in dramatic works.
- *Interpersonal communication* is the exchange of messages between two people. Examples are conversations, dialogues, or interviews in which two persons interact (others may also be present as audience). An author communicates *interpersonally* with his or her reader, who is always present as a silent audience in the author's mind while writing. A letter is also an example of interpersonal communication between the writer and the person to whom it is addressed.
- *Group communication* can be among small or large groups, such as an organization, club, or classroom, in which all individuals retain their individual identities.
- *Mass communication* is when a message is sent to large groups of people, for example by newspaper, radio, or television. In this process, each receiver is a faceless individual with almost no opportunity for response or feedback.

Any communication that involves the use of words—whether it consists of speaking, listening, writing, reading, or thinking—can be classified as *verbal communication.*

Communication can also be classified on the basis of the medium employed.

- *Verbal communication* means communicating with words, written or spoken. Verbal communication consists of speaking, listening, writing, reading, and thinking.
- *Non-verbal communication* includes the use of pictures, signs, gestures, and facial expressions for exchanging information between persons. It is done through sign language, action language, or object language.

  Non-verbal communication accompanies the acts of speaking and writing. It is a wordless message conveyed through gestures (signs), movements (action language), and pictures/clothes (object language). Further, non-verbal

*Non-verbal communication* includes the use of sign language, action language, or object language. It is present in all acts of speaking and writing.

communication is characterized by personal space (proxemics), body language (kinesics), touch (haptics), eyes (oculesics), sense of smell (olfactics), and time (chronemics).

All these aspects of non-verbal communication need to be understood as they affect and, at times, contradict verbal communication. We shall discuss them in detail in Chapter XX.

- *Meta-communication* is when the speaker's choice of words unintentionally communicates something more than what the words themselves state. For example, the remark, "I've never seen you so smartly dressed" could be a compliment, but could also mean that the regular attire of the listener needs improvement.

## BASIC ELEMENTS OF COMMUNICATION PROCESS

The process of communication begins with a person's desire to share or exchange an idea, thought, or feeling with another person or persons. It basically involves a sender, a message, a medium, and a receiver.

### The Linear Concept of Communication

The earliest conceptualization of communication by Harold Lasswell involved the following five basic questions:

1. Who?
2. Says what?
3. To whom?
4. In which channel?
5. With what effect?

> Communication was considered a one-way process marked by the flow of information from a sender to a receiver.

Early ideas of communication considered it a one-way (linear) process marked by the flow of information from a sender to a receiver (see Exhibit 1.3).

According to this linear view, the receiver passively receives the message and acts as directed or desired by the sender. Communication is intended to control/manipulate the receiver. It is assumed that the message, while passing through the medium chosen by the sender, reaches the receiver without any distortion or change.

Sender → Message → Media → Message → Receiver → Action

**Exhibit 1.3** The Linear Model of Communication

### The Shannon–Weaver Model

C. E. Shannon and W. Weaver[3] were the first to point out that in actual practice, messages can be changed or blocked. Shannon's model of communication was first published in the *Bell System Technical Journal*. It was based on the mathematical or mechanistic view of the communication process, in which the basic problem is that the message received is not the same as the message sent. He attributed the loss to noise. The Shannon model, co-authored with Weaver, was brought out later in *The Mathematical Theory of Communication* in 1949. Weaver introduced the idea of feedback as a corrective counter to noise. However, in the Shannon–Weaver model, feedback was not considered to be an integral component because the model conceived the communication process as a linear act and feedback

> **2**
> Understand the communication process and its elements.

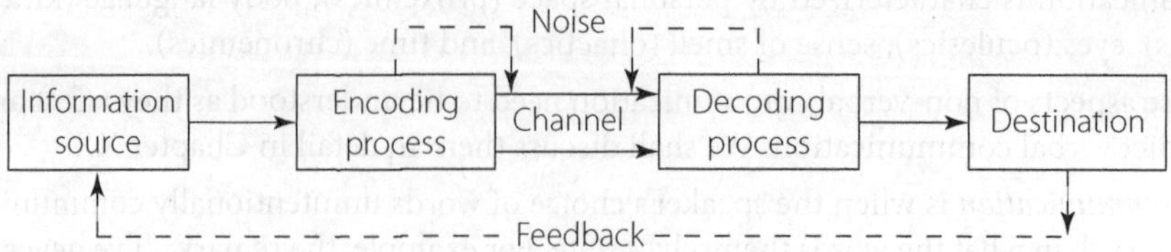


**Exhibit 1.4** A Diagram Based on the Shannon–Weaver Model

*Source:* Based on C. Shannon and W. Weaver, *The Mathematical Theory of Communication* (Urbana, IL: University of Illinois Press, 1949), 5.

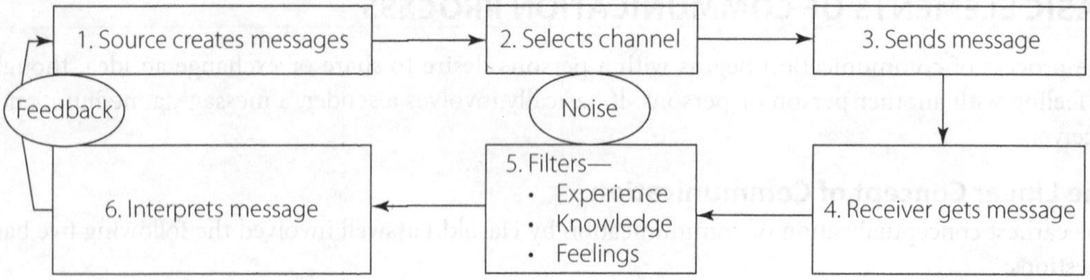


**Exhibit 1.5** How Communication Takes Place

as a new act of communication. This is why in the Shannon–Weaver model shown in Exhibit 1.4, feedback is represented by dotted lines.

The model is based on the idea that communication occurs only when the message has been received and that it should be received unchanged, as far as possible. This is, of course, a theoretical concept of perfect communication. In real life, filters in the minds of both the sender and the receiver affect the content of the message. To an extent, feedback corrects the distortions and helps complete the cycle of communication (see Exhibit 1.5).

The Shannon–Weaver model comprises the following basic elements:

- *Information source (ideation):* The communication process begins with the information source. The sender has some raw information in the form of outside experience. His or her intent changes that information into a message to be communicated. The source of a message, therefore, is the information source of the communication process.
- *Encoding (transmitter):* After having thought about the message, the sender puts it into words (verbal symbols or any other symbolic form of expression). This process is called encoding.
- *Channel (transmission):* An appropriate medium—oral, written, or electronic, in code, or a signalling system—chosen to send the message is known as the channel.
- *Receiver (decoding):* The receiver gets the message through decoding—by receiving, understanding, and interpreting the message.
- *Acting:* The communication process ends with the receiver putting the interpreted message into action, as intended by the sender.

> The communication process begins with the information source.

We see that communication completes a full circle, bringing together the sender and the receiver to become two aspects of a single purpose. It is this unifying process and role of communication that has made modern management organizations consider communication as an essential skill for successful managers. According to Davis[4], "The only way that management can be achieved in an organization is through the process of communication."

A group of people are involved in completing the cycle of communication, in which the receiver also acts as the sender of the feedback to the transmitter (sender).

- *Noise:* The process of communication is, however, open to "noise", which prevents or distorts communication. Noise may be described as any distortion or hindrance that prevents the transmission of the message from the (mind of) the sender to the (mind of) the receiver.

  For some communication theorists, noise basically refers to any external disturbance in the physical environment surrounding the act of communication, or noise in the machine used for communicating the message, such as telephone disturbances, poor print, or bad handwriting.

  Communication distortions caused by subjective factors, such as the mindset of the sender or the receiver, are attributed to filters.

- *Filters:* Filters are mental in nature. They include attitudes, beliefs, experiences, consciousness of personal status, and the ability to think clearly. Misunderstandings and different problems may arise as the message is transmitted through the filters of both parties, such as low interest or involvement in the message or distraction and fatigue causing loss of concentration.

## The Elements of Communication

The various elements of communication are briefly described to explain the process of communication.

The most important characteristic of a message as an element of communication is that it is organized, structured, shaped, and selective—a product of the pre-writing or pre-speaking stage.

- *Message:* The message is the information, written or spoken, which is to be sent from one person to another. Here, the word *person* represents the two ends of a system and may represent an individual, a group of individuals, or even electronic machines.

  The most important characteristic of a message as an element of communication is that it is organized, structured, shaped, and selective—a product of the pre-writing or pre-speaking stage. It exists in the mind of the sender (communicator).

- *Sender:* The person who transmits, spreads, or communicates a message or operates an electronic device, the one who conceives and initiates the message with the purpose of informing, persuading, influencing, or changing the attitude, opinion, or behaviour of the receiver (audience/listener). He or she decides the communication symbols, the channel, and the time for sending the message after carefully considering the total context in which communication takes place.
- *Encoding:* Encoding is the process of changing the message (from its mental form) into symbols, that is, patterns of words, gestures, or pictorial forms or signs. In short, it means putting ideas, facts, feelings, and opinions into symbols, which can be words, actions, signs, and pictures. The communication symbols are selected by the sender keeping in mind the receiver's ability to understand and interpret them correctly.
- *Receiver:* A receiver is the targeted audience of the message. The receiver understands, interprets, and tries to perceive the total meaning of the message as transmitted by the sender.
- *Decoding:* This is the act of translating symbols into their ordinary meanings. However, the total meaning lies in the meanings of the words (symbols) together with the tone and attitude of the sender as reflected by the structure of the message and the choice of words used by him or her (the sender).

- *Acting:* Communication manipulates the receiver to act in a desired manner. A receiver's response action shows that he or she has understood the message. Finally, the receiver completes the chain of communication by responding to the message.
- *Feedback:* This is the loop that connects the receiver with the sender, who, in turn, acts as a feedback receiver and, thus, learns that communication has been accomplished. Feedback plays an important role in communication. It helps the communicator know if there are any corrections or changes to be made in the proposed action. It also ensures that the receiver has received the message and understood it as intended by the sender.

In management, the decision-making process is greatly helped by receiving feedback from those who are directly concerned with the changes proposed in the communication.

In management, the decision-making process is greatly helped by receiving feedback from those who are directly concerned with the changes proposed in the communication. The process of feedback assures the initiator of the action of its correctness and impact.

## TWO-WAY COMMUNICATION

More recent conceptualizations of the communication process look at communication as a two-way process. A group of people are involved in completing the cycle of communication, in which the receiver also acts as the sender of feedback to the original transmitter (sender). Thus, both the sender and receiver play reciprocal and reversible roles, as in telemarketing or call-centre communications. Consider the two-way flow of communication illustrated in Exhibit 1.6.

The two-way concept of communication is more contemporary. It considers communication essentially to be a reciprocal process and a mutual exchange of messages.

The two-way concept of communication is more contemporary. It considers communication essentially to be a reciprocal process and a mutual exchange of messages. It makes no sharp distinction between the roles of the sender (source) and the receiver, because the same person plays both roles, often simultaneously.

The two-way communication process is also known as *transactional communication.*

The earlier linear view treated the sender as the determiner of the message and its meaning. The two-way concept involves the receiver as an active agent in constructing the meaning of the message. The meaning of the message is perceived in the context of the receiver's experiences, beliefs, and feelings. The intended and received meanings may result in common interpretations of situations, ideas, schemes, and events to the extent that people live and work together and develop common attitudes and viewpoints with regard

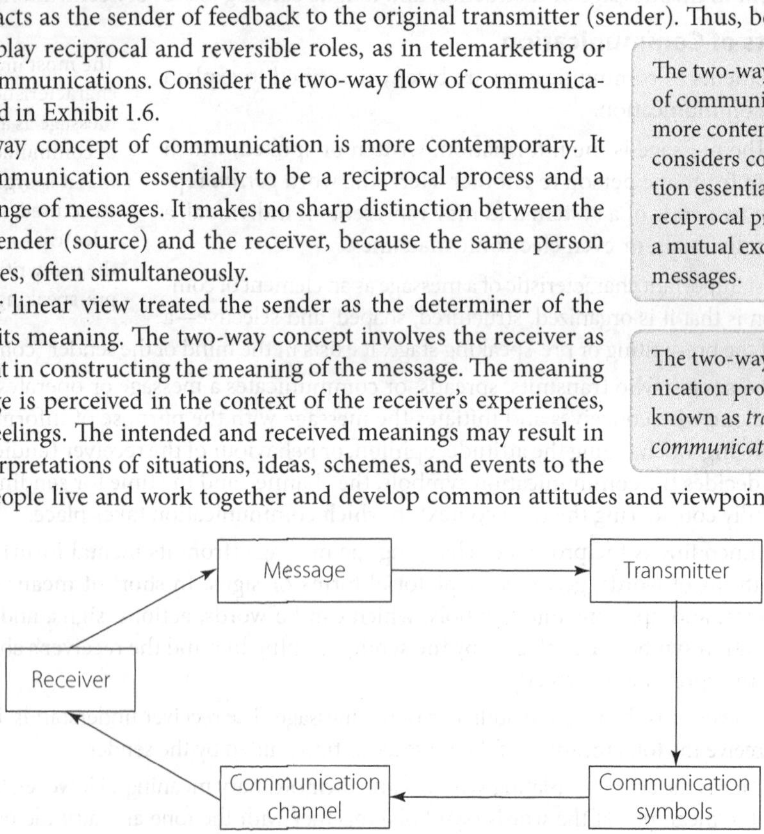


**Exhibit 1.6** Two-way Flow of Communication

| | |
|---|---|
| Communication source | An organization's news bulletin containing a policy to be circulated among all employees |
| Encoder | The editor/person who writes the policy |
| Message | The content (policy details) and the words/pictures used to convey the policy to employees |
| Channel | The medium—in this case the news bulletin |
| Decoder/receiver | The audience of the message—those for whom the policy is intended and who read the bulletin |
| Feedback | Impact/effectiveness of the communication in achieving its objectives |

**Exhibit 1.7** Transactional Communication

to their organization or society. The two-way communication process is also known as *transactional communication*, which has been explained in Exhibit 1.7.

Communication is purposive in nature. It achieves success by manipulating the target audience through information and persuasion to effect the intended action.

## VALUE AND SELF DEVELOPMENT

The skills of effective communication do not come automatically to most people. As a result, human beings are often poor communicators. Many people rarely realize that failure to achieve one's objectives in relationships, negotiations, or decision-making processes, is, to quite a large extent, owing to a failure in communicating one's purpose and ideas accurately to others. This may be a failure to communicate the content of the message, the form of the message, or both. Instances of such failures in communication are common in personal and organizational communications. It is common to hear colleagues or friends say something like, "Sorry, I did not realize that you wanted me to…", "I would have changed the arrangement, but nobody told me...", or even, "Well, I did not know you were to leave so soon…" and "But what was the point of this discussion?" Each of these remarks indicates the regret and disappointment felt by the speaker for having failed to live up to what was expected of him or her. Such remarks indicate a failure in communication. And when communication fails, the intended result is adversely affected. For instance, consider a situation in which the vice-president of a company asks his secretary to call an urgent meeting of all the managers, but, to his surprise, learns that the meeting has been scheduled for the next morning instead of the same day as he had expected. The secretary thought the "urgent" meant "serious" and not "immediate". In this instance, the receiver missed the purpose of communication because the vice-president did not clearly and precisely specify the time of the meeting. The secretary must have regretted that the vice-president's intended purpose was not accomplished because of this miscommunication. Sometimes, the failure to communicate successfully can be very disappointing, as can be seen in Communication Snapshot 1.1.

3

Understand how cultural context affects personal behaviour and business communication.

Executives seeking global business shores often join formal classes to get a feel for local cultures. Sensitivity to local cultures is necessary to stay in business. For instance, dinner diplomacy in China is often more effective than boardroom meetings for securing business. Those who understand this, like M&M, often manage to clinch deals over less-sensitive rivals.

**Communication Snapshot 1.1** An Instance of Unclear Communication

Ritushree is a regional sales manager with Titan in Chennai. She reads about an upcoming B2B international trade conference in Mumbai. She is interested in attending it and immediately writes to the national sales manager, Sumit Chakraborti, at the head office in Bangalore, describing the conference and its relevance to their work. Her note is given in Exhibit 1.8.

Sumit Chakraborti
National Sales Manager
Titan India Limited
Bangalore 560001

Dear Mr Chakraborti,

An international conference on B2B trade, which would be of great importance for us, is being held in Mumbai. The enclosed brochure shows that the business information to be shared at the conference would be of great value in expanding our corporate sales business. The registration fee is only Rs. 5,000, and the cost of travel and stay is about Rs. 8,000. Hence, Rs. 13,000 will be required per person. I am informing you about the conference now so that you can take a decision in time for me to make the necessary arrangements for train/flight bookings and hotel accommodations.

Ritushree

**Exhibit 1.8** Ritushree's Note

The national sales manager was thrilled to receive the memo and wrote back immediately to Ritushree. His response is given in Exhibit 1.9.

Dear Ritushree,
Thanks for informing me about the B2B conference in Mumbai. I will certainly attend it. Please make all the necessary arrangements for me as suggested in your memo.

Sumit Chakraborti

**Exhibit 1.9** The Response to Ritushree's Note

This response left Ritushree feeling quite frustrated. She was perplexed about her supervisor's decision to exclude her and instead attend the conference himself. Unfortunately, she did not realize that her message to him was not precise and clear. It was ambiguously worded, using phrases such as "importance for us" and "expanding our business". She was looking for permission to attend the conference herself, but she had failed to clearly say so in her memo. She started her communication by praising the conference, but instead, she should have begun by directly asking for permission to attend the conference.

Awareness about a client's cultural sensitivities often results in a positive advantage in business relationships. The phrase "cultural sensitivity" was first used in the *Harvard Business Review* in 2004, in the context of the cultural intelligence quotient (CQ). Shital Kakker Mehra, founder of Soft Skills International, defines cultural sensitivity as "an ability to interpret unfamiliar and ambiguous gestures in the way compatriots of the same culture would." Here, the term *gestures* stands for the whole range of non-verbal cues that accompany verbal communication between persons from two different cultures. In interpreting gestures, one can consider the human body to be part of the code for communication of symbolic messages that reveal an individual's thoughts and feelings. Gestures are often expressive of cultural context.

Here, it is important to understand that culture is not just behaviour. Culture is the received and accepted set of rules guiding human behaviour. These rules are absorbed and eventually become engrained in each individual's mind to the point where they are second nature. Persons with similar sets of social rules tend to behave in the same manner, which then becomes the normal behaviour expected in different situations. It is interesting to know that an individual's behaviour is noticed only when it deviates from the norm and becomes a noticeable behaviour in a particular culture. Thus, cultural sensitivity, which is measured by the cultural intelligence quotient, helps us to understand cultural differences. It enables us to interpret different gestures according to the rules of normal behaviour in that culture.

For example, here is a scenario illustrative of significant differences between cultures: a man travelling alone in a cab in New York will sit in the back seat, but in Australia, if a man is travelling alone in a cab, he will occupy the front seat next to the driver. According to Beatty and Takahashi, most New York cab drivers hold that if a single male attempted to get in the front seat, next to them, they would get out of the cab. For them, such an act would likely mean that the entering passenger is a thief. Australian cab drivers, on the other hand, feel that a man getting in the back seat alone is rather unfriendly and distant.[5]

Cultural sensitivity is considered to be very important in helping a person adapt to a foreign culture. This is why most nations include questions about their culture in their citizenship tests, assuming that a person who is aware about their culture will be able to adapt to it successfully. Exhibit 1.5 shows a few sample questions that a person may be required to answer as part of a U.K. citizenship test.

## Meetings and Social Visits

People's behaviour at meetings and social gatherings is nearly a ritualized act in various cultures. At a formal meeting between two persons or groups from different cultural backgrounds, people might behave according to their own culture. For example, in English one may say "Pleased to meet you" or "How do you do?", whereas in Japanese one says "Hajimemashite" (it is beginning). Differences in cultures are seen in the way people from different cultures behave on meeting someone for the first time. Japanese executives first exchange business cards instead of verbally introducing themselves. The card is handed over to the receptionist, without an introduction. The purpose of giving or showing the card is to announce the visitor's arrival for the appointed meeting. No verbal exchange takes place because the Japanese believe that verbal exchange should be for prolonged interactions. The exchange of visiting cards involves no time as such. American businesspeople find this practice rather surprising. Americans and Europeans usually approach the receptionist and verbally announce, "I am so and so" and "I have come to meet so and so". On meeting the person concerned, they would greet them with a "Good morning/afternoon/evening" and "how are you doing?", which is followed by an introduction

> Differences in cultures are seen in the way people from different cultures behave on meeting someone for the first time.

## Group Behaviour

Cultural differences are also noticeable in the way people in groups act when they are joined by a new person. In America, when a group of persons is talking and someone joins the group, the group drops the ongoing discussion as it is believed that the newcomer would have little interest in it or would fail to join in the discussion. In this matter, the Japanese follow the practice of continuing with the ongoing discussion and wait for the moment when the newcomer is able to join the conversation.

Several nations ask immigrants to take citizenship tests that examine their knowledge of the culture they hope to live in. Below is a sample citizenship test for the United Kingdom.

1. The United Kingdom has a vibrant popular culture. Which of the following is **not** a British musical group?
   - Westlife
   - Mis-teeq
   - So Solid Crew
   - Busted
2. Queen Elizabeth II, the head of state, celebrates an "official birthday", the date of which changes every year. What is her actual birthday?
   - 23 April
   - 14 June
   - 1 April
   - 21 April
3. You have a bought a kettle from a High Street electrical retailer. Under what circumstances can you demand your money back?
   - You changed your mind; you don't want it anymore.
   - It keeps switching off before the water boils.
   - You discover that a friend has already bought one for you.
   - All of the above.
4. The United Kingdom has a devolved government, which means there are special groups of elected officials who currently meet in both Edinburgh and Cardiff. Who is the first minister of the Welsh Assembly?
   - Rhodri Morgan
   - Jack McConnell
   - Peter Hain
   - Denzil Davies
5. Under working time regulations, after six hours of work, you are entitled to a break of how long?
   - 20 minutes
   - 30 minutes
   - 60 minutes
   - 90 minutes

**Exhibit 1.10** Sample Citizenship Test

4

Know the main characteristics of low-context and high-context cultures.

Of course, if the newcomer has high status, the group drops the discussion to pay attention to the newly arrived person. Thus, one could say that "Americans regroup, whereas Japanese join an existing group." Our attitudes, values, beliefs, social behaviour, and language crystallize in the crucible of culture. Therefore, to be able to act and respond correctly in intercultural situations, it is important to know the other individual's cultural background.

Verbal and non-verbal communication should be explained with reference to their cultural contexts. Edward T. Hall, an anthropologist, propounded the theory of strong linkage between culture and communication. While teaching intercultural skills to foreign service personnel in the 1950s, he developed the concepts of "high-context culture" and "low-context culture."

The kind of communication that dominates in a given culture relates directly to the type of the culture it is or, to be more precise, to the role of social context in that culture. Social context is interpreted as the network of social expectations that determine a person's behaviour. The rules act as social context and guide behaviour almost spontaneously, with little conscious effort on the part of the participants in the interaction. Context is a key factor in determining the effect of culture on communication. It implies consideration of the framework, background, and surrounding circumstances in which communication takes place.

## High-context Cultures

In a *high-context culture*, there are many contextual elements that help individuals understand the rules. Much is taken for granted while communicating. A person who does not know the unwritten rules of the culture may find communication confusing. High-context cultures are found in many Asian countries and much of the Middle East, South America, and Africa. People from these countries are more likely to be relational, collectivist, intuitive, and contemplative. This means that people in these cultures emphasize interpersonal relationships. Developing trust is an important first step to any business transaction. According to Hall[6], these cultures are collectivist, preferring group harmony and consensus to individual achievement. People in these cultures may be less governed by reason than by intuition or feelings. Words are not as important as context, which might include the speaker's tone of voice, facial expressions, gestures, posture, and even the person's family history and status. A Japanese manager explained his culture's communication style to an American in the following words: "We are a homogeneous people and don't have to speak as much as you do. When we say one word, we understand ten, but here you have to say ten to understand one." High-context communication tends to be more indirect and more formal. Flowery language, humility, and elaborate apologies are typical.

> In a *high-context culture*, there are many contextual elements that help individuals understand the rules. Much is taken for granted while communicating. A person who does not know the unwritten rules of the culture may find communication confusing.

> **5** Learn how to communicate across cultures with different concepts of formal and social behaviour, time, and space.

## Low-context Cultures

In a *low-context culture*, very little is taken for granted. Therefore, explicit statements and explanations are required. The chances of misunderstanding by those outside that culture are minimized. Low-context cultures include those of North America and much of Western Europe. These cultures tend to value rationality, logic, action-oriented behaviour, and individualism. They emphasize reason, facts, and directness. Solving a problem means lining up the facts and evaluating them. Decisions are based on facts rather than intuition. Discussions end with actions. Explicit contracts conclude negotiations. Communicators are expected

> In a *low-context culture*, very little is taken for granted. Therefore, explicit statements and explanations are required. The chances of misunderstanding by those outside that culture are minimized.

| **Low-context Cultures**<br>Examples: North-America, Germany, France | **High-context Cultures**<br>Examples: Japan, China, Greece, Arab nations |
|---|---|
| • More emphasis on accurate and correct information<br>• Detailed information and precise documents are crucial; the context is relatively unimportant<br>• Listeners try to gain as much information as possible<br>• The interpretation of the message should be unambiguous<br>• Decisions based on information and facts; objective data valued | • Seeks to appeal to emotions<br>• Lack of detailed information and precise documents, much information depends on the context<br>• Relaxed speaking and listening, no interference from listeners<br>• Listeners are free to interpret the message<br>• Decisions based on emotional factors; subjective relationships valued |

**Exhibit 1.11** Communication in High-context and Low-context Cultures

to be straightforward, concise, and efficient in explaining all actions literally. This is very different from communication in high-context cultures, which depend less on precise language and legal documents. Businesspeople from high-context cultures may even distrust contracts and be offended by the lack of trust they suggest. Knowledge of the culture of one's business associates helps set realistic expectations regarding the type of communication that is likely to happen. Exhibit 1.11 compares the characteristics of high and low-context communication.

## Time As a Cultural Factor

According to Hall, another significant characteristic of a culture is how time is viewed in that culture. In his book *The Silent Language*, Hall coined the terms *polychronic*, to describe the ability to attend to multiple events simultaneously, and *monochronic*, to describe individuals and cultures with a preference for doing things sequentially. The main differences between the two are highlighted in Exhibit 1.12.

### *Monochronic Time*

M-time, as Hall calls it, means doing things in a sequential manner, one thing at a time. Monochronic people tend to carefully plan and schedule their work. They are known for their time management skills. A monochronic sense of time is more common in low-context cultures.

### *Polychronic Time*

In a *polychronic culture*, human relationships are valued more than time. Polychronic people do not hurry to get things done, and they get things done in their own time. They are high-context people in their overall attitude towards information sharing.

> *Monochronic time* means doing things in a sequential manner, one thing at a time.

| **Monochronic Cultures**<br>Examples: North-America, Germany, France | **Polychronic Cultures**<br>Examples: France |
|---|---|
| • Do one thing at a time<br>• Concentrate on the job at hand<br>• Think about deadlines and when things must be achieved<br>• Put the job first<br>• Seldom borrow or lend things<br>• Emphasize promptness | • Do many things simultaneously<br>• Are highly distractable and subject to interruptions<br>• Think about what will be achieved<br>• Put relationships first<br>• Borrow and lend things more easily<br>• Base promptness on relationship factors |

**Exhibit 1.12** Differences Between Monochronic and Polychronic Cultures

> In a *polychronic culture,* human relationships are valued more than time. Polychronic people do not hurry to get things done, and they get things done in their own time.

Within western cultures people have different attitudes towards time. For instance, Americans and Germans are highly monochronic, whereas the French tend to be largely polychronic. Hence, being late to a business meeting is a much bigger faux pas for a German or American executive than for a French executive.

## Space As a Cultural Factor

Different cultures vary in their concern for space and social relationships within it. Hall calls the study of human concern for space *proxemics.* Concern for space primarily suggests personal body space. But, it also relates to space in other situations such as in one's room, in traffic, and in the office.

People are extremely sensitive to any intrusion into their personal space by others. But, the area of personal territory differs from culture to culture and relationship to relationship. This concern for proper personal space will be discussed in greater detail in Chapter XX. However, here we will consider it as one of the cultural factors affecting human relations and levels of comfort. For instance, a Japanese person may need less space and may stand too close for an American's comfort without realizing it.

This concern for space may extend to the level of territorial possessiveness. In fact, perhaps all territorial feuds and wars result from an overzealous concern for space. This is often seen in offices, where some individuals with territorial tendencies fight for exclusive use of their office desks, behaving as if they possessed the desk and were not simply using it.

People of high territoriality tend to be from low-context cultures. People of low territoriality tend to have less of a sense of ownership of personal space and, accordingly, boundaries have less meaning for them. They readily share their territory and space. For example, in buses or trains some persons offer to share their seats with others with little hesitation.

This cultural analysis should help us understand an individual's actions in the context of the type of culture to which he or she belongs. For example, the reason for a person being late to a meeting may not be laziness or lack of respect, but, rather, his or her having a polychronic cultural background and a more flexible attitude towards timings.

## MEDIA OF COMMUNICATION

Channel is the vehicle or medium that facilitates the sending of the message to the receiver. The medium of communication can be written, oral, audio-visual, or live. Again, the written medium can be in the form of letters, memos, reports, manuals, notices, circulars, questionnaires, minutes of meetings, and so on. Similarly, the oral medium can be in the form of a dialogue, a face-to-face interview, a telephone conversation, a conference recording, and so on. The channel (medium) can also be visual, such as hoardings, posters, slides, documentary films, television programmes, and advertisements.

### Communication and Electronic Media

The electronic media have made communication instantaneous and immediate across the world. The use of telephones, voice mail, phone conferencing, video conferencing, cell phones, and e-mail as preferred modes (channels) of communication has greatly accelerated the decision-making process at all levels. Their use connects the sender and receiver in a timeless and spaceless web of communication. In a way, the online message and its immediate feedback give distant communication the force and advantages of face-to-face communication.

In business, all these electronic modes of communication are used according to the need and purpose of the communicators. E-mail, however, is the most commonly used global medium of interaction today. Even within the same organization, managers and executives prefer to communicate via e-mail instead of phone calls. These modes of communication will be discussed in detail in Chapter XX.

### Communication and Social Media

Social media, according to Dave Evans[7], "involves a natural, genuine conversation between people about something of mutual interest, a conversation built on the thoughts and experience of the participants. It is about sharing and arriving at a collective point, often for the purpose of making a better or informed choice." These emerging online social media, according to Susan Bratton, richly reward[8] "our innate desire to connect with each other at a human level."

Internet forums, weblogs, Twitter, message boards, Wikis, podcasts, picture-sharing sites, and other online media connect and share information in a collaborative manner. Examples of social media applications are Google (reference, social networking), Wikipedia (reference), MySpace (social networking), Facebook (social networking), Last.fm (music), YouTube (video sharing), Second Life (virtual reality), and Flickr (photo sharing).

As a social web participant, the channels one is likely to use today are SMS (texting), blogs and microblogs, video sharing, photo sharing, personal social networks, event services, e-mail, white label social networks, Wikis, podcasts (audio) and collaborative tools.

Social media are popular because they allow collaboration and creativity. The audience of social media can participate by adding comments or changing the stories themselves. The empowerment and freedom of the audience to add or create new content makes social media a process and not a static medium. Unlike direct mail or television advertising, social media are "a collaborative process through which information is created, shared, altered, and destroyed."[9] In business, politics, and personal life, social media act as a "feedback loop". As the audience, we listen to it, learn from it, and follow it. For example, in the purchase funnel of "awareness—consideration—purchase", social media influence the customer's consideration to quite an extent by offering the experiences of other customers of that product. Participants believe the social message because it is based on natural, genuine conversation informed by the experience and wisdom of the multitude.

## REVIEW YOUR LEARNING

1. Why is communication important for good relationships and effective management?
2. Do you believe that the English used in business translations is a separate kind of English? Give reasons for your view on business English.
3. What is meant by standard English? Discuss its chief characteristics, with examples.
4. Discuss communication as a two-way process of exchange of ideas.
5. Comment on the importance of feedback in communication.
6. Discuss Shannon–Weaver Model of Communication.
7. Analyze the elements of communication.
8. Discuss the major difficulties in having effective exchange of ideas, information, and feelings.

## REFLECT ON YOUR LEARNING

1. Why have communication skills become an essential requirement for a successful career in any profession? Discuss with examples.
2. How does an interview/discussion conducted on television become an act of communication? Explain.
3. Show how feedback acts as an essential element in the communication process.
4. "The principle of completeness in communication requires that we answer all questions that may be put to us." Elaborate.
5. Why are human beings, in general, poor communicators? Can communication skills be improved?

## ENDNOTES

1. George T. Vardman. *Effective Communication of Ideas* (New York: Van Nostrand Reinhold Company, 1973), p. 3.
2. Keith Davis and John Newstrom. *Organizational Behavior: Human Behavior at Work*, 9th ed. (New Delhi: Tata McGraw-Hill, 1993), p. 399.
3. C. Shannon and W. Weaver, *The Mathematical Theory of Communication* (Urbana, IL: University of Illinois Press, 1949), p. 5.
4. Keith Davis and John Newstrom, *Organizational Behavior: Human Behavior at Work*, 9th ed. (New Delhi: Tata McGraw-Hill, 1993), p. 399.
5. Beatty and Takahashi, *Intercultural Communication* (New Delhi: Biztantra, 2003).
6. Edward T. Hall, *Hidden Differences: Studies in International Communication* (Hamburg: Grunder and Jahr, 1985).
7. Dave Evans, *Social Media Marketing* (New Delhi: Times Business Services, Wiley India, 2008), p. 31.
8. Susan Bratton, foreword to *Social Media Marketing*, by Dave Evans (New Delhi: Times Business Services, Wiley India, 2008), x, iii.
9. Ibid., p. 34.

# 2 Communication Barriers and Methods to Overcome Them

*Upon completion of this chapter, you should be able to:*

1 Learn about the different barriers in the process of our communication.

2 Understand the conditions for successful communication.

3 Realize the role of personality in the act of communication.

4 Learn how to improve ourselves as communicators.

5 Know the principles of effective communication.

## THE MAJOR DIFFICULTIES IN COMMUNICATION

The following are the main difficulties usually experienced by communicators:

- Ensuring that the interpreted meaning affects behaviour in the desired way
- Achieving accuracy in communicating the message
- Ensuring that the message conveys the desired meaning

The purpose of two-way communication is to establish understanding and rapport between the sender (speaker) and receiver (audience). However, the communicators (sender/receiver) generally experience the following difficulties:

- *No perceived benefit to the audience:* The receiver (listener) finds the message of no relevance or interest and, therefore, remains unresponsive.
- *Noise, outside disturbance:* To receive the message correctly, the receiver needs to remain attentive without being disturbed by any kind of physical, environmental, or psychological disturbance.
- *Variations in listening skills:* The ability to listen with comprehension is not equally developed in all persons. Some individuals, therefore, respond to communication by missing parts of the complete message.
- *Cultural differences:* The word *culture* refers to the entire system of an individual's beliefs, social customs, and personal values. It includes the individual's educational background and family nurturing. The problem of proper understanding arises in situations of intercultural communication because of the differences in cultures across the world.

- *Complexity of subject matter/message:* A difficult and involved message acts as a barrier to a smooth understanding of the message.
- *Time restraints, real or perceived:* Both the sender and receiver lose organized exposition and reception of the message if they are pressured by a lack of time.
- *Personal biases or hostility:* Prejudice and resentment towards the speaker condition the understanding of the message.
- *Difficult questions:* Questions regarding personal behaviour and management policies and practices may not be easy to answer. They are to be responded to with carefully considered honesty and frankness if the questioner is to be satisfied with the answer.
- *Sensitive issues:* A situation or subject that involves the other person's feelings and problems needs to be dealt with sensitively and carefully, because the matter may upset people. However, it may sometimes be difficult to avoid such sensitive issues entirely.

## Barriers to Communication

In communication, a psycho-semantic process, the word *barrier* implies, mainly, something non-physical that keeps people apart or prevents activity, movement, and so on; examples are social, ethnic, and language barriers or lack of confidence. These negative forces may affect the effectiveness of communication by acting upon any or all of the basic elements of the communication process and the sender/receiver/channel. The more commonly experienced communication barriers are lack of planning, incorrect assumptions, semantic difficulties, and cultural differences. Some other barriers of communication are:

> In communication, a psycho-semantic process, the word *barrier* implies, mainly, something non-physical that keeps people apart or prevents activity, movement, and so on.

- Socio-psychological barriers
- Emotions
- Selective perception
- Information overload
- Loss by transmission
- Poor retention
- Goal conflicts
- Offensive style
- Abstracting
- Slanting
- Inferring

Broadly speaking, some of these barriers can be attributed to the sender and some to the receiver. Barriers attributable to the sender are:

- Lack of planning
- Vagueness about the purpose of communication and objectives to be achieved
- Poor choice of words, resulting in a badly encoded message
- Unshared or incorrect assumptions

- Different perceptions of reality
- Wrong choice of channel

Barriers attributable to the receiver are:

- Poor listening skills
- Inattention
- Mistrust
- Lack of interest
- Premature evaluation
- Semantic difficulties
- Bias
- Different perceptions of reality
- Lack of trust
- Attitudinal clash with the sender
- Unfit physical state

A common barrier for the sender and the receiver can be created by the absence of a common frame of reference affecting the smooth interpretation of thoughts, feelings, and attitudes from the sender to the receiver in a specific social situation.

A common barrier for the sender and the receiver can be created by the absence of a common frame of reference affecting the smooth interpretation of thoughts, feelings, and attitudes from the sender to the receiver in a specific social situation.

Identification of a well-defined social context in which communication takes place helps both the sender and the receiver perceive the content of the communication in a similar way, with similar implications and meaning.

The physical noise and other faults in the surroundings and the instruments of transmission of the message relate mainly to the channel, but they may not necessarily distort the overall meaning of the total message.

Many of the barriers listed here are easy to understand. But, a few of them may still need further explanation.

### *Incorrect Assumptions*

All communications from one person to another are made under some assumptions, which are not necessarily communicated to the other party. They may turn out to be incorrect and, thus, result in communication failure. For instance, we often assume that others:

- see the situation as we do.
- should feel about the situation as we do.
- think about the matter as we do.
- understand the message as we understand it.

All such assumptions may be incorrect; therefore, one should try to verify them whenever possible. That would help the communication to be more effective.

### *Psychosocial Barriers*

There can be many types of psychosocial barriers to communication. The key barriers are discussed here.

### *Status*

Consciousness of one's status affects the two-way flow of communication. It gives rise to personal barriers caused by the superior–subordinate relationship. A two-way vertical channel is present in most organizations, yet few subordinates choose to communicate with their superiors.

> Consciousness of one's status affects the two-way flow of communication. It gives rise to personal barriers caused by the superior–subordinate relationship.

Similarly, superiors may be unwilling to directly listen or write to their subordinates and seldom accept hearing that they are wrong. Though organizations are culturally changing and adopting flat structures, the psychological distance between superiors and subordinates persists.

> The most important aspect of human communication is the fact that it takes place in the world of reality that surrounds us.

### *Perception and Reality*

The most important aspect of human communication is the fact that it takes place in the world of reality that surrounds us. This world acts as our sensory environment. While we are engaged in the process of communicating, our sense organs remain stimulated by the different sensations of smell, taste, sound, forms, and colours around us. All these sense perceptions received by our brain through our senses recreate within each one of us the world that exists within our mind as its content. Thus, there are two aspects of the same reality—one that actually surrounds the communicator from outside and another that is its mental representation (in his or her mind) as he or she sees it.

> Know why communication succeeds or fails.

The objects that excite our five sense organs/perceptions—eyes, ears, nose, tongue (taste), flesh (touch)—are called *signs*. Our senses respond to these signs and we receive sensations that pass into the brain through a network of sensory nerves. Our perceptions—the mental images of the external world—are stored in our brains and form our viewpoints, experiences, knowledge, feelings, and emotions. They constitute what we really are, how we think of something, or how we feel or respond to something. These stored perceptions colour and modify whatever our brain receives from any signs, data, thoughts, or messages. That is why these conditioning perceptions existing in the brain are called *filters*. The mind filters the message received from the signs and gives it meaning, according to individual perception.

> The objects that excite our five sense organs/ perceptions—eyes, ears, nose, tongue (taste), flesh (touch)—are called *signs*.

It is obvious that each individual's filter would be unique. No two individuals have the same or similar experiences, emotional make-up, knowledge, or ways of thinking. Because filters differ, different individuals respond to signs with different understandings. The sign may be a word, gesture, or any other object of nature; each individual will respond to it in his or her own way and assign the total meaning to that sign according to his or her filter.

> Our perceptions—the mental images of the external world—are stored in our brains and form our viewpoints, experiences, knowledge, feelings, and emotions.

The presence of a unique filter in each sender and receiver of a communication causes a communication gap (distortion) in the message.

In face-to-face communication, this gap can be more easily removed. In most cases, the speaker does realize that he or she has not been correctly understood through the listener's facial expressions, gestures, or other forms of body language. Alternatively, the listener might say, "Sorry, I didn't get you". Of course, much depends on how formally/informally the two are related to each other in the office, workplace, or life.

But in situations in which the audience is invisible, as in written communications—letters, memos, notices, proposals, reports, and so on—the semantic gap between the intended meaning and the interpreted meaning remains unknown to the communicator and also to the unsuspecting

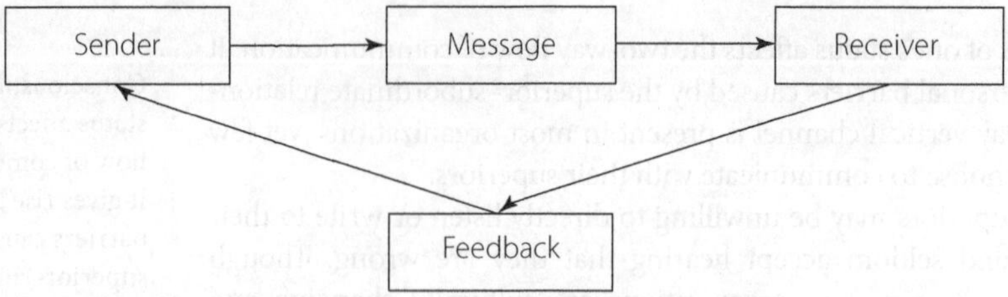


**Exhibit 2.1** Successful Communication

receiver who misses the total meaning in terms of the tone, feelings, and seriousness of purpose of the sender. The feedback does help the sender, but it may be too late.

### Improving Communication

Essentially, to communicate is to share information in its widest sense with others, in an intelligible, participative form through the medium of words (spoken or written), gestures, or other signs.

Two basic things stand out here. One, the message is to be both "known" and "understood" by others. Two, communication is a symbolic act, whether it is verbal or non-verbal. These two aspects—the purpose and nature of communication—act as the two determining influences in the practice of communication in all contexts of speaking or writing.

Herein lies the crucial difference between effective and ineffective communication. If something is communicated and is not fully understood by the receiver, then communication has been ineffective, not fully serving the condition of being understood. If the message has been understood, the response of the receiver—the feedback—indicates this.

Keith Davis[1] lays down the *Rule of Five* to guide the receiver to be an effective element of the communication process. "In the communication process, the role of the receiver is, I believe, as important as that of the sender. There are five receiver steps in the process of communication—receive, understand, accept, use, and give feedback. Without these steps being followed by the receiver, no communication process would be complete and successful."

Thus, communication can be considered successful when:

- the message is properly understood.
- the purpose of the sender is fulfilled.
- the sender and the receiver of the message remain linked through feedback (see Exhibit 2.1).

## PRINCIPLES OF EFFECTIVE COMMUNICATION

### The Seven Cs of Communication

Francis J. Bergin[2] advocates that there are seven Cs to remember in verbal communication. These are also applicable to written communication. They are:

1. *Candidness:* In all business transactions, one's view of a matter should be honest and sincere and should reject prejudice or bias. The guiding principle should be fairness to self and to others involved in the situation. Phrases that qualify observations with the words "my honest opinion" or "frankly speaking" indicate an attempt to be candid, open-hearted, and sincere. Honesty implies consideration of the other person's (listener's)

2

Recognize the techniques that help in communicating a message accurately.

interest and his or her (the listener's) need to know objective facts. Thus, sharing of thoughts should be characterized by the "you" attitude.

Candid talk also exhibits the speaker's self-confidence. In oral communication, confidence is a key element in creating an impact. When something is said without hesitation, it expresses a confident manner.

In everyday life and in business, we may see persons in power doing things, such as appointing relatives to important positions, neglecting merit in assigning jobs/functions, or becoming inappropriately close to an individual or a group of individuals. Such actions are bound to emotionally alienate others from that person. Out of consideration and concern for that person's long-term image and relationships in the organization, it is important to communicate one's view of such administrative unfairness in an unbiased manner.

2. *Clarity:* The principle of clarity is most important in all communications, especially in face-to-face interactions. It is not always easy to verbalize ideas accurately on the spot during conversations, presentations, or other oral forms of interaction.

   Clarity requires the use of accurate and familiar words with proper intonation, stresses, and pauses. Spoken language should consist of simple words and short sentences. Thoughts should be clear and well-organized. The speaker should know what to say and why. It is a clear mind that can talk clearly and effectively.

   > It is not always easy to verbalize ideas accurately on the spot during conversations, presentations, or other oral forms of interaction.

   However, in case of doubt or uncertainty due to lack of clarity of thought or expression, the listener can, in a one-to-one oral communication, seek immediate clarification from the speaker.

3. *Completeness:* Clarity is ensured also by completeness of message. In conversations or oral presentations, one can easily miss some parts of the communication. It is, therefore, essential that oral presentations, discussions, or dialogues should be, as far as possible, planned and structured. Therefore, when the speaker begins the presentation, dialogue, or address, he or she should ensure that all the necessary information that listeners need or expect has been provided.

   > In a situation where the interviewee has no information or answer or is unwilling to discuss a particular question, they should frankly express their inability to answer.

   The principle of completeness requires that speakers communicate whatever is necessary, provide answers to all possible questions that could be raised, and add additional information, if necessary, as footnotes. For example, in an interview, if an interviewee fails to answer a question completely, it could imply that he or she is deliberately sidestepping a particular issue. It could also raise doubts in the audience that there is something to hide regarding that matter. In a situation where the interviewee has no information or answer or is unwilling to discuss a particular question, he or she should frankly express their inability to answer.

4. *Conciseness:* In business and professional communication, brevity is important. One should avoid being repetitive. It is a common but erroneous assumption that repeating whatever has been said in multiple ways adds emphasis to the message.

   The examples in Exhibit 2.2 are show that spoken language tends to become wordy. Fewer words should not mean less meaning. Rather, it is possible to achieve intensity and concentration without sacrificing essential meaning.

5. *Concreteness:* Concreteness means being specific and definite in describing events and things. Avoid using vague words that don't mean much. In oral communication, one cannot draw figures, tables, or diagrams to illustrate one's point. But, one can choose precise words and speak with

| Superfluous Statements | Concise Statements |
|---|---|
| At this point of time . . . | Now . . ., or at present . . . |
| As regards the fact that... | Considering . . . |
| Because of the fact that... | As . . ., or because . . . |
| Are in need of . . . | Need . . . |
| In due course of time . . . | Soon... |
| Not very far from here . . . | Nearby . . ., or close by . . . |

**Exhibit 2.2** Examples of Superfluous and Concise Statements

proper modulation and force to make sounds reflect the meaning. For example, in oral communication passive voice is avoided because active voice reflects force and action. It also sounds more natural and direct. For example, no one says, "you are requested by me to visit us". A more vivid way to express the same sentiment is, "I request you to visit us".

6. *Correctness:* In the spoken form of communication, grammatical errors are not uncommon. The speaker can forget the number and person of the subject of the verb if the sentence is too long. Sometimes even the sequence of tenses is incorrect. And most frequently, the use of the pronoun is incorrect, especially in indirect narration or reported speech (see Exhibit 2.3).
7. *Courtesy:* In conversational situations, meetings, and group discussions, an effective speaker maintains the proper decorum of speaking. One should say things assertively, but without being rude.

| Incorrect Statement | Correct Statement |
|---|---|
| He said to me that I will surely go there. | He told me that he would surely go there. |
| Kindly explain to me this poem of Keats. | Kindly explain this poem of Keats to me. |
| I consider her as my sister. | I consider her my sister. |
| She shut the TV and then opened the taps for her bath. | She turned off the TV and then turned on the taps for her bath. |
| The stars walk as if the whole world belongs to them. | The stars walk as if the whole world belonged to them. |
| Shahzad has also claimed that a Bihar-based former junior minister and prominent Mumbai politician helped him evade arrest. | Shahzad has also claimed that a Bihar-based former junior minister and a prominent Mumbai politician helped him evade arrest. |
| The dealer agreed to either exchange the shirt or to refund the money. | The dealer agreed either to exchange the shirt or to refund the money. |
| How long has it been since you had your last promotion? | How long is it since you had your last promotion? |
| The crowd cheered him making double century. | The crowd cheered his making a double century. |
| Being an experienced manager, we are sure you can resolve the conflict. | As you are an experienced manager, we are sure you can resolve the conflict. |
| Sohan and her are equally brilliant. | Sohan and she are equally brilliant. |
| His wife is taller than him. | His wife is taller than he (is tall). |
| She is looking for who? | Whom is she looking for? |

**Exhibit 2.3** The Necessity of Grammatical Accuracy for Effective Communication

Courtesy demands not using words that are insulting or hurtful to the listener.

Courtesy demands not using words that are insulting or hurtful to the listener.

In business discussions, it is necessary to respect the other person by listening to him or her patiently and without interruption.

The speaker's tone should reflect respect for their listener or audience. The pitch and tone should be level and measured rather than aggressive; they should not suggest that the speaker is talking *at* the listener.

## UNIVERSAL ELEMENTS IN COMMUNICATION

There are some universal elements in all human communication:

3

Understand the universal elements in communication.

- *The communication environment:* All communicators act within the sensory environment around them, from which their senses receive competing stimuli impinging upon the content of communication.
- *Use of symbols:* All communicators use verbal symbols and signs such as words, body movements, facial expressions, and so on, to encode (and to decode) messages.
- *The mental filter:* All communicators/receivers of a message have to register, organize, transmit, receive, and interpret through their uniquely structured minds that have varying "filters", which consist of their experiences, thoughts, and feelings.

To understand communication better, we should know the following basic facts regarding its process:

- *Perfect communication is impossible:* Human communication is essentially imperfect. All our communication encoding and decoding acts are conditioned by the fact that a common mental filter is not possible. Meanings differ because filters differ. Therefore, no two persons involved in an interaction will perceive the exact same meaning from a message. What they tend to have is a "workable understanding", as Vardman puts it in his definition of communication discussed earlier.

The fact that the symbols used for communicating are imprecise in their associative meanings further contributes to the imperfection of communication.

Besides the filters, the fact that the symbols used for communicating are imprecise in their associative meanings further contributes to the imperfection of communication. Choosing correct symbols to encode an idea, thought, or feeling is not an easy task. We tend to often pick up imprecise symbols for encoding. This tendency increases the chances of misinterpretation or miscommunication between the sender and the receiver (see Exhibit 2.4).

Even the same symbols put in a different order or sequence may change the overall meaning of the message (see Communication Snapshot 2.1). Therefore, both parties, the sender and the receiver,

> Mr Balakrishnan, a heart patient, was considering two medical procedures: bypass surgery and angioplasty. His surgeon had told him that the angioplasty would cost slightly more than the bypass surgery. The bypass cost Rs 2.5 lakh. Mr Balakrishnan did not mind spending slightly more for the angioplasty, so he opted for it. But he was shocked to later get a bill for Rs 6.5 lakh. He was left wondering what exactly his surgeon's "slightly more" meant.

**Exhibit 2.4** An Example of Miscommunication

**Communication Snapshot 2.1** How Sentence Structure Affects Meaning

Consider the following sentences:

1. The letter has been dispatched by me.
2. I have dispatched the letter.
3. The police chased the crowd.
4. The crowd was chased by the police.
5. What are you doing here?
6. Here, what are you doing?
7. The dog wagging the tail.
8. The tail wagging the dog.
9. Only you have to be there.
10. You have only to be there.
11. You have to be only there.
12. Also, Abhinav is going to Paris.
13. Abhinav is going to Paris also.
14. Manisha too is tired.
15. Manisha is too tired.

The first sentence answers the question "Has the letter been dispatched?", whereas the second is an answer to "Who has dispatched the letter?". There is a change in the emphasis: the first sentences emphasizes the act (of dispatching), while the second emphasizes the doer of the act (the dispatcher). To understand this subtle shift in the overall meaning of the statement, equal levels of linguistic competence are required by both the questioner and the respondent.

Similarly, in the third sentence, we are talking about the police, whereas if we change the sequence of the symbols, as we have done in the fourth sentence, the crowd becomes the subject of communication. This can further be understood by considering the fifth and the sixth sentences. Though these sentences sound alike, they convey different meanings. The fifth sentence communicates the speaker's surprise about a *person's* presence, whereas the sixth is about the place where the person is present.

The seventh sentence indicates that the person is quiet, docile, and easily controlled. As opposed to this, the eighth sentence says that an unimportant thing/person is wrongly controlling a situation.

The ninth, tenth, and eleventh sentences show how meaning changes by changing the position of the word *only*. In the ninth sentence, the speaker talks about the *person* (you) who alone is required—meaning nobody else is required. In the tenth sentence, the speaker says that the person (you) would "do nothing" but simply be present; and, finally, in the eleventh sentence, the speaker wants the person (you) to be "there" only and nowhere else. The shift in significance relates to *who*, *what*, and *where*. (It may be noted that *only* modifies the word that immediately follows it.)

Similarly, the word *also* modifies the word that follows it or is placed next to it. In sentence 12, *also* is used to indicate that in addition to some other persons going to Paris, Abhinav too will go to Paris. In sentence 13, the change in position of *also* changes the meaning of the sentence. Here, *also* is used to indicate that Abhinav is going to Paris in addition to other places. In sentence 12, it signifies "in addition to the other persons"; in sentence 13, it means "in addition to other places".

In sentences 14 and 15, the shift in the position of the word *too* changes the meaning completely. Sentence 14 implies that Manisha is tired, like other people. But, sentence 15 implies that Manisha is overtired, or that she is so tired that she cannot do any work now.

Try to imagine real-life situations in which you would communicate a feeling of surprise or delight on unexpectedly meeting a friend when you did not expect to see them.

should possess the same ability to interpret the meaning of symbols (words) and their structure (the order in which they are used).

- *Meaning is not out there:* By now, it must be obvious that the meaning of a sentence or paragraph is in the mind and not in the symbols. Symbols (except onomatopoeic words) are arbitrary. They have no intrinsic meaning. They stand for things, but are not the things themselves. Their meaning is conventional, commonly shared by the people belonging to a linguistic community. But the literal meaning is something that is printed in the pages of a dictionary.

  Communication is a living act, performed in specific contexts, in particular situations, and with a definite goal. Thus, an effective communicator creates new meanings of symbols (words) by structuring them in strings of images of his or her mind or mental landscape.

  > An effective communicator creates new meanings of symbols (words) by structuring them in strings of images of his or her mind or mental landscape.

  Understanding this fundamental aspect of communication can help all receivers look for the meaning of the words (the message) that the sender thought of when choosing them. A receiver should not be satisfied with, "I think it means . . .". Instead, he or she should search for what the words must have meant to the sender.

- *Personality communicates:* Walt Whitman[3], in his famous *Song of Myself*, poetically brings out the dimension of communication. Of his poetic process, which is an act of communication, he says,

  I celebrate myself,
  And what I assume you shall assume,
  For every atom belonging to me as good belongs to you.

  In fact, communication in its final analysis can be seen as a projection of "myself"—how I think, feel, believe, perceive, and respond to reality. If communication is anything, it is indeed a mental representation of reality. The symbols of communication represent the perceptions of the communicator.

  In this regard, the complexity of communication further arises from a truth so aptly projected by O. W. Holmes[4] in his collection of essays, *The Autocrat of the Breakfast-Table*:

  There are three Johns:

  1. The real John; known only to his Maker.
  2. John's ideal John; never the real one and often very unlike him.
  3. Thomas's ideal John; never the real John, nor John's John, but often very unlike either.

  The real problem in communication is caused by Thomas's ideal John.

  In fact, it is difficult for people to communicate effectively unless they have a correct knowledge of themselves. Understanding how we see ourselves is the first step in improving our ability to communicate; we can improve this understanding by closely examining our own self-concept.

  According to psychologists, there are three aspects of self-concept:

  1. The me that I know.
  2. The me that I wish I were.
  3. The me that I want others to see.

Some people are so perfect in projecting images of themselves to others that the real person is never displayed. This art can be advantageous to a manager and his or her personal communication skills, but if practised to the extreme can prevent effective communication and understanding.

> Some people are so perfect in projecting images of themselves to others that the real person is never displayed.

To be effective as the audience (receiver), one should follow Whitman's wisdom and practise "what I assume you shall assume". This process is also known as "empathy"—the power or the state of imagining oneself to be another person and sharing his or her ideas and feelings. Empathy is needed for listening, and is also a necessary state of mind while encoding. It allows the communicator to realize the audience's (receiver's) expectations, fears, emotions, needs, level of learning/knowledge, and, above all, state of mind. It is only through reciprocal empathy that people can communicate effectively in different contexts of life and business.

## REVIEW YOUR LEARNING

1. Discuss some important barriers in the communication process.
2. Explain the element of noise as one of the psychological barriers in perfect communication.
3. Do you accept that perfect communication between two human beings is impossible to achieve?
4. Discuss how barriers can be largely overcome.
5. Discuss the three conditions when communication can be considered to be successful.
6. Explain Francis J. Bergin's concept of clarity as a principle of effective communication.
7. What is conciseness? Give some examples of concise statements.
8. Discuss how a change in the order of words changes a statement's meaning.

## REFLECT ON YOUR LEARNING

1. Communication is a way of changing other person's way of thinking. Discuss.
2. "Meaning of a message is not out there," it is in the receiver's mind. Discuss.
3. Consider the role of personality in communication.
4. "The principle of completeness in communication requires that we answer all questions that may be put to us". Discuss.
5. "Sender can improve effectiveness of communication by planning the whole thing". Mention the things the sender should plan.

## ENDNOTES

1. Keith Davis and John Nemstorm, *Organizational Behaviour: Human Behaviour at work*, 9th ed. (New Delhi: Tata McGraw-Hill, 1993), pp. 402-403.
2. Francis J. Bergin, *Practical Communication* (New Jersey: Financial Times Prentice Hall, 1981).
3. Walt Whitman, *Leaves of Grass* (New Delhi: Allied Publishers, 1959), p. 25.
4. O. W. Holmes, "Autocrat of the Breakfast-Table", *The Atlantic Monthly* (1857).

# 3 Oral Communication

*Upon completion of this chapter, you should be able to:*

1. Understand the nature and importance of oral communication in human transactions in business and social life.
2. Learn the key skills of oral communication for effective conversation.
3. Study the prosodic features of English speech.
4. Learn to use the falling or rising tone as required by the nature and purpose of our statement.
5. Know the characteristics and principles of successful oral communication.

## WHAT IS ORAL COMMUNICATION?

Oral communication, also known as verbal communication, is the interchange of verbal messages between a sender and receiver. It is more immediate than written communication. It is also more natural and informal.

1 Understand the nature and importance of oral communication in business transactions and personal interactions.

In human development, speech precedes writing. Children first learn to speak, and then, much later, develop the ability to read and write. The ability to speak/articulate single words and later speak groups of words in meaningful sequence comes to children in the course of their growth. This ability develops from listening to verbal sounds (words). As compared to written communication, therefore, the ability to communicate through the spoken word (speech) is a naturally developing ability (barring medical abnormalities).

In business, oral communication is used more than written communication. A study of executive working hours showed that 70 per cent of an executive's time is spent on communicating. Forty-five per cent of this time is spent listening, 30 per cent is spent on speaking, 16 per cent on reading, and 9 per cent on writing. As 75 per cent executive communication is oral, it is advisable that executives develop their listening and speaking (oral communication) skills.

## IMPORTANCE AND OBJECTIVES OF ORAL COMMUNICATION IN BUSINESS

A manager's maximum time is devoted to oral communication. He or she is often engaged in one of the following tasks: meetings, discussions, negotiations, seminars, presentations, interviews, peer conversations, providing instructions, and telephone conversations. All these business activities, except telephone conversations, involve *face-to-face* verbal communication. A telephone conversation is one-to-one oral communication that requires skillful control of tone, voice, and pitch, and precise use of words.

In business transactions that involve face-to-face interaction between individuals or groups of individuals, it is not enough to be able to talk, discuss, converse, argue, or negotiate an issue. A manager should be able to do all these persuasively, effectively, and convincingly. But, to be convincing, he or she must know and apply the skills of oral communication.

A manager should be able to converse or discuss persuasively, effectively, and convincingly.

| ***Oral Communication*** | ***Written Communication*** |
|---|---|
| | ***Advantages*** |
| More personal and informal | Better for complex and difficult subjects, facts, and opinions |
| Makes immediate impact | Can be read at the receiver's convenience or pleasure |
| Provides opportunity for interaction and feedback | Can be circulated |
| Helps the speaker correct himself or herself (and his or her message) according to the feedback and non-verbal cues received from the receiver | Provides opportunity to refer back to a more permanent record |
| Better for conveying feelings and emotions | Better for keeping records of messages exchanged |
| | Can be revised before transmitting |
| | ***Limitations*** |
| Demands ability to think coherently while speaking | Immediate feedback is not available for correction on the spot |
| A word once uttered cannot be taken back | Many people do not like reading, especially official or business messages |
| Hard to control voice pitch and tone, especially when stressed, excited, or angry | More impersonal and remote |
| Very difficult to be conscious of body language | The reader is not helped by non-verbal cues that contribute to the total message |
| | Do not know if the message has been read |
| | Is more time consuming[1] |

**Exhibit 3.1** Comparative Advantages and Limitations of Oral and Written Communication

Managers face difficulties in resolving the problems of workers and influencing others through dialogue and personal discussions. They need oral communication skills that include being able to:

- Solve problems
- Resolve conflicts
- Influence people to work together
- Persuade others to be involved in organizational goals
- Be assertive without being aggressive
- Listen thoughtfully
- Negotiate effectively
- Make proposals

These skills include developing the necessary tact to work effectively for mutual satisfaction in complex situations. Broadly speaking, one has to know when to talk; when not to talk but to listen; how to talk (the tone, pitch, and modulation); how to interpret the listener's facial expressions, physical gestures, movements, and attitude; and how to be aware of one's own *body talk* (leakage), which consciously or unconsciously sends signals to the listener. It is said that it does not matter what you say, but rather, how you say it. This includes one's choice of words, level of confidence, and sincerity.

> It is said that it does not matter what you say, but rather, how you say it.

## USE OF ENGLISH IN ORAL COMMUNICATION

Most educated Indians understand and write English sufficiently well. But, they often face difficulty in speaking in English fluently and in following British/American and other foreign speakers effortlessly and correctly. They tend to miss the intended meaning communicated by the speaker's stress on words, phrases, and sentences, and deliberate pauses in between the utterance of words and sentences. This limitation of Indian speakers of English is natural.

Basically speaking, English should not only be read, but also carefully listened to as a rhythm of rising and falling sound patterns. Its rhythmic movement is meaningful. It is produced by word stress and sentence stress, and pauses.

### The Phoneme

Phoneme is the smallest unit of speech that can be used to make one word different from another word, such as the "b" and "p" in "big" and "pig". The first need of spoken English is that we hear and speak the sounds of English speech correctly and distinctly. Otherwise we may hear big as pig and pig as big.

### Sounds of English Speech

There are 44 sounds of English speech corresponding to 26 letters (alphabet) of written English.

Just as there are five vowels (a, e, i, o, u) and twenty one consonants in the written form of English, there are twenty vowel sounds and twenty four consonant sounds in spoken English, called phones. They form phonemes which are the smallest meaningful units of sound that distinguish one word from another (e.g., p, b, d, t in the English words pad, pat, bad, bat). Therefore, we receive a different word if we hear "p" for "b" or "b" as "p".

## Phonetic Symbols: The IPA Symbols

These 44 English sounds are graphically represented by phonetic symbols, developed by a body of experts, known as International Phonetic Association. To distinguish the letter from its sound, the IPA symbol of the sound is written between two strokes. For example, the sound of letter "m" is written as |m|. Therefore, m refers to the letter and |m| refers to its sound.

## Classification of Sounds

All speech sounds are normally divided into vowels and consonants. The 44 sounds of English are divided into 20 vowels and 24 consonants. The vowels are sub divided into 12 pure vowels and 8 diphthongs. The 24 consonants are divided into 15 voiced and 9 unvoiced consonants.

### *The Description of Vowels*

When a vowel is spoken, the air passes through the mouth freely. The air passage remains open and the production of vowels is not accompanied by any sound of friction. All other sounds are classified as consonants.

### *The Description of Consonant Sounds*

The twenty four consonant sounds in English are described according to the nature of the air-stream. the place and manner of articulation, and the vibration of the vocal chords.

(i) Pulmonic air-stream: If the air stream moved the lungs it is called Pulmonic air. It is known as egressive, that is, coming out, or ingressive, going in.
All English sounds are produced by egressive air stream mechanism.

(ii) Voiced/voiceless sound: Do the vocal chords vibrate or not? Voiced sounds are produced by using the vocal chords. For example, |d| and |g| are voiced consonants. The vocal chords vibrate while speaking them. Voiceless sounds are produced without using the vocal chords. For example, |p| and |k| are voiceless consonants. Other voiceless consonants are : |p, t, k, ts, f Q, s, S, h|.
The rest are voiced.

(iii) Oral sounds

(iv) Nasal sounds

(v) Nasalized sounds

(vi) Place of sound

(vii) Manner of articulation

The above classification of sounds is technical. It is based on the mechanics of producing different sounds of English speech. It is a subject of study by itself, known as Phonetics. Here, our purpose, however, is not to go into details of phonetics as such. We seek to know how a word and its meaning change by the change of a single sound segment.

## The Study of Phoneme

Phoneme, the smallest unit of speech, capable of creating a new word may be known by you by forming minimal pairs of words which differ in terms of only one sound segment like: mat, hat, get, set, big, fig, reed, need, debt, wet. We have got from this set of words ten English phonemes |m, h, g, s, b, t, f, t, r, n, d, w|. You can learn more phonemes by forming similar pairs of words.

## The Syllable

After phoneme, the next higher unit of sound is syllable. Syllable is defined as a unit of pronunciation uttered without interruption, forming the whole or a part of a word and usually having one vowel sound often with a consonant. For example, there is one syllable in man, there are two in woman, and three in womanly. Practice hearing the number of syllables in each word. For example, im-por-tance – 3 syllables, animal – 3 syllables, quiet – 2 syllables.

## Prosodic Features of an Utterance

English speech is rhythmic. A lot of meaning is gained by the study of speech rhythms. In spoken English the patterns of sounds and rhythm form a part of meaning of words. It is studied under the following prosodic features of an utterance:

1. Length
2. Stress
3. Pitch and Intonation

### *Length*

Length is shown by the duration and movement of an utterance. For example, hear the following two utterances, both having 5 syllables each:

(i) My aunt is away. (5)

(ii) Watch dogs catch much meat. (5)

The second utterance about watch dogs takes more time to complete than the first utterance about aunt.

The pace of movement of speech depends on the shape of words. For instance, in the first utterance, 3 words begin with vowel sounds which are swiftly uttered, whereas in the second utterance, all the words begin with consonants which require repeated adjustment of mouth. From the communication point of view, pace of movement of speech shows the movement of the speaker's ideas. The length of an utterance is a non-verbal clue to the speaker's sense of urgency and haste.

### *Stress*

The term stress describes the force or intensity or air pressure in uttering a word or a part of a word or a sentence. Stress is used to lay emphasis on the word and its meaning.

### *Word Stress*

The stressed part of a word is marked with a raised stroke before it, like, 'conduct, con-'duct, 'pre-sent, pre-'sent, pro-'duction, 'management, 'always, 'asking. The place of stress in single syllable words is fixed. We should practice to pronounce the single words according to the stress they have. But, we do not speak in monosyllabic words alone. Our speech is a continuous rhythmic flow of stressed and unstressed syllables. In continuous speech, the stressed syllables are spoken with emphasis and length and the unstressed syllables uttered between the stressed syllables are shortened because they are weak. The common practice is to stress the word or its part according to the force or importance we attach to it. It is important to know that communication suffers in its clarity and effectiveness if the right word or if its right part is not rightly stressed.

For example, the meaning of the following sentence changes as we change the stress from one word to another:

1. **You** have to go there. (no one else)
2. You have **to go** there. (do nothing else)
3. You have to go **there**. (not to any other place)

This aspect of stressing the significant segments of speech (utterance) needs to be understood for effective communication.

### *Stressed and Unstressed Parts of Speech*

As a general guidance, you may remember the following classification of parts of speech which usually are stressed or unstressed. Words which are not stressed:

- articles
- personal pronouns
- helping verbs
- conjunctions
- prepositions

In continuous speech, the above words are spoken in their weak forms. Like and is spoken as |on|, or of as |or|.

The words which receive stress are:

- nouns
- main verbs
- adjectives
- adverbs
- interrogatives
- demonstratives
- negative markers
- interjections
- numerals

## Pitch and Intonation

Pitch and intonation, the rise and fall in voice while speaking is the most meaningful element in oral communication. The manner of utterance conveys more than the verbal meaning of words spoken. The speaker's intonation pattern, the sing-song way, the rhythm of speaking communicate his/her mood, attitude, sincerity, and seriousness towards the listener and the subject being discussed.

## The Rhythmic Patterns of English Speech

English is spoken in a rhythmic way. The speaker's voice keeps rising and falling continuously in a partnered way. There are several rhythmic patterns of English speech. But the two patterns which are of interest to us are:

(i) The falling tone
(ii) The rising tone

As the terms falling and rising indicate, in the case of falling tone the level, that is to say, the pitch of voice falls at the end of the sentence, and in the case of rising tone, the pitch rises at the end. In fact, the nature of the tone depends on the stress pattern of the last stressed syllable in the sentence-uttered. These two tones communicate two opposite attitudes of the speaker. Their appropriate use is of crucial importance in business transactions. The lack of knowledge about the meaning conveyed by the tone would result in imperfect communication between the speaker and listener. Therefore, to avoid creating false impressions, it is necessary that both the speaker and listener know the significance and meaning of tone.

## The Choice of Tone and Its Significance

The choice of tone is deliberate. And each tone is associated with the nature and purpose of the utterance. In the falling tone, the voice starts high and ends low. It is reversed in the rising tone.

### *The Falling Tone*

The falling tone is associated with the following types of utterances:

- **Commands:**
  Bring here.
  Come nere.
- **Statements:** Statements can be sincere expressions or just formal utterances. For example, "thank you" can be a sincere expression of gratitude or it can be just a statement of formality. The difference in the nature of the statements in expressed by the falling or rising tone of the speaker. If spoken with falling tone, it shows the person really feels grateful. This falling tone means sincere gratitude. But, if "thank you" is said with rising tone, that is, it begins with low pitch "thank" and high pitch "you", the statement shows a formal, rather a casual acknowledgement of thankfulness.

  The choice of falling or rising tone is crucial in the context of your relationship. Suppose you wish to thank your friend sincerely for a nice stay you have had at his place and you thank her in rising tone, she is very likely to feel offended. And, if you happen to be abroad and chance to thank a taxi driver in the falling tone, he would be surprised by your sincere sense of gratitude.

In business, the distinction between the low ending and high ending tones is crucial. The two tones signify as follows:

**The falling tone** conveys business like objectivity, sincerity, excitement, certainty, and command.

The rising tone conveys courtesy, request, politeness, doubts, questions, and protest.

For effective spoken English in business, these shapes of tones are necessary to be understood and practised.

Further examples of falling tone:

(i) **Statements**
Our children don't like the way we run the world for them.
You'll have to come with her now.

(ii) **Exclamations**
Well done!
How difficult!

(iii) **Choice questions**
Do you want to go out or stay?
Would you have tea or some cold drink?

(iv) **Interrogative statements**
Statements with question words. What places did you visit this time?

(v) Question tags as an extension of meaning.

A phrase, such as 'isn't it? or won't it!' or 'does she?' that we add at the end of a statement changes it into a question to find out that some one agrees with us or not. For example,

You're from Delhi, aren't your?

You've got its copy, haven't you?

***The Rising Tone***

The rising tone is used for the following kinds of statements:

(i) **Requests**
- Post the letter, please.
- Leave the passage free, please.

(ii) Apologies
- We feel so sorry.
- I deeply regret the lapse.

(iii) **Yes/No questions**
- Did the test begin on time?
- Is our office open?

(iv) **Statements left incomplete**
- Before I meet her ...
- I was trying to suggest …

(v) **Protests**
- The government could have consulted the opposition as well.
- I never meant that.

(vi) **The statement implied to be a question.**
- You're going to the movies straight?
- I believe you see the implications of this order?

(vii) **Question tags as real questions**
- Customers can be attracted, can't they?
- The meeting can be postponed, can't it?

## Pause

In spoken language the function of comma, fullstop, semicolon, dash, which act as marks of punctuation in the written language, to suggest a short or long stop, is done by a short break in speaking. A speaker stops between words or after a group of words depending on (i) the length of his breath and (ii) the meaning or sense of words. The breath pause comes naturally after a long utterance. But, the semantic pause, which is taken by the speaker according to the sense of words, clarifies meaning by separating the two utterances.

Consider the following two utterances with two different pauses:

- A small/bearded person was looking for you.
- A small bearded/person was looking for you.

In the first sentence, the person is small, in the second the beard is small. Pauses are significant in other ways also. They mean that the speaker is careful in his words, and wants the listener to receive the words with serious attention.

## Fluency in Spoken English

Fluency mean saying words/group of words smoothly, without hesitating or halting between the words. While speaking English, we should not allow gaps between the words or within the group of words. In continuous speech, words remain connected with one another. The end of one word flows into the beginning of the next word. The whole utterance is an unbroken chain of sounds.

### *Method of Increasing Your Fluency of English Speech*

Your fluency depends upon the length of group of words you are able to speak/say without gaps or hesitation. Therefore, the way to improve your fluency is to practise to increase the length of the word groups you can speak at a time. For example, consider the following utterance:

She came back – by the Monday – evening – flight.

There are three breaks in the utterance. Now, as J.D. O'Connor suggests (Better Pronunciation, 1970) begin by saying the short group "she came back" smoothly. When you find you speak it with no gaps in between the three words, you add the next three words and say, "she came back by the Monday" and speak the words unhesitatingly. After doing it successfully, you now add one more word "evening" to the group of words and say the whole thing in a running manner. She came back by Monday evening. After repeating it several times to be able to speak without stumbling, finally add the last word "flight", and speak a continuous form, "she came by the Monday evening flight".

For practising fluency you may use the following exercises of lengthening word groups to be spoken as shown above.

1. Who was that- pretty lady - you danced with - at the party?
2. It was the beginning - of the holidays when - I went - to Muscat last month.
3. She wants to know how-long she should wait for you-to reach-here.
4. Come and have – tea-with us-on Saturday-this weekend.
5. I want to know – how-you finished it-so fast-miss Nalini.

### *Factors Affecting Fluency of Foreign Speakers of English*

***Lack of confidence*** Many foreign learners of English fail to speak English smoothly. They lack confidence. They communicate in their regional language/ mother tongue fluently, with ease. But, they find it difficult to interact in English.

They hesitate to speak in English because of lack of practice in speaking English.

To overcome this hesitation, they should practice loud reading to prose passages smoothly and unhesitatingly. They should follow the punctuation marks for long and short pauses. They should gradually increase the speed of reading the text.

## Pronunciation

The special difficulty of foreign speakers of English is owing to the fact that, unlike Indian languages, English words are not always pronounced according to their spelling. That is to say, in English the pronunciation of a word does not necessarily follow its spelling. For example, see the spelling and pronunciation of the following words:

| Spelling | Pronunciation | Spelling | Pronunciation |
|---|---|---|---|
| dough | (do) | cough | (coff) |
| rough | (ruff) | trough | (traff) |
| through | (throo) | quay | (kei) |
| bough | (bow) | doubt | (daut) |

Further, to be able to pronounce a word correctly, we should know not only the correct sounds which form the word, but also the correct word stress – the syllable on which the stress falls. In the case of single (mono) syllabic words, there is no difficulty. The words with more than one syllable follow the following patterns mainly:

(i) words of two syllables with stress on the first syllable:
'fa-ther, 'tea-cher, 'he-ro, 'lett-er, 'sis-ter, 'pai'nter

(ii) words of two syllables with stress on the second syllable:
con-'sist, be-'hind, be-'gin

(iii) words of two syllables having both the syllables stressed:
'arm-'chair, 'half-'term, 'thir-'teen

(iv) words of three syllables having stress on the first syllable:
'pos-i-tive, 'per-i-od, 'print-a-ble

(v) words of three syllables having stress on the second syllable.
Com-'mi-tee, re-ac-tor, ho-'ri-zon

(vi) words of three syllables with stress on the third syllable:
dis-ap-'point, in-ter-'fere, dis-re-'gard, in-di-'rect.

(vii) In words having four or more syllables, the stress usually falls on the third from last:
pho-'tog-raph-er, ge-o-'met-ri-cal, de-'moc-ra-cy.

## Change of Meaning by the Stress Shift

A shift in the position of stress in a word changes its function and meaning. For example, the word convict with stress on the first syllable 'con is a noun and it means a person who has been proved to be guilty of a crime and sent to prison. If the stress shifts to the second syllable, the word becomes a verb and means to prove by trial in a court that someone is guilty of a crime: con-'vict.

We have to be careful about the correct position of stress in words because change in stress position changes the form and meaning of the word. The following list of word illustrates this point:

(i) 'ob-ject (noun), a thing that we can hold, touch, or see, but that is not alive, for example, a chair.
ob-'ject (verb), to oppose or disapprove of something

(ii) 'mi-nute (noun), one-sixtieth of an hour
mi-'nute (adjective), very small

(iii) 'content (noun), the thing contained in a book or utensil
con'tent (adjective), satisfied

(iv) 'abstract (adjective), not concrete
abs'tract (verb), to separate

(v) 'convert (noun), a person who adopts a new religion
con'vert (verb), to change from one thing to another

(vi) 'escort (noun), a guard who goes with someone as a protection
es'cort (verb), to accompany as a guard

(vii) 'invalid (noun), a sick person
in'valid (adjective), not valid

(viii) 'frequent (adjective), often
fre'quent (verb) to go to a particular place often

(ix) 'desert (noun), a sand place
desert (verb), to run away
(x) 'attribute (noun), a quality
attribute (verb), to assign as a reason or motive to someone for doing something.

These distinctions of accent (stress) indicate the nature and meaning of words of multiple syllables. To help you learn this aspect of spoken English, the International phonetic symbols for twenty vowel sounds and twenty four consonant sounds are given below:

## The English Phonemic System and Its Notation

### *Vowels and Diphthongs*

The English vowels and diphthongs are conveniently considered in five groups (A, B, C, D, E below). There are certain differences between RP and GenAm, both in realization (vowel quality) and in the system (vowel inventory).

The **short** vowels are:

**A**

ɪ kit, bid
e dress, bed
æ trap, bad
ɒ (RP) lot, odd
ʌ strut, bud
ʊ foot, good

The **long vowels** and **diphthongs** are:

**B**

iː fleece, see
eɪ face, day
aɪ price, high
ɔɪ choice, boy

**C(RP)**

uː goose, two
əʊ goat, show
aʊ mouth, now
ɒʊ *near-RP variant in* cold *(see 3.6)*

**D(RP)**

ɪə near, here
eə square, fair
ɑː start, father
ɔː thought, law, north, war
ʊə cure, jury, poor *(if not* ɔː*)*
ɜː nurse, stir

The **weak** vowels are:

**E**

i (happ)y, (rad)i(ation), (glor)i(ous)
ə a(bout), (comm)a, (comm)o(n)
u (infl)u(ence), (sit)u(ation), (biv)ou(ac)
– although the weak vowel system also includes
ɪ i(ntend), (rabb)i(t) *(if not* ə*)*
ʊ (stim)u(lus), (ed)u(cate) *(if not* ə *or* u*)* and the syllabic consonants (see below).

***Consonants***

The English consonants are p, b, t, d, k, g, ʧ, ʤ, f, v, θ, ∂, s, z, ʃ, ʒ, h, r, l, j, w, m, n, ŋ.

The symbols p, b, t, d, k, f, v, h, r, 1, w, m, n stand for the English consonant sounds usually so spelled. Keywords for the remaining consonant sounds are as follows:

| | | | |
|---|---|---|---|
| ʧ | church | ʤ | judge |
| θ | thin, author, path | ∂ | this, other, smooth |
| s | cease, sister | z | zone, roses |
| ʃ | ship, ocean | ʒ | vision |
| j | yet | ŋ | sing, long, thanks |
| g | go, give, gag | | |

**Stress** is shown by a mark placed at the beginning of the syllable in question, as in the following examples:

primary word stress re'MEMber
secondary stress ACa'DEMic; 'BUTter FINgers
in prefixes) stressed, but level undefined: primary or secondary as appropriate.

## How to Improve Your Pronunciation

The type of pronunciation to be spoken is known as received pronunciation (RP). In business interactions, this is the model followed by educated executives.

***Some Common Errors of Pronunciation to Be Avoided***

The correct sound of "r". Some of us roll it too much. For pronouncing "r" correctly, the tongue is slightly curled from the sides and drawn back slightly to touch the ridges of the teeth. The single "r" in the middle and at the end of the words is mostly silent in English, whereas Indians mostly pronounce it clearly. Try to pronounce the following words without "r"

army, car, carpet, iron, barge, merger, finger, corner, market, soldier, shoulder, border, hired.

***Exceptions*** Single "r" is pronounced in the middle of words when it appears before vowel sounds. For example: career, paragraph, various.

***Double "rr" must be pronounced*** "rr" in a word is to be pronounced. For example, "Ferret", "curry", "barrage", "sorry".

The "r" at the beginning of a word is pronounced, but it should not be rolled.

Say this aloud.

Round the ragged rock, the ragged rascal ran.

Notice the position of the tongue while you say these rs at the beginning of the above words. It is not curled.

Avoid mixing up "w" and "v" sounds. For example the words, "vine" and "wine" or "water" and "vendor" should not be spoken in the same way, "v" should not sound like "w". In the above words "v" is pronounced with lower lip touching the upper row of teeth, but "w" is pronounced with lips in the rounded form. To practice the distinction between the sounds of "v" and "w" say these words:

Love-low, shove-show, cove-cow, cover-cower, hovel-howl, ever-ewer.

Avoid unclear pronunciation of "T" and "D". Say the following words: Time, dime, candour, bridal, demand.

Finally, the test of effective spoken English is easy in intelligibility of words and their quickest response in the desired manner.

## CHARACTERISTICS AND PRINCIPLES OF EFFECTIVE AND SUCCESSFUL ORAL COMMUNICATION

There are three communication situations in which oral communication takes place:

1. Face-to-face
2. Intercultural
3. Via electronic media

Oral communication is indispensable in any group or business activity. Here are some of the characteristics and principles of effective oral communication:

- *Purpose:* The purpose of talking effectively is to be heard and understood by the listener.
- *Lively rhythm:* Oral communication should, first of all, have a lively rhythm and tone.
- *Simple words:* It is important to use language that is free from long-winded sentences, clichés, and old-fashioned words and phrases. It is best to employ commonly used words and short and simple sentences.
- *Pitch:* The pitch of the speaker's voice should take into consideration the distance between the listener and the speaker.
- *Tone and body language:* The speaker's tone should be marked by sincerity and confidence. The listener, unlike the reader of a written communication, has the advantage of watching the speaker in the act of verbalizing his or her ideas and feelings, and is able to note subconscious body language that may contradict the intent of the spoken words. Therefore, in face-to-face communication, the message is both heard and seen. A speaker has to be very careful, both about his or her choice of words and the manner of speaking them. The manner of speaking is, at times, more important than the actual words, which communicate only 7 per cent of the total meaning of the message. Albert Mehrabian's research reveals astonishing facts about how exactly different factors contribute to a speaker's total message:

  - Verbal factors (words): 7 per cent
  - Tone of voice and modulation: 38 per cent
  - Visual factors (facial expressions, body movements, and gestures): 55 per cent

  Effective speakers learn to control and use their tone and body language to support their words.
- *Pace of speaking:* Unlike the written word, the spoken word is ephemeral and short-lived. Listeners cannot refer back to the spoken word as readers can in case they missed something. This is an inherent limitation of speech. To overcome this limitation, the listener has to listen closely and attentively and the speaker should converse slowly, with proper semantic pauses, to enable the listener to receive and register what is said. There should be a correlation between the pace of

speaking and the rate of listening. Research has established that an individual speaks nearly 125 words a minute, but the listener can process the information nearly 4–5 times more rapidly than this. If the gap between hearing and registering is too wide or too narrow based on the pace of speaking, comprehension will too be adversely affected. Hence, an important principle of oral communication is to speak fluently, without long pauses or without rushing.

Research has established that an individual speaks nearly 125 words a minute, but the listener can process the information nearly 4–5 times more rapidly than this.

- *Fluency:* Fluency is described in the *Oxford English Dictionary* as "the quality of being able to speak or write a language easily and well." A fluent speaker is one who is heard with ease. The listener does not have to strain his or her mind to receive, register, and interpret the message. Listening is activated and helped when the speaker delivers his or her words in an ordered manner. Each word is distinctly heard and easily connected with other words to form the structure of the message.

Listening is activated and helped when the speaker delivers his or her words in an ordered manner.

### Guidelines for Effective Oral Communication

Oral communication should provide a platform for fair and candid exchange of ideas. The communicator should keep in mind the following tips and guidelines:

2 Learn key skills of oral communication.

- Consider the objective.
- Think about the interest level of the receiver.
- Be sincere.
- Use simple language and familiar words.
- Be brief and precise.
- Avoid vagueness and generalities.
- Give full facts.
- Assume nothing.
- Use polite words and tone.
- Eliminate insulting implications.
- Include some information that is interesting and pleasing to the recipient.
- Allow time to respond.

## BARRIERS TO EFFECTIVE ORAL COMMUNICATION

Managers have to communicate individually with people at different levels—superiors, subordinates, peers, customers, and public figures. The oral mode of communication is easy, efficient, and functionally helpful in resolving issues. But, oral communication demands great control and communicative competence to be successful. The foremost barrier to oral communication is poor listening. Listening is a psychological act affected by several factors, such as the speaker's status, the listener's receptivity and retention, language barriers, and so on.

### Language Barrier

The language of communication should be shared by the speaker and the listener. In business, English is widely used in most parts of the world. The ability to converse in English is essential for executives in a multi-lingual country like India. English is now the global medium for conducting business, and the lack of knowledge and practice of spoken English acts as a barrier to verbal communication.

The listener should also be familiar with the accent of the language in use, as a new accent can often be difficult to follow for those unfamiliar with it. For instance, in India, even those who speak English fluently need special training to work in call centres so that they can understand what overseas callers say over the phone. Workers involved in outsourced businesses tend to overcome their initial language barrier through training and exposure to the foreign accent.

The effects of most of these barriers that interfere with the proper response to oral messages can be reduced or even removed through effective listening. In order to develop good listening skills, we must first identify and understand the characteristics of effective listening.

Besides the barriers in listening discussed in this section, there may be other factors that affect listening. For instance, many studies show that men listen mostly with the left side of the brain while women tend to use both sides. Further, studies also suggest that left-handed people may use a part of the brain to process language that differs from their right-handed counterparts. Such differences in brain dominance and lateralization could affect listening, either positively or negatively.

## TO BE ASSERTIVE WITHOUT BEING AGGRESSIVE

### Being Assertive Without Being Aggressive

At the workplace, hierarchy may make some individuals submissive. Sometimes, asserting one's point of view runs the risk of being perceived as rude. In such a situation, the skills of assertive conversation become useful.

To be assertive is to be confident. An assertive person does not say "yes" when he or she means "no". Assertive individuals can say "no" in a positive and firm manner; being firm requires stating one's point of view clearly and without hesitation. This is the key to being assertive. It is important not to fumble or be indirect when conveying one's concerns.

An assertive and firm person should be able to analyze the situation as he or she sees it, and should indicate relevant concerns by drawing the attention of seniors to the consequences. Firm communication with seniors or supervisors compels them to evaluate their assumptions, even if there is to be no change in the line of action to be taken.

In business, you have to be assertive when you strongly believe that someone's course of action involves risk and danger and may have undesirable consequences that you might be held responsible for. In such situations, say what you must say.

> Negative thinking results from a negative attitude or negative perception, which, at times, is part of a person's personality.

Negative thinking results from a negative attitude or negative perception, which, at times, is part of a person's personality. Some persons always focus only on the dark side of a situation. They say things, such as "This is impossible", "It is too difficult", or "This is useless".

When negative consequences are foreseen as a result of an expert's critical thinking, their assertion is valuable to discussion. Sometimes, even pointing out loopholes in assumptions is necessary. For example, take the case of the Bhopal gas tragedy that took place on 2 December 1984. The internal reports of the U.S.-based undertaking, Union Carbide, show that the officials were aware of the growing safety and maintenance problems since 1982 when management cut staff at the methyl isocyanate (MIC) facility from twelve to six operators and reduced the number of maintenance workers. Faulty safety devices remained unattended for weeks. In fact, a 1982 report by a group of Carbide's U.S. engineers had listed the problems, but the parent corporation made no effort to ask the Indian executives responsible for running the plant to correct them.

Obviously, the U.S. engineers failed to assert the need for safety. The Indian executives, also responsible for day-to-day operation of the plant, failed to point out the loopholes in the management's extensive cost-cutting plans. The management was attempting to reduce losses by cutting maintenance costs. The failure of engineers and executives to be assertive on the subject of safety measures led to one of the worst disasters of the twentieth century.

## CONVERSATION

### What Is Conversation?

3

Know the meaning and social purpose of conversation.

The art of conversation is an essential interpersonal skill that helps build a pleasing personality. Effective conversation helps in getting friendly cooperation in social and professional situations. Conversation involves speaking and listening in a sequence. It is an oral exchange of sentiments, observations, opinions, and ideas. The *Longman Dictionary of Contemporary English* defines conversation in the social context, which is the ordinary context of everyday life, as "an informal talk in which people exchange views, feelings and thoughts". The *Merriam-Webster Dictionary* defines conversation in the professional context as "an informal discussion of an issue by representatives of governments, institutions or groups".

What distinguishes ordinary conversation from other forms of oral communication, such as debates, public speaking, negotiations, or business discussions, is its informality, in the sense that it is relaxed and friendly without being restricted by the rules of formal behaviour. Conversation, in general, is spontaneous, friendly, and casual. The use of direct, informal, and commonly used phrases constitutes the conversational style.

### Social Conversation

4

Learn how to break the ice and start conversations.

Social conversation, also known as *chit-chat* or *small talk*, attempts to establish a sociable atmosphere. At a tea-party or social gathering, the conversation reveals feelings of togetherness, rather than communicating ideas or any specific meaning. Words are used in symbolic ways, as verbal social gestures. This social use of words is known as *phatic communion*.

The words and phrases used in phatic communion, such as "It was a pleasure meeting you", "Do come again", or "How is your family?" can be best described as expressions of togetherness and camaraderie and an indication of the speaker's culture and sensibility as a social being. Hayakawa points out that it is regarded as a social error not to say these things, even if the speaker does not mean them, and that it is completely impossible for us in society to talk only when we "have something to say"[2]. According to Hayakawa, "the *togetherness* of the talking is the most important element in social conversation; the subject matter is only secondary".

Greetings and farewells, such as "Good morning", used to greet someone in the morning; "Take care", used to wish good luck while parting; or "How do you do?", used when being introduced to someone, do not carry literal meaning and are phatic in nature. According to Bronislaw Malinowski, phatic communion is a type of speech in which ties of union are created by a mere exchange of words. The words fulfil a social function and "that is their principal aim, but they are neither the result of intellectual reflection, nor do they necessarily arouse reflection in the listener". The *Oxford English Dictionary* explains phatic communion by saying, "they [the words] are used to convey general sociability rather than to communicate a specific meaning; for example, *Nice morning isn't it?*" Similarly, the phrase "How are you?" is not a question about the listener's state of health, and "Take care" is not a warning against danger. Phatic utterances are used to break silence. Their purpose is to initiate conversation. This type of conversation does not aim at discussing an idea that may provoke disagreement. Instead, the conversation is usually about some common, shared feeling that can be instantly appreciated, such as appreciation of fine weather or natural beauty. Fuller communication can grow from small, ice-breaking remarks made upon making someone's acquaintance.

Fuller communication can grow from small, ice-breaking remarks made upon making someone's acquaintance.

Exhibit 3.2 illustrates how small talk and informal, friendly conversation about unimportant subjects creates a relaxed atmosphere for discussing business.

Social conversation in the form of chit-chat, small talk, or phatic communion is not bound by any rigid order or sequence of subject matter. Its order and nature depends on the extent of both parties' desire to establish a relationship. People who are drawn to each other talk with the goal of reaching a stage where

Divya Mehra, an architect and the owner of her firm, Interiors, has commissioned an advertising agency to create an ad brief for her new business plan. The plan involves creating modern office spaces for corporations and businesses. Daniel, who has been given the task of crating the brief and presenting it to Mrs Mehra, visits her to show her the draft and get her feedback.

**Daniel:** Good morning, Mrs Mehra. How have you been?

**Mrs Mehra:** Good morning, Daniel. Very well, thank you. Did you have a nice weekend?

**Daniel:** Yes, indeed. I met a couple of old friends, so we had a good time. How was your weekend?

**Mrs Mehra:** Not bad at all, thank you. A friend took me to see some of the beaches close to Mumbai. It all looks so lush green during the rains!

**Daniel:** Yes, some of the beaches in Maharashtra are very pretty, aren't they?

**Mrs Mehra:** You don't come from this part of the country, do you?

**Daniel:** No, I'm from Delhi. But, I like it here very much.

**Mrs Mehra:** I'm glad to hear that. Well now, back to work! How's the brief coming along?

**Daniel:** I thought I'd show you the draft I've created. Would you please take a look at it and let me know what you think?

**Mrs Mehra:** Sure, I've been waiting to see the draft. Let's see the text first:

> "Interiors create spacious and comfortable workspaces for you…easy-to-install fittings, employee-friendly workspaces, all at an affordable price…cut your costs by half…"

That last one's a bit of a tall claim, isn't it? Should we retain something so far-fetched?

**Daniel:** You're right, Mrs Mehra. I shall delete that part, go over the whole thing once more and show it to you in a couple of days.

**Exhibit 3.2** How Small Talk Facilitates Business Conversations

The ability to connect with others through small talk can lead to big things, according to Debra Fine, author of *The Fine Art of Small Talk* (Hyperion 2005). A former engineer, Fine recalls being so ill at ease at networking events and even the 10 minute coffee break during a meeting that she would hide in the restroom. Now a motivational speaker, Fine believes the ability to develop relationships with people through small talk is an acquired skill.

**Fine offers the following tips for starting—and ending conversations:**

- Come up with three things to talk when preparing for a function along with a couple generic questions that will get others talking.
- Be the first to say "hello." Smile first and always shake hands when you meet someone.
- Take your time during introductions. Make an extra effort to remember names and use them frequently. Exhibit host behaviour by introducing others that join the group to each other.
- Get another person talking by leading with a common ground statement regarding the occasion or location and then asking a related open-ended question. For example, you can also ask them about their trip in or how they know the bride or groom.
- Show interest in your conversational partner by actively listening and giving verbal feedback. Maintain eye contact.
- Listen more than you talk.
- Be prepared to have something interesting to contribute. Staying on top of current events will provide you with great conversation builders, leading with "What do you think of?" Have you heard?"
- Be aware of your body language. People who look or act ill-at-ease make others uncomfortable.
- Have a few exit lines ready, so that you can gracefully move on. For example, "I need to check in with a client over there," or "Who do you know at this meeting that could help me with ...?

*Source:* Extracts from Debra Fine, "Tips for Making Small Talk Success", available at http://www.debrafine.com/art_tipsForSmallTalkSuccess.html, accessed 15 September 2010.

Debra Fine is the author of *The Fine Art of Small Talk* (Hyperion). She presents keynotes and seminars on conversational skills and networking techniques internationally. Contact Debra at 303-721-8266 or visit her Web site at www.DebraFine.com.

**Exhibit 3.3** Tips for Successful Small Talk

they have a better understanding and exchange of ideas. This is achieved by avoiding subjects that would lead to disagreements. With each point of agreement, no matter how commonplace or obvious, doubt and suspicion of the new acquaintance wear away and the possibility of friendship increases. And finally, when more intimate conversation reveals common tastes, opinions, and views, friendship replaces misgivings and communication in the real sense is made possible. Thus, social conversation is psychologically structured, beginning in casual chit-chat and developing into genuine communication expressive of friendship and cooperation. Exhibit 3.3 shows how one can make small talk and break the ice.

In their daily interactions, people are constantly involved in the exchange of facts and opinions. In these conversations, it is important to avoid what is known as the *binary mode* and adopt a *multi-valued* approach. Sometimes, people tend to present facts and opinions in a binary manner, in which they try to prove that what they are saying is correct and what the other person has to say is totally wrong. This view tends to antagonize both participants and can lead to arguments. In some conversations, there may be a visible attempt at what Stephen Potter calls "one-upmanship"—an attempt to make oneself seem better than other people. A valuable part of a conversation is wasted when the participants want to prove that they are correct; instead, they should use the opportunity more profitably to exchange facts and opinions.

Rational human beings should follow what Karl R. Popper says, "Faith in reason is not only a faith in our own reason, but also and even more in that of others. Rationalism, is therefore, bound up with the idea that the other fellow has a right to be heard and to defend his arguments". According to this view, no person is wholly wrong even if we do not accept him or her as correct. Rationally speaking, reality cannot be truly categorized into an "either–or" system of thinking. Reality is not simply right or wrong, or good or bad. This perception is further refined when truth is viewed in terms of a scale of values, such as 0 to 5 or 0 to 100. To value reality as 0 and 1 is to miss the vast design of reality that consists of numerous shades, not just black and white. Conversation should be inspired by the multiple possibilities of truth/reality and be characterized by tolerance and positivity.

## Effective Conversation

Humans begin conversing from the time we begin to prattle as children. From infancy, we develop the basic tool of conversation that is language. Gradually, we become familiar with complex uses of language suited to our purpose: to inform and to persuade. However, even though we naturally pick up the ability to converse, we may lack the skills of a good conversationalist, which include knowing how to speak as well listen. Conversation is not a monologue, it's a dialogue. Good conversation is characterized by the following features:

1. It has natural directness and spontaneity.
2. It is live in the sense that it takes place face-to-face, and the participants can see and hear each other at the same time. The live presentation of conversation is enriched and made effective with the added power of body language—a great source of communicative effectiveness.

> Conversation is not a monologue; it's a dialogue.

3. It is sensitive and flexible in that it can change quickly according to the participants' reactions.

These characteristics are clearly illustrated in Communication Snapshot 3.1, which is a conversation between Catherine and Linton in Emily Bronte's *Wuthering Heights.*

**Communication Snapshot 3.1** Effective Conversation: An Example

Linton sat in the great arm-chair half asleep. Walking upto him, Catherine began in a serious tone: "As you don't like me, Linton, I'll not come any more. Let us say good-bye and tell Mr Heathcliff that you have no wish to see me and that he mustn't invent any more falsehoods on the subject." "Sit down and take your hat off Catherine", he answered. "You are so much happier than I am. Believe me, if I could be as happy, I would also be like you; but Papa talks of my defects so much and shows such scorn for me that I believe I am worthless, bad tempered, bad in spirit and I cannot help showing my nature to you, though I regret it and repent it till I die!"

Catherine is strong-willed and passionate. She talks to Linton in an impulsive, vehement way. "As you don't like me… let us say good bye." Linton on the other hand is cool, sad, and bares his heart, which is filled with remorse. He changes Catherine's negative thoughts and feelings by his moving self-expression. This is seen when Catherine tells Ellen, "I felt he spoke the truth; and I felt I must forgive him, and though we should quarrel the next moment, I must forgive him again."

Linton's words are full of genuine feelings of love and remorse for Catherine. When he narrates how scorn and bad temper were driven into his nature by his father's constant treatment of him as a worthless fellow, he sounds very earnest and convincing. Catherine is persuaded to change her opinion by the touching facts of Linton's helplessness, everlasting regret, and repentance.

## REVIEW YOUR LEARNING

1. Give five reasons for choosing the oral mode of communication instead of the written form.
2. What skills does a speaker need to be successful in communicating with others? Give an example of difficulty or failure in oral communication.
3. Discuss some of the principles of effective oral communication.
4. In intercultural conversation, both how you talk and what you say is equally important for building good professional relations. Give examples and explain.
5. Why do conversations go wrong? Illustrate your answer with analysis of a situation you have actually experienced.
6. Explain the nature and purpose of "phatic communion". Describe an example of such a conversation in your personal life.
7. What is conversation control? Discuss with examples.
8. "A key conversation skill is to know the difference between opinion and fact and to use it to your advantage". Discuss.
9. Discuss the principles of successful oral communication.

## REFLECT ON YOUR LEARNING

1. "You can be assertive without being aggressive". Discuss.
2. How important is informality in conversation?
3. How important is it to notice the pauses and speech pace to understand the speaker's state of mind?
4. How would you improve your fluency of spoken English?
5. Give five reasons for choosing oral mode of communication, instead of written form.

## ENDNOTES

1. Albert Mehrabian, "Communication Without Words", *Psychology Today* (September 1968), 53–55.
2. S. I. Hayakawa, *Language in Thought and Action* (New York: Harcourt, Brace & World, Inc., 1964), 72.

# 4 Written Communication

*Upon completion of this chapter, you should be able to:*

1. Understand the basic difficulties in writing clearly, simply, and correctly.
2. Identify the different purposes of writing.
3. Learn to plan written communication by paying special attention to the needs and expectations of prospective readers.
4. Know the essential principles of effective written communication.
5. Write effective business letters, memos and reports.

## THE ART OF WRITING

Writing is a mode of communicating a message for a specific purpose. It reveals one's ability to think clearly and to use language effectively. A manager is responsible for a variety of written communications, such as replies to clients, enquires, memos recording agreements, proposals for contracts, formal or informal reports to initiate action, and so on. A manager should be able to convey information, ideas, instructions, decisions, and welfare proposals in written form, in keeping with the level of the people who receive and read them. However, a manager's objective in writing a particular document is only met when readers understand exactly what is intended to be communicated to them. A manger, therefore, should be able to write down his or her thoughts simply and concisely.

1 Understand the basic difficulties in writing clearly, simply, and correctly.

### The Skills Required in Written Communication

Effective writing does not come by chance. It does not just happen. There is a set of skills required to write simply, clearly, accurately, and concisely.

Writing skills are as essential as the other knowledge and skills that form an executive's professional qualifications and requirements. The skills required for business writing are essentially the same as those required for general written communication. Business writers should carefully check the grammar, punctuation, and spellings; ensure that sentences and paragraphs are structured logically; and follow the principles of sound organization—clarity, simplicity, and directness.

## THE PURPOSE OF WRITING

The first task for writing effectively is to identify the purpose of the communication. There are mainly two goals of communication in business situations—to inform and to persuade.

### Writing to Inform

When the writer seeks to provide and explain information, the writing is called *informative writing*. It is also called *expository writing* because it expounds on or expresses ideas and facts. The focus of informative writing is the subject or the matter under discussion. Informative writing is found in accounts of facts, scientific data, statistics, and technical and business reports.

2 Identity the different purposes of writing.

*Informative writing* presents information, not opinions. Its purpose is to educate and not persuade. It is written with maximum objectivity.

Informative writing presents information not opinions. Its purpose is to educate and not persuade. It is, therefore, written with maximum objectivity. For example, consider the passage in Communication Snapshot 4.1.

Exhibit 4.1 presents a list of questions that must be answered in the affirmative to determine if a piece of writing is effective.

**Communication Snapshot 4.1** Informatory Writing

The passage in Exhibit 4A is a piece of informative or expository writing. It successfully transmits a message about ants to readers. In the passage, the writer's opening sentence expresses the main idea. The subsequent sentences give information that supports the main idea, namely unusual facts about the social lives of ants.

As indicated, the purpose of the writer is to inform a reader objectively, with little bias. The information is logically arranged and clearly written.

Ants have strange social lives. Like mediaeval feudal lords, some ants keep slaves to do their work. They attack other ants' nests and capture them. The victorious ants bring back the defeated groups of ants to their own nests and force them to work as slaves. Surprisingly, ants do not live alone in their nests. Hundreds of other small creatures, like beetles and crickets, dwell with the ants in their houses as inmates. Some of these small creatures do useful work for the ants. They serve the ants by keeping the nests clean and performing other duties. However, others seem to live without doing anything in return. Why the ants allow them to stay in their nests is a puzzling question. Is it just benevolence or is it the feudal spirit of keeping a large retinue of servants?

**Exhibit 4A** Ants

1. Does the write-up focus on the subject under discussion?
2. Does it primarily inform rather than persuade the reader?
3. Does it offer complete and precise information?
4. Can the information be proven?
5. Does it present information logically and clearly?
6. Does it flow smoothly?

**Exhibit 4.1** Informative Writing: A Checklist

## Writing to Persuade

> *Persuasive writing* is found in opinion essays, editorials, letters to editors, business and research proposals, religious books, reviews, or literature belonging to a certain political party.

*Persuasive writing* aims at convincing the reader about a matter that is debatable; it expresses opinion rather than facts. This writing is also called argumentative, as it supports and argues for a certain viewpoint or position. The matter at hand generally has two or more sides to it. The writer seeks to influence and convince the reader to accept the position he or she has put forth.

Persuasive writing focuses on the reader. The writer attempts to change the reader's thinking and bring it closer to his or her own way of thinking. Persuasive writing is found in opinion essays, editorials, letters to editors, business and research proposals, religious books, reviews, or literature belonging to a certain political party.

Persuasive writing does more than just state an opinion—that is not enough. The opinion must be convincing. There must be supporting evidence or facts to back the writer's opinion or point of view. Moreover, the writer's point of view should be well argued, meaning his or her reasoning should be logical and clearly arranged. Let us consider the example of "Alternative Sources of Fuel" shown in Communication Snapshot 4.2.

**Communication Snapshot 4.2** Persuasive Writing

The case built in Exhibit 4B for considering alternative sources of fuel is well argued. The final paragraph clinches the argument for finding substitutes for fuel oil by convincing readers that, although it is not easy to solve the energy problem, the real need is "to find substitutes for fuel oil" and "replacement energy forms are available to fill that need".

Faced with today's high energy costs and tremendous consumer demand, we need to find alternative energy forms. During the past five years, consumers have tried conservation as a means of defence against high fuel (petrol and home-heating) prices. They purchased smaller, more fuel-efficient cars and insulated their homes with storm windows and doors. While these conservation measures improved the efficiency of oil consumption, they had no effect on continually increasing oil prices. Since conservation alone is not the answer, what alternatives are available now?

One readily accessible substitute energy form is solar energy, produced by the sun. Solar collectors—made of insulation, serpentine tubing filled with water, and glass—absorb heat from the sun and distribute it to radiators or baseboard heaters. Hot water for bathing is available through this same process.

Gasohol is another alternate fuel. Gasohol is a mixture of 10 per cent alcohol and 90 per cent gasoline. Cars travel more efficiently on this fuel due to its high octane content. In fact, Henry Ford designed the Ford Model-T to run on pure alcohol. Gasohol should be carefully considered as an alternate fuel, because the alcohol needed is easily derived from just about anything, such as corn, wood, or organic garbage.

We could also look to another natural resource—the wind. Some experimentation is being conducted in the Midwest using windmills to generate electricity. As a matter of fact, at least one major store sells windmills across the country.

Coal and wood should also be considered as substitute fuels. People heated their homes with wood stoves and coal furnaces long before oil was available as a home-heating fuel.

Although there are no easy or comfortable ways to get around our energy problems, comfort has to be placed after our real need, which is to find substitutes for fuel oil. Replacement energy forms are available to fill that need.

---

*Source:* Based on Diana Hacker and Betty Renshaw, "Alternative Source of Fuel", *A Practical Guide for Writers*, 2nd ed. (Boston: Little, Brown and Company, 1982) 183–184.

**Exhibit 4B** Alternative Sources of Fuel

1. Does it focus on the reader?
2. Does it basically seek to convince rather than inform?
3. Does it support its argument by providing facts or valid reasons?
4. Does it follow a logical arrangement of thought and reasoning?
5. Does it evoke the intended response from the reader?

**Exhibit 4.2** Persuasive Writing: A Checklist

Exhibit 4.2 presents a list of questions that must be answered in the affirmative for a passage to be considered persuasive.

## PRINCIPLES OF EFFECTIVE WRITING

An important requirement for effective writing is to recognize the needs, expectations, fears, and attitudes of the audience or receiver and the reader of the written message. Written communication is one-way—from the sender to the receiver. The receiver cannot immediately clarify doubts or confusion if the message is unclear. Therefore, communicating clearly is especially important when it comes to written communication.

3

Learn to plan written communication by paying special attention to the needs and expectations of prospective readers.

A manager works out schemes and projects, a scientist or engineer solves a technical problem. As the "doer", he or she is clear about what is in his or her mind. But the moment someone takes up a pen and starts writing to communicate ideas, he or she must keep in mind that the structure of his or her thoughts has to follow the structure of language, that is, the format of sentences, paragraphs, and the composition as a whole. Writers must follow the principles of unity and coherence that bind words into sentences, sentences into units or paragraphs, and paragraphs into essays (the full composition). When this transformation of thought into language is not effected under the guiding principles of language, the muddy clutter hides the meaning and makes it difficult to understand the writer's thoughts.

When the transformation of thought into language is not effected under the guiding principles of language, the muddy clutter hides the meaning and makes it difficult to understand the writer's thoughts.

Although letters have remained the most common means of written communication for a very long period, their importance is frequently overlooked. Authors often dictate or write down a few scattered sentences in the hope that the reader will get the message. However, the message may be buried under a mountain of unnecessary words, or an unnatural style may conceal the writer's true intentions. Instead of letting business letters be friendly, interesting, and persuasive, such writing makes them overly formal and dull.

Although the letter, for a long time, remained the most common means of written communication, its importance is frequently overlooked. Authors often dictate or write down a few scattered sentences in the hope that the reader will get the message.

Exhibit 4.3 shows a well-written sample letter that has the flavour of easy conversation. Notice the use of everyday words, such as "hope", "remember", "regret", "send", "says", "provide", "charge", "believe", "make", and so on that give the letter the simplicity of the spoken word.

The written word often gets cluttered with complex construction of sentences. Communication Snapshot 4.3 presents an example of a paragraph whose meaning is lost because of complex sentences. It also shows how this paragraph can be rewritten to bring clarity.

12 August, 2009

The Service Manager
Customer Satisfaction Division
Samsung India Limited
Nehru Place
New Delhi

Dear Sir,

I hope you remember our discussion last Monday about the servicing of the washing machine supplied to us three months ago. I regret to say the machine is no longer working. Please send a service engineer as soon as possible to repair it.

The product warranty says that you provide spare parts and materials free, but charge for the engineer's labour. This sounds unfair. I believe the machine's failure is caused by a manufacturing defect. Initially, it made a lot of noise, and, later, it stopped operating entirely. As it is wholly the company's responsibility to rectify the defect, I hope you will not make us pay for the labour component of its repair.

Thanking you,

Yours faithfully,

Mrs Roli Chaturvedi

**Exhibit 4.3** A Well-written Sample Letter

**Communication Snapshot 4.3** Examples of Clear and Unclear Writing

After reading Exhibit 4C, the only facts that a reader can be sure about are that the owners of the land were contacted on July 25 and that the president will be returning on August 25. The important information about the possible sale of the block is completely concealed by the excess of words. It is likely that the writer wanted to say something along the lines of Exhibit 4D.

When the owners were contacted on July 25, the assistant manager, Mr Rathi, informed the chief engineer that they were considering ordering advertising Block 25 for sale. He, however, expressed his inability to make a firm decision by requesting this company to confirm their intentions with regard to buying the land within one month, when Mr Jain, the president of the company, will have come back from a business tour. "This will be August 25."

**Exhibit 4C** The Original Paragraph

The chief engineer contacted the owner on July 25 to enquire if Block 25 was on sale. He was informed by the assistant manager, Mr Rathi, that the company was thinking of selling the block. He was further told that decision would not be made until the president, Mr Jain, returned from a business tour on August 25. Mr Rathi asked the chief engineer to submit a written proposal for sale.

**Exhibit 4D** The Revised Paragraph

The purpose of business writing is to achieve the understanding and reaction needed in the quickest and most economical way. To do this, one must follow the principles and structure of effective writing.

4

Know the essential principles of effective written communication.

Effective written communication is achieved by following the principles of (a) accuracy, (b) brevity, and (c) clarity, in addition to others. As we have already discussed clarity, let us focus on other important principles of effective writing here.

## Accuracy

To achieve accuracy, the writer should check and double-check:

- All facts and figures
- The choice of words
- The language and tone

For example, whether a communication is formal or informal, one should always write "between you and me", not "between you and I". In this case, the choice is simple as it is guided by the objective rules of grammar. But in other cases, word choice may not be as clearly indicated. The correct choice of words is determined by the appropriateness of the word for the subject, audience, and purpose of a particular piece of writing.

A message should be communicated correctly in terms of grammar, punctuation, and spelling. Of course, it is not always easy to be accurate in expression; however, some obvious pitfalls can be avoided by being alert to the following:

A message should be communicated correctly in terms of grammar, punctuation, and spelling.

- Follow the rules of grammar.
- Pay attention to punctuation marks.
- Check words for spelling and usage.

Only a few samples are given here to indicate the danger of overlooking the technical aspects of writing. Detailed study of the grammatical rules will be discussed in Appendix 1.

To avoid incorrect usage, it is important to check the suitability of the words used. Exhibit 4.4 presents a list of words that are often confused or used incorrectly.

## Brevity

Brevity lies in saying only what needs to be said and leaving out unnecessary words or details. Being brief does not mean saying less that what the occasion demands. Brevity is not to be achieved at the cost of clarity. Nor is brevity to be gained by sacrificing proper English.

Brevity lies in saying only what needs to be said and leaving out unnecessary words or details.

To achieve brevity, avoid wordiness. This can be done in the following ways:

1. Do not use four or six words when one or two will do. It is not necessary to qualify one word with another word that basically means the same thing. For instance, in the phrase, "worldwide recognition by all", it would suffice to say just "worldwide" or "by all". Exhibit 4.4 lists phrases that are examples of wordiness; they can each be reduced to one or two words.

| *Wordy Constructions* | *Concise Constructions* |
|---|---|
| Along the lines of | Like |
| In the event of | If |
| For the purpose of | For |
| In the neighbourhood of | About |
| For the reason that | Since/Because |
| With a view to | To |
| In the event that | If |
| In as much as | Because |
| With reference to | About |
| In the case of | If |
| With regard to | About |
| With the result that | So that |

**Exhibit 4.4** Examples of Wordy and Concise Constructions

2. **Wordiness can also be avoided by changing long clauses into phrases. Here are a few examples:**

Wordy: The vast majority of farmers in India are poor in a greater or lesser degree.

Concise: Most Indian farmers are quite poor.

Wordy: The special difficulty in my case arises in relation to the fact that I live so far from my institute.

Concise: I am specially handicapped by living so far from my institute.

Wordy: In this connection, it is not without interest to observe that, in the case of many states, no serious measures have been taken with a view to putting the recommendations of the HRD minister into practice.

Concise: Most states have done little to implement the HRD minister's recommendations.

Wordy: Mr Singh, who was a newcomer to the city mentioned earlier in this report, proved to be a very able administrator.

Concise: Mr Singh, a newcomer to the above-mentioned city, proved to be a very able administrator. (Here a clause has been reduced to a phrase and a phrase reduced to a single word.)

Wordy: She is so honest that she will not tell a lie.

Concise: She is too honest to tell a lie.

Wordy: The wind is so cold that we cannot go out at present.

Concise: The wind is too cold for us to go out at present.

3. Drop "which" and "that" clauses when possible. For example:

   Wordy: I need cards that are of formal type.
   Concise: I need formal cards.
   Wordy: She received a shirt that was torn.
   Concise: She received a torn shirt.
   Wordy: She cleared the debts that her husband had taken on.
   Concise: She cleared her husband's debts.
   Wordy: I am sure that I shall be able to help you.
   Concise: I am sure I can help you.

4. Do not overuse the passive voice. For example:

   Wordy: Technology can be used by children also.
   Concise: Children also can use technology.
   Wordy: The post of Prime Minister of India is held by Dr Manmohan Singh.
   Concise: Dr Manmohan Singh holds the Prime Ministership of India.
   Wordy: Many great lands had been seen by Ulysses.
   Concise: Ulysses saw many great lands.

Communication Snapshot 4.4 illustrates a wordy and tedious business letter and one way to make it more concise.

The letter in Exhibit 4E can be rewritten in a brief and concise form, as shown in Exhibit 4F.

**Communication Snapshot 4.4** Rewriting a Letter

Dear Sir,

We are in receipt of your letter dated June 25 and have pleasure in informing you that the order you have placed with us will receive our best and immediate attention and that the fifteen ACs you require will be provided to you as soon as we are able to arrange for and supply them to you.

We are, however, very sorry to say that our stock of these ACs is, at this moment of time, quite short. Owing to the extremely hot summer and the consequent increase in demand, we have been informed by the manufacturers that they are not likely to be in a position to supply us with further stock for another three weeks or so.

We are extremely sorry not to be in a position to satisfy your requirements immediately, but we wish to assure you that we will always try to do everything we possibly can to see that your order for fifteen ACs is met as soon as possible. If you are not able to obtain the ACs you need from elsewhere, or if you are able to wait for them until the end of the next of month, you are requested to inform us in a timely manner.

Once again expressing our sincerest regret at our inability to fulfil your esteemed order on this occasion with our usual promptness and trusting you will continue to favour us in the future,

Yours truly,

*PAhuja*

Prem Ahuja

**Exhibit 4E** A Wordy Letter

Dear Sir,

We thank you for your order of 25th June, but regret that due to the exceptional demand for ACs thanks to the prolonged hot spell, we are currently out of stock of the brand you ordered. The manufacturers, however, have promised us further supply by the end of this month, and if you could wait until then, we would ensure the prompt delivery of the fifteen ACs you require.

We are sorry that we cannot meet your present order immediately.

Yours truly,
*PAhuja*
Prem Ahuja

**Exhibit 4F** The Rewritten Letter

## PLANNING, WRITING, AND REVISING: BUSINESS MESSAGES

The writers of letters and other forms of business communications are advised to follow the three steps of successful writing to communicate clearly and accurately: (1) planning, (2) writing, and (3) rewriting (revising).

- *Planning:* Writing a letter or memo is a one-way communication exercise. The words written on the page are all that convey the message. The reader does not have other non-verbal means to interpret the message. Usually, the reader is not in a position to immediately clarify something that is unclear. For example, suppose you write a letter to the Hill View Resort to make arrangements for a business meeting and lunch three days before the event. You would need to give complete information about everything the manager would need to know before making arrangements for the meeting and lunch. This includes the number of persons, the time, duration, and size of the conference, the hall desired, the number of collar microphones needed, the seating plan, the duration of the meeting, the kind of food needed, the number of vegetarians and non-vegetarians, the beverages and snacks required, and so on.

  Hence, to write a complete and short letter, plan before writing it. In addition, it is generally helpful to write a draft first.

  The writers should always consider:

  - The reader
  - The purpose of writing
  - The situation (context)

  These three elements determine the choice of the letter's/memo's/report's content, organization, and format.

*Revision* is a process of clarifying ideas, meanings, and purpose. It involves eliminating clutter that hides the writer's true intentions.

- *Rewriting and revising:* Writing is a mode of thinking. Rewriting or revising what has been written or dictated is a mode of improved thinking. Revising the first draft is not just useful for fixing grammatical errors. It is also an attempt to check if the writer has been able to say what was intended in the best manner possible. *Revision* is, therefore, a process of clarifying ideas, meanings, and purpose. It involves eliminating clutter that hides the writer's true intentions.

Very few people are capable of expressing themselves accurately in the first draft. This is not due to poor command of the language. It is related to the process of accurate thinking. Writing is an act of transcribing ideas into words. The transcription will be accurate only when the thinking is accurate. Each revision sharpens the writer's thinking and thereby helps tighten his or her expression to a close transcription of what is in his or her mind.

How rewriting changes the thinking and message of a manager from verbiage to intent, eliminating wordiness, correcting the tone, and revising the policy itself can be explained with the help of the example discussed in Communication Snapshot 4.5.

**Communication Snapshot 4.5** Redrafting a Memo

The management of Excel Corporation is concerned about the misuse of office telephones by its employees. In the past few months, expenses have soared because employees have been using their desk phones to call friends and relatives. In fact, employees have been making outstation calls for personal conversations. Lisa Christopher, the head of administration, drafts a memo (Exhibit 4G) to stop employees from misusing their office telephones, which has cost the company a lot of money and employee time.

**Excel Corporation**

INTERNAL MEMORANDUM

To: All employees

From: Lisa Christopher, Head, Administration

Subject: Misuse of office telephones

We have noticed that, in the past few months, the company's expenses have been soaring because employees have been misusing their desk phones. Office telephones are being used for personal communication.

The use of office telephones for personal calls is against company policy. Employees are advised to use their desk telephones (and other office phones) for official purposes only. The use of office phones for personal calls must stop with immediate effect. The management will take strict action against anyone who is found guilty of misusing office telephones, and their employment may be terminated.

Please feel free to contact me if you have any queries about the issue.

Lisa Christopher

**Exhibit 4G** The Original Memo

Before signing the memo, Lisa reads it a few times. She wonders if she will be able to change the behaviour of the employees by writing such a stern memo. She revises the memo a couple of times, until it is in the final form. The redrafted memo is shown in Exhibit 4H.

**Excel Corporation**

INTERNAL MEMORANDUM

To: All employees

From: Lisa Christopher, Head, Administration

Subject: Misuse of office telephones

In view of the soaring administrative costs, we have revised our policy on the use of office telephones. So far, our policy has been to discourage the use of office telephones for personal purposes because of the costs involved. We realize that this may not be a convenient solution, so employees can now use office telephones for personal calls by paying for each call.

The details of charges for local and outstation calls have been put up on the notice board.

Lisa Christopher

The revised memo is certainly better. The writing is simplified, the wordiness is removed, the tone of the memo is made courteous, and the revised policy is clearly stated. In short, the purpose is exactly and effectively communicated.

If you very carefully compare the first and final versions of Lisa's memo, you will discover a basic change in her thinking on the use of office phones. Lisa had first considered the use of phones for personal matters to be misuse of office phones (see the subject line of the memo). Now, she treats it as regular use of phones. This psychological shift in Lisa's perspective has improved the tone of her memo and her attitude towards other employees in the company, who now become part of "we". Her tone now is free of harshness and the threat of termination.

Work out the changes in Lisa's mind as she moves from a poor first draft to a final revision that has simplicity, brevity, courtesy, and the you-attitude. Notice the following steps in Lisa's process of revising and reaching the final draft, which are a part of all successful revisions.

- Focusing on intent
- Eliminating wordiness
- Correcting the tone
- Revising the policy itself

For realizing how rewriting sharpens thinking and changes both content and form, you should trace each one of the above changes in the two memos. This exercise will improve the effectiveness of your written business communication.

**Exhibit 4H** The Revised Memo

## LETTERS AND MEMOS

Letters, memos, and e-mails are brief pieces of communication. They are so short that most people hardly think it necessary to spend much time planning them before writing. It is common to just jot down one's thoughts—the basic information needed to communicate. In fact, it is important to be careful when writing letters, memos, and e-mails, because these small pieces of communication are used in less formal contexts. They tend to affect the receiver's feelings and thoughts with great immediacy and power. Writers should, therefore, consider two questions before writing:

1. What is the exact message?
2. How will it affect the receiver? That is, what would be the receiver's reaction—would he or she be pleased or displeased, interested or not interested? These four kinds of reactions should guide the writer. They determine the sequence of information in letters.

## Memos: Format and Appearance

Persuasive letters partly share the form and intimacy of memos, which are frequently written to persons within the office/organization to communicate routine matters. A memorandum, often referred to as a memo, is a form used by a person known to the receiver personally. Therefore, it is less formal in tone and does not have formal elements, such as the salutation, subscription, greeting, or even a signature at the end. It directly states the subject after mentioning the following:

From ________ Subject ________

To ________ Date ________

Alternatively, it can have the following format:

To ________ Date ________

From ________

Subject ____________________________

### *How to Write a Memo*

A memo addresses the subject under discussion immediately. It is short and written in a friendly tone. All business messages and information solicit a friendly, cooperative, and positive response from employees, clients, or senior or junior colleagues. For this purpose, the memo writer (manager) should write in a friendly and cooperative tone. A harsh or unfriendly tone will dishearten the reader of the memo and lower his/her morale.

> A harsh or unfriendly tone will dishearten the reader of the memo and lower his/her morale.
> - Do not assume that everyone knows everything related to the issue discussed in the memo.
> - Explain the causes of problems or reasons for changes being suggested.
> - Be clear, concrete, and specific.
> - Be pleasant rather than commanding or authoritative. Use you-attitude.
> - Ask for feedback or suggestions.

For example, consider the following memorandum from a works manager to the supervisors working with him.

> "Every Saturday morning all supervisors in my plant must meet and report on the clean-up of their individual shop floors. All reports must be submitted by afternoon."

In this memo, the tone is of distrust and authority. The works manager uses "all" and "must" twice. It shows that he does not consider any of his supervisors responsible. The use of "must" indicates that he doubts their sense of duty. The manager can direct his supervisors without doubting their sense of duty. Further, the memo is vaguely worded. The reader will not know which Saturday the meetings begin and when they are to be held—*morning* is a long period of time and is not specific. In addition, questions such as where the meetings are to be held are not addressed. No reference of place is made. Again, *afternoon* is a vague deadline. The manager should indicate the specific time by which the reports are due. Finally, the phrase "clean-up" does not completely convey all that is to be considered while inspecting the work. Such vagueness should be avoided by observing the following principles of writing memos:

In the case discussed here, show how the supervisors would benefit from the proposed change. Explain the need to hold a Saturday supervision meeting to discuss and report on the clean-up of the shop floors. Ask for feedback. It is necessary to know supervisors' ideas on the monitoring and reporting of the clean-up. If they are invited to give their views, they will have sense of participation and involvement in the decision-making and execution processes.

### *Uses of a Memo*

The various functions of memorandums are given in Exhibit 4.5.

A memorandum acts as a permanent record of whatever is communicated.

As a written record of business decisions, policies, institutions, and so on, a memorandum acts as a permanent record of whatever is communicated. Therefore, it should be written with great care and skill.

| *Function* | *Example* |
|---|---|
| To provide information | I attended the meeting of the executive committee. The main points discussed were… |
| To issue an instruction | Staff members are requested to attend the orientation session to be held in the conference room at 11 a.m. today. |
| To convey a policy decision | The executive committee has decided to pay one day's salary for working on a Saturday. |
| To offer suggestions | I think in-house training should be a regular feature for all cadres. |
| To record/report an agreement | During the meeting held on August 5, it was decided that we buy 3 LCD projectors. |

**Exhibit 4.5** Functions of a Memorandum

**Part A: The Original Memo**

TYC

May 12, 2008

To: Lab Personnel

From: Sushil Kumar

Subject: Final Report Requirements

Beginning Monday, December 19, *all* our final test reports must indicate:

1. Test results
2. Dimensions in metric terms
3. Photos in proper order—also identify each one on its reverse
4. The distribution list
5. Write the report immediately after the test
6. Be sure all terms are spelled correctly
7. Complete formulas

**Exhibit 4.6** Ineffective and Effective Sample Memos

**Part B: The Revised Memo**

TYC
May 12, 2008
To: Laboratory D-66 Personnel
From: Sushil Kumar, Supervisor
Subject: Final Test Report Requirements

I've received some requests for changes in our test reports from the chemical engineers who use them. Therefore, beginning Monday, December 19, all final test reports must include the following:

1. Full test results at each stage of the testing process
2. Dimensions stated in metric terms
3. Photos in proper order and each identified on its reverse
4. The distribution list
5. Correctly spelt terms
6. Full formulas

Please write your reports immediately after completing the test while the data are fresh in your mind. I'm sure with these minor adjustments in report style, we can give the engineers what they need.

**Exhibit 4.6** *Continued*

The two versions of the memo in Exhibit 4.6 show the difference in the effectiveness of a well-written memo and a poorly written one. The revised memo is specific and friendly in tone. It gives adequate details and explains why the change is needed and how it would help the engineers.

## Office Memorandum

Letters or any form of such written correspondence are vital organs of an office. An official letter is different from the types of business letters that have been discussed. It can be both internal and external. Some of the examples of official letters are memorandum, notice, circular, and e-mail.

### *Memorandum*

A memorandum or memo is a document used for internal communication in an organization. The plural form of memorandum is either memoranda or memorandums. A memo may be addressed to one person or a group. The writer and the readers of a memo are well acquainted, and therefore a memo does not require formal elements, like salutations, greetings, or even signatures at the end. A memo usually records events or observations on a topic or provides information about any development in the organization. Since it is only about communicating some important information related to the functioning or processes of the company, it is usually quite direct in approach, to the point, focusing sharply on what the reader needs to know.
The format of a memo is fairly simple. The standard features of a memo are listed here:

1. The word 'Memo' or 'Memorandum' at the top of the page; though not mandatory, it helps to make clear, right at the beginning, the nature of the communication
2. The date of the issue of the memo
3. The name of the receiver/s, followed by "To:" and the name of the sender, followed by "From:"

4. The names of the receiver/s and the sender/s should be followed by their full title and the department.
5. A subject line following the word "Subject:" or "Sub:", clearly identifying the topic
6. The content or message of the memo

The content of the message should be brief, to the point, giving specific dates and time, if any. The language should be polite, pleasant, and friendly. It should not sound bossy and instructive; it should be participative and tactfully articulated. A memo is generally used to convey a policy decision, to issue an instruction, to provide information, or to record an agreement.

**An example of a Memo**

P&L Consultants<br>2/35, Block E<br>Pitampura, Delhi

MEMO

Date: 18.06.2010

To: Marketing Executives, Exhibition Division

From: Director–Marketing, Exhibition Division

Subject: Change in the report of the marketing team

I have received some requests for change in our reports from the marketing team to the project management team. Therefore, beginning Monday, 21 June 2010, the marketing executives should include the following topics in their reports and have them in the order as given below:

1. The client company's name
2. Complete address
3. Office phone and fax number
4. The contact person and his designation
5. The contact person's cell number
6. Their choice of hall number and stall size
7. The status of the deal

You are advised to submit your reports every Thursday before 4 p.m. I'm sure these minor adjustments in the report template will facilitate the project management team's operations.

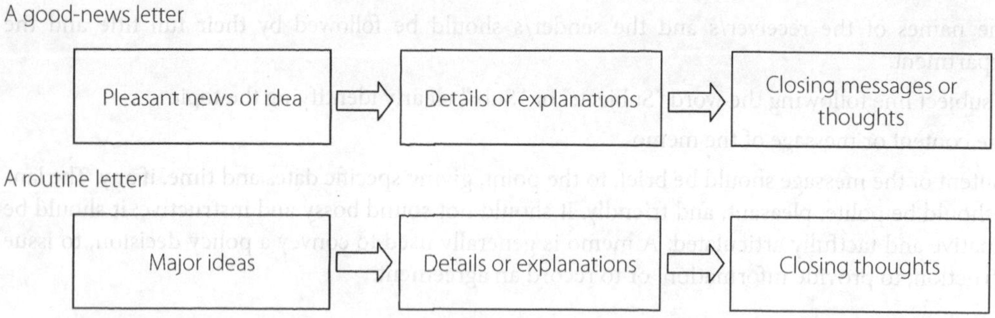


**Exhibit 4.7** Sequence of Presentation of Ideas in Routine and Good-news Letters

## Good News and Routine Letters

Letters that please the receiver are called *good-news letters*. Those that neither please nor displease, but are received with interest are known as *routine letters*. Both follow the same sequence of presentation of ideas and have a deductive pattern, which is a direct organization of ideas (Exhibit 4.7).

The direct organization of ideas in good-news and routine letters follows human psychology. A pleasant or interesting idea will always hold the receiver's attention. Hence, good news can be given in the very first sentence, followed by details and the final message.

This basic plan of presenting ideas can be used in many business situations. These situations include:

1. Routine claim letters and "yes" replies
2. Routine request letters and "yes" replies
3. Routine order letters and "yes" replies

### *Routine Claim Letters and "Yes" Replies*

A *claim* is a demand or request for something to which one has a right. Examples are a refund, payment for damages, a replacement for something defective, exchanges, and so on. A claim letter is, thus, a request for adjustment. When a writer thinks that because of guarantees or other specified terms and conditions, the request for adjustment will be automatically granted without delay or without requiring persuasion, he or she writes the letter in the *routine* form. When the writer believes that a direct statement of the desired action will get a positive response without arguments, he or she can use the following sequence/pattern of ideas:

1. Request action in the opening sentence.
2. Give reasons supporting the request or action.
3. End by appreciating or thanking the addressee for taking the action requested.

The writer of the claim letter in Exhibit 4.8 obviously thought that his routine request for an exchange would be granted. He, therefore, stated his claim in the very first sentence without any complaints. Similarly, the person replying to a routine claim letter knows that the recipient will be glad to know that his or her request has been granted, therefore, the writer states an expression of willingness in the first sentence of the response. The details and closing sentence follow the opening. This is demonstrated in Exhibit 4.9.

The "yes" reply in Exhibit 4.9 grants the request, but the writer does not use the word "grant". Moreover, there is no reference to the letter being answered as a claim, though these words are often employed

| | |
|---|---|
| Directly states claim | Please send me another copy of *How to Communicate Under Pressure* to replace the copy returned herewith. |
| Gives reasons | This is the latest edition, but this copy has four pages, from page 60 to page 64, wrongly sequenced, which is confusing and annoying. |
| | The enclosed receipt was packed with the book sent to me. |
| Ends with a confident repetition of action desired | I shall appreciate an early replacement. |

**Exhibit 4.8** A Routine Claim Letter

> Date…
>
> Dear…
>
> A copy of *How to Communicate Under Pressure* is on its way to you. You will not be charged for its mailing. You should receive it within a few days. Our catalogue for the latest arrivals in Communication Strategies/Studies is also enclosed.
>
> Sincerely,

**Exhibit 4.9** A "Yes" Reply to a Routine Claim

for referring to such letters. Phrases such as "your request is granted" or "we are granting your request" may convey to the receiver "we see ourselves as superiors and in a position of power". Similarly, "we are adjusting your claim" can also suggest "We are responding to your dissatisfaction". Therefore, words such as "grant" and "claim" are not used in such letters.

The recipient of a claim letter should always try to view the complaint positively. He or she should not be angered by customers, clients, or defective products. Business letters in all situations should be written with politeness and respect for the other party. Negative expressions should be avoided, though it is easy to react sharply when people complain about something one has done, said, or sold. Neither the writer nor the person replying should use expressions of accusation, such as "because of your careless packing, several pieces of the crockery set sent to me are broken" or "I have been cheated by you because the colour of the shirt, which was guaranteed to be fast, has completely faded".

> Business letters in all situations should be written with politeness and respect for the other party.

Instead of using the harsh language used in Exhibit 4.10, the writer can simply state the facts of the situation and the action desired. For example, it is more businesslike to say:

> "I have received the sunglasses I ordered from your company. I find that there is a scratch on the right lens; perhaps it happened in transit. I would appreciate an early replacement of the sunglasses as I am going on a trip to Rajasthan at the end of the month."

508, Sector 9
Faridabad
June 18, 2010

Agfa Company
531, Linking Road
Bandra, Mumbai – 400 052

Dear Sir,

I am returning a pair of Rayban sunglasses, which you sent me per my order of June 6, 2010.

You will notice there is a scratch on the right lens. As the lens is guaranteed against imperfections, I am returning it to you.

Will you send me a new pair of sunglasses as soon as you can? The enclosed receipt was packed with the sunglasses when they were mailed to me.

I shall appreciate an early exchange as I am going on a trip to Rajasthan at the end of the month.

Yours truly,

**Exhibit 4.10** A Businesslike/Impolite Routine Claim

Another example of a businesslike claim is,

> "I am returning the Easy Knit shirt that I purchased from your shop a week ago. Its colour has faded after washing by machine. The colour was guaranteed as long as the shirt was not exposed to the sun. I request you to exchange it with a new shirt of the same colour."

The "yes" reply letter in Exhibit 4.11 directly grants the request, reassures the buyer that he made a wise choice when he chose Easy Knit, and goes on to explain how to maintain the product. The reply avoids negative language. Through positive language, the customer is made to see his mistake. The letter also suggests ways to prevent future trouble and finally expresses hope for a con-

Date...

Dear Mr...,

One long-lasting, pink Easy Knit shirt is being sent to you against the one you returned to us. Compared with other shirts, Easy Knit shirts do not normally fade in colour and remain wrinkle-free. But, for best results, they must be washed by hand and without using any strong bleach.

Our Special Discount sales catalogue is being mailed to you separately.

Truly,

**Exhibit 4.11** A "Yes" Reply to a Businesslike/Impolite Routine Claim

tinuing relationship by informing the buyer of discount sales. The "yes" letter is carefully written to guarantee customer confidence in the product and full satisfaction in the transaction. The letter has a direct, positive approach.

## Request Letters

### *Routine Request Letters and "Yes" Replies*

Now that we know how routine claim letters and replies to them should be written, let us take a look at *routine requests*. A letter to, say a vendor, requesting information about a product, should state clearly and completely what information is desired. A request for information should not suggest that the writer wants to place an order. Exhibit 4.12 shows a sample routine request. Exhibit 4.13 shows how a "yes" reply to a routine request should be written.

### *Routine Orders and Their "Yes" Replies*

*Routine orders* should be explicit and thorough. In addition, they should be very clear about what they expect by giving complete details of the desired product. This includes specifying the time of delivery and the mode of shipment. There should be no ambiguity or chance of confusion or misunderstanding. A sample of a routine order letter is presented in Exhibit 4.14.

*Pearls Repair Service*

155, Kashmere Gate
New Delhi
"If they make it, we repair it."

April 30, 2010

Mr Abhishek Chaturvedi
Order Department
MML Electronics Suppliers, Inc.
135 C, Kolkata

Dear Mr Chaturvedi,

Re: Order No. 497; Shipment No. 246032

In our order of April 10, 2010, we included a request for an electron tube X518E. The shipment we received today does not include the tube we ordered, but does include a proton tube. Upon checking your catalogue, I discovered that you intend this tube to be a replacement for the tube X518E, which you have discontinued from your product line.

The supervisor of our repair shop, however, says that he cannot use the replacement tube sent by you. Because of this, we are returning this item from the shipment.

Please credit our account for Rs 2,000 for the tube we did not order and have returned.

Sincerely yours,

Ajay Saxena
Administrative Manager

**Exhibit 4.12** A Routine Request Letter

**NEW INDIA TILE COMPANY**
444, New Main Street
Charki Dadri – 120072

April 12, 2002

Ms Sonia Suri
General Manager
Escorts Medical Hospital
Neelam Bata Road
Faridabad, Haryana

Dear Ms Suri,

We will be more than happy to replace the Durafinish tiles in front of the elevators and in the lobby area of Escorts Hospital as you requested in your letter of March 28, 2002.

When we installed the tile (Model 520) in December 2000, we guaranteed the no-fade finish. The tile you selected is imported from Italy and is one of our best-selling products. Recently, the manufacturer added a special sealing compound to the tile, making it more durable.

Our sales representative, Mr Deepak Rai, will call on you in the next few days to inspect the tiles and make arrangements for replacing them, at no additional cost. I appreciate your calling this situation to our attention because we are always eager to know how our products are performing. We guarantee our customers' full satisfaction.

Sincerely yours,
Mokshit Sharma
MS:tk
cc: Mr Deepak Rai

**Exhibit 4.13** A "Yes" Reply to a Routine Request

Since the response to the letter in Exhibit 4.14 is positive, the "yes" response should follow the pattern shown in Exhibit 4.15.

### *Guidelines for a "Yes" Reply*

The guidelines a writer needs to follow while drafting a "yes" reply to a routine claim, request, or order are summarized here:

1. The beginning should state the reason for writing the letter and the main idea.
2. The middle paragraphs should give details of the good news, reaffirm the guarantee if any, describe the product offered, and explain why the replacement would satisfy the receiver.
3. The end should draw the reader's attention to the conditions, if any, attached to the positive response. The letter should close on a positive note of thanks for the original order and hopes for continuing good relations with the buyer.

### *Guidelines for a "No" Reply*

In business, at times we have to say "no". In some situations, it may not be possible to grant the writer's request or deliver what he or she has ordered. On such occasions the goal of the person who is responding should be to write a "no" letter inoffensively, while stating facts and giving reasons as convincingly as possible. A refusal is a refusal. It is bound to disappoint the reader. However, the goal is to reduce the negative emotions as much as possible. The writer of a "no" reply cannot convey an unfavourable deci-

*Maria Interiors, Inc*

12, Andheri West
Mumbai – 400 012

July 1, 2001

Silvania Office Products
B-27, Lajpat Nagar
New Delhi

Attention: Order Department

Dear Sir,

Please send me the following office supplies as listed and priced in your summer catalogue 91:

| | | |
|---|---|---|
| 8 pkgs | D33E-886 | Colour-coded files with heavy manila folders—letter size |
| 4 boxes | D33E-276 | Square box-files—capacity 2 |
| 24 | D33E-3325 | Large capacity 3-ring binders—letter size |

Please charge these to the Maria Interiors account. I would appreciate quick delivery of these items. Please ship by the fastest freight available.

Sincerely,

Akshay Sharma
Office Manager

**Exhibit 4.14** A Routine Order Letter

sion in an unfavourable way if he or she wants to retain the customer's goodwill. Thus, he or she must be able to write "no" while minimizing the reader's disappointment. To achieve this objective, the information should be patterned as follows:

> The goal of the person writing a "no" reply is to reduce the negative emotions as much as possible. The writer of a "no" reply cannot convey an unfavourable decision in an unfavourable way if he or she wants to retain the customer's goodwill.

1. The letter should begin with a paragraph that describes the general situation as the context in which the reader's request was considered. It should indicate in a neutral or friendly tone the reasons that led to the negative information or a refusal.

   Some possible methods to do this are:

   - Assuring the receiver that his or her matter was considered with great understanding and care.
   - Making the reader believe that it is the circumstances or situation and not the merit of his or her request that is responsible for the "no" response. (For example: "This session, there are more than ten thousand admission requests from your country.")
   - Agreeing with the reader in some way. (For example: "You are right that the guarantee period is one year.")
   - Giving a sincere compliment. (For example: "Your CAT score is quite high…")

*Silvania Office Products*
B-27, Lajpat Nagar
New Delhi

July 12, 2009

Mr Akshay Sharma
Office Manager
Maria Interiors, Inc.
12, Andheri West
Mumbai - 400012

Dear Mr Sharma,

The following items were shipped to you today by Worldwide Express, rush service:

| | | |
|---|---|---|
| 8 pkgs | D33E | Colour-coded files with heavy manila folders—letter size |
| 24 | D33E-3325 | Large capacity 3-ring binders—letter size |

Enclosed is the invoice for Rs 4,000, which includes sales tax. Your order for four boxes of square box-files—2 in capacity (D33E - 276) should reach you within 14 days, also by Worldwide Express. Because of the great popularity of these durable, high-capacity hole punchers, they are currently out of stock. A shipment from the supplier is due shortly, and when it arrives, we will fulfil your order immediately.

Thank you for your order, and please let me know if I can be of service in the future. For your convenience, I am enclosing a preview copy of the new catalogue, No. 107, which will be mailed to our customers in early December.

Sincerely,

Rajesh Bhatia
Sales Manager

RB:rb
Encl. : Catalogue No.107
: Invoice

**Exhibit 4.15** A "Yes" Reply to a Routine Order

- Showing (without raising false hope) that the possibility of fulfilling the request was there. (For example: "Your plan for opening a business school of international caliber sounds excellent.")
- Mentioning good news of interest to the reader. (For example: "The government has passed a bill to open new credit banks for farmers.")

2. The "no" letter should give facts and provide reasons and factors for refusal. (For example: "The manufacturer's instructions have not been strictly followed.")
3. The refusal should be mentioned in the same paragraph. It is important not to highlight the refusal. Therefore, no separate paragraph should be given to this negative point, instead, it should just be stated at the end of the paragraph that mentions the reasons for it.
4. The end of the "no" response seeks to maintain good business relations with the reader by suggesting an alternative course of action or a better deal in the future.

The aim of indirectly organizing a "no" response letter is to assure the reader that the bad news or the unfavourable decision was arrived at after careful consideration of the total situation and facts that could not be altered by the writer (the decision-maker). The purpose of indirect organization is to ensure that the reader does not believe that the refusal is based on arbitrary, subjective, or personal reasons.

Consider Exhibit 4.16, a letter of refusal written by New India Tile Company to the replacement request. Exhibit 4.13 is a "yes" response to the same request, but the factors involved in making the decision are different in this situation. Hence, the company's response to replacing the tiles is "no". The letter seeks to convey the negative message through indirect organization.

**NEW INDIA TILE COMPANY**
444, New Main Street
Charki Dadri – 120072

April 13, 2002

Ms Sonia Suri
General Manager
Escorts Medical Hospital
Neelam-Bata Road
Faridabad, Haryana

Dear Ms Suri,

You are certainly correct that we guarantee our tiles for 20 years after installation. We always stand behind our products when they are used according to the recommendations of the manufacturers and design consultants.

When I received your letter, I immediately studied the sales contract and checked the reports of the design consultant. Our records show that the consultant did explain on December 6, 2000 that Paloma Tile (Model 520) was not recommended for heavy traffic. Although another tile was suggested, you preferred to order the Paloma Tile, and you signed a waiver of guarantee. For your information, I'm enclosing a copy of that page of the contract. Because our recommendation was to use another tile, our usual 20-year guarantee is not in force in this situation.

For your needs, we recommend the Watermark Tile, which is specially sealed to withstand heavy traffic. The Watermark Tile is available in a design that would complement the Paloma Tile that is already in place. Our design consultant, Mr Ramesh Singh, would be happy to visit Escorts Medical Hospital and recommend a floor pattern that could incorporate a new Watermark Tile, without sacrificing the Paloma Tile that does not show wear. Enclosed is a brochure showing the Watermark designs. Mr Singh will call you for an appointment this week, and because you are our customer, we will be happy to schedule prompt service for you.

Sincerely,
Mokshit Sharma
Production Installation Manager
MS/dc

Encl.: Watermark brochure
Contract page

cc.: Mr Ramesh Singh

**Exhibit 4.16** A "No" Reply (to a Routine Request)

## Persuasive Letters

Persuasion is used when the writer suspects that the reader will not be interested in the message and the action to be taken. In such a situation, the writer may use the device of startling the reader by informing him or her about something unexpected at the beginning of the letter. This way, the reader is made to see right away why he or she should accept the letter's proposal. The letter goes on to show how the reader will greatly benefit by taking the suggested action. Such letters, which arouse the reader's interest and induce him or her to act as directed, are essentially letters that sell ideas to others. They are called *persuasive letters*. Writing them well requires skillful patterning of information. The persuasive pattern, also known as persuasive organization, involves the following sequence of ideas:

5 Write simple, complete, and persuasive letters and memos.

Letters that arouse the reader's interest and induce him or her to act as directed are essentially letters that sell ideas to others. They are called *persuasive letters.*

1. The opening sentence in a persuasive business letter (usually sales) catches the reader's attention by saying one of the following:
   - A startling statement of fact—"Every second, 6 children die of malnutrition in our country."
   - A remedial measure to a problem—"At last, you can build your own house."
   - An alarming question—"Would you like to die without providing for the safety of your children and spouse?"
   - A special product, scheme, or plan—"Within the next 14 days you should expect to receive important authorized mail from our sweepstakes manager."
2. The middle section of a persuasive letter gives details regarding the product or scheme that is being promoted. This section mainly describes the benefits to the reader. It explains why the reader should accept the proposal.
3. After arousing the reader's interest in the proposal, the letter then requests action, such as a "yes" response to the proposed request.
4. The last paragraph acts as a reminder to the reader of the special benefits he or she would gain by acting as urged and requests action within the given deadline.

Such persuasive sales letters are also known as *form letters*. They differ from other business letters in the following ways:

1. They may not be dated: These letters can be used by the company for many months. Therefore, the date of the form letter (sales letter) may not be necessary and relevant.
2. There may be no personal salutation: The sales letter is not addressed to a specific individual. The receiver's name is superimposed as a mailing device.

   Dear Friend,
   Dear Reader,
   Dear Valued Customer,

   The opening sets a pleasant tone by saying that the reader is known for his or her interest in the kind of proposal made.
3. There is usually a postscript message to remind the reader of the action to be taken by the specified deadline or to highlight the benefits or any other important point.

4. Most persuasive sales letters include some mention of further material to be received by the reader. For example, the box with the word "important" in the sales letter shown in Communication Snapshot 4.6 highlights that two sweepstakes entry cards would be sent in the near future.

**Communication Snapshot 4.6** How Sentence Structure Affects Meaning

The focus of the letter in Exhibit 4I is "be advised". The advice is in bold and is placed at the centre of the letter in an eye-catching position. The letter bears no date. It has no personal salutation. The expression "Dear Valued Customer" establishes a friendly tone at the very outset. It goes on to arouse the reader's curiosity by stating, "expect to receive important authorized mail".

The middle paragraph gives details of the reader's undoubted chance to win the Rs. 1,000,000,00 First Prize. This paragraph uses strategy to hold the reader's attention and interest by saying, "You already stand ahead of many…". This paragraph also gives details of how the reader is going to benefit from this message.

In a friendly tone, the writer calls this letter a "pre-disclosure". It motivates the receiver to act further by disclosing that "You already stand ahead of many…". The letter does not include the usual "Subscription offer", "yours sincerely", and so on. Instead, it ends on a sincere note of advice: "Be sure to reply as instructed". This sample letter is an actual letter written by the sweepstakes committee of the magazine Pottery Weekly. It is a good example of a persuasive sales letter. The organization, language, and sales strategies followed by the writer persuade and urge the reader to participate in the sweepstakes.

**Pottery Weekly**

Dear Valued Customer,

In the next 14 days, expect to receive important authorized mail from *Pottery Weekly's* sweepstakes manager. This mail will provide you with details on your current sweepstakes eligibility status.

You should know that as of June 2009, there is no doubt that you are enviably well positioned to have a shot at our Rs. 1,000,000.00 First Prize. You already stand ahead of many who have not been invited to participate in *Pottery Weekly's* 2-million-rupee sweepstakes.

**Be advised that the sweepstakes documents that are due to arrive at your address have strictly controlled deadlines!**

**This is why you are entitled to receive this pre-disclosure—to provide you sufficient notice to reply on time. The post office has assured expedient delivery of the package to you.**

**IMPORTANT**

Please watch out for a red envelope from *Pottery Weekly,* marked with the same package code as in this letter. It contains two sweepstakes entry cards. Then, reply in strict conformance with the instructions provided therein.

This is the only step required of you to secure your eligibility to enter the 2-million-rupee sweepstakes for your chance to win well over Rs. 1,000,000.00. Please do not discount the vital importance of this pre-disclosure. Be sure to reply as instructed.

**Exhibit 4I** The Letter

***Konnect Cellphone***

Mr P. D. Apte
508, Sector 9
Faridabad, Haryana 121006
31 July 2010

You have been a valued member of the Konnect Cellphone family. As you may be aware, Konnect Cellphone is now a part of Konnect Telecom, one of the largest cellular operators in India and the third largest in the world. We have taken the leadership in launching new and exciting tariff plans in Delhi, thereby making cellular telephony more affordable.

As per the Honourable TRAI ruling dated 25 January 2001, an amount of Rs. 595.36 is refundable against your contract number 00124813301 and mobile phone number 9811071974. This refund is on account of a reduction in license fees. This amount will be refunded to you via an account payee cheque at the address mentioned above.

If you have any queries regarding the same, please feel free to contact us on our toll-free hotline number, 9811398133, and we would be glad to address the same.

Keep smiling!

***Joydeep Chatterjee***

Joydeep Chaterjee
GM—Customer Services
Konnect Telecom
Nariman Street, Fort,
Mumbai 400001

**Exhibit 4.17** An Alternative Style for a Persuasive Letter

Most persuasive sales letters include some mention of further material to be received by the reader.

There is another style of formatting a persuasive form letter, which is shown in Exhibit 4.17. To look more informal, the letter leaves out the salutation completely. It also drops the formal ending "subscription". Instead, it closes with "best wishes" from the writer of the message.

## Collection Letters

Collection letters are letters sent to customers who do not pay accounts promptly. In such letters tone is very important. The way you write such letters will depend on such factors as the age of the debt, whether the customer is habitually late in settling accounts, and any previous reminders issued.

| | |
|---|---|
| | **KHAN ASSOCIATES**<br>VIDEOCON TOWER, 7th FLOOR<br>E -1, JHANDEWLAN EXTN<br>NEW DELHI - 110055<br><br>TEL.: 22618685-90 |
| You may prefer to use lower case for your initials | GK/sat |
| | 2 November 200- |
| | Arvind Sinha<br>B1/14, Chaitanya Marg<br>New Delhi - 43 |
| Use 'Dear Sirs' when writing to the company | Dear Sirs |
| Appropriate heading | ACCOUNT NUMBER FT384738 |
| State background details and amount owing | According to our records the amount shown on our statement dated 30 September 2000 has not been paid. The amount owing Is Rs 43,752.00. |
| The customer is given the benefit of the doubt in this case | If payment has already been made by the time you receive this letter please accept my apologies for troubling you. However, if payment has been overlooked, I hope you will settle this account as soon as possible. |
| | Yours faithfully |
| | GEETIKA KAPOOR<br>Accounts Manager |

If a polite letter like this fails to produce a response, a firmer letter is sent.

A firm tone will be accepted as a professional approach while a letter with impolite tone may result in losing a customer.

## Examples

### *Letter of Confirmation*

The main purpose of this letter is to provide a written record of arrangements made between the sender and the recipient in person or by telephone. These letters are usually very short.

**China Centre for Rural Development**
**11, Ashoka Road**
**Chand Crossing**
**New Delhi - 110004**
**Tel: 011-24716065-96**
**Fax: 011-24317921**

TWB/cfb

18 September 200–

Prof Abdull Rizvi Khan
Manager
Tie & Dye Fabrics
IFFCO Chowk
Gurgaon - 110075

Dear Mr Rizvi

I am pleased to comfirm our meeting at 11:45 a.m. on Friday, 18 November 200– at our head office in New Delhi. Our Director from China, Mr Ong Chee Lee, will be in New Delhi at that time and he will also join us in our meeting.

As I mentioned to you on the e-mail, I am very interested in seeing your new range of fabrics and hope you can bring some samples with you.

I look forward to seeing you again.

Yours sincerely

Anand Kapoor
Dy. General Manager

## Letter of Acknowledgement

We acknowledge receipt of something when a written record is appropriate. An acknowledgement letter may also be sent to acknowledge receipt of another letter or document which requires further attention. As such you would clearly state that you will look into the matter and reply in more detail at a later date.

**Magic Photo Studio**

**56, Ist floor**
**Shree Ram Towers Netaji Marg**
**Kanpur - 226001**
**INDIA**

**Tel: 2288361-68** **Fax: 0522-2288376**

HMY/LK

25 April 200–

Mr. Vinay Chaturvedi
203, Silver Oaks
Vasundhara Vihar
Noida - 62

Dear Mr Chaturvedi

Thank you for your letter of 22 March addressed to our VP, Mrs Gurpreet Kaur.

Mrs kaur is overseas on business and will not be in the office again until 7 July. I shall be in contact with Mrs Kaur and shall inform her about your letter, which I am sure will receive her prompt attention.

Please let me know if I can be of any help.

Yours sincerely

Pooja Jain (ms)
PA to Gurpreet Kaur
V.P.

Some organisations use printed cards for this purpose, which can be completed easily.

**Dev Chand and Sons, Ambadeep Building, Janpath, New Delhi - 110001**

---

**We acknowledge with thanks the receipt of**

**which will receive careful attention.**

---

***Telephone - 011-24367510*** ***Fax - 011-24366702***

### *Letter of Enquiry and Reply to Enquiry*

Enquiries for information about goods or services are sent and received in business all the time. In your letter remember to state clearly exactly what you want – information? a catalogue? a price list? a quotation? Keep your enquiry brief and to the point.

The sender's personal address looks good when balanced at the top right

56 Windsor Avenue
Vasundhara Enclave
Noida
Sec-63

When you write your own personal letters a reference is not necessary, just a date

20 February 200–
Pearson Education
Knowledge Boulevard
Sector 62
Noida
U.P.

When writing to a company use the salutation 'Dear Sirs'

Dear Sirs

Introduction

My neighbour, Mr Ram Kapoor, has recently recommened your high-end textbook to me. He and his wife have often bought books and speak very highly about them.

Details

My wife and I are thinking of opening a collage in August.

Response required

Please send me a copy of your current brochure showing the cost of your books together with contact details of the persons whom I can contact.

Close

I hope to hear from you soon.

Match the complimentary close with the salutation

Yours faithfully

Mohan Pandey

### *Reply to an Enquiry*

Enquiries are potential business. They must be acknowledged promptly. If the enquiry is from a present customer, say how much you appreciate it. If it is from a prospective customer, thank her/him for the enquiry, give all the relevant information and express the hope of good business relations.

| Annotation | Letter |
|---|---|
| Letterheaded paper | **Pearson Education**<br>*Tel: +91-120-542 5555*<br>*Fax: +91-120-555 4444* *Email: info@pearson.com* |
| Reference and date | 22 February 200– |
| When replying to a letter use the appropriate courtesy title before the name in the inside address | Mr Mohan Pandey<br>Pearson Education<br>Knowledge Boulevard<br>Sector 62<br>Noida<br>U.P. |
| Use the personal 'Dear Mr Farrelly' rather than 'Dear Sir' | Dear Mr Pandey |
| Introduction | Thank you for your letter of 20 February enquiring about our books on higher education. I am pleased that you have heard favourable comments about our titles. |
| Details | I enclose our catalogue giving full details of this year's list of titles. Your attention is particularly drawn to page 49 which gives contact details for each sales representative. |
| Response required | As there is usually a heavy demand for these titles, I suggest that you should book early, particularly as you propose to start a collage during the peak season. |
| Close | Please do not hesitate to contact me and I shall do my best to ensure that your titles are delivered before the opening your new collage. |
| Match the complimentary close with the salutation | Yours sincerely |
| | Swati Suri<br>Sales Manager |
| Don't forget Enc | Enc |

### *Letter of Complaint and Reply to Complaint*

In business, there are bound to be occasions when you have to make a complaint, or deal with one. When you have a genuine complaint, you will feel angry, but remember that the other party may not be to blame. They may have a perfectly good reason. Therefore, your complaint should be confined to a statement of the facts, followed by an enquiry about what the company will do about it or your suggestion of how you expect the matter to be dealt with. At all costs, avoid rudeness.

K. Prasad
29.B Upvan
Eage
Borivali (East)
Mumbai -
400078
022 3587095
022 2543326

*Note that a telephone number is included with the sender's address*

15 November. 2011
Mr Dhraj Misra
General Manager
New Age Builders Ltd.
Western Lane
Mumbai - 400004

Dear Mr Misra

BUILDING AT NANDAN BAN SOCIETY ROAD, MUMBAI

*Introduction and reason for writing – tone is firm but courteous*

I signed the contract for a two bed room flat in Nandan Ban in July, 2010. At that time it was estimated that the work would be completed and the flat would be ready for occupation in a year. That was 15 months ago and the work is still only half finished.

*Inconvenience is emphasised*

The delay is causing a great deal of inconvenience not only to me, but also to my present land lord. Obviously, I cannot shift until the Nandan Ban flat is ready for my possession.

*Action expected*

Please let me know the progress and status of the construction and completion of my flat.

Yours sincerely

K. Parsad

Most companies wish to hear if customers have cause to complain. It gives them an opportunity to improve, to explain, and to put things right. Here are some general rules for dealing with complaints:

(i) Acknowledge a complaint promptly. If you are unable to reply fully give a brief reply and say they will hear in detail soon.

(ii) The customer is not always right, but it is good practice to assume that the customer may be right.

(iii) Be polite and try not to offend, even if the complaint is unreasonable.

(iv) Admit blame readily if appropriate, then express regret and state how you intend to put matters right.

(v) Thank the customer for bringing the matter to your attention.

(vi) Do not apologise if you are not at fault.

**New Age Builders Ltd**
26 Western Lane
Mumbai - 400004

Tel.: 022 - 3996685

21 November 2011

K. Prasad
29 B, Upvan Eage
Boriveli East
Mumbai 400004
Tel.: 022 - 3996685

Dear Mr Prasad

BUILDING AT NANDAN BAN, MUMBAI

Acknowledge letter and express regret — Thank you for your letter of 15 November. I am sorry that the estimated period for completion of your flat has already been exceeded. I realise how much inconvenience this delay must be causing you.

Circumstances are explained fully — I would like to point out the severe labour shortage Maharashtra is facing. This has been a major factor for the delay. Secondly, there was a nationwide shortage of building material earlier this year, from which the trade is only now recovering. Had it not been for these two unforeseen difficulties, the estimated completion in period of 12 months would have been met.

Assurance that the situation will improve — Fortunately, the labour situation has improved a lot in recent weeks and as such work on your flat is now proceeding smoothly. Unless there are any other unforeseen delays, we hope that the flat will be ready for your possession the end of March 2012.

Courteous close — Please do not hesitate to telephone me if you have any further questions.

Yours sincerely

Dhiraj Misra
General Manager
DM/cp

***Collection Letters***

Collection letters are letters sent to customers who delay payment of dues. In such letters tone is very important. The way you write such letters will depend on factors, like the period of the debt, whether the customer is habitually late in clearing accounts, and earlier reminders issued.

| | |
|---|---|
| | **JAIN ASSOCIATES**<br>Sunrise Building<br>C-2 New Ashok Nagar<br>New Delhi - 110096<br>Tel.: 22714552 |
| You may prefer to use lower case for your initials | 2 November 2011 |
| | Mr. Govind Bakashi<br>D2, Mandir Lane<br>New Delhi - 11 |
| Use 'Dear Sirs' when writing to the company | Dear Sirs |
| Appropriate subject line | ACCOUNT NUMBER NBC 2564 |
| State background details and amount due | As per our records the amount of Rs 90,000 shown on our statement dated 12 Aug. 2011 in your account is still outstanding. |
| The customer is given the benefit of the doubt in this case | If payment has already been made by the time you receive this letter, please ignore this letter. However, if payment has been overlooked, I hope you will clear this payment as soon as possible. |
| | Yours faithfully |
| | Geeta Kalia<br>Account Manager |
| | GK/sat |

If a polite letter of this kind, fails to act, a firmer letter is sent. The second letter is firm but polite.

A firm tone will be appreciated as a professional approach, while a rude letter may result in losing the customer.

## Application Letter

An advertisement that attracts your attention, check carefully to note whether application should be hand-written. If it is not mentioned, you may print your letter. Keep the application letter short and concise, give your main particulars listed in an enclosed curriculum vitae (sometimes called a resumé). This saves your letter from becoming very long.

**JAIN ASSOCIATES**
Sunrise Building
C-2 New Ashok Nagar
New Delhi - 96

Tel: 22714552

30 December 2011
Mr Govind Bakshi
D2, Mandir Lane
New Delhi - 11

Dear Sirs

ACCOUNT NUMBER NBC 2564

*Give background details again and repeat sum due*

On 2 November, we wrote to remind you that our August 2011 statement showed a balance of Rs 90,000 outstanding and due for payment.

*The tone is firmer here*

Settlement of this account is now almost 4 months overdue. Therefore, we suggest that you further either send us your payment without delay or let us know the reason for this delay.

An earlier reply will be greatly appreciated.

Yours faithfully

Geeta Kalia
Account Manager

Gk/st

Some advertisements require that you should request for an application form, in which case just write a simple letter of request in the standard form. Larger organizations because by having specific headings the company can be assured of obtaining the same information about each applicant.

| | |
|---|---|
| Your personal address | 6/102, Easy End Apartment<br>Mayur Vihar Phase 1 Extn<br>Delhi - 96<br>Tel: 0115 987654 |
| | 12 July 2011 |
| Address to person named in the advertisement | Mrs Kavita Seth<br>Human Relations Manager<br>Airtel<br>Aurora Camp<br>Temple Road<br>Delhi |
| | Dear Mrs Seth |
| Use job title as the heading | TELEPHONE EXECUTIVE (MARKETING) |
| | I am interested in applying for this post as advertised in today's Hindustan Times. |
| Give some brief details of what you are doing now | I have been employed as part-time Administration Assistant in Delhi Technical College for the last 6 months while studying there on a Business Administration course. My course finishes very soon and I am keen to join a progressive company such as Airtel. |
| Enclose your CV | My full particulars are shown on my enclosed Curriculum Vitae. I shall be happy to attend an interview at any time. Look forward to hearing from you soon. |
| | Yours sincerely |
| | Signature<br>Manisha Kaur (miss) |
| Don't forget Enc | Enc: |

### *Letter for Interview Invitation*

A letter inviting shortlisted applicants to attend all interview should be fairly short, simply thanking the person for his/her application and giving a day/date/time for the interview.

***Interview*** The interview is an essential stage in the recruitment process. Unit 2 gives full guidelines on how to prepare for interviews. Perhaps you can arrange for some mock interviews to be held in your class.

**Airtel**
**Aurora Camp**
**Temple Road**
**Delhi**

| | | | |
|---|---|---|---|
| **Tel** | **0207 345375** | | |
| **Fax** | **0207 453678** | **E-mail** | **kavita@airtel.com** |
| **Mobile** | **09890 333444** | **Website** | **www.airtel.com** |

LD/ST

28 September 2011

Don't forget to include the courtesy title — Miss Manisha Kaur
6/102, Easy End Apartment
Mayur Vihar Phase 1 Extn
Delhi - 96

Tel: 0115 987654

Personalised salutation — Dear Miss Kaur

Acknowledge the letter — Thank you for your letter of 12 July applying for the post of Telephone Executive Marketing post.

State date and time for interview — I hope you can attend an interview at 10:30 a.m. on Friday 16 October an our Airtel office Delhi.

Suggest how alternative arrangements can be made — If this date or time is inconvenient, please telephone my secretary to make alternative arrangements.

Yours sincerely

Kavita Seth (Mrs)
Human Relations Manager

### *Letter of Offer of Employment*

After all the candidates have been interviewed, a shortlist may be drawn up and second interviews held. Once a decision has been made on the successful candidates, a formal offer of employment will be sent to the successful applicant(s). Depending on the size of the organisation, a separate contract of employment may be drawn up. Here we will deal with a simple offer letter, enclosing a job description.

**Airtel**
**Aurora Camp**
**Temple Road**
**Delhi**

| | | | |
|---|---|---|---|
| **Tel** | **0207 345375** | | |
| **Fax** | **0207 453678** | **E-mail** | **kavita@airtel.com** |
| **Mobile** | **09890 333444** | **Website** | **www.airtel.com** |

LD/ST

3 November 2011

Miss Manisha Kaur
6/102, Easy End Apartment
Mayur Vihar Phase 1 Extn
Delhi - 96

Tel: 0115 987654

Dear Miss Kaur

TELEPHONE EXECUTIVE (MARKETING)

Thank you for attending the recent interview.

*Offer the job and state commencement date*

I am pleased to offer you this post commencing on December. 3, 2011.

*Enclose job description and contract of employment (You may prefer to give salary in the offer letter)*

Full details of the post are shown on the attached Job Description. The terms and conditions of employment will be as laid down in our Contract of Employment which is also enclosed.

*Request written confirmation*

Please let me have written confirmation of your acceptance of this post as soon as possible.

*Give other relevant details and state instructions for first day of work*

Two other Telephone Executives will start work on the same day so the morning of 2 August will be spent on an induction training course. Please report to our reception at 09:00 a.m. and ask for my Secretary, Miss Rupa Kaur.

*Finish with a welcoming close*

I look forward to welcoming you to the staff of ST International plc.

Yours sincerely

Kavita Seth (Mrs)
Human Relations Manager

*Don't forget Encs and Copy if necessary*

Encs

Copy: Anand Kumar, Marketing Manager

***Letter of Acceptance***

It is usual to write a formal letter to the company accepting the post. Keep it simple.

6/102, Easy End Apartment
Mayur Vihar Phase 1 Extn
Delhi - 96
Tel: 0115 987654

25 July 200–

Mrs Kavita Seth
Human Relations Manager
Airtel
Aurora Camp
Temple Road
Delhi

Be consistent – display all your letters in the same style — Dear Mrs Seth

TELEPHONE EXECUTIVE

Thank you for your letter of 20 July 2000.

I am pleased to confirm my acceptance of this post as detailed in the Job Description and Contact of Employment.

Finish appropriately — I shall look forward to joining the staff of Airtel.

Yours sincerely

Manisha Kaur (Miss)

***Letter of Resignation***

When you have been in employment and wish to leave for whatever reason, it is usual to write a formal letter, resigning from your post.

6/102, Easy End Apartment
Mayur Vihar Phase 1 Extn
Delhi - 96
Tel: 0115 987654

25 July 200–

Mrs Roshni Chopra
Human Relations Manager
Airtel
Aurora Camp
Temple Road
Delhi

Dear Mrs Roshni

Express regret and state last day of work — Further to our discussion today, I regret to inform you that I wish to give one month's notice of my resignation from the company. My last day of work will be Friday 30 July.

Explain tactfully and courteously — I have been very happy working here and found my work very varied and enjoyable. I have gained a lot of experience in many areas which I am sure I shall find useful in furture employment.

Give thanks — Thank you for your help and guidance.

Yours sincerely

Manisha Kaur (Miss)

### *Letter of Recommendation*

It is helpful to ask previous employers for testimonials as they will be useful when applying for jobs in future.

**Airtel**
**Aurora Camp**
**Temple Road**
**Delhi**

| | | | |
|---|---|---|---|
| **Tel** | **0207 345375** | | |
| **Fax** | **0207 453678** | **E-mail** | **kavita@airtel.com** |
| **Mobile** | **09890 333444** | **Website** | **www.airtel.com** |

HB/GB

28 June 200–

Use this heading in place of an inside address

*TO WHOM IT MAY CONCERN*

State position and duration of employment

Miss Manisha Kaur has been part-time Administration Assistant in our General Office from 24 May 1999 to 28 June 2000. We asked her to join us on a permanent part-time basis after she had been with us for several short periods of work experience during her Business Administration course.

Mention the duties performed

Miss Kaur carried out a wide range of general office duties including opening and distributing mail, photocopying, filing, dealing with general telephone, and walk-in enquiries and entering data into our computer systems.

State the employee's working attitude and how work was carried out

A conscientious, hard-working, and reliable employee, Miss Kaur, set herself very high standards in her work. She had a pleasant telephone manner and was always courteous when dealing with her colleagues and external contacts. She was a good timekeeper and had a good attendance record.

Mention personal qualities

Miss Kaur has a friendly, outgoing personality, a good sense of humour, and she works well as part of a team.

Give a recommendation

I feel sure that Miss Kaur will be an asset to any organization.

No salutation and complimentary close are necessary

Roshni Chopra (Mrs)
Senior Executive Human Relations

## Sales Letters

Sales letters are a very selective form of advertising. They aim to sell a company's goods or services, or they persuade readers to take up special offers. All sales letters must:

- arouse interest
- sound convincing

- create a desire
- encourage action.

In this sales letter Aurora Mobile enclose a newsletter and make everything sound appealing and attractive.

**SPECTRA MOBILE**

**STAY**

**CONNECTED**

Dear Valued Customer

With the introduction of our new Connect Card, Spectra Mobile has brought a new era of convenience in mobile communications. With the Connect Card you can enjoy all the benefits of Spectra Mobile's leading-edge network without worrying about monthly bills. Find out how in this month's issue of stay connected.

Stay connected also introduces you to our vastly expanded international roaming services - Roam-a-Round - which allows you to roam to all corners of the globe. Stay connected.

Many more features can be found inside.

- generous savings when you call another Aurora Mobile customer
- what's new at our website
- see and read about our performance at a recent Communications Exhibition

Inside stay connected, we have also included an exciting contest for you to win fabulous prizes, such as a free subscription to our value-added services, a free Connect Card worth Rs. 200, and restaurant privileges in leading restaurants.

With your continued support we have become India's leading network service provider.
Yours sincerely

Madan Rao
Senior Director
Marketing, Sales and Customer Service

**Spectra Mobile, Main Camp, Temple Road, Noida**
**Tel: 208 542 4444 Fax: 208 555 4444 Email: info@spectramobile**

Remember these important principles when writing sales letters:

1. Try to get on the same wavelength as your reader in the opening paragraph.
2. Present the advantages of the product or service showing relevance to the reader.
3. Write in a positive, convincing style without being aggressive.
4. Encourage the reader to respond by placing an order, completing a reply form or card, requesting further details.
5. Use singulars rather than plurals, e.g.

| | | | |
|---|---|---|---|
| ✓ Dear Customer | *not* | Dear Customers | ✗ |
| ✓ I know you will appreciate this unique product | *not* | I know everyone will appreciate this unique product. | ✗ |

***Quotation Letter***

A quotation is an offer for a specific product or service for sale. It states exactly how much a product/service will cost.

S.R.K and Company
Modern Metals Furniture
12, Civil Lines
Bokaro (Jharkhand)

8 August, 2010

The Manager
Style Fittings and Furnishings
9, Cross Lane, Smith Street
Kolkata (W.B.)

Dear Sir,

Thanks for your letter No. SFFI 10-7110, dated 26 July 2010, asking for our latest catalogue of our steel furniture and list of their prices for a bulk purchase of selected furniture. We are glad to enclose our latest collection coloured illustrated catalogue and price list of luxury furniture for homes and offices.

We use high-gauge imported steel sheets and metal pipes for our luxury furniture and guarantee the lasting quality of our products.

The enclosed catalogue and price list describe our products and normal rates. You will get a detailed idea of the range of products on bulk purchase of any of the luxury products, a special discount of 20 per cent will be offered on the normal discount of 15 per cent, if the total order exceeds one lakh fifty thousand. If you need any further information regarding transportation or payment conditions, kindly do let us know.

We look forward to further hearing from you in this regard. The desired catalogue and price list are enclosed for your perusal. Keep enjoying high quality products.

Yours faithfully,

A.K. Bose
Sales Manager

### *Application for Bank Credit Card*

The application for getting the credit card is made by filling an application form of the issuing bank/organization. Generally, the form calls for information about your name, address, contact number, and other personal details, such as age, nature and place of employment, annual income, outstanding credits, and expenses and other financial information to assess your credit worthiness. When the application is granted, the credit card is mailed to you with a letter of thanks and details of conditions for utilisation of credit allowed.

### *Credit Letter from the Bank for Issuing of Credit Card*

*July 25, 2010*

*Mr. S Pathak*
*133, 29 sector*
*Noida, U.P.*

*Dear Mr. Pathak,*

*Welcome to the membership of ICICI Bank Credit Card holders group. We are delighted to send you a gold ICICI bank credit card, free of any charges for it.*

*Your credit limit is 1 lac. Your monthly statement will be generated on the 7th of each month and your payment is due on the 25th of the following month. If you pay the total amount due, no interest will be levied. If you choose to pay only the minimum amount due, you will pay charges and fees as indicated in the credit statement mailed to you every month.*

*Please read them.*

*We all wish you to enjoy our credit card facility with a sense of empowerment and satisfaction.*

*Sincerely yours*
*K. Kumar*
*Credit Manager*

### *Bank Loan for Business*

*20 November, 1999*

*Mr. D Sharma*
*Senior General Manager*
*Canara Bank*
*Delhi Gate*
*Agra, U.P.*

*Dear Mr. Sharma*

*In January 2010, I propose to construct the second floor of my showroom, Kids Korner, Mishra compound, Bulandshahar. I would like to have a personal loan of 10 lacs to finance its construction and furnish it back. Our present annual turnover is over 50 lacs. We need the loan before 15th December. We shall pay, through 12 monthly EMI's.*

*We solicit an early consideration and action.*

*With kind regards,*
*Rajat Mishra*
*Kids Korner*

## DRAFTING AN APPLICATION LETTER

An application letter is planned like a sales letter: it gains attention and interest and asks for action. The application letter demonstrates the applicant's communication skills and functions as an interview request when it impresses the potential employer with the applicant's abilities and education. It needs to be written very skillfully.

6

Write job applications/ cover letters properly.

### The First Paragraph

The first paragraph identifies the objective exactly. In the first paragraph, the applicant should specifically state the position/job he or she is applying for and how he or she came to know about it—usually through an advertisement or a contact. Sometimes, an applicant may apply without knowing that a position exists or is available. He or she can use the opening paragraph to show what kind of position he or she is qualified for and also state the reasons for his or her interest in that particular company.

### The Second Paragraph

The second paragraph gives evidence of the applicant's ability/qualifications. In the second paragraph, the applicant should explain he or she is qualified for the position/job. It is important not to repeat what has been written in the résumé. Instead, the application letter points out the particular facts relevant to the position applied for. It can highlight important courses or special projects that have enriched the applicant's preparation and enhanced his or her suitability for the position. It can also describe any extra-curricular activities that show leadership or the ability to organize and coordinate. Lastly, it can also show how the various projects, industrial visits, and work experiences listed in the CV are related to the position.

It is important not to repeat has been written in the résumé. Instead, the application letter points out the particular facts relevant to the position applied for. It can highlight important courses or special projects that have enriched the applicant's preparation and enhanced his or her suitability for the position.

### The Third Paragraph

The third paragraph asks for an interview. At the end of the letter, the applicant can suggest that he or she come in for an interview at the employer's convenience. The purpose of the letter is to convince the prospective employer to interview the applicant.

### General Tips

While writing an application letter, the applicant should remember that he or she is selling those merits which the employer needs. The following principles are key to writing an effective application letter:

- Coherence
- Concreteness
- Simplicity
- Emphasis
- Originality
- Sincerity

While writing an application letter, the applicant should remember that he or she is selling those merits which the employer needs.

- Empathy
- Convention

Application letters should be brief. Like the résumé, they should be spotless, free of errors, typed, and well formatted on a standard white sheet. As far as possible, the application letter should be addressed to a specific person. Also, the applicant should sign the letter before mailing it. Exhibit 4.18 shows a sample application letter, and Exhibit 4.19 lists some pitfalls to avoid when writing an application letter.

6/102 East End Apts
Mayur Vihar Phase I
Delhi 110096
April 6, 2009

Shri N. K. Varma
Sales and Marketing
LG Electronics India Pvt. Ltd.
Surajpur–Kasna Road
Greater Noida (U.P.)

Dear Mr Varma,

Please consider me as a candidate for the position of Assistant Marketing Manager, advertised in the *Times of India* on 1 April 2009. The position is especially attractive to me because I feel that my education and work experience have prepared me to work with a company like LG, which offers a wide variety of household durables.

As my résumé shows, I received my MBA with a major in marketing from Bombay University in 2008. During my summer and final terms, I performed various duties in the marketing department of Samsung, including consumer research for new products.

In June 2007, I joined Samsung as a management trainee. While at Samsung, I gained a great deal of experience in marketing research and product design under excellent supervision.

I am a hardworking person who enjoys the challenges of marketing. I love travelling. Enclosed is my résumé for your consideration. I do hope that I shall have an opportunity to appear for an interview for the position of Assistant Manager Marketing at LG Electronics India.

Yours truly,

Arunav Chandra

Enclosure: CV

**Exhibit 4.18** Example of an Application Letter

## ESSENTIALS OF GOOD BUSINESS LETTERS AND MEMOS

7

Know the essentials of good business correspondence.

Businessmen and women do not have time to read long letters and messages. They want to know facts, results, and important details. Therefore, business letters should provide only what is essential in the shortest space. The key is to keep to the point and be simple.

Simplicity, clarity, and conciseness are interrelated concepts. "Simple", according to *The Pocket Oxford Dictionary of Current English*

- Don't use your present employer's stationery.
- Don't beg or ask for a favour.
- Don't be unduly humble, and avoid phrases like "I beg to state that…".
- Don't overuse the words *I*, *me*, and *my*.
- Don't sound casual.
- Don't boast about yourself.
- Don't criticize your present employer.
- Don't repeat information that is already in the résumé.
- Don't use vague or general terms.
- Don't just say you are qualified for the job/position; instead give evidence.
- Don't use hackneyed and worn-out expressions.
- Don't copy a letter written by another applicant.
- Don't forget to check the following before sending the letter:
  - The letter should be addressed to the appropriate person and, in the case of e-mails, the e-mail address should be correct. In case of multiple submissions, no other e-mail addresses should be visible.
  - There should be a proper subject line.
  - The letter should be precise and well formatted.
  - There should be no spelling or grammatical errors in the CV and the cover letter.
  - It should be signed with the applicant's full name and complete contact address.

**Exhibit 4.19** Some Don'ts for Writing Application Letters

(1998), means, "(1) understood or done easily and without difficulty (2) not complicated or elaborate; plain (3) not compound or complex (4) absolute, unqualified, straightforward." Most writers want their written communication to be simple in all the four senses. In fact, clarity and conciseness result from simplicity.

## Simplicity

> Simplicity in writing essentially means plainness.

Simplicity in writing essentially means plainness and saying exactly what one means. The writer should not bring in irrelevant details or information. Instead, he or she should be straightforward and choose just one word instead of many whenever possible. Unnecessary adjectives and adverbs should be avoided. Qualifiers, adjectives, adverbs, and other unnecessary words often creep in without the writer realizing their presence. It is commonly believed that to be clear, the writer should be elaborate and repetitive, using several words with the same meaning. However, this creates clutter in writing instead of providing clarity. The key to writing simply, clearly, and concisely is to tighten the writing. Hence, while writing business letters, memos, or reports, one should choose one from among several nearly identical possible words and only use those that convey the message exactly. This basic principle of choosing one word carefully is usually called the principle of "unity"—the unity of thought and expression. This basic principle is discussed here:

- *One main subject in one letter:* Practical wisdom tells us if we have to write about two different subjects to the same company, department, or office at the same time, we should write two letters discussing each subject separately. Why? Two separate subjects placed together may adversely affect each other's importance. The two subjects may belong to two different sections and after taking action on one of the subjects, the department may just file the letter, resulting in the other subject being forgotten.

Only when two subjects are related and are to be considered for action by the same person, should they be discussed in the same letter. In all other situations, it is better to write separate letters.

- *One thought in one sentence:* Each sentence should be formed so that it contains a single, complete thought. Complicated (complex and compound) sentences are confusing in a business letter. For example, compare the following sentences:

  Complicated: The benefits that he derived from his early training were soon lost and he began to do things as he was accustomed to doing them.

  Simple: The benefits of his early training were soon lost. He started doing things in his usual way.

- *One idea in one paragraph:* Each paragraph should open with a sentence that summarizes the central idea of the paragraph. The sentences that follow should support, illustrate, and develop the thought by providing additional information.

Each paragraph should open with a sentence that summarizes the central idea of the paragraph.

## Clarity

The clarity of a business letter is two-fold:

1. *Clarity of message:* Ideas should be logically sequenced in a coherent way.
2. *Clarity of form:* Presentation of matter, format, paragraph divisions, layout, margins, and spacing between the lines should be done neatly. The letter should appear well organized and properly formatted.

## Conciseness

It is best to be "short". This means writing short letters, choosing short words, forming short paragraphs, and constructing short sentences. The goal is to give only relevant information in the fewest possible words.

Besides simplicity, clarity, and conciseness, there are many other issues that need to be kept in mind while writing business letters and memos. These are discussed here.

## Standard and Neutral Language

Writers of business letters should use standard, neutral language and should avoid jargon, technical terms, and slang. They should also eliminate hackneyed and old-fashioned expressions from their writing.

## You-Attitude

Writers should keep in mind the point of view of their readers (customers and clients). All writing is for a specific reader, and it is at his or her level that the letter or correspondence should be written.

In addition, the writer should know his or her readers' expectations, fears, beliefs, and feelings about the matter at hand. The writer should be able to visualize the readers' reaction to the message before writing.

## Sincerity and Tone

The writer's tone and sincerity reflect his or her personality. These two aspects of a letter or memo are important to convince readers that the writer really means what he or she is saying. The tone of the letter should reflect the writer's personality. Today, good writers believe that a business letter should be characterized by confidence, directness, enthusiasm, and humanity.

- *Confidence:* Before writing a letter, the writer should have complete information on the subject and should be certain about the facts that will be discussed. If the writer is definite about what he or she is saying, the letter will not be evasive or vaguely worded with indirect expressions and passive verbs. Passive verbs are weak. They convey withdrawal in the writer's subconscious mind. In contrast, active verbs are strong. Expressions such as "it is recommended that" (I recommend), "it was considered that" (I considered), "it was felt that" (I feel), "it is an indication of" (it indicates), "conducted a survey of" (surveyed) show hesitation and should be replaced with their active forms, which show directness and confidence.

> Passive verbs are weak. They convey withdrawal in the writer's subconscious mind. In contrast, active verbs are strong.

- *Directness:* Directness in letters results from confidence. One's letters should not only say what is intended, but should say so in a straightforward and courteous manner. However, while directness is desirable, one should not be abrupt.
- *Enthusiasm:* The writer should be enthusiastic in his or her sincerity. The letter should make the reader feel that the writer is genuinely interested in him or her. This cannot be done by just saying something like "Believe me I am really interested in solving your problem." Instead, the writer must choose words that show interest in the reader.
- *Humanity:* Business letters are generally written in a stiff, formal, and mechanical manner. They often lack personal warmth and the feeling of speaking to another living being. To counter this, writers should use the personal pronouns "we", "I", "you", "he", "she", and "they". These give a personal touch to business letters. For achieving the right tone, the letter and other forms of business correspondence should be written in a simple, formal, and friendly way. Remember that criticizing or apologizing should be done carefully, as should complimenting.

> Write your letters in short and simple sentences. Use simple, familiar and short words. Avoid abstract words. Choose verbs that express forceful action.

## Emphasis

In business correspondence, specially a letter or memo, ideas must be placed in order of their importance. The main idea must be stated at the beginning. Even in the case of a sentence or paragraph, the rule is to place the main idea first. Position reflects importance. Emphasis can be indicated also by repetition, use of punctuation, and the mechanical devices of using bold letters or underlining.

> 8
>
> Plan written communication by first considering the needs, levels, and expectations of readers.

## WRITING E-MAILS

E-mail is the most commonly used mode of interaction among executives and departments, and between a company and its customers, clients, distributors, retailers, suppliers, and vendors. It is the quickest channel of written communication. Any amount of information, documents, pictures, and so on, can be sent to the recipients as attachments.

### Receiver's E-mail Account

For e-mail connectivity, one needs to have just the e-mail address of the intended receiver. Many persons have more than one e-mail account—an official account and a personal account. Therefore, the sender of the e-mail should know which address is appropriate to use. In addition, one has to be careful in typing the address. For example, in the address mukesh.chaturvedi@bimtech.ac.in, if there is any mistake, say an extra space, a spelling error, or a missing dot, the mail would not be delivered.

### Subject Line

In an e-mail, the subject line is the first thing that is noticed by the receiver. Therefore, it should be composed as precisely as possible. The writer needs to carefully work out the wording of the subject line so that the title and context are clear and the reader gets the gist of the message. Examples of good subject lines are "Visit postponed to next Monday" and "Annual report to be ready this Saturday".

### Sending Copies

The sender may need to send a copy of the e-mail to several persons at the same time. This is generally simpler if group e-mail IDs are provided. For example, if a company has internal group IDs set up, then by writing "marketing" in the "To" line, an e-mail can be sent to all the people in the marketing department. Usually, this is an internal facility. In external e-mails, the e-mail addresses of all intended receivers are listed in the "Cc" line. A "blind carbon copy" of the e-mail can also be sent to one or more persons without the knowledge of other receivers, by entering their addresses in the "Bcc" line. However, caution should be exercised in marking blind carbon copies as this can lead to difficult situations. For example, if the sender marks a copy to a person without the knowledge of the receiver and the person marked in the "Bcc" field hits "Reply All" in response to that mail, it places the sender in a difficult spot.

An e-mail is like a memo that needs neither a salutation nor a closing subscription. However, if the two persons are communicating for the first time and do not know each other personally, the sender may indicate a favourable disposition towards the receiver by being friendly. Exhibit 4.20 shows an example of a short, friendly, and clear e-mail written by a famous Bollywood actor and youth icon in response to an invitation from a business school.

Exhibit 4.20 shows a series of e-mails between the COO of Time Industries and one of his former employees.

The following is a summary of the broad guidelines that need to be followed while writing business letters, memos, and e-mails:

- Consider the readers' (receivers') needs and expectations.
- Understand the purpose for writing the message and the total context in which it is being written.
- Put essential information first.
- State each point clearly and directly.

To... preti@gcc.co.in
Cc...
Bcc...
Subject: Re: An invitation from GCC Business School

Thank you for the invitation Preity, but I am not in Mumbai and am shooting in Dholpur, Rajasthan, till the 22nd of this month and then in Roorkee till 21st April.

The address where you can send the invite is:

172 Yugdharma Towers
Opp. Inorbit Mall
Goregaon (West)
Mumbai 400062

**Exhibit 4.20** A Series of E-mails

**Communication Snapshot 4.7** How Sentence Structure Affects Meaning

The style of the e-mail in Exhibit 4.10 is businesslike, formal, and brief, but not brusque. It is written with conversational ease, in a pleasant tone. The closing sentence reassures Abhinav that the issues he raised in his e-mail (Exhibit 4.11) would be addressed.

To... c.abhinav@hotmail.com
Cc...
Bcc... chrischacko@time.com
Subject: RE: An Urgent Appeal!

Dear Abhinav,

Many thanks for your message. May I request you to contact Chris Chacko? He will be your single point of contact in Time to resolve this matter. He will also advise you regarding whom you should meet to obtain clarifications relating to the various areas highlighted by you.

We are committed to ensuring that you obtain a full and fair response.

Kind regards,

Harish

**Exhibit 4J** Harish's E-mail to Abhinav

To... harish.g@time.com
Cc... chrischacko@time.com
Bcc...
Subject: An Urgent Appeal!

Dear Sir,

This is with reference to Mr Chris Chacko's mail of 19 July regarding the issue of clearance. Mr Chacko asked me to get in touch with OneCommercial. According to him, OneCommercial reported a mismatch of Rs 38,000 for the WOT–TDI Mall project. As per his advice, I got in touch with the commercial team at OneCommercial on the 19th. However, on 27 July, I received a mail from Mrs Chopra stating that there was a shortage of Rs 1,50,350, seemingly held against me. In addition, some stock reports were sent to Mr Aakash in OneCommercial by WOT–TDI Mall between 31 May and 21 June with some other figures altogether.
I sent a detailed message to Mrs Chopra regarding this, along with the necessary supporting documents. To bring to your notice the kind of ambiguity there is in the system, I have also sent you and Mr Chacko hard copies of the entire set of supporting documents, which should reach you in a day or two.
I am deeply pained because it seems that there is some intention to implicate me. I shall be very grateful if you could please advise me how I should proceed with the matter.

Regards,
Abhinav Chaturvedi

**Exhibit 4K** Abhinav's Original Message to Harish

An e-mail should be written the way we talk. This makes the writing vivid. It should read like the sender (writer) and the receiver (reader) are conversing face-to-face. Exhibit 4L is an example of a conversational style of writing an e-mail; it is from Chris Chacko to Abhinav in response to Abhinav's e-mail (Exhibit 4M).

To... c.abhinav@hotmail.com
Cc... harish.g@time.com; saumya.shah@OneCommercial.com
Bcc...
Subject: Re: An Urgent Appeal!

Hi Abhinav,

There has been stock mismatch worth Rs 38,000 that has been reported by OneCommercial for TDI Mall, which is being looked into.

I too do not know under what head the amount of Rs1,947 has been credited to your account. I am surprised to hear that you have not received any response regarding this from OneCommercial despite your follow-up. Could you tell me whom you spoke to? Saumya Shah, the Regional HR Manager, confirms that you have not spoken with her.

I cannot give any timeline regarding when your clearance will come through, as it is was clearly mentioned that clearance formalities need to be completed by you, and you have not obtained clearance from OneCommercial. Please take this up with OneCommercial directly as you need to get your clearance formalities completed to settle your accounts.

Regards,
Chris

**Exhibit 4L** Chris's Message to Abhinav

The opening phrase of Chris's e-mail in Exhibit 4K, "Hi Abhinav", sets an amiable tone. Further, the use of passive voice does not allow him to sound accusatory. In addition, Chris shares the chain of his thoughts in a candid manner with Abhinav. Chris's e-mail is written in a style that makes the official communication between a senior executive and a junior business manager more like a personal chat.

To... chrischacko@time.com
Cc... harish.g@time.com
Bcc...
Subject: An Urgent Appeal!

Dear Sir,

It has been three weeks since I wrote to you about my clearance. On the 13th of July, I received an amount of Rs 1,947 from Time Industries Ltd, but I am unable to find out from OneCommercial what head this amount has been credited under.

Also, despite sending a reminder on 9 July, I am still waiting for my clearance. Could you please help me determine how long this will take?

Regards,
Abhinav

**Exhibit 4M** Abhinav's Original E-mail to Chris

In fact, the success and popularity of e-mail in the world of global business is partly because e-mail has the speediness of a telephone conversation and the crispness of a well-written memo.

- Use conventional formats.
- Be courteous.

## CIRCULARS AND NOTICE

### Notice

A notice is written to give information or warnings to people. We come across notices at most of the places we visit, for instance, educational institutions, shopping centres, railway stations, hospitals, parks, housing societies, etc. They are usually put up on notice boards, which are assigned as notice boards. The notice boards in educational institutions and business organisations are usually indicated as staff notice board/faculty or employee notice boards. They can be further sectioned into games, meetings, general activities or time table, working hours, quality policy, or any other important matter, such as safety precautions.

A notice is given not only for the benefit of the information of others, but as a precautionary step taken by the organization to claim, if required, that proper information in this regard was communicated to all by a notice, dated such and such. And the workers, visitors or students are supposed to read the notices as a routine.

The organization makes particular persons responsible for attaching the notice to the notice board and removing it after a specified time.

### *Drafting a Notice*

A notice should be short, simple, and precisely written. It should communicate only the amount of information required by the reader to act or know for doing a particular thing.

A notice should have the following details:

1. Heading of the notice. Subject and purpose to be mentioned in the heading clearly.
2. Date on which the notice is written.
3. The persons for whom the notice is written.
4. Give the name of the authorising person who is issuing the notice.
5. Give briefly other necessary information, such as date, time, and place if it is notice of a meeting seminar or some other work.
6. Designing the notice in a way that it attracts the attention of people who pass by the notice-board.
7. To attract attention, leave enough white space on all the four margins.
8. Double space each line.
9. Choose the positive and polite tone. Avoid negative implications, for an effective drafting of notices.

### *Designing Notices*

When designing notices, your aim must be to ensure that your notice is seen and acted upon where necessary. Long, rambling paragraphs will not achieve this aim. When designing notices, bear in mind these guidelines:

Give the notice a clear heading.

1. Use different size print for emphasis.
2. Use sub-headings to break up the main information logically.

25 July 2010

**Notice of department meeting**

"A meeting of all the members working in the workshop department will be held on Saturday, 31st July 2010, at 3.30 p.m. in the workshop to discuss the proposed changes in the working hours and duties of the workshop staff. All must attend punctually." M.K Raghunath, Head Works Department.

Comments: The first part of the notice is factual. It informs the department members of the workshop about the day, date, time, place, purpose and expected participants.

Consider the second part of the notice. It is negative in tone. First, what does the phrase "all must attend" imply? It shows that the writer believes that all may not attend the meeting. Hence, this anxiety and order to ensure that everybody attends it.

Second, the word "punctually" is often used in the notice, without realizing that it insults those who are never late; besides, again it shows doubt that some may come late, perhaps as usual.

Hence, you should draft the notice in a positive form. State your request directly and simply. Just write: "All are requested to attend it."

3. Use asterisks/bullet points to display points on separate lines.
4. Use the paper effectively to display the notice attractively.
5. Include the name of the writer at the bottom as well as a reference and date.

Example of a notice generally issued in organizations. The notice is placed on the workshop notice board.

### Circular

A circular is a form of a written communication to inform or advise the reader about something. It can be written like a letter which is sent to several persons. It is usually written once, but used in the same form at different times. It is, therefore, not dated. And it is addressed in a general manner not to any particular person,

> Dear Valued Customer,
>
> Within the next 14 days you should expect to receive important authorised mail from our Sweepstakes Director. These documents outline in detail your current Sweepstakes eligibility status,
>
> You should know that as of June 2003, there is no doubt that you are in an enviable position to have a chance to win our Rs. 1,000,000 in Gold First Prize. You already stand ahead of many who have not been invited to participate in the Readers' Digest 2 million Rupees Sweepstakes.
>
> THE SWEEPSTAKES DOCUMENTS DUE TO ARRIVE AT YOUR ADDRESS HAVE STRICTLY CONTROLLED DEADLINES. THIS IS WHY YOU ARE ENTITLED TO RECEIVE THIS PRE-DISCLOSURE—TO PROVIDE YOU WITH SUFFICIENT NOTICE TO REPLY ON TIME.
>
> BE ADVISED THAT
>
> THE POST OFFICE HAS
>
> ASSURED EXPEDIENT DELIVERY
>
> OF THE DUE PACKAGE TO YOU.
>
> Please watch out for a yellow envelope from Reader's Digest Books & Home Entertainment marked with the same package code as above. It contains your 2 Sweepstakes Entry Cards. Then, reply in strict conformance with the instructions provided therein.
>
> This is the only step required of you to secure your eligibility to enter the 2 million Rupees Sweepstakes for your chance to win well over Rs. 1,000,000 in Gold. Please do not discount the vital importance of this pre-disclosure. Be sure to reply as instructed.

## REPORT WRITING

### What Is a Report?

After the letter and the memo, the report is the most used form in business writing. A report can be defined as a communication in which the writer (or speaker if it is an oral report) provides information to some individual or organization because it is his or her responsibility to do so.[1] It is an assigned communication for a purpose and for a specific receiver/reader.

The common element in all reports is the element of responsibility. The writer is obliged to communicate what he or she knows to those who need this information, as a part of an assigned, clearly defined, time-bound task.

- Other forms of writing, such as essays, are subjective in nature. They reflect the writer's personality.
- An essay can be factual, but it remains subjective in its treatment and presentation. The essayist does not usually offer evidence for his or her writing, nor does the reader look for it. The reader of a report, on the other hand, looks for facts and evidence.
- As a form of creative writing, an essay's purpose is largely self-expression for the author and providing entertainment or enjoyment for the reader.
- An essay is rooted in the writer's imagination, whereas a report is rooted in investigation and analysis. This is why an essay has a beginning, but may not have a report's logically derived conclusion. Moreover, it has no signposts, headings or sub-headings, or bullet points to indicate a coherent structure that moves from the beginning, through the middle, to the end.

> The common element in all reports is the element of responsibility.

- Reports generally draw on outside sources. They present facts, conclusions, and recommendations based on investigation and analysis of data obtained by observation of facts.
- The word "paper" can mean several things, such as an article, a detailed report, or a project report. However, it most commonly refers to research writing.
- Reports have a highly structured format.
- Each part of a report is numbered and captioned with headings and sub-headings.
- The language of a report is concise and concrete.
- Reports contain recommendations and conclusions.
- They make use of tables and graphs.
- Reports are usually preceded by a summary.
- Reports can be oral or written, but essays are always written.

Thus, a report is distinct from an essay or any other form of writing.

> Understand that a report and an essay are two distinct forms of written communication and be able to differentiate between their physical structures and the styles in which they are written.

## Purpose of a Report

While collecting data, the investigator should remember that the report is not a descriptive statement of facts, events, or future possibilities. For example, the purpose of a report is not fulfilled if it speaks about "the possibility of change of work site". Instead, the report should explain the reasons for changing the workplace, discuss the need for doing so, compare the relative advantages of different choices available, and choose and recommend the best option. The basic purpose of a report is to help the management identify the reasons underlying a specific situation. The factors responsible for the problem, the alternatives available for solving it, and the best course of action to take emerge from a thorough study of all relevant facts and factors. The main purpose of report is to present specific conclusions regarding the problem's existence and solution.

> The basic purpose of a report is to help the management identify the reasons underlying a specific situation.

## Types of Reports

Reports vary in style, subject matter and presentation. They may be classified on various bases such as:

- Presentation—oral and written reports
- Length—short and long reports
- Nature—informal and formal reports
- Purpose—informational and analytical reports
- Time Duration—routine/periodic and special reports

Know the various types of reports and their essential elements.

1. **Oral Reports:** An oral report is a face-to-face communication about something seen, observed, experienced or investigated. It generally consists of impressions, observations and experiences. It is simple and easy to describe, quick and immediate to present and gives first-hand information, but it may not be as objective and as detailed as a report has to be. It saves time for the reporter, but may be strenuous for the listener as he/she has to listen and memorise each and every word at the moment. Moreover, it lacks authenticity and is difficult to preserve. An oral report may not be used for taking vital decisions, but it is beneficial in judging speculations and impressions and can be used to take an immediate action.
2. **Written Reports:** A written report provides a permanent record; so, it is always preferred to an oral report. Moreover, a written report is accurate and precise while an oral report may be vague at times. There are no chances of distortion of facts while transferring information from one source to another. A written report is more formal than an oral report and is generally used to communicate complex facts. It is a visual aid to communication as the reporter may organize message into paragraphs highlighting the main points.
3. **Short Reports:** Short reports can be presented in the form of a letter or a memo. They are concerned primarily with day-to-day business problems as well as their solutions. A short report consists of three parts—an opening, body and ending. Short reports, generally include periodic, situational and progress reports.
4. **Long Reports:** Long reports describe a problem in detail. They include the process of preparing the outline of the topic, collecting data, making a rough draft, logical and organized presentation of facts, thorough revising, editing, and preparing the fair draft, etc. These reports require a detailed study of an issue. The important parts of a long report are—preface, introduction, summary, abstract, description, conclusion, appendices, glossary, and index.
5. **Informal Reports:** Certain business reports can be short and informal. In current business dealings, informal reports are more frequent than the formal ones. Basically, informal reports perform the same function as the formal reports—transmitting information, facts or data to someone for taking decision. However, informal reports are quite brief (around one to five pages), that too when you have supplementary material, such as bibliography, appendices, etc. The style of writing is positive, personal, and conversational. Depending on the requirement, they may have heading, illustrations, footnotes, etc., but may not include all the details like formal reports. Informal reports are written in the form of memo reports or letter reports.
   - **Memo Reports:** Memo reports play a significant role in an organization. These reports are generally written to: (1) co-workers to give information, express opinion or to state a viewpoint, (2) subordinates to provide information, explain a policy or a procedure, give instructions or to

announce changes, and (3) your boss to give information, make a request, propose recommendations, give suggestion, or to confirm an agreement. The memos are important because they ensure smooth flow of information in all directions in all the organizations.

- **Letter Reports:** Reports written in the form of letters are called letter reports. The letter reports combine the features of a business letter as well as a formal written report. They follow the format of a business letter, convey technical information to a company, contain factual information, and they are written from the perspective of the readers. However, the purpose of a letter report unlike a business letter is to provide information as it is a technical document in content as well as in tone.

6. **Formal Reports:** A formal report is the result of thorough investigation of a problem or situation. Formal reports are generally detailed and elaborate. These reports follow a fixed format. The length of the report may vary according to the requirement. Formal reports include informational, analytical, routine, special, technical, project, research reports, etc.
7. **Informational Reports:** An informational report presents facts, situations, or problems required to take vital decisions. The writer collects relevant information, compiles, and organizes it in an orderly manner and presents it as objectively as possible. Informational reports record happenings such as conferences, seminars, tours, and so on and supply details for future planning.
8. **Analytical Reports:** Analytical reports present data along with an analysis of it. The writer studies facts, situations, or problems neutrally, evaluates the information, draws suitable inferences, and puts forward his/her recommendations and conclusions. Project reports, feasibility reports, and market search reports fall in this category.
   - **Project Reports:** Project reports usually provide pre-investment information required for investments before setting up the project. These reports are based on small investigations. Cost, goods, machinery requirements, etc., given in the report are rough calculations. They also keep the organizations regularly updated about the progress of the long-term projects or bring an important issue in the limelight.
   - **Feasibility Reports:** A feasibility report evaluates a proposal in terms of the difficulty in carrying out a plan. Generally, a feasibility study precedes technical development and project implementation. Market feasibility study involves testing geographic locations for a real estate development project. It takes into account the importance of the business in the selected area. Authorities often require developers to complete feasibility studies before they approve a permit application for retail, commercial, industrial, manufacturing, housing, office or mixed-use project.
   - **Market Search Reports:** These reports contain guidelines for the promoters of the new products, policies, organizations, etc. Market research is an organized effort to gather information about markets or customers. It is done for discovering what people want, need, or believe or how they act. Once that research is completed, it can be used to determine how to market the product. This report collects data on market trends, users and prices of different commodities.
9. **Routine/Periodic Reports:** Routine reports, also known as form reports, are usually written on a prescribed proforma. The main purpose of these reports is to record the progress of a task, evaluate the performance of its employees and to record the success or failure of a policy. As these reports are written periodically, they are also called periodic reports. They generally include laboratory reports, progress reports, inspection reports, production reports, monthly sales reports, annual confidential reports, etc. All the organizations, institutions, companies, and research establishments depend on routine reports for various decisions.

- **Laboratory Reports:** A laboratory report records the experimental work done in a laboratory to analyze a theory, conclusion, or validity of a particular research. One has to record the process, reactions, and results accurately to arrive at a convincing conclusion. These reports include title, experiment number, date, purpose, apparatus used, procedure adopted, observations, conclusions, and signature.
- **Progress Reports:** A progress report informs the readers about the progress and status of a long-term project. The project may be about installation of a factory, construction of a bridge or a residential colony, or some research work carried out in an organization. These reports are written at the various stages of the project. The essential details included in these reports are title of the project, total work to be done, time allotted, date, work already done, work to be done, time required, future plans, remarks, name, signature, and designation of the reporter.
- **Inspection Reports:** Inspection reports are written to ascertain whether or not the work is going on satisfactorily, infrastructure facilities are sufficient or the quality fulfils the required specifications. These reports are written in factories as well as in educational organizations to check and ensure the quality.
- **Production Reports:** To control the budget and expenditure, standards are set for a production department based on the capacity of machines, time needed, and the manpower employed. To ascertain the efficiency of a factory, production report is prepared. These reports normally give details of the standard production decided in a given time frame, actual production, or the comparison of the standard time required, and the time utilized.
- **Monthly Sales Reports:** Monthly sales reports track the sale of a product in the market. They report increase or fall of sale in a particular time period as well as the factors responsible for it and give their recommendations accordingly.
- **Annual Confidential Reports:** Annual confidential reports are written to evaluate the performance and the general conduct of the employees in an organization. Such reports may be subjective as the human qualities, such as alertness, zeal, confidence, etc., may not be measured. However, these reports are used to determine their efficiency, critically appraise their achievements, and assess their usefulness before granting them increments or promotions.

10. **Special Reports:** Special reports are written to convey special information related to a single condition, situation, occasion, or problem. These reports do not contain repeated information as they are written about the specific situations. Like other reports, these reports also help in decision making as some of the most important decisions are taken on the basis of special reports. Special reports include inquiry reports, research reports, thesis, dissertations, etc.
    - **Inquiry Reports:** These reports are prepared by the special committees appointed by some government or private organizations to investigate the cases of mishap, carelessness on the part of the officials, charges of corruption, or some antisocial activity. Such reports are prepared in groups because they demand thorough investigation of an issue, objective interpretations and recommendations, and systematic presentation of information. These reports are very common in administration as no action can be taken against any one without proper justification.
    - **Research Reports:** Research reports are prepared by the researchers and scholars of various universities, colleges, and research organizations to present a concrete proof of the conducted research. While preparing a research report, you must aim at clarity, organization, and content. Research reports are all the more same like technical reports, laboratory reports, and scientific papers which follow a consistent format to display information clearly.

### *Factors Determining the Choice of the Form of Report*

In the world of business, a report can be a short information account of the present state of work, say a project (essentially a memo), to a long, formal, well-documented report of a corporate or government department.

Each organization, normally, has its own "in-house" method of presentation, which will always be adhered to by its report writers. The writer of a report in an organization is guided by:

- a specific layout—sequence of information
- its own cover—organization, code number, and other related information about the author, subject, and details of submission.

**Layout:** Recommendations and conclusions may precede discussion.

**Assigning a Report—Terms of Reference:** In an organization, the task of producing a report on a specific problem can be assigned to an individual or a team. The problem, purpose, scope/limitations, budget, cultural consideration, if any, related to ethical or ethnic values of the organization, and the date for submission (time-limit) are clearly given while authorizing the person responsible for submitting the report. These specification guide the report writer. They from what is called 'Terms of Reference'. The one who needs the report to be prepared sets down these terms.

> The writer has to first investigate the problem, search for facts, gather evidence for the facts observed, and then analyse before presenting observations, conclusions and suggestions as solutions to the problem.

The process of writing a report is left entirely to the writer. Report writing involves Research and Analysis and Presentation. The writer has to first investigate the problem, search for facts, gather evidence for the facts observed, and then analyze before predestining observations, conclusion, and suggestions as solutions to the problem. The writer can, however, choose from various methods of enquiring into the problem—visits, interviews, questionnaires, data banks, studying record of the organization, consulting existing literature and documents as relevant sources of information. The writer also needs to know the total context and background of the subject of investigation. Background study and data collection may sometimes pose difficulties, but without this effort, a report will not be authentic.

## Objectives of a Report

A report is primarily a source of information that helps in decision-making. It can also be used to offer a solution to a business problem. Its objective can be:

> A report is primarily a source of information that helps in decision-making.

- To give information about a company's activities, progress, plans, and, problems.
- To record events for future reference.
- To recommend a specific action.
- To justify and persuade readers about the need for action in controversial situations.
- To present facts to the management to help decide the direction the business should choose.

The study and report should be comprehensive. They should examine all aspects of a problem and the potential solutions. The recommended solution and its advantages or disadvantages should be analyzed in relation to management as a whole, not just the entrepreneur. All groups—workers, staff, customers, and so on whose interests may be affected in different ways by a change should be considered.

The report writer should consider the objectives of the report from the point of view of its recipients and ask the following questions as guidelines:

- For whom is the report written?
- What is their level of information and education?
- How much do they already know about the problem?
- Why do they want the report?
- What do they want to know, and in how much detail?
- How does the report's result (conclusion) help them?

## Writing Reports

A report presents facts, conclusions, and recommendations in simple and clear language, and in a logical and well-defined structure. The elements (parts) of a full report, in the order of their sequence in a long, formal report are:

- Cover
- Title page
- Acknowledgements
- Table of contents
- Executive summary
- Introduction
- Discussion/description
- Conclusions
- Recommendations
- Appendix
- List of references
- Bibliography
- Glossary
- Index

The first five elements (cover, title page, acknowledgements, table of contents, and executive summary) constitute the front matter; the next four elements (introduction, discussion, conclusions, and recommendations) form the main body; and the last five elements (appendix, list of references, bibliography, glossary, and index) constitute the back matter.

### *Structure of a Report*

In the *normal arrangement*, the conclusions and recommendations are positioned after the discussion. However, this is not the case in the *alternative arrangement* of a report. Business executives are usually short of time and are, therefore, more interested in knowing the conclusions and recommendations of the study. A detailed description of the discussion may, therefore, appear after the conclusions and recommendations in the alternative arrangement.

> Business executives are usually short of time and are, therefore, more interested in knowing the conclusions and recommendations of the study.

| Elements | Level |
|---|---|
| Summary<br>Introduction | Non-technical |
| Conclusions<br>Recommendations | Partly technical |
| Discussion<br>Appendix | Fully technical |

**Exhibit 4.21** Order of Elements in a Formal Business Report

The order of elements in a formal business report may be as given in Exhibit 4.21. The researcher should also keep in mind the non-technical background of his or her readers and demarcate certain parts differently as shown in Exhibit 4.21.

***Basic and Subsidiary Parts of a Report***

The basic and subsidiary parts of a report are delineated in Exhibit 4.22.

Some subsidiary elements—the table of contents, the bibliography and references, and the glossary—are used only in long, formal reports. The cover and title page in short reports are replaced with the heading and other similar devices.

> Learn how to write both long and short formal reports in a clear, objective style, using the appropriate layout.

***Short Management Reports*** A short report is usually written either in the form of a memorandum (memo) or a letter. Usually, reports meant for persons outside the company or clients are written in letter form. The short report:

- Uses the title page or just the report's title as the heading or subject.
- Is usually in direct order, beginning with a summary or a statement summarizing the content.
- Presents findings, analysis, conclusions, and recommendations.

***Memos***

Memos are used as internal messages in companies. They are informal and need very little introductory or background information. Their goal is to address and solve an internal problem. An example of a memorandum is given in Exhibit 4.23.

***Letters***

Letters are usually written to deal with smaller problems and are organized in an indirect order. They usually end on a note of goodwill. An example of a letter report is given in Exhibit 4.24.

| ***Basic Parts of a Report*** | ***Subsidiary Parts of a Report*** |
|---|---|
| Executive summary<br>Introduction<br>Discussion<br>Recommendations<br>Appendix | Cover<br>Title page<br>Table of contents<br>Bibliography/references<br>Glossary |

**Exhibit 4.22** Parts of a Formal Report

**MEMORANDUM**

To: All departments
From: Debasish Roy, HR
Date: 19 August, 2010
Ref: MR/ 02/ 06
Subject: **Pest-Control Problems**

On 17 August 2010, I inspected the company office as part of my routine monthly inspection. The inspection concentrated on two main aspects—hygiene and maintenance issues in the office.

1. **Hygiene:** Standards of hygiene in the office need to be improved. Cleanliness and pest-control are becoming difficult issues because:
   - Despite the fact that employees are allowed to carry only beverages to their desks, we constantly find food particles in the carpeted area. This attracts a lot of pests.
   - Food left over after team get-togethers is frequently stored in the fridge and left there for days.
   - Used coffee mugs and glasses left on desks and spilled sugar near the coffee machine attract ants.
2. **Maintenance Issues:** A little involvement on the part of employees can go a long way in helping reduce waste.
   - Lights are not switched off as employees leave the office for the day.
   - The printer is often overloaded because of multiple-page printouts. This also delays other peoples' work. There is also a lot of wasted paper around the printer.

**Recommendations**

1. Employees are requested to avoid carrying food to their desks. Used coffee mugs and glasses should be returned to the pantry at the end of the day. Food stored in the fridge should be consumed in a day, and the maintenance team should be informed if coffee/sugar is spilled.
2. Employees are requested to switch off their cabin lights at the end of the day. To help save electricity, computer monitors can be switched off when not in use. Employees should not print more that 30 pages at a time using the common printer. Further, everyone is requested to take two-sided printouts if possible.

**Exhibit 4.23** A Memorandum as a Short Report

**Report on the Fall in Profits at *Mom and You*, Noida**

30 August 2009

**Terms of Reference**

At the request of the General Manager, *Mom and You*, in his letter of 16 July 2009 (ref PO/ST/24/03), I was instructed to:

1. Investigate the reasons for the fall in profits at *Mom and You*, Noida, during the period 1 January 2009 to 30 June 2009.
2. Suggest corrective steps in light of the findings.

**Exhibit 4.24** A Letter as a Short Report

**Procedure**

1. The sales records for the period 1 January 2009 to 30 June 2009 were inspected and compared with those for the second half of 2008.
2. Two hundred customers were interviewed over seven days (2nd to 8th August).
3. The shop and its vicinity were carefully inspected.
4. The store manager, sales assistants and cashiers were interviewed.
5. Recent developments in Noida and the surrounding area were observed.

**Findings**

1. A study of the sales records show that profits fell from a monthly average of 8 per cent in the second half of 2008 to an average of 6 per cent in the first 6 months of 2009.
2. The factors responsible for the fall in profits can be divided into internal and external factors.

*A. Internal*

1. A new manager, Mr N.M. Shah, joined *Mom and You* in late 2008. Soon after joining, he went through a prolonged period of illness, which has clearly affected his efficiency in dealing with a new store.
2. Two of the sales assistants —Arun Sharma and Prem Kumar—have been uninvolved in their dealings with customers. A majority of the customers interviewed complained of their brusqueness and unhelpful attitude.
3. The cashier appointed between December and April to replace the previous cashier is inexperienced. The regional manager found that accounts books have not been maintained systematically, and there are gaps in some areas.

*B. External*

1. The prolonged construction of a flyover in Noida has affected the area. Customers prefer to avoid the dust and the traffic in this area and go to the new market that has opened in Sector 43.
2. The opening of Mother's Angels in GP Mall has diverted some of the customers. The new mall has a big food court, multiplex and parking space, and this seems to have attracted some loyal customers.

**Conclusions**

1. The decline in profits is because of external developments—competition from a children's store in the new mall and restricted access to the store because of ongoing construction activities.
2. The performance of the manager, along with the inexperience of the cashier and the discourtesy of some of the staff, is a factor that cannot be ignored.

**Recommendations**

1. Mr Shah should be consulted to help raise his efficiency and to provide him any support that may help him resolve his health issues. His performance should be reviewed again after six months.
2. Arun and Prem should be warned about their behaviour.
3. The cashier should be provided training.
4. The store and its offers should be given coverage in local newspapers. Special offers and children's activities should be organized to promote the store and increase footfall.
5. The viability of the store be reviewed in December 2009.

P. Misra
Regional Sales Manager
MandY Group of Stores

**Exhibit 4.24** *Continued*

***Writing Elements of a Long Formal Report***

Some of the elements of a long formal report are discussed in detail in this section.

***Title Page*** The title page includes the following:

- The heading (title of the report), which should be short, clear, and unambiguous
- The name and affiliation of the author(s)
- The department and date of issue

An example of a title page is given in Exhibit 4.25.

**Identification of Market Potential and Entry Strategy for Consumer Paper Bags**

Submitted to
Mr Suresh Kumar
Director and Chief Executive

By
Anil Gupta
Marketing Manager

PPL Feedback Packaging Ltd
Thane, Maharashtra
September 29, 2003

**Exhibit 4.25** Example of a Title Page

***Acknowledgements*** The writer of the report should thank everyone associated with the assignment and preparation of the report. He or she should be generous in expressing gratitude. An example is:

I thank my organization, PPL Feedback Packaging Limited, for giving me the opportunity to conduct this research project. A special word of thanks to Mr Suresh Kumar (Director and Chief Executive), Mr Nitin Khanna (DGM), and the executives of PPL Feedback Packaging Limited for giving me the necessary guidance and help.

I also thank all the respondents of the survey, who gave me valuable information to carry out the study.

Finally, I wish to thank my colleagues in the marketing department, whose inputs were invaluable to the research.

***Cover Letter*** The cover letter is usually written by top management or project guides as a preface or foreword to a report, reflecting the management's policy and interpretation of the report's findings, conclusions, and recommendations. It introduces the report and tells readers why it is being sent to them. The cover letter is usually placed between the cover and the title page. It is never bound inside the report. It can be written in the form of a memo, a letter, or a forwarding certificate.

***Letter of Transmittal*** Many times, a formal report is accompanied by a letter to outside readers. Although the letter of transmittal is usually placed after the title page, it functions as a greeting to the reader. The letter summarizes the findings, conclusions, and recommendations and gives an idea of what is in the report. It is best written in a direct, conversational manner.

1. It begins by directly talking about the subject of the report. For example:

   Dear Ms Singh,

   Here is the report you requested on August 20 regarding a plot of land for your proposed playschool in Greater Noida.

2. It then gives a brief review of the contents of the report.
3. It acknowledges the contribution of others to the study, if any.
4. The letter ends by thanking the person or body who authorized the report and expressing hope for future interaction. This letter should be written in the personal style of a business letter—that is, using personal pronouns, first person, and active voice. The tone should reflect sincerity. Nowadays, a cover letter is generally preferred to a letter of transmittal.

> The table of contents indicates the hierarchy of topics and their sequence.

***Table of Contents*** Long reports must have a table of contents placed after the acknowledgements and before the executive summary. The table of contents is an important element in a long, formal report as it identifies the topics and their page numbers in the report (or any long document). The table of contents also indicates the hierarchy of topics and their sequence and mentions the main sections of the report exactly as they are worded in the text. An example is given in Exhibit 4.26.

### *Abstract and Executive Summary*

> Know how to write abstracts and summaries, introductions, final recommendations, and conclusions.

An abstract or executive summary comes immediately after the list of tables in the table of contents or on/after the title page itself. Normally, a report has either an abstract or an executive summary, based on the length of the report and expectations of readers. A company practice may be to have both an abstract and an executive summary with long reports.

A summary:

- Should give the context of the report
- Should provide the most important findings, conclusions, and recommendations
- Should act as a time-saver for busy management executives

> A *descriptive abstract* only mentions the topics discussed in the report. It does not give details on these topics. Busy executives have little patience with such a skeletal account of a report's important conclusions and recommendations.

Usually, management reports use executive summaries instead of abstracts. An *abstract* is a summary of a report's most important points. It can be either descriptive or informative and is generally written in about 200 words and in one paragraph. An *executive summary* gives a

## TABLE OF CONTENTS



**Exhibit 4.26** Sample Table of Contents

more detailed overview of a report than an abstract does. It can run into one or two pages. It presents the reader with a preview of the report's findings, conclusions, recommendations, and impact on the company. Management executives sometimes need to know just the main contents of a report, specially its conclusions and recommendations, and a detailed synopsis in the form of an executive summary serves this purpose.

***Descriptive Abstract*** A *descriptive abstract* only mentions the topics discussed in the report. It does not give details on those topics. For details, the reader has to go through the report. Busy executives have little patience with such a skeletal account of a report's important conclusions and recommendations. Therefore, descriptive abstracts are less popular with writers of business reports. For example, consider a descriptive abstract of the report "Identification of market potential and entry strategy for consumer paper bags". It would be as follows:

> The study finds that the market potential for paper bags is not picking up due to the price of paper bags when compared to polybags. It is recommended that the company PPL Feedback supply paper bags at a lesser cost to compete with polybags.

***Informative Abstract*** An *informative abstract* discusses the main subject and presents conclusions and recommendations. Formal reports and scientific and technical articles often use an informative abstract. An informative abstract for the report "Identification of market potential and entry strategy for consumer paper bags" would read as follows:

An *informative abstract* discusses the main subject and presents conclusions and recommendations.

> This report explores new ways to expand the company's (PPL Feedback and Packaging Limited) business, from industrial bags to consumer bags, to meet its growth targets.
>
> The objective of the study was to study the market potential of consumer paper bags for rice and to identify entry strategies for the company. It was found that the market potential for paper bags for rice is about 27 million bags per annum at present; there is an interested segment whose requirement is 27 million bags. The recommendation is that PPL Feedback should price paper bags lower than polybags.

A descriptive abstract only mentions the topics discussed in the report. It does not give details on these topics. Busy executives have little patience with such a skeletal account of a report's important conclusions and recommendations.

This abstract provides more details of the report's contents than the descriptive abstract.

***Executive Summary*** An executive summary covers all the major elements of a report's content:

1. Background of the problem
2. Major topics
3. Important details
4. Main conclusions
5. Recommendations
6. Discussion of how implementation of the recommendations would affect the company.

An executive summary of the PPL report is shown in Exhibit 4.27.

Stiff environmental regulations have brought up new concerns in packaging. These concerns include hygiene, safety, disposability, and recyclability in a developed world. Paper, being eco-friendly and having a premium image, has replaced other packaging materials, such as tin, plastics, and so on for packaging goods for export.

The export market is highly volatile and so is the demand for packaging material. Last year, that is, in 2009, exports were low in the first half of the year as compared to the second half. Also, in segments like carbon black where paper packaging is used, the demand is almost saturated.

Considering these factors, the company (PPL Feedback and Packaging Ltd) is exploring new ways to expand business from industrial bags to consumer bags to meet its growth targets. The more lucrative segments are shopping bags and consumer bags for rice, for which there is a steady demand.

The aim of this research was to study the market potential of shopping bags and consumer paper bags for rice to identify entry strategies for the company. To calculate the market potential, the consumer sample survey method, explained in Chapter IV, was adopted. Chapters I and II provide details about the existing business of the company. Chapter III provides details about the significance of the study for the company, the research objectives, the scope of the study, and data sources. Chapter V explains the design and methodology of the study. To estimate the market potential, the questionnaire approach was followed and the respondents were interviewed personally for relevant details about paper bags. Chapter VI provides details of the results and conclusions reached by the study. The market potential for paper bags for rice is about 27 million bags per annum at present. There is an interested segment whose requirement is also for 27 million bags. The main factor working against the popularity of paper bags is their price in comparison to polybags. However, PPL can supply bags at a lower cost as it has an existent idle capacity to manufacture bags and its machines are fully depreciated. The consumer paper shopping bags market has a potential of about 32.4 million bags per annum at present. If the company invests in mechanized operations at this stage, then the operations may not be profitable for the company in the short run as per the break-even capacity utilization for the machine (discussed on page 35). The operations, however, may be viable in the long run.

This study was for the corporate retail segment only; there is another segment of individuals and retail showrooms who also use paper bags. At the time of market testing for corporate retail segments, the company could also study this segment under the set conditions of product mix explained in Chapter VI, to calculate the size of the market for retail showrooms. At the time of test marketing, which is essential for entry-strategy finalization, the company should test the various possibilities identified in the marketing mix and specifications for the final product launch, which are explained in Chapter VI.

**Introduction**

The introduction of this executive summary states the details of the:

- Authorizing person or body requesting the report
- Author or group of authors responsible for investigation (and submission of the report)
- Purpose or reason for the report
- Methods of enquiry (the research method used)
- Arrangement or grouping of data
- General background of the report's subject

**Exhibit 4.27** Executive Summary of the PPL Report

**Findings**

The findings present the results of the investigation.

**Conclusions**

The conclusions of the executive summary:

- States the results of the investigation
- Offers answers to questions raised in the beginning of the report.
- Contains no new information

**Recommendations**

The recommendations of the executive summary:

- Are the action centre of the report
- State how the conclusions should be acted upon.
- Make clear and definite suggestions/proposals.
- Mention the need for further investigation as a condition for a more comprehensive study of the problem if required.

It is not possible to have a report without recommendations, even if recommendations were not specifically requested when the report was assigned. Recommendations flow from conclusions, as conclusions flow from the discussion.

**Exhibit 4.27** *Continued*

### *Discussion of Findings and Analyses*

This is the main body of the report. It discusses findings and analyzes results. The information is developed in one of the ways discussed here.

Recommendations flow from conclusions, as conclusions flow from the discussion.

***Chronological Development*** The information can be arranged in the order in which the events happened. This is the simplest method of presenting information—as a story with a beginning, middle, and an end. Chronological development requires relatively little planning and organization. The writer selects and arranges the major topics in the order of their occurrence. Non-significant events are left out.

Chronological development requires relatively little planning and organizing.

This method is usually used for writing short reports, progress reports describing the status of a project, and investigative reports that discuss investigations conducted over a long time and at different places.

By discussing each event step by step, the cumulative effect of a variable (factor/thing) can be seen through the conclusions drawn at suitable intervals. The organization of information is easy to determine, as the report writer is guided by the order in which events actually took place.

### *Subjectwise Development*

The information can also be arranged according to the subjects or topics discussed within the report. The subjects are grouped in a predetermined order. This arrangement makes the presentation of information coherent and logical.

When a report involves the study of two or more variables acting upon something, the writer has to arrange the discussion by subject. The writer could describe the effect of one variable on the subject and then proceed in chronological order to determine the cumulative effect of the variable on the subject. Then, in a similar manner he or she would study and describe the effects of the other variable, and record chronologically its cumulative effect.

The question that then concerns the writer is regarding the sequence in which each variable should be discussed if there are several variables of equal importance. The writer has to choose the sequence according to the variable he or she wants to recommend or emphasize. The report can move in increasing order of suitability or move from the most suitable to the least suitable. Before structuring the information, the writer should make the order clearly known by stating whether ascending or descending order is being followed.

Suppose an automobile dealer wants to recommend the most suitable model of luxury car to an executive. He or she will follow the descending order. After evaluating the price, fuel consumption, speed, automation, seating capacity, space, and after-sales guarantees for different models of luxury cars, the dealer would then recommend the model most suitable for the customer. In this case, the dealer has, in fact, made a comparative study of the essential parameters that determine a buyer's choice of a car and presented the information accordingly.

### *Concept Development*

The information can be organized "concept-wise". This means that the writer develops his or her argument and reasoning on the lines of his or her thoughts.

> The logic of the argument guides the organization of the report. Each part or stage of the project is seen as part of a well-linked procession of ideas forming a complete concept.

A report writer can arrange the report by following the logical sequence of the investigation. The writer can develop the topic by describing each step in sequence with the step that follows it, in a series of steps that builds up his or her argument. The logic of the argument guides the organization of the report. Each part or stage of the project is seen as part of a well-linked procession of ideas forming a complete concept.

In the concept-wise method, the writer tells the reader how he or she arrived at the results and why they are valid. This method should be employed when the topic is complex and reasoning and careful consideration are required to explain the various concepts used in reaching the conclusion. When the best result can be selected by a simple and direct analysis, for instance the choice of a car or a site for a new house, subject-wise development would be more appropriate than concept-wise development. Whatever the method of developing the main argument, the report should be logically organized and the narration interesting and convincing.

### *Glossary*

The glossary is the list of technical or special terms used in a report or technical paper and is placed at the end of a report, before the index. It alphabetically lists words or phrases that need special attention. It explains the usage of technical terms peculiar to the industry. A glossary of usage includes rules for forming compound words, abbreviating technical terms, and writing unusual or difficult words. A glossary also acts as a dictionary for some select words that are often confused, misused, or wrongly spelled. These are:

> A glossary of usage includes rules for forming compound words, abbreviating technical terms, and writing unusual or difficult words.

- Words that are often confused because they are similar in meaning or spelling; examples are *diplex* and *duplex*, *ground floor* and *first floor*, *postpone* and *cancel*, or *imply* and *infer*.
- Common errors of usage, such as *many a times* (should be *many a time*), *one of the best option* (in place of *one of the best options*), *comprised of* (for *comprises*).
- Words that tend to be wrongly spelled; examples are *agism* (correct spelling is *ageism*), *accomodation* (instead of *accommodation*), *seprate* (should be *separate*).

- Words having more than one acceptable spelling, such as *program* and *programme*. In case of words like *symposiums* and *symposia* where both versions are in use, both are given in the glossary and a choice is indicated for one of them.
- Words like *data*, which is often wrongly used as singular or as *datas* for the plural, are specially entered in the glossary and their usage is fully explained. *Data* is plural (but is also treated as singular, although the singular form is *datum*). In scientific, philosophical, and general use, *data* generally means a number of items and is thus, regarded as plural, with *datum* as the singular. But, in computing and related subjects, it is taken to denote a mass or collective noun and is, therefore, used with words like *this*, *that*, and *much* and with singular verbs (for example, "useful data has been gathered"). The glossary, like the *Oxford English Dictionary*, will draw our attention to the meaning as well as usage of the word *data* and point out that although some people consider the use of *data* with a singular verb incorrect, it is now in common use. It will also point out that *data* is not a singular countable noun and should not be preceded by words, such as *a*, *every*, *each*, *either*, or *neither* or be given the plural form *datas*.

> In scientific, philosophical, and general use, *data* generally means a number of items and is thus regarded as plural, with datum as the singular.

### Appendix

The *appendix* is used to give a variety of information separately when its inclusion in the main body could interfere with the smooth reading of the report. It usually includes the text of questionnaires or other instruments of survey. Tables, flow charts, maps, summaries of raw data, and details of mathematical formulation are generally included in the appendix. Each appendix is numerically or alphabetically labelled to help the reader identify the material. Sometimes a descriptive title is given. The word "annexure" is sometimes used for the appendix.

The appendix may also include the distribution list. When a report is sent to several persons, it will contain a list of all the persons who receive a copy. The distribution list is placed according to its size or the customer's or company's practice. However, it seems proper to place it as a separate appendix if the list happens to be long. A short distribution list can appear at the foot of the table of contents.

### Index

An index (plural *indexes* or *indices*) is an alphabetical list of subjects, names, and so on, with references to page numbers where they occur in the report or book. It is usually placed at the end. It should not be confused with the table of contents, which always appears at the beginning of the report or book.

In long reports and voluminous works, an index helps the reader locate a subject easily wherever it has been mentioned or discussed in the text. For example, "Order refusals 115" entered in a report's index means one can find order refusals mentioned on page 115. In a book's index, the entry "Research questions 34 a—675" means that the topic of research questions is discussed on page 675 under section 34a.

Normally an author's note about the symbols used in indexing subjects appears at the beginning of index entries, which helps the reader follow the way entries are made. For more information, see Lynn Quitman Troyka's note on indexing in the *Handbook of Writers*.[2]

***Framing an Outline***

Some guidelines for framing an outline include:

1. *Introductory and concluding sentences:* These do not form part of a formal outline. The *thesis* or the topic statement is placed before the first sentence.
2. *Numbers, letters, and indentations:* The formal outline begins with the capitalized Roman numeral I, which numbers the first main idea and is followed by the Roman numerals II, III, and so on, which are used to indicate major subdivisions of the topic. Indented capital letters (A, B, C, and so on) are used to mark the next level of generality, while small letters (a,b,c, and so on) indicate a further level of generality, if any. This arrangement is based on the principle that each subdivision is placed above the next level of specific detail given by the outline. It may be noted that in a sentence outline if an entry is longer than one line, the second line is indented by one word. That means that the second line begins under the second word of the first line.
3. *At least two entries at each level:* In an outline, there can be a topic numbered "I" only if there is "II" that follows it, and similarly, there can only be an "A" when there is a "B". Without at least two parts, no category can be divided. Where a category has only one subdivision, it should either be left out or reclassified, or expanded to include at least two subdivisions.

   For example:

   **Incorrect**

   I. Standards of hygiene in the canteen not satisfactory

   A. Food left over from lunches

   II. Fridge not defrosted frequently

   **Correct**

   I. Standards of hygiene in the canteen not satisfactory

   II. Safety issues regarding electrical sockets in the canteen

   **Correct**

   I. Standards of hygiene in the canteen not satisfactory

   A. Food left over from lunches

   B. Fridge not defrosted frequently

   II. Safety issues regarding electrical sockets in the canteen

4. *Levels of generality:* All subdivisions should have the same level of generality. A main idea and a supporting detail cannot be placed at the same level.

   **Incorrect**

   I. Starting an IT centre

   II. Conducting computer courses

   **Correct**

   I. Starting an IT centre

   II. Opening a health resort

5. *No overlap:* There should be a fresh point under each heading. The same idea should not be repeated in different places.

**Incorrect**

I. People move away from villages
   A. They go in search of jobs
   B. They go to seek their livelihoods

**Correct**

I. People move away from villages
   A. They go in search of jobs
   B. They often change their outlooks

6. *Parallelism:* All statements (divisions and sub-divisions) should have grammatically parallel construction. For example, if one item begins with the *–ing* form of the verb, other items should also begin with form *verb* + *–ing*.

   **Incorrect**

   I. Negotiating peace
   II. Promote understanding

   **Correct**

   I. Negotiating peace
   II. Promoting understanding

7. *Punctuation and capitalization:* Only the first word or a proper noun should be capitalized in each entry. Please note that a full stop should be used at the end of each entry only when it is a sentence outline. No punctuation mark is used at the ends of entries in a topic outline.

Outlining is the key to organization; it is essential for writing any form of business communication. To determine the sequence of ideas (or presentation) in any piece of writing, the writer has to consider the level of importance of the information and also the order in which it should be known. For instance, when writing a report, one could mention the problem first and then discuss the method used to solve it, followed by findings and conclusions.

Since the reader of a report is more interested in the findings and conclusions, it is better to give more importance to these elements. The details of the problem and the methodology used to solve it receive less attention as they are of less interest to the reader. However, they provide the necessary background for the findings and conclusions. One could have an outline including all the four elements of a report in the form shown in Exhibit 4.28.

I. Introduction
   A. Definition of the problem
   B. Description of the methods used
II. Findings
III. Conclusions

**Exhibit 4.28** A Sample Outline

As the statement of the problem and description of research methodology are of lesser interest to most readers, they can be put together as two elements under the same entry, *Introduction*. As the other two elements, *findings* and *conclusions*, are of greater interest, they are entered separately as item II and item III.

The effort and time devoted to forming an outline are rewarded by the gain in clarity and understanding of the levels of significance of different elements in the composition.

The effort and time devoted to forming an outline are rewarded by the gain in clarity and understanding of the levels of significance of different elements in the composition.

### *Bibliography*

All published and unpublished sources of information used in preparing the report are listed in the bibliography. All reference documents, previous reports, books, periodicals, and even letters written and received by the writer are mentioned in it. In using written material from secondary sources, report writers must always mention the source of the information by citing it as a footnote or endnote. Failing to document sources amounts to plagiarism.

Rules for bibliographies vary. In a report, the bibliography should conform to the style of documentation followed by the concerned company, just as a technical article or paper conforms to the form followed by the journal or society that is publishing the material. Though each organization usually has its own standard format of documenting sources, the general system followed is either that of the Modern Language Association (MLA) or the American Psychological Association (APA).

Documentation of cross-references should be done in a way that does not disturb the flow of the argument. The writer can provide references in footnotes at the end of each relevant page or can describe all references together in endnotes, which is the list of all references at the end of the report. In both cases, the reader can find all the details about sources mentioned in the report and can check the accuracy of facts by consulting the original sources. Endnotes are usually preferred as they are easy to refer to when desired. Also, footnotes create the problem of spacing the material on the page.

It is to be noted that each reference to be cited in the endnotes is numbered consecutively as 1, 2, 3, and so on. Each reference should have the same number when mentioned in the body of the discussion. The various styles for documenting the sources are discussed in greater detail in Appendix 12.

### *Diagrams in Reports*

Report writers use tables and graphics, such as bar charts, line charts, and pictograms to explain ideas briefly and vividly. Diagrams, like all visual aids, communicate information clearly and effectively. For example, written instructions supported by illustrations to show how an eye-drop should be opened and applied would be far more effective than plain instructions in words alone.

Diagrams, like all visual aids, communicate information clearly and effectively.

***Use of Tables*** A table presents numerical or topical data in rows and columns. A report writer should know some of the techniques of preparing tables for clear presentation of content. The most important technique is to label each table in a manner that allows the reader to locate the desired table easily. Some tips are given here:

1. **Numbering all tables:** The writer should number all the tables in the report consecutively by calling them "Table 1", "Table 2", "Table 3", and so on. When referring to them, one can simply say, "as shown in Table 1, …" or "… in the following table". This makes cross-references simple and clear. The table number should be written at the top of the table.

2. **Labelling each table:** There should be a complete heading or title for each table that clearly describes the contents of the table for the reader. As headings, the table titles can be as long as they completely describe the table's contents. The title can even run into two lines. It may mention sources of data, numbers included in the figures in the table, and the subject of the table. An example is: "Segmentation of market (5–20 kg) based on the usage of bags in the total market of 3,150 million". For emphasis, the title of the table can be written in bold letters.
3. **Column heads and sub-heads:** Column heads and sub-heads should be used to classify information when several columns are given. For example, if the column head is "Cities" and the column lists several cities, they may be segregated by sub-heads that classify the cities under various zones, such as "North", "South", and so on.
4. **Rows:** Similarly, the subject of each row should be indicated by identifying its contents. For example, in a column that lists various sectors of the economy, the subject of the row should be identified as "Economic Sector".
5. **Footnotes:** Footnotes are used to explain or qualify specific entries, if required.
6. There should be sufficient space between columns so that the data remain well separated.

Exhibit 4.29 is an example of a table with various parts labeled; it illustrates the layout, title placement, and headings for the vertical columns and horizontal rows effectively. Notice that if the table is taken exactly from some other source, the source must be mentioned.

Understand the role and use of graphics in reports.

**Table 1** Choke Points: Highest Pollutant Levels in Various Parts of Delhi on Diwali Day (2003)

**Column Heads**

Row subject

| **Parameters** | **Location** | **Permissible Levels (mg/m³)** | **Actual Levels (mg/m³)** |
|---|---|---|---|
| SPM | Meera Bagh | 100 | 2,292 |
| Respirable SPM | Meera Bagh | 200 | 4,772 |
| Carbon monoxide | Karawal Nagar | 100 | 8,000 |
| Sulphur dioxide | Vasant Kunj | 80 | 201 |
| Nitrogen dioxide | Meera Bagh | 80 | 174.8 |

*Source details* → *Source:* Delhi Pollution Control Committee

*Notes* → *Note:* The data was collected at 11 p.m.

**Exhibit 4.29** A Sample Table

## Attributes of a Good Report

An effective reporting calls for professionalism, profound knowledge of the subject, attentiveness and outstanding writing proficiency. A good report is essentially:

- Brief and accurate—facts and figures should be presented in an accurate manner.
- Clear and logical in structure—indicates clearly where the ideas are leading
- Relevant and appropriate—concentrates on the particular problem and includes no irrelevant details or misleading ideas.
- Well-organized, systematic and definite in presentation of facts.
- Rational, persuasive, and specific in analysis and recommendations.
- Comprehensible—covers all vital details and conveys understandable information.
- All inclusive—What is the main problem? Who is/are involved in it? When did it arise? Where will the report be presented? How can it be presented the best?
- Highly objective—no place for prejudices, distortion of facts, or personal opinions.
- Written in good English—uses short sentences, correct grammatical structures, and spellings (In report you don't get marks for writing correct language, but you lose for writing wrong English.)
- Using appropriate layout and professional style.
- Neat and attractive in style and appearance—should make a good first impression.

## Methods of Reporting

There are two methods by which individuals can write reports:

### *The Letter Method*

It may take the form of an ordinary letter. That means that usual formality of heading, address, inside addresses, salutation etc. should be maintained in the report. Below the salutation, the title of the report should come.

The next paragraph should show what procedure the report writer followed and what persons he interviewed. The rest of the paragraphs should show the findings and the last paragraph should give the conclusions or the considered opinion of the report writer. In short, it is just a more systematically written letter.

### *The Schematic Method*

This method is more common in committee reports.

Here, the title of the report is given first. Then, the contents of the report are given under the following subtitles.

1. **Terms of reference:** This section should give the source or the authority that ordered the report. It also describes the scope of the report and its objectives.
2. **Procedure:** This section should give the method followed by the report-writer. It may mention the places visited, persons interviewed, etc.
3. **Findings:** The facts as they exist are presented in proper order here.
4. **Recommendations or conclusion:** This section should give the considered opinion of the report-writer based on the facts as interpreted by him. It has got to be an expert opinion based on incontrovertible facts.

The end may have the signature and designation of the report writer.

The following is a report presented in both the letter method and the schematic method:

1. Report on workers' discontent presented in the Letter form

**DECCAN ENGINEERING CO. LTD.**
2-2-344, Balanagar, HYDERABAD 500 011
Ph.040-27938966/67/79

April 24, 2003

The Directors,
Deccan Engineering Co. Ltd.
Balanagar,
HYDERABAD 500 011

**Report on workers' discontent at the Company's auxiliary unit**

In accordance with the instruction given to me on April 9, 2003, I visited the auxiliary unit of the Company in order to find out the cause and extent of discontent among the workers.

I interviewed supervisors, plant-operators and 25 workers, selected at random, in this context.

I found out the following facts that are responsible for this trouble:

There seems to be widespread discontent amongst workers. Several other personnel pointed out that the number of incidents of breach of discipline and general non-cooperative attitude had gone up considerably. They expressed the view that the situation was deteriorating and that a serious outbreak of misbehaviour might result. The workers, on their part also had some complaints. According to them, the supervisors were inadequate; the workers were given long hours on the production line and skilled personnel were not eager to explain the working of the machinery to apprentices. There were other avoidable lapses that the workers resented. The skilled personnel, to save their own time, leave the machines dirty so that the unskilled workers have to clean them. Safety precautions in the machine room are continually being ignored. There is a widespread belief that the rates paid to workers are the lowest in the area.

I am of the opinion that immediate action must be taken to prevent further disturbances. It is also felt that there is evidence that all the complaints are well-founded. In particluar, ignoring safety precautions is an offence against the Factories Act and must be stopped.

Regarding pay and allowances, it is necessary to bring to the notice of the workers that our rates compare favourably with those paid to apprentices in other similar units. It is, therefore, my considered opinion that the following suggestions will go a long way in reducing the discontent:

- A special officer may be appointed and he should be asked to draw up a systematic program for the unit.
- All supervisors must be strictly advised to keep machinery clean and observe all safety precautions.
- The Personnel Officer must point out to the workers that the rates of payment enjoyed in this factory are very favorable.

Yours faithfully,

Sd/-
Trivikrama Rao
Company Secretary

2. Report on workers' discontent in the Schematic form

The same report can be presented in the schematic form with sub-headings for different points.

**DECCAN ENGINEERING CO. LTD.**
2-2-344, Balanagar, HYDERABAD 500 011
Ph. 040-27938966/67/79

**Report on workers' discontent at Company's Auxiliary Unit**

*Terms of reference:* In accordance with the instructions given to me on April 9, 2003, I visited the auxiliary unit of the Company in order to find out the causes and extent of discontent among the workers.

*Procedure:* In this connection, I interviewed supervisors, plant-operators and 25 workers selected at random.

I found out the following facts that are responsible for this unrest.

*Findings:* There seems to be widespread discontent amongst workers. Several other personnel pointed out that the number of incidents of breach of discipline and general non-cooperative attitude had gone up considerably. They expressed the view that the situation was deteriorating and that serious outbreaks of misbehaviour might result.

The workers, on their part, also had some complaints. According to them, the supervisors were inadequate, the workers were given long hours on the production line and skilled personnel were not eager to explain the working of the machinery to workers. There were other avoidable lapses that the workers resent. The skilled personnel, to save their own time, leave the machines dirty so that the unskilled workers have to clean them. Safety precautions in the machine room are continually being ignored. Further, there is a wide spread belief that the rates paid to workers are the lowest in the area.

*Conclusion:* I am of the opinion that immediate action must be taken to prevent further discontent and ill will. There is evidence to believe that all complaints are well-founded. Deliberately ignoring safety precautions is an offence against the Factories Act and must be stopped.

Regarding pay and allowances, it is necessary to bring to the notice of the workers that our rates compare favourably with those paid to apprentices in other similar units.

*Recommendations:* It is therefore my considered opinion that the following suggestions will go a long way in reducing the discontent:

- A special officer may be appointed and he should be asked to draw up a systematic program for the unit.
- All supervisors must be strictly advised to keep machinery clean and observe all safety precautions.
- The Personnel Officer must point out to the workers that the rates of payment enjoyed in this factory are very favorable.

Sd/-
Trivikrama Rao
Company Secretary

April 24, 2003

## REFERENCE STYLE

### Books

***One author***

Basu, A (1963), Consumer Price Index: Theory, Practice and Use in India, Modern Book Agency, Calcutta.

***Two authors***

Singh, M. and Pandya, JF (1967), Government Publications of India, Metropolitan Book Co., Delhi.

***Three authors***

Mote, VL; Malya, MM and Saha J (1968), Tables for Capital Investment Analysis, Indian Institute of Management, Ahmedabad.

***Edited book***

Basu, G (ed.) (1962), Indian Tax Laws and Foreigners Having Investment in India or Having Business Connections in or with India, Oxford Book & Stationery, Calcutta.

***Government publication***

Ministry of Law, Government of India (1960), The Copyright Act, 1957, The Manager of Publications, Delhi.

***Journal paper***

Jain, SK (1967), World Class Manufacturing, International Journal of Operations Management, Vol. 6, No. 12, pp. 11–31.

pp. stands for page number.

***Article in a newspaper***

Gandhi, VP (1968), Will the Budget Achieve Its Aims? Certain Doubts, The Economic Times, Mar. 8, pp. 5–6.

***Conference paper***

Bhattacharya, S.K. (1967), Control Techniques and Their Applicability, paper presented at the Ahmedabad Management Association, Ahmedabad, Nov. 22, pp. 11–17.

## CV WRITING

A résumé of a recent graduate lists:

- Personal/biographical details
- His or her educational background
- Details of his or her work experience
- References

The résumé briefly communicates all relevant and important biographical information about an applicant. The application letter interprets the information.

A new college graduate's résumé is generally just one-page long. It includes the applicant's career objectives, education details, work experience, and school/college activities. It is attached with the application letter. Because it is a fresh graduate's résumé, educational qualifications are placed first and have a position of prominence. All information in the CV should be under bold, clear headings, so that the reader can easily find the desired information. Headings given in upper and lower case are easier to read than those entirely in capital letters.

There are several styles for writing a student résumé. For an example of a CV in the commonly used chronological format.

## Heading

The heading should include the applicant's name, address, date of birth (if age limit is mentioned), telephone number, and e-mail address.

## Objective

In this section, the applicant should mention the specific, desired position that suits his or her educational qualifications and experience. The objective should be stated in practical terms, not in a vague manner such as "I am anxious to join a challenging position in a renowned organization where I can prove my ability." Employers want to know practical objectives, not the ambitions of the applicant.

## Education

Should the list of educational qualifications begin from the school level and end with graduate and postgraduate qualifications, or should the more recent degrees be mentioned first? The chronological order may not be very impressive, and the highest qualification is generally the most important and relevant. It should, therefore, be emphasized by placing it first and listing the degrees in reverse chronological order.

It is not necessary to include school certificates, but the résumé should mention any short-term training or special certificate programmes taken in addition to coursework if they are relevant. It is especially important to specifically mention those courses or skills that are particularly important for the kind of position the applicant is applying for. Overall grades, along with grade points in different courses, should be listed if they are significant. The applicant should also list any specializations or majors with the grade point average. Any honours or distinctions should also be listed under a separate heading, along with other details of educational degrees, such as year of graduation, name of university or college, and subjects taken.

## Work Experience

Relevant work experience should be listed in reverse chronological order. This category can include all experience, part-time as well as full-time, if the applicant's experience is not very extensive. However, someone who has worked in their field for several years need not list part-time positions.

For each position listed, the following details should be provided: the job title, the company's name, the location, and the duration of employment. There should be a brief description of the applicant's role, responsibilities, and accomplishments, particularly at those jobs that are most closely related to the applicant's career goals. It is important to remember that descriptions of responsibilities become more powerful with the use of action words, such as *designed*, *prepared*, *developed*, *coordinated*, *supervised*, *directed*, and so on. When mentioning the duration of employment, the exact day, dates, or months need not be given. The names of terms and vacations, with relevant years, are sufficient.

> There should be a brief description of the applicant's role, responsibilities, and accomplishments, particularly at those jobs that are most closely related to the applicant's career goals.

Applicants should remember that potential employers are not interested in simply reading a list of positions they have held. They want to know the specific methods, techniques, and processes used in different positions as well as any concrete accomplishments. Applicants should never write that they have no work experience. Fresh graduates may have had little opportunity to acquire professional work experience, but graduate students can gain some experience organizing functions, running student clubs, associations, and societies, managing events, undertaking industry visits, and so on. Graduates at management or technical institutes undertake summer projects or term/semester-long industrial training. In addition, some students earn money working part-time job(s) in their institutions. All such exposure forms a fresh graduate's "experience". Instead of writing that they have no experience, it is better for recent graduates to mention all activities in which they have been involved as students. And while explaining their student experiences, they should emphasize how these experiences qualify them for the job.

### Awards and Honours

The résumé should include a mention of all scholarships, prizes, and awards won in college. School awards show that the applicant has been consistently meritorious. Professional prizes can also be mentioned.

### Activities

In this section, the applicant should mention his or her college activities. For instance, he or she can highlight a position as president, secretary, or coordinator in a student organization. The applicant can also mention any significant hobbies, such as playing a musical instrument or being an accomplished athlete.

### References

Under references, the applicant should list the names of two or three persons who know that they are being listed as references. The full name, business address, e-mail address, and telephone number should be provided for each reference. References are expected to honestly speak about the applicant to the employer confidentially. Thus, they should be familiar with the applicant and his or her work and are usually professors or previous employers. They should not be related to the applicant. Sometimes, under references, one can write: "references available on request".

### Summary

Individuals with a lot of experience sometimes begin with a summary of their qualifications in place of a job objective. The recent practice is to place a summary of all major achievements and specializations below the name. The summary is supposed to help the reader of the résumé find the most relevant and important information about the applicant immediately. For the candidate, it acts as a strong preface or foreword to his or her experiences.

> Individuals with a lot of experience sometimes begin with a summary of their qualifications in place of a job objective.

### Essentials of a Good CV

A good CV provides basic information to the recruiter in a systematic form. It enables the employer to evaluate the applicant's qualifications and strengths in just a few minutes and shortlist or reject the applicant based on this initial review. A good CV, by opening the door to an interview, can, therefore, mean a lot for one's career.

General "Do's" for writing a good CV include:

- Indicate a specific job objective or a summary of your qualifications.
- Highlight your accomplishments.

- Emphasize education/training/experience related to your job objective.
- Give details of professional activities that are supportive of your career objective.
- Proofread your CV and, ideally, also have someone else check it for typing errors.
- Ensure that all contact information is current and correct.

General "Don'ts" for writing a good CV include:

- Do not use first person or second person pronouns in the résumé.
- Do not use an uncommon format.
- Do not mention the expected salary.
- Do not leave any unexplained gaps in your experience.
- Do not give reasons for leaving earlier jobs.
- Do not use coloured paper.
- Do not send a handwritten résumé.
- Do not mention personal details, such as the number of children, marital status, or other details that are not relevant to the job.
- Do not be too brief or too lengthy.

> A CV should begin with the category that the applicant wishes to emphasize. If an applicant has little work experience but a good education profile, then he or she should begin with education.

### Suitable Organization

The conventional method is to begin with personal details and end with references. But, a more practical method is to begin with the category that needs to be emphasized. For instance, if an applicant has little work experience, but a good education profile, then he or she should begin with education. Conversely, if an applicant has extensive work experience, then he or she should begin with work experience and bring up educational qualifications afterwards. Personal details can then appear as the last category, to be placed before references. Employers will be more interested in an applicant's qualifications and work experience than in his or her biographical details.

> Employers are more interested in an applicant's qualifications and work experiences than in his or her biographical details.

### Appropriate Length

The CV of a fresh graduate should be neither too brief nor too long. One page is the ideal length. Experienced candidates have more information under each category. Hence, their CVs can be two to three pages in length. After several years of work experience, people do not list college activities and, instead, emphasize memberships in professional bodies and related professional activities. The résumés of highly experienced individuals may run into several pages, even up to 15 to 20 pages. There is no prescribed length; the length of such CVs is based on the needs of each individual candidate and job. These résumés may have more categories of information such as:

- Major qualifications
- Major achievements
- Activities and professional memberships

## WRITING MINUTES OF MEETINGS

Minutes are a precise summary of the discussions and decisions made at a meeting.

### Elements of Minutes

General formats of minutes include the following important details about a meeting:

1. Heading: The name, number, time, place, and date of the meeting whose proceedings are recorded
2. Lists of members present and that of the members invited, but absent
3. Any special invitees
4. Name of the chairperson who conducted the meeting
5. The starting time and the closure time of the meeting
6. All major decisions taken. The details of discussions are left out. Only the final conclusions reached are recorded.
7. Any follow up actions to be taken and the names of the persons designated for the purpose, if any
8. Suggestion for any further meeting on the subject, if any

In the format of minutes followed by some organizations, minutes record in detail the discussions, with the names of persons who contributed some important points or made significant observations.

The minutes are drafted very clearly and systematically with headings and subheadings. If any member presents tables or charts, the same are attached. (in copy form) Since the minutes are recorded for the reference and action of the participants, they are circulated among all the members or posted on the internet that they easily reach all the members of the organization.

## PARAGRAPH AND ESSAY WRITING

For successful written communication, we should be able to choose proper words, construct effective sentences, develop well- organized paragraphs, and join them to produce longer themes, reports, proposals, or letters. The quality of written communication depends on the clarity and correctness of expression. Here, attention is given to expression in terms of: paragraph building, sentence construction, and use of words.

### What Is a Paragraph?

A paragraph is a unit of thought consisting of many sentences, each of which is the smallest unit of the theme of the paragraph.

We are aware of a paragraph only as readers of a written communication. Typographically, or even in hand written text, it stands out indented by five spaces or by double space between two paragraphs, written without indentation if presented in block form style.

As listeners, we are aware of just words, the speaker's pitch of voice, and tone. There are no units of paragraphs, in oral communication. However, as readers we are concerned with different units of thought: paragraphs, sentences, and words.

***Definition***

Paragraph is the unit of written composition next larger than the sentence. It is a unit of composition in the sense that contains only one subject expressed in one main idea. The main idea is also known as central idea. And, it is this single central idea around which a paragraph develops, supported by other subordinate ideas. Unity is a paragraph's essential feature of composition.

***Kinds of Paragraph***

Paragraph can be of two kinds:

(1) **Topical** paragraph, (2) **Special** paragraph

The topical paragraph develops a topic or an idea. Special paragraphs introduce, conclude, or modulate the ideas developed in an essay.

The art of writing a proper paragraph, specially as a unit of a larger theme, is most important for knowing how to write well organized and unified essays, articles, reports, and themes (assignments).

***The Topic Sentence***

The main idea of a paragraph is found stated in a sentence called the topic sentence. The topic sentence states the subject of the paragraph. Usually, topic sentence is placed at the beginning of the paragraph. This gives focus to the sentences, which follow the opening sentence as developers of the main idea.

***Sentence Functions in Paragraph Development***

The sentences in most well written paragraphs may be analyzed into four general functions. First, there are paragraph introducers, which are sentences that establish the topic focus of the paragraph as a whole. Second, there are paragraph developers, which present examples or details of various kinds that support the ideas set forth by the paragraph introducers. Third, there are viewpoint or context modulators, which are sentences that provide a smooth transition between different sets of ideas. Fourth, there are paragraph terminators, which logically conclude the ideas discussed in the paragraph in a psychologically satisfying manner. Not all pieces of writing will conform to this analysis, however, most successful paragraphs usually contain some combination of these four sentence types.

(Source: Maurice Imhoof and Herman Hudson, From Paragraph to Essay, Longman, London, 1976, p.1)

An analysis of the model paragraph given above will tell you that each sentence of the paragraph has a key idea. Each key word (idea) is given in italics. You should write down these italicized words from each of the six sentences. Further,

1. State the theme of the model paragraph as a whole.
2. Point out the function of the opening sentence in the paragraph given above.
3. Mention the four paragraph developers used in the above paragraph.
4. Do you find the last sentence in the paragraph as a good closing sentence? Give reasons for your answer.

You must have noticed that the paragraphs you have read are built around a single idea, which is usually stated in the first sentence of the paragraph.

In writing your paragraphs, use this method of placing the topic sentence at the beginning of the paragraph. This will help you in achieving unity of ideas in your paragraph. The statement of the main idea/ theme at the beginning will also help your reader to know the subject at the very outset.

This is the most common pattern of paragraph formation. The main idea is stated first, then explained, illustrated, developed, and supported with examples or details in the subsequent sentences. Here is another example of this simple pattern. Note its main idea and see how it is further developed and repeated at the end.

**Note:** But, it is possible for a writer to place his topic sentence even at the end of the paragraph or in the middle of the paragraph. Sometimes, the topic may not be clearly and specifically stated in a particular sentence. In that case, the reader has to infer the main topic of the paragraph as he goes on reading it as a whole. For example, please consider the following paragraph on Growing Food:

**Growing Food**

"Farming provides most of the food we eat in India. Our chief food crops are cereals or grains. Cereals include maize, rice, and wheat. We also grow barley and gram. We can claim to be 70 per cent self-sufficient in food."

If you read the above paragraph to see how the sentences are arranged, you will not fail to notice that the paragraph begins (its first sentence) by stating first its topic (growing food). Farming is the means of most of the food we need. The remaining sentences 2, 3, and 4, further develop the paragraph by giving details of what we grow- our food crops, which include cereals or grains given in sentences 3 and 4. Sentence 3: rice and wheat. Sentence 4: barley and grain. All sentences are connected to the main topic.

The first sentence (the opening sentence), which states the topic of the paragraph is known as the "topic" sentence or introducer that establishes the topic focus of the whole paragraph. Now, read the following paragraph. Try to follow both the meaning and organization of the ideas discussed.

**Our Deadly Enemies**

"Flies are our deadly enemies because they feed upon dirt and rubbish. When they come and crawl over the meat, sweetmeats and cakes with their dirty legs they leave all kinds of germs behind them and thus, poison our food. To keep away flies we must clean our homes and yards. We must always put the lids on our dustbins. We must not throw rubbish into the streets, but put it into the dustbins. We must cover our food so that no flies can settle on it. We must never let flies sit on milk, or they will poison it."

1. What are the two main ideas about flies in the paragraph?
2. Does the paragraph have unity of idea?
3. Where do you find a different idea starting in the paragraph?
4. Will you like to divide the given paragraph into two separate paragraphs? Why?_

### *Forms of Paragraph*

A paragraph is a unified and coherent structure of sentences. It can run from a single word or a single sentence to several pages long like 'Charles Lamb's Dream Children: A Reverie', an essay in a single paragraph spread over several pages. Normally, paragraphs contain four to ten sentences. Business letters usually contain short paragraphs so that readers can grasp each single idea quickly, uninterrupted. The two words unified and coherent, used to define the form of paragraph, are the guiding features for the composition of a good paragraph.

When you read a paragraph, look for its single topic. Its central idea expressed in a particular sentence. The sentence that expresses the central idea is called the thesis, or topic sentence.

### *Variety in Paragraph Forms*

The topic sentence is normally placed at the beginning of the paragraph. It helps the writer to organize the paragraph by first introducing the main idea and then develop the main idea with the help of other sentences stating the supportive ideas. Writers create variety in their writing by shifting the topic sentence from the opening position to the middle or at the end. Sometimes, the writer may leave the main idea unexpressed, simply implied. The shifting of the topic sentence breaks the monotony of reading paragraphs of the same form, a kind of deductive movement of ideas.

### *Examples of Different Patterns of Paragraph Development*

### *The main idea stated first and then repeated at the end*

**Example:**

"In technical writing, you report factual information objectively for the practical use of your readers. This information is usually specialized and directed towards a specific group of people. It is based on your experience, observations, and interpretations in a certain field. The purpose of technical writing is to inform and to persuade by providing facts (and opinions based on facts) that help readers answer question, solve a problem, make a decision, or perform a task. Such writing does not seek to entertain, to create surprise, or to stimulate emotions. It does seek to give readers the information they need – clearly and objectively."

Notice how the main idea stated in the first sentence is restated at the end of the paragraph. Can you tell, why?

### *Topic Sentence in the Middle*

**Example:**

"An American writer, called Thoreau, said, 'It takes two to speak the truth - one to speak, and another to hear.' This is a very important saying, and it would save a great deal of argument and annoyance in life if people paid attention to it. 'It takes two to speak truth'. You cannot speak the truth by saying what you think is the truth. You have to express it differently for different people. To some people 'socialism' means taking money from those who have money and giving it those who have none. To other people 'socialism' means state control of industry and commerce. We cannot tell a man 'the truth about socialism' until you know what he understands by the term. If you say, 'I believe in socialism', and he understands that you mean you believe in robbery, you must not speak the truth. If a man says to a friend, 'good morning, Mr. A', and the friend replies 'it's not a morning at all', is that the truth, even if the morning is bad?"

(Source: J.C. Hill, *Introduction to Writing English*)

### *Topic Sentence at the End*

**Example:**

"I have collected a considerable number of papers and letters of national and historical interest. Many of these, connected with various phases of our national struggle for freedom, were unfortunately destroyed or mislaid during the long years when we were in prison. Still some remain. There are other papers and documents as well as letters relating to the subsequent period after I took office, which have also considerable historic value. All such important papers and documents and letters should be offered to the national library or the national archives."

—Jawahar Lal Nehru

### *Main Idea Implied, Not Stated in any Sentence*

**Example:**

"Experiments are sometimes made by experts to find out how many errors people do make in their statements. Here is one experiment, which was tried. Some students at a university were shown on a screen a picture of a bullfight. They were then asked to write short account of what they had seen. When this was finished, they were told to put a number on every statement made-**1** if they thought so; **2** if they were fairly sure about it; **3** if they were quite sure; and **4** if they were prepared to swear to the statement on the oath. Every student had at least ten per cent errors in the statements he was prepared to swear to an oath, and considerably more than ten per cent in all the other groups."

In this paragraph, the main idea implied is whenever you are arguing with some one about a point, remember that there is quite a good chance that you are wrong, however confident you feel about it.

### *Logical Order of Ideas: Coherence*

There are two distinguishing features of a paragraph: Unity: presence of one single main idea; and, the other, Coherence: logical order of ideas.

No matter where the main idea (the topic sentence) is placed, the ideas are logically sequenced to form a single unified whole. The ideas are related to each other in a reasonable way.

**Example:**

Read the following conversation. There is a proper flow of ideas. The whole dialogue can be easily understood by you. Find out the words which are working as connectives between different arguments:

"I tell you", said the man with the bicycle, speaking to a sergeant of police, "when I started from my house this lamp had plenty of oil in it. When I left the canal after my swim, I lighted the lamp with my own hands. Don't you see a wind is blowing, it might have been blown off at any time between here and canal."

**Analysis:**

The material of this paragraph follows the logical order. A statement is made and then supported by means of examples; reasons are given which take us to a conclusion. The whole statement is based on a cause- effect relationship and the events are presented on the simplest method of order of time or the chronological order of events. These two methods of arranging the material of the paragraph, (1) cause-effect relation and (2) order of time, have given the paragraph its coherence.

Notice the repeated use of "when" to convince the sergeant that the lamp might have been blown off at any time between here and canal.

This paragraph also uses one more method of making the argument logical and convincing. The use of spatial arrangement: started from 'home' – reaching the 'canal' – being caught here.

The three methods of logically arranging the materials of a paragraph are:

1. Order of time (sequence of events)
2. Spatial order (distance, nearer)
3. Cause - effect relation

These methods can be used separately or together as seen in the short paragraph discussed above.

### *Lack of Coherence and Unity*

Read the following paragraph and point out the different ideas placed together in a single paragraph.

"The police are always on the look out for bad characters and lawbreakers. Their chief duty is to maintain law and order in the country. If a man breaks a law, he must be punished. There are many types of anti-national and anti-social elements in our society, but the worst are terrorists who kill innocent human beings belonging to a particular community. Communalists who incite communal riots in the country are the enemies of the nation. Terrorists and communalists who want to destroy the unity and integrity of the nation are traitors and should be awarded the most severe punishment."

The paragraph's topic sentence establishes our focus on the chief duty of the police. But, in the later sentences, the paragraph drops this idea and begins to discuss the anti-national and anti-social character's activities. It ends by suggesting punishment for those criminals and the sentences do not logically follow from one to another. This lack of logical progression of ideas is known as lack of coherence. Each sentence in the paragraph should be well connected to the central idea and also linked with the previous sentence logically.

**Activity**

Read the following paragraph and point out the source of its coherence.
How is the material arranged?

"I had the good fortune of growing up with a sense of kinship with nature in all its manifestations. Birds, plants, stones were companions and, sleeping under the star-strewn sky, I became familiar with the names and movements of the constellations. But my deep interest in this our "only earth" was not for itself but as a fit home for man."

(Source: Indira Gandhi, Human Environment, 1972).

**Activity**

Read the following paragraph and say if you find in it unity and coherence. Give reasons for your analysis. Discuss its development from the topic sentence to the end-sentence.

"I took the tattered object in my hands and turned it over rather ruefully. It was a very ordinary black hat of the usual round shape, hard and much the worse for wear. The linning had been of red silk, but was a good deal discoloured. There was no maker's name, but as Holmes had remarked, the initials 'H.B' were scrawled upon one side. It was pierced in the brim for a hat securer, but the elastic was missing. For the rest, it was cracked, exceedingly dusty, and spotted in several places, although there seemed to have been some attempt to hide the discoloured patches by securing them with ink."

(Source: Arthur Conan Doyle, *The Adventure of the Blue Carbuncle*)

## How to Write a Paragraph and Beyond

To construct a good paragraph, follow the guidelines given hereunder:

- Have a purpose – a single idea. State it in a topic/thesis sentence.
- Relate throughout to this central idea; it must not introduce any new or unrelated idea (which logically belongs to another paragraph).
- Develop logically from beginning to end; sentences must follow logically one upon another.
- Move smoothly from beginning to end, there must be a smooth change between sentences.
- Avoid construction of long paragraphs that contain too many ideas.

(On a larger scale, each paragraph must contribute to the whole essay in the same way as each sentence contributes to the whole paragraph. Therefore, the central idea of the whole paragraph must relate to the central idea of the whole essay.)

- The development from paragraph to paragraph must be logical.
- The transition between paragraphs must be smooth.

## Paragraph Development

### *Development by Listing: List Paragraph*

The simplest way to develop the paragraph is by enumerating details to support the main idea. Its examples you have seen in paragraph on Food Grains and the one on the Sentence Functions in Paragraph Development. The first sentence mentions four general functions of sentences in a paragraph. The subsequent sentences enumerate all the four functions: introducers, developers, context modulators, paragraph terminators with the description of each function. In the model list paragraph, notice the use of transitional words first, second, third, fourth, which help the smooth flow of ideas.

***Development by Examples: Example Paragraph***

**Example:**

"Now, here is one of the most surprising things in life: no man really understands himself. What a lot of argument and anger we should save if people would only understand this. Suppose, for example, you saw a motor accident and were giving evidence about what happened. You would feel perfectly confident, perhaps, that the car which knocked the boy over was a blue car; another person would be equally confident that it was a gray car; and someone else that it was a black car."

This paragraph has all the essential elements of introducer, the developers, and modulator. But, in addition to providing transition, the word "suppose" develops the idea that no man really understands himself with different illustrations of self-delusion through perfect confidence.

Again, consider the following paragraph:

"It is not always easy in company to speak frankly, if you don't want to be considered a bad mannered person. You have to watch constantly for signs. It is not easy, for example, to listen for long to any one person. Try, in company, to take only a fair share of the conversation. If there are two of you, take half of it. When you have said a little, keep quiet, and give your friend chance to say something. If he does not talk, he probably does not want you to talk either. Many a young man or woman talks away, thinking the company is delighted to hear him or her, and everyone is really exhausted and angry."

It is a list paragraph and reads also as an example paragraph. It also differs somewhat from the two paragraphs you have read earlier. It has two sentences, which act as paragraph introducers. The first sentence introduces the topic, which is to be developed in the paragraph. The second sentence - the topic sentence- "You have to watch constantly for signs", further defines the subject more specifically. The sentences that follow as developers, elucidate the topic with examples of good manners for a person who does not want to be considered a bad mannered person when speaking in a company.

Again, read the following paragraph and notice the technique of developing the topic of all writing is for use of readers through different examples of purposes:

"All technical <u>writing is for</u> readers who would use your information <u>for some purpose</u>. You might write to describe something - as to an architectural client who wants to know what a new addition to his home will look like. You might write to explain something—as to a fellow stereo technician who wants to know how to eliminate base flutter in your company's new line speaker. You might write to <u>persuade</u> your vice-president in charge of marketing, who wants to know if it is a good idea to launch an expensive advertising campaign for a new lubricant. You might write to define something – as to an insurance customer who wants to know what variable annuity means. In short, as a technical writer, you do not write for yourself. You write to inform others."

It is an excellent example of a paragraph's unity and coherence. The key ideas in the first and the following sentences are given with underlines. Consider their relationships among different sentences. Also comment on the nature of the last two sentences.

**Activity**

Now try to write an example paragraph with the topic sentence given below:

"The ability to write short, clear and correct sentences and well organized paragraphs is necessary for an undergraduate's success in all courses."

**Activity**

The following sentences of an example paragraph are not written in their logical order in relation to the topic sentence. Read them carefully and list them in order of their function as topic sentence or developers with modulators and terminators:

Thus, crime reporters become the heroes of the newsroom. A house collapse is regarded as the saviour of the front page and a power cut becomes a national calamity.

The preferred option is the big local story blown up on page one day after day.

Usually newspapers cope in one of three ways. The silly season, which is a major journalistic term for a period when there is no major news to report and fill their front pages.

The second option – not preferred by most journalists, but usually successful in increasing sales – is to go tabloidesque and focus on celebrity stories, such as a Bollywood heroine's marriage failure or a rising tennis stars back hand or a threat to former Cricket Captain's life.

The third option is to find a political story and paste it on the front page to show that despite our concern for celebrities we are still a serious newspaper.

### *Paragraph Development by Comparison: Comparison Paragraph*

To form a paragraph by comparison, we list the examples belonging to one subject and compare them with the examples of another subject. The topic sentence introduces and states the point of comparison between two objects. Then, sentences that function as developers of comparison are written in respect of both the objects separately. Modulators may be used to change the point of view or move from one set of ideas to another. Terminator, finally, sums up the main point of comparison.

**Example of a paragraph developed by comparison:**

"Wordiness – the failure to achieve economy is a common writing problem. Essays can be wordy because of scanty planning, corrected through global revision, or a monotonous style, corrected through better use of coordination and subordination. To eliminate wordiness within a sentence entails local revision. The two most common methods are deleting words and phrases and substituting more economical expressions for wordy ones."

(Source: Trimmer, McCrimmon, *Writing With A Purpose*, Boston: Houghton Mifflin Co., 1988.)

### *Paragraph Development by Contrast: Contrast Paragraph*

The paragraph development by contrast lists the dissimilar aspects of the two subjects. For example, the following paragraph contrasts the differences between mediocre art and great art in terms of complexity and difficulty:

"The difference between a simple folk melody or a hymn and the work of art that a Bach and Beethoven will then make of this tune is simply that the artwork is vastly more complex. Both the folk tune and the Beethoven sonata ultimately confirm the same laws of tonality and harmonies of the diatonic. The difference is that Beethoven will test the limits of the diatonic or work against the expectations of the diatonic for dramatic effect, or even leave that confine for brief and startling moments. We admire Beethoven and his fellow adventures for this, and hold them to be 'great', in part, because our culture admires the performance of difficult feats."

[Source: Curtis White, The Middle Mind: Why Americans Don't Think for Themselves (London: Allen Lane 2003), p85.]

Paragraph development by contrast uses the same pattern of using a topic sentence as introducer of the main idea that the artwork differs from the folk tune in being vastly more complex than the simple folk tune. The following sentences function as developers of the details of specific differences between the artwork and folk tune. The paragraph terminates by culturally accounting for our natural admiration for the work of Beethoven and his group.

***Paragraph Development by Definition: Definition Paragraph***

Define means to give the definition of something and, in doing so, to separate it from similar things. Accordingly, a definition paragraph describes, explains, or defines an unknown term by relating it to a known term. It uses the methods of comparison, contrast and synthesis, generally, at the same time.

**Example of a paragraph developed by definition:**

"It is only stupid people who take remarks too literally, as we say; that is, who do not look for the real meaning in the statements people make. Thus, when a friend says, 'you will not be going past the post office, will you?' he may mean, 'I should be grateful if you would post a letter for me if it is not too much trouble for you. If you say, 'No' to the question because you are not going past the post office, it means to your friend that you are not willing to go out of your way even a little to oblige him."

This paragraph does not define stupid persons in terms of its dictionary definition as unintelligent fellows. The stupid people are literal in their understanding of things. They lack intelligence. They miss the contextual connotation of the statements people make.

The definition paragraph is usually written at the beginning of a chapter or long paper to describe a subject, such as communication, economics, or business management. It is a paragraph that in a way summarizes the concept in terms of its major concepts.

A definition paragraph is frequently used to explain a general concept, such as stupidity, good manners, photosynthesis, and the like by describing a particular example of the concept. Thus, an abstract term becomes concrete.

**Activity**

Here is a definition paragraph on "A Good Relationship". The writer has used comparison to explain the real meaning (connotation) of the concept of good relationship. First, give the literal meaning (denotation) of the term good relationship, and then describe what you really understand about it from its comparison with the dancing partners.

"A good relationship has a pattern like a dance and is built on some of the same rules. The partners do not need to hold on tightly, because they move confidently in the same pattern, intricate but cheerful, swift and free, like a dance of Bharatnatyam or Manipuri. To hold tightly would be to break the pattern and cut the movement, stop the continuously changing beauty of its unfolding. There is no place here for the possessive clutch, the clinging arm, and the heavy hand; simply the barest touch in passing. Now together, arm in arm, now back to back, now face to face or parted – it matters little. For they know they are partners moving to the same rhythm, creating a pattern together, and being visibly nourished by it."

(Adapted from *Gift from the Sea* by Anne Morrow Lindberg)

***Paragraph Development by Classification: Classification Paragraph***

Classification is the technique used to arrange into groups on the basis of shared characteristics.

**Example:**

*Paragraph Forms*

"A paragraph has many forms. It can be one word long or several pages long. Most paragraphs are three to ten sentences. Newspaper stories generally have short paragraphs to help readers easily resume from where they were, after being interrupted. Magazine articles, usually, have longer paragraphs than newspapers, but shorter paragraphs than many novels. The author decides the paragraph's length because each paragraph has one subject expressed in one main idea. The length follows the principle of <u>Unity of a Paragraph</u>."

To reinforce your understanding of the paragraph development by classification, answer the following questions based on the model paragraph by classification.

What is classified in the paragraph? Point out the sentence in the paragraph that defines a classification paragraph.

How does the author classify paragraphs in different forms?

What is the common feature in all the forms of paragraph?

### *Paragraph Development by Space: Space Paragraph*

All paragraphs that describe objects, scenes, costumes, and so on, logically, list details in spatial order because objects occupy space. One can describe an object, or a painting, or a landscape from inside to outside, front to back, top to bottom, or any other order in which the space is logically perceived.

**Example:**

***The City of Mandalay***

"And so it happened, that at the age of eleven, walking into the city of Mandalay, Rajkumar saw, for the first time, a straight road. By the sides, of the road there were bamboo – walled shacks and palm – thatched shanties, pats of dung and piles of refuse. But, the straight course of the road's journey was unsounded by the clutter that flanked it; it was like a causeway cutting across a choppy sea. Its line's led the eye right through the city, past the bright red walls of the fort to the distant pagodas of Mandalay hill, shining like a string of white bells upon the slope."

(Source: Amitav Ghosh, *The Glass Palace*)

This paragraph illustrates two features of descriptive writing:

1. Use of concrete words of form and colour.
2. Organization of the description by logically arranging the space from near to distant reach.

The paragraph's last sentence could be taken as a good example of descriptive power of words. Language's power to evoke visual image as a picture or painting does.

### *Paragraph Development by Time: Time Paragraph*

It is easy to develop a paragraph by describing things in order of their happening. The chronological order provides a clear chain of successive events.

**Example:**

***Background of Manufacturing in India***

"The presence of traditional Indian skills in medicine, metallurgy, construction, textiles, hydraulics or early shipbuilding was an integral part of our innovativeness in ancient and medieval times. Witness the splendid metal icons and monuments, like the Taj Mahal that were created employing intricate human skills and human/animal power. India was renowned for her prowess in skills as diverse as surgery and muslin weaving. We were advanced in the use of fire and metallurgy. Still, the invention of machines that generate their own locomotive power by burning external fuels eluded medieval India. The internal combustion engine, the cornerstone of the industrial revolution in Europe, reached India only in the colonial period. India was a latecomer in learning the new manufacturing techniques invented in Europe. It was only in the late nineteenth and the first half of the twentieth century that India established a few sugar factories, steel and textile mills and began to think in terms of ambitious projects, like shipbuilding and aircraft and automobile manufacture. Thanks to visionaries like Walchand Hirachand."

(Source: A.P.J. Abdul Kalam, *India 2020*)

The model paragraph, without mentioning specific dates, traces the presence and development of Indian skills in various areas of manufacturing from ancient to the beginning of modern times by mentioning them in chronological order.

***Paragraph Development by Describing Processes and Mechanisms: Processes and Mechanism Paragraph***

Process description follows definite steps in a given order in producing, operating, or manufacturing a thing. It is like following the various steps in conducting a scientific experiment.

**Example:**

***When You Receive a Picture Message***

"To view the message immediately, press View. Press back to discard the message. To view the message later, press Exit and save the message in the folder. When you save a new picture message, you may need to replace the factory installed picture message in the picture's folder."

(Source: Nokia 2100, User's Guide)

Notice that the process description is written, generally, in an impersonal form. In scientific description of an experiment, the sentences are written mostly in passive form. For Example, nobody says, "I take a beaker and fill it with 250 cc of Sulphuric acid and heat it for some time." Instead, we write it in its passive form, "A beaker is taken and filled with 250 cc of sulphuric acid and heated for some time."

In such a description, the focus is on the process, not the doer of the act. Hence, the passive form is chosen to describe the method of doing the thing.

## Features of a Good Paragraph

### *Unity*

In the last section, you have seen that a paragraph can be developed in a number of ways. But, a paragraph remains a unit of composition with a central idea developed through supporting details. A badly written paragraph would lack unity; that is to say, it would have more than one central idea. The test of a good paragraph is that its theme can be stated in a single sentence.

Read the following paragraph and see if its structure needs improving. Do it, if you think so:

"As soldiers, hikers and students can testify, it takes energy to haul around a heavy backpack. Now, researchers have developed a backpack that turns that energy into electricity. It does not crank out a lot of juice – just a bit more than 7 watts – but that's enough to run things, like an MP3 player, a personal data assistant, night goggles, a handheld global positioning system or a GSM cell phone. The development could eventually allow field scientists, hikers, explorers, soldiers, and disaster workers to produce their own electricity."

The following paragraphs lack unity. Some sentences of the paragraph are unrelated to the central idea. Cut out such sentences that should not be used in this paragraph:

"As a student, Rahul had one obsession in life – cricket. He talked about cricket, he read about cricket, and he dressed up like cricketers. He had pictures of cricketers from all countries on the walls of his study room. He did not care for football. Football is very popular in West Bengal, and many other parts of the world. Rahul thought of cricket as a royal game."

"After the vedic era, the works of the renowned physicians Charka and Susruta, namely the Charka Samhita and Susruta Samhita, deal with about 700 drugs of daily and specific uses. Between the sixteenth and seventeenth centuries India witnessed great upheavals in the development of medical botany and some of the most widely used herbal drugs came to light in this period. For this reason, the period is also called the Age of Herbal Medicine. Since time immemorial, Himalayan Flora has been a major source of medicinal plants."

### *Coherence*

A paragraph may have unity, a single idea as its subject, stated in a good topic sentence, developed by supporting details, and yet it may not be a well-constructed paragraph. It could be lacking in coherence, the device that makes the ideas hold together. The sentences should be properly interrelated. One sentence should lead the reader to the next, and there should be an unbroken logical progression of thought. The movement of ideas should be smooth. The mind should not jump from one idea to some other idea that is not related to the earlier idea. For achieving coherence, paragraph writers use the following methods to make all sentences hold together:

1. Repeating key words
2. Using synonyms – words having the same meaning as other word
3. Referring back to the ideas expressed in earlier sentences
4. Signaling coming of new ideas

The following paragraph uses all the above devices:

"Employers first judge your writing skills by the quality of your application letter and resume. If you join a large organization, your retention and promotion may depend on decisions by top executives you have never met. In this case, the quality of your letters, memos, progress reports, work orders, requisitions, recommendations, and instructions will be regarded as indicator of the overall quality of your work. This is hardly time to hide your competence beneath carelessly written reports. Good writing skills give you advantage in any field. And, as you advance, your ability to communicate increases in importance while your reliance on your technical background may correspondingly decrease. The higher your professional goals, the better communications skills you need. Your value to any organization depends on how well you can convey to others what you know."

(Source: John M. Lannon, Technical Writing)

Just analyze the sources of coherence in this paragraph:

The key phrase "writing skills" is used two times, and it is implied third time in "communication skills".

The word "top executive" is a near synonym for "employers".

In the third sentence, the use of "In this case" takes your attention back to the earlier sentence – "... your retention and promotion may depend on ...." Consider the use of "this" in the fourth sentence. It refers the reader back to the situation stated in third sentence: "the quality of your letters, (etc.) will be regarded as indicator of the over all quality of your work".

The use of "And" to begin a fresh sentence signals the addition of a further point of equal importance as stated in earlier sentences.

The paragraph has both unity and coherence. All the sentences in this paragraph stick together through the device of repetition of key words, and reference to earlier ideas. This paragraph talks about a single central idea - the value of communication skills for young professionals.

Now, try to identify the sources of coherence in the following paragraph:

"Your ability to communicate useful information increases your chances for success. As jobs become more complex and specialized, the demand for effective communication grows. In fact, much of the communication in the working world is carried out in writing. Therefore, few of us can afford to write poorly."

## ESSAY WRITING

### Beyond Paragraph: Unity and Coherence

So far we have studied how a sentence or a paragraph is constructed and the twin principles of unity and coherence. As we move to longer composition, known as essay, we have to follow unity and coherence at beyond-paragraph level. An essay, like a paragraph, is a well-organized composition in which several paragraphs are coherently linked to develop the main subject – the theme of the essay. A good essay has a central theme stated in a paragraph, usually placed at the beginning of the essay.

## Essay Structure: Beginning, Middle and End

Just as in paragraph, a sentence functions as an introducer, a developer, a context modulator or a terminator, a paragraph, in relation to an essay, acts as introducer, developer, context modulator, and terminator.

An essay should be a well organized single whole. It should have a beginning, middle and it should logically reach end. According to Aristole, beginning is that before which there is nothing, and every thing follows it. The beginning paragraph(s) should introduce the reader to the main topic to be developed in its scope and focus – the point of view. Introduction may need more than one or two paragraphs. For, in many longer research papers, introduction states the subject/problem of the research, its essential background, its scope and methods of investigation. Each of these points of information is covered by separate paragraphs that together form the introduction part of an essay (dissertation).

The middle paragrphs develop the argument using the devices discussed for developing a paragraph.

There can be context modulator or viewpoint modulator paragraphs too, used to present another perspective on the main theme of the essay.

Finally, the terminator paragraph brings the whole argument to a logically arrived end. The end must be conclusive in the sense that the questions raised at the beginning should be answered fully.

### *Coherence in an Essay*

Use of words showing transition and repetition words.

**Transition words**: Between the paragraphs, we need words which link them as bridges for moving form one thought to another.

| *Transition Words* | *Functions/Uses* |
|---|---|
| First, second, third,<br>finally, in addition,<br>besides, also, furthermore,<br>and, or, nor, moreover | Used to connect and add ideas. |
| Likewise, for example,<br>similarly, for instance | They are used before illustrations and examples. |
| In other words, in short,<br>so, thus, therefore,<br>hence, and so, consequently | These words are used to indicate consequences or a summary. |
| Because, for, since | They are used to connect a statement with a reason. |
| Nevertheless, still, yet,<br>but, however, on the contrary | These words show a reversal, an exception or a change in direction of the argument. |

**Repetition words:** Sense of coherence between the paragraphs is created also by repeating words to indicate continuity of thoughts. For instance, a word in the last sentence of one paragraph is repeated in the sentence of the next paragraph, so that, while reading, you can move easily from the subject of the first paragraph to the subject of the next.

**Example:**
"Bad language and four letter words should be banned at work, a business group says."

"The Institute of Directors, which represents 50,000 executives, wants a ban on everything from stress-induced outbursts to crude jokes because they might offend more sensitive employees."

The word 'ban' connects the ideas expressed in the above two paragraphs.

***Thesis Statement in Essay***

Usually, the opening paragraph of essay states the theme of the essay. It is expressed at the end of the first paragraph. Sometimes, like in the case of paragraph, the thesis statement is left implied.

**Essay topic:** Distractions Haze Memory

**Thesis statement:** Memory loss in older adults owes more to surrounding distractions than to an inability to focus on relevant information.

***Guidelines in General***

In writing sentences, paragraphs or essays follow the principles of unity, coherence, order, and completeness. Each paragraph should read as a unit of a single well-organized whole essay.

Like a sentence functions in a paragraph - introducer, developer, modulators of context, and terminator, the paragraph in an essay introduces, develops, modulates, and terminates the thought of the essay.

## PRÉCIS WRITING

A précis *(pronounced pray-see/pl. pray-seez; comes from French word 'Précis' that literally means 'precise')* is a brief summary of the essential ideas contained in a large piece of writing. The Oxford Dictionary defines it as "a short version of a speech or a piece of writing that gives the main points or ideas". It is not just paraphrasing, which merely represents the original text in different and simple words nor is it listing the main points. The basic idea is reproduced in brief form, retaining the mood and tone of the author. It is summarizing that insists on the economy of words and an exact reproduction of the facts with logic, organization, and emphasis of the original material. A précis is useful while dealing with lengthy passages that demand careful attention to the logic and organization of an argument.

### The Benefits of Précis Writing

Précis writing is a difficult skill. It develops one's analytical, and critical, reading abilities; together with writing skills of condensing and synthesizing. Students need summarizing to write a synopsis or an abstract, to remember the essential details of a long written material and to gain an insight into the underlying meaning of a text. It assists them to develop the cut of condensing a longer text into a brief summary that tells precisely the essence of the original. At workplace, it is a great help in writing the "executive summary" of a technical report in clear, correct, and concise English.

### Qualities of Good Précis

A good précis has the characteristics of the 5Cs, that is, completeness, conciseness, coherence, correctness, and clarity. Completeness: A précis contains all the major points of the original text. Conciseness: It is brief and precise and its length is approximately one-third of the original passage, but one should be very careful not to lose or distort the original meaning. Coherence: (unity of thought)

The ideas and the sentences are well knit and well linked to one another. Presentation of ideas in a précis should not be done through disjointed or unlinked sentences. Correctness: It is grammatically correct with right spellings. Clarity: The ideas are expressed distinctly so that even a reader who does not have enough time to read the original text has no trouble getting the message.

## Guidelines for Making the Summary/Précis

Here are some steps that may be followed to write a useful summary:

Step 1

- First read the whole passage carefully to get a general idea of the subject as a whole. Note down the main topic and the author's purpose of writing the passage. The main topic or the central idea, that may be traced from the first few or the last few lines, can be in the form of a short phrase or a word.

Step 2

- Then re-read paragraph wise to know the supporting. Each paragraph has one key point. That develops the main points an ideas that develop the main point as a cause on result on example of the main idea.
- Keep only, the main idea and the relevant details and leave out all the non-essentials, such as: (a) repetitions, (b) examples and illustrations, (c) anecdotes, stories, etc., (d) adjectives, (e) abbreviations, contractions and slangs, (f) clichés, (g) proverbs, quotations and idiomatic phrases, (h) comparisons, (i) rhetorical and flowery expressions.
- After you have understood the main idea of the paragraph, you should re-write it concisely and clearly in your own words in a single sentence.
- Always give the name of the article/document, the author and the source (whether it is from a magazine, a book, an encyclopaedia, or a technical report, etc.).
- Exhibit unity and coherence by arranging the key sentences in a logical order.
- The same process is followed in summarizing the remaining paragraphs. Thus, the complete précis of the passage will be found by putting together all the sentences you have got for the paragraphs. Combine the key ideas into one or more smooth paragraphs, maintaining the unity of thought. Make sure that you retain the order of the original points in your précis, but sometimes, you may have to change the order for the sake of unity and logicality. However, as the author's view point and attitude are the most important aspects, see that they are conveyed in the right point of view.
- Avoid using the vocabulary used in the original except for certain key words, which you may find necessary.
- Do not refer to the original text or begin with the expressions as "In this article", "The author says" or "The paragraph means." Begin as though you were summarizing your own writing.
- A précis is written from the point of view of the author whose work is being summarized. So, you should not use phrases, such as "I think" or "in my opinion".
- If the text is subjective in nature and the writer has used the first person "I" for himself or herself, it has to be changed into third person he/she, only if the gender is known, otherwise use the term "the author".
- All the sentences given in the direct speech should be changed into indirect narration and past tense.

- Note that the summary should not contain anything that is not given in the text. You should not make any interpretation nor should give personal opinions or any introduction/conclusion about the original text.
- Capture the tone or feeling of the original, particularly if it is humorous, satirical, aggressive, or moralistic.

When the original narrative is related by one of the actors, it is usual in the précis to re-tell it from the point of view of an onlooker or a reporter. Snatches of dialogue or conversation may be interspersed in the original, but the whole of the précis should be in the indirect form and written in the third person. *E.g.*, "When Pericles beheld his own armour, he said, 'Thanks, Fortune ! after all my crosses you give me somewhat to repair myself. This armour was bequeathed to me by my dead father, for whose dear sake I have so loved it, that whithersoever I went I still have kept it by me; and the rough sea that parted it from me, having now become calm, hath given it back again, for which I thank it, for since I have my father's gift again, I think my shipwreck no misfortune.'" (88 words.)

The gist of this extract could be expressed in a précis thus:-

Pericles was relieved to recover his armour, and thanked Providence and the sea for restoring his father's bequest from which he had never before been parted. (26 words.)

- The length of the précis should be around one-third of the original passage. Check the length. If it is more than the limit, edit it. You can also borrow a supporting idea kept in reserve, in case the length is shorter than the limit.
- Review the summary for completeness, clarity, conciseness, coherence, and correctness of grammar, spelling and punctuation.
- Check all important points for irrelevancy.
- Write down the fair draft of the précis of the original text.

**Summer Camp for Children**

Thirty or forty years ago, there were few summer camps for children. Because even those few were very expensive, only the wealthy could afford to send their sons and daughters to them. Within the past ten years, however, the number of camps has greatly increased. Those privately owned are still too costly for most parents, but the rates charged at many others, such as those operated by churches, by fraternal orders, and by the Boy Scouts and Girl Scouts, are not beyond the average family income. To underprivileged boys and girls, similar recreational facilities are offered free of charge by many civic organizations.

Parents, therefore, not only can but should send their children to a summer retreat, for there is no place of greater benefit to them. Camps provide peaceful living away from the danger, noise, and heat in the city. Good food, clean air, and proper rest make their bodies strong and healthy. Purposeful activities, carefully planned, teach them how to work, play, and live with others. These activities give them a better understanding of right and wrong than they could obtain in any other way. Through the training given in arts, crafts, and sports, children progress mentally and physically. Certainly, then, for the full development of their sons and daughters, Indian parents ought to give them the benefits of a summer in a modern camp.

**Précis**
All parents, whether rich or poor, can now send their children to one of the many private or free public camps established during the past decade. All children, therefore, should be given the advantages of the social, mental, moral, and physical development provided in safe and healthful modern summer camps.

## Strategies for Reducing the Number of Words

Practise economy in the use of words by learning to avoid round about expressions (circumlocutions), pointless repetitions, passive constructions, and prepositional phrases. The following strategies may be useful for reducing wordiness:

1. Circumlocutions: The most common round-about expressions are those formed by adjectives, adverbs, abstract nouns, prepositions, and conjunctions. For example:

   Adjective: use pleasant for of a pleasing soul, nature or kind character.

   Adverb: use briefly for in a brief manner or way. Considerably for to a considerable extent, or degree, seldom for on few occasions, or cases, often in place of in many cases, on many times.

   Abstract Nouns use Connection, reference, respect, regard for the following expressions with regard to, in reference to, and in respect to.
2. Avoid pointless repetition: For example (i) It continued to rain throughout the last night without stopping, till it was morning. Notice the unnecessary repetition of the same idea of continuous rain till morning. The sentence can be re-written in less words as: Last night, it rained continuously. (ii) Example: It was decided that entries for the musical event should be restricted to club members only and that competitors from outside should not be allowed to participate in it. Cut out the repetition that follows after club members only. It is wrongly believed that repetition makes the expression forceful. There is no loss of force of meaning by writing the sentence precisely as follows, "It was decided that entries for musical event should be restricted to the club members only."
3. Avoid using passive constructions as they create wordiness. Compare "***The child was hit by a car***", with "***A car hit the child***".
4. Avoid using too many prepositional phrases, for example, "***the dog of Mr. Rams***" say "***Mr. Ram's Dog***".
5. Use connectors such as—that, unless, and, which, whereas, but, so that, etc., to reduce the number of words and to link ideas. For example, "***The work would be over. It was our hope. Our hope was correct,***" can be reduced to "***Our hope that the work would finish, was correct***".
6. Use word substitution for achieving conciseness. "***She on her own offered her help***", may be replaced by "***She volunteered her help***".
7. Learn the art of reducing a clause to a phrase, for example, "***The thief confessed that he was guilty***"—"***The thief admitted his guilt***".
8. Cut down a list of same category words to a common term—"*taps, pipes, bends, joints, and water seal*"—can be condensed to "*plumbing material*".

## Using Words for Phrases

There are many expressions in the English language that are long-winded and could be expressed in a simpler or shorter way. This exercise will help you recognize such expressions, when summarizing.

Reduce the expressions shown without changing the meanings. Use the number of words shown in brackets:

1. in the near future (1) ____________
2. it appears that (1) ____________
3. put up with (1) ____________
4. the same amount of (1) ____________
5. in modern times (1) ____________
6. as a result ____________
7. because of this (1) ____________
8. always bear in mind (1) ____________
9. a lot of ____________
10. at all times (1) ____________
11. at the beginning of each day (2) ____________
12. owned by private individuals (2) ____________
13. equipment should be checked (2) ____________
14. make a record of all appointments (3) ____________
15. on the day of the interview (3) ____________

## Give One Word Substitution

Summarizing means saying the same thing, but in not so many words. In these sentences replace the section in italics by providing just one word.

1. When the meeting is over, you must produce the accurate transcript of the main discussions which took place and the decisions made. ____________
2. She's not interested in work – only in tennis, swimming, hockey, golf – anything requiring physical activity. ____________
3. The next meeting of the Board is coming up soon. I must prepare the list of items to be discussed at the meeting. ____________
4. The person who greets visitors to an organization must portray a good impression. ____________
5. When goods have been purchased, it is usual to send out an itemized statement informing the buyer of the quantity, description and price of the goods which were bought. ____________
6. We must send out a document to all the customers on our mailing list. ____________
7. This is a list of all the duties which the employee may be required to perform. (2 words) ____________
8. Some job advertisements require applicants to send a separate schedule showing their education, qualifications, employment history, and other personal details when applying for jobs. (2 words) ____________

## Substitution and Generalization

Summarizing anything requires the ability to find and remove unimportant details. Choose words which will convey a general impression of a number of particulars.

Consider the following examples:

A. The chairman received the deputation of workers. He listened patiently to a long statement of grievances made by the leader and promised to give careful considerations to the points he emphasised. But they came back with a vague feeling of satisfaction and dissatisfaction and were by no means sure that the chairman meant what he said.

   Précis: The chairman's courteous and sympathetic hearing left the deputation convinced of his sincerity.

B. It does not follow that because a fact has been generally accepted as true, we are under no obligation to find only whether there is any real foundation for it.

   Précis: General belief in a fact does not absolve us from the duty of investigating its truth.

## Count the Number of Words

Summary assignments normally state the number of words to be used. This will usually be expressed in one of two ways:

1. Use no more than 160 words

   In this case, do not exceed 160 words. 150–160 will normally be accepted, but anything less than 155 will be penalized.

2. Use approximately 160 words

   Here, 155–165 will not be penalized.

### *What to Count*

When counting the number of words used, do not count the words in the heading or any numbers used in your display. Sub-headings, however, should be included in your word count.

## Sample Précis

### *Ex. 1*

All the secretaries in your organization use audio transcription, as the employers prefer not to use shorthand dictation. In informal talks with many secretaries personally, you know there is a considerable amount of frustration because of poor audio dictation technique by their employers. You recently came across the following article in a secretarial magazine, and feel it includes helpful advice for employers on effective audio dictation techniques. You decide to write a Précis, as a checklist for employers to follow when dictating, and to send it to the editor of the staff magazine asking him to consider it for inclusion in the next issue. Use approximately 100 words.

Using dictation machines saves considerable time, as the secretary does not need to be present, thus it leaves the secretary free to deal with her other responsibilities while the boss dictates his correspondence. But how many secretaries out there continually bang your head against the office wall in frustration because the boss has coughed loudly in your ear? Does your boss mumble, talk too loudly occasionally and then almost whisper? How many times have you rewound and listened to an unfamiliar word 20 times and just wished the boss had the sense to spell it out?

Well maybe your boss is an admirable Accountant or a marvellous MD, but good dictation technique requires considerable practice. I hope this advice will be helpful—perhaps you can casually put it on your boss's desk with his coffee in the morning, but don't admit where it came from of course!

Before starting dictation, it is essential to be organized. All the necessary papers should be at hand. Otherwise you'll get frustrated and start scrambling about in the midst of dictation and it will be especially infuriating for your secretary if you forget to switch off the mike during this process!

Interruptions will affect your train of thought during the dictation. So try to time your recording when you know you have some time free and do it in a room which is free from noise.

Once these preparations have been made, you're off. Before starting dictation on each piece of correspondence, do state the exact nature of the document, e.g. 'short letter', 'long report', etc. Also give an indication of the number of copies which will be required. This type of information is invaluable to your secretary as to the correspondence to be transcribed.

As for the dictation—the microphone is not a lollipop, so don't try to eat it! Hold it two or three inches away from your mouth. If you hold it too close, your speech will be blurred; too far away and you won't be heard at all. Don't mumble into the mike, but try to ensure your speech is clear. And please don't go like a bull at a gate—a secretary will not thank you if you dictate at 50 miles an hour!

When you have dictated the first sentence or so, listen to it again by playing back the recording, so that you can make any necessary adjustments—the sound may be too high or too low, so it's much better to correct it at this point than deafen your secretary later!

If the volume's OK, then go ahead. We all need to pause for thought now and again, so when you find it necessary to do so, or when the phone rings, remember to switch off the mike. Your secretary doesn't want to listen to a few minutes of nothing, or to a conversation with your wife about what's for dinner!

Wherever you can, try to include a mention of new paragraphs, and give clear instructions to your secretary regarding headings and any items which need to be numbered.

Your secretary will also need to clarify things with you every few minutes if you don't spell out personal names, place names, foreign names—anything which she may be unfamiliar with. Numbers too—prices, sums of money, percentages, etc.

When you've successfully reached the end of a document, mark the length of the document on the index slip—this will be a valuable reference tool for your secretary on the size of paper to use for the correspondence.

Finally, make sure you keep any letters, memos, reports, files, and other relevant documents connected with the dictation in a special pile, and pass all this to your secretary with the recording. In this way all the information she needs will be just where she can find it, and she won't need to bother you with queries.

If you follow the above advice, it should save your secretary much frustration—and a happier secretary makes your life easier too, doesn't it?

Happy dictating!

***Ex. 2***

You have been asked to give a talk on how to hold effective meetings, and the text of your speech is printed below. You have also been asked for a one-page Précis of your speech for inclusion in the seminar booklet which delegates will keep for future reference. Using an appropriate format, make your Précis in not more than 150 words.

Meetings form an essential part of business life and, as managers, our role is to ensure that they are organized and administered efficiently, and that all the paperwork is dealt with correctly. I would like to talk to you today on the various things we have to think about when preparing for meetings, and the documentation involved.

Once it has been agreed that the meeting will take place on a particular day, there are many practical tasks you should attend to. First of all make sure you block the dates and time in your diary. This will, of course, avoid the risk of a clash of appointments at a later date. Then check the venue for the meeting, and if there is a regular room make sure it is available. This may be the company's own board room, or in the case of a departmental meeting perhaps you will use the manager's office. You then need to prepare and circulate the notice of meeting and agenda.

Any additional documents for distribution, such as reports, statistics, etc., should be circulated with the notice and agenda, so that members may become thoroughly familiar with their contents prior to the meeting. Remember also to make additional sets of such documents—isn't it always the case that someone forgets to bring their copies on the day of the meeting, and we end up having to get extra copies for them at the last minute! If you take extra copies to start with, you will avoid this last-minute rush.

In consultation with your Chairman you should then produce a draft of the Chairman's agenda which he may amend as necessary. The Chairman's agenda is a little more detailed than the ordinary members' agenda. It is for use only by the Chairman, containing extra notes for his own reference in helping him to conduct the business of the meeting efficiently.

So much for the preliminary documentation, what about other matters? If you have a regular caterer, a provisional order should be made for refreshments at this stage, which will be confirmed when the number of participants is known nearer the date.

Any equipment which may be required at the meeting should be arranged, including making sure any visual aids required will be available if necessary. (Does anyone require the overhead projector, spirit pens, video recorder, etc.?)

Place names should be prepared if these are needed to identify the participants at the meeting. Obviously these will not be necessary at a departmental meeting where everyone knows everyone else, but at more formal meetings they may be useful.

Once these provisional arrangements have been attended to, you can more or less relax until the day of the meeting itself. Then you will need to make sure everything is organized as efficiently as possible, using a bit of the foresight we are supposed to develop as managers. First of all, arrange the meeting room, attending to such things as seating arrangements, water and glasses, writing paper and pencils. Any documents to be used during the meeting should be laid out on the table. Spare copies of the agenda and minutes of the last meeting should be at hand, as well as the official minute book and any other reports which I mentioned earlier. You should also check that any equipment and accessories required are in the right place and in working order. Please see that the presentations are loaded on the "O" drive and the laptop is properly connected. Remember those meetings where in the middle of the meeting, the presenter, wanting to support his point with facts, struggles to locate the file while others exchange glances!

Next reconfirm that refreshments will be served at the appropriate time, and give any last-minute instructions regarding the number of members attending the meeting.

The switchboard and receptionist should also be given a list of participants at the meeting, together with instructions for diverting their calls as necessary. Perhaps a colleague will be called upon to take all calls, or the switchboard operator herself may be required to take messages. Whatever the arrangements, make sure the relevant people know what is required of them.

If you are attending the meeting as secretary, gather your own paperwork together with suitable materials to take down the minutes. Ensure that you have your own and your boss's diaries available to check details of appointments when future dates have to be arranged during the meeting. Finally, place a 'meeting in progress' notice on the door. This will ensure no one walks in and disturbs the progress of the meeting. I will not mention anything about Minutes here because my colleague will be discussing that with you in detail later in the programme.

Arranging meetings can be a bit of a headache—collating all the reports and material for the meeting, making sure all the documentation is issued at the appropriate time, and all the various other matters which we have to attend to. But, if you think them through logically, step-by-step, and use the summarized checklist which I have included in the seminar booklet, you can ensure that nothing is overlooked.

So whether you are organizing your first meeting or your fiftieth, I wish you success.

## REVIEW YOUR LEARNING

1. What is the difference between unity and coherence?
2. What is the relationship between brevity and clarity?
3. Give some important characteristics of effective writing in business.
4. What is "you-attitude" in business writing?
5. Explain the function of tone in making communication truly effective.
6. Define the role of the reader in determining the form and style of business letters.
7. How do we make our writing natural?
8. To what extent does clarity of writing depend on the clarity of thinking?
9. Why should we avoid using jargon and clichés in business letters or memos?
10. Discuss the importance of form and layout of different parts of a business letter.

## REFLECT ON YOUR LEARNING

1. Why do most of us find it difficult to convey our thoughts in written form? How can we overcome these difficulties?
2. Do pre-writing thinking and post-writing revising help the writer? Please discuss.
3. "It is simple to be difficult, but very difficult to be simple while writing." Elucidate.
4. How does extensive reading help in writing effectively?
5. Reflect on the value of short and simple sentences in creating a lucid style.

## ENDNOTES

1. Theodore A. Sherman and Simon S. Johnson, Modern Technical Writing (New Jersey: Prentice-Hall, 1975), p. 141.
2. Lynn Quitman Troyka, Handbook of Writers (New York: Simon & Schuster, 1987).

# 5 Non-verbal Communication

*Upon completion of this chapter, you should be able to:*

1 Know the meaning and characteristics of non-verbal communication.
2 Understand the function of body talk in fully interpreting the underlying message of words.
3 Learn positive gestures, body movements, and facial expressions.
4 Recognize different cues and clues indicated by facial expressions, gestures, postures, body movements, and eye contact.
5 Understand silence as a mode of communication.
6 Learn how to build rapport.

## WHAT IS NON-VERBAL COMMUNICATION?

*Non-verbal* means not involving words or speech. Thus, non-verbal communication refers to the wordless messages received through gestures, signs, body movements, facial expressions, tone of voice, colour, time, space and style of writing, and choice of words.

1 Know the meaning and characteristics of non-verbal communication.

Animals communicate their deepest feelings of love, anger, joy, hunger, and desire for mating through gestures, cries, whistling, body movements, and many other signals known through instinct. Of course, the exact interpretation of such signs and gestures does vary, but they are mutually understood within their species.

It is we human beings alone who have evolved the language of words to convey our thoughts in a structured manner. Still, in moments of excitement, we tend to convey our feelings and emotions of joy, love, anger, and hatred by smiling, shouting, frowning, or using other wordless clues. Such non-verbal expressions of feelings come spontaneously. However, at times, we can deliberately lace our words with expressive tones, gestures, and facial expressions to heighten and modify the meaning of our words.

Some non-verbal message usually accompanies a verbal message. The verbal and the non-verbal together form the total meaning of the message communicated. In addition to the words uttered by the speaker, there is also usually something unsaid and implied, so to fully understand the message, the listener should pay attention to body language and non-verbal signals.

Unspoken messages are transmitted by non-verbal clues and signs (body movements and gestures). They exist in the form of kinesic communication (body talk) and meta communication. The receiver's response to them influences the interpretation of messages received through words. Body language is not mind-reading. Rather, it involves instant revelations—flashes that are communicated from one subconscious to another. There is no deliberate attempt to give or receive non-verbal messages. The exchange happens spontaneously.

## CHARACTERISTICS, IMPORTANCE, AND FORMS OF NON-VERBAL COMMUNICATION

A writer's style or a speaker's tone of voice and facial expressions indicate his or her attitude and feelings beyond what is being expressed through words.

2

Understand the function of body talk in fully interpreting the underlying message of words.

- Non-verbal communication occurs via instrumental body movements. When someone moves their hands to perform some function, such as wash their face, it is an instrumental movement and not a symbolic clue. Most body movements, with the exception of instrumental movements, have meaning and communicate something. Communicative movements act as non-verbal clues. For example, wiping one's mouth when confronted by an authority figure communicates nervousness and using the hand gesture to wave goodbye communicates courtesy and friendship.
- Non-verbal cues may be conscious or unconscious. They reveal the speaker's state of mind and inner feelings and emotions, which may be real or affected. Trained actors and orators intentionally use gestures, facial expressions, body movements, and postures to create the intended impact on their audience. Effective writers use stylistic devices to convey hidden feelings and attitudes.

  However, in real-life, most people betray their inner thoughts and feelings through unconscious signs. The speaker may not realize that he or she is conveying these feelings. For example, consider the following statement on bilateral talks between two unfriendly countries made by the representatives with tense facial expression or without a smile: "The meeting has made history."
- The interpretation of non-verbal clues differs from person to person. For example, if a listener maintains continuous eye contact, the speaker may take it as a sign of perfect attention and full acceptance, but to someone else it could be a sign that the listener feels helpless or trapped.

  The visible is usually more convincing than what is heard as it may support or contradict the verbal message. Non-verbal clues are often taken as indicators of reality. For example, the pale face of a person in danger contradicts his or her claim of fearlessness. The trembling of a speaker indicates nervousness even though the speaker may say, "I feel encouraged and inspired to stand before such a learned audience." Dress or language can also reveal the communicator's status or education.
- The same gestures may also be interpreted differently in different circumstances. For example, consider two colleagues, A and B, who are good friends. When A pats B on the back endearingly to congratulate her on a successful project, the pat is taken as a friendly gesture. Now, suppose A is the chairperson of a promotions committee and B is a candidate for promotion. To create a misunderstanding between A and B, someone tells B that A, as chairperson, opposed her promotion. When, on meeting her the next evening, A congratulates B and as usual pats her on the back, she recoils. This example shows that the relationship between two people also determines how they interpret each other's gestures.

| *Non-verbal Acts* | *Possible Unspoken Idea* |
|---|---|
| A senior looks at his watch while you are talking | "Your time is over, go away." |
| A person winks after saying something | "Do not believe what I just said." |
| An executive is always late for meetings | "I am always very busy."<br>"I am not bothered about your time." |
| A speaker prefers to speak from the floor rather than the dais. | "I want to show my sense of equality with you (the audience)." |

**Exhibit 5.1** Some Examples of Kinesic Communication

## KINESICS

*Kinesic communication* is the message conveyed through non-verbal acts in the form of body movements, such as gestures, winking, smiling, posture, and appearance from the style of dressing and grooming, which send out a message that supports or contradicts the verbal message.

*Kinesic communication* is the message conveyed through non-verbal acts in the form of body movements, such as gestures, winking, smiling, posture, or style of dressing and grooming, which send out a message that supports or contradicts the verbal message.

Kinesic communication is also known as body language or body talk. It includes the entire non-verbal behaviour of the communicator. A non-verbal act is often subconscious. It transmits unstated feelings and attitudes and hidden intentions. Non-verbal signs offer clues to the receiver, and help the receiver understand and correctly perceive the total meaning of the message.

A non-verbal message conveyed through body movements is known as *leakage*. A successful receiver is able to observe and interpret the leakage. Though it is not possible to have an exhaustive account of all leakages and what they signify, a few examples that illustrate the modifying effect of body movements on communication are given in Exhibit 5.1.

## META COMMUNICATION: BODY LANGUAGE AND PARALANGUAGE

*Meta-communication* is an implied meaning conveyed by the choice of words, tone of voice, fumbling, silence, or omission. It is a message communicated not by words, but along with words. Meta-communication can be intentional or unintentional. For example, consider the following statement: "Try to reach the airport well on time." The remark offers sound advice. But, the sentence, without stating it explicitly, implies that the listener is not punctual or is habitually late. Similarly, when someone wishes another person "best of luck", it generally conveys good wishes, but also implies a sense of anxiety or fear that something untoward may happen.

*Meta-communication* is an implied meaning conveyed by the choice of words, tone of voice, fumbling, silence, or omission. It is a message communicated not by words, but along with words.

Meta-communication also occurs through the use of paralanguage. *Paralanguage* includes pitch, loudness of voice, and speech breakers such as "er", "ah", and "uh", which show hesitation or caution. Just as a normal or low pitch of speaking shows calm and control, a loud voice

*Paralanguage* includes pitch, loudness of voice, and speech breakers such as "er", "ah", and "uh", which can show hesitation.

communicates displeasure or anger. Prolonged gaps, pauses, or silence are also forms of paralanguage. When a leader speaks slowly with many uses of "er" and "uh", he or she is usually being very careful and suspicious.

## PROXEMICS OR SPACE LANGUAGE, TIME LANGUAGE AND SURROUNDINGS

Besides non-verbal gestures that convey wordless messages through body language and facial expressions, there are other wordless signs of power, position, taste, and culture, such as decoration and size of one's office, dress, grooming, and so on. These are called lateral gestures and include the following broad categories: (a) physical setting, (b) dress—clothes and shoes, and (c) personal space.

### Physical Setting

An executive's position of power may be gauged from the size and furnishings of his or her office. The quality of furniture adds to the impression created by the setting of the room.

In an office, the executive's table is usually placed a few steps away from the door. This compels visitors or subordinates to walk up to him or her and feel his or her presence. Space is one of the factors involved in indicating the proximity of a relationship.

> Besides the non-verbal gestures that convey wordless messages through body language and facial expressions, there are lateral wordless signs of power, position, taste, and culture such as decoration and size of one's office, dress, grooming, and so on.

### Dress

Clothes can define a person. It is one of the first things people notice. A person's clothes—their texture, colour, design, style, and stitching—reveal their taste and aesthetic sense.

In business, it is important to pay attention to one's clothes, especially at an interview or presentation. While one should look impressive, it is important not to be overdressed. Instead of highly fashionable and trendy designs and styles of suits, business executives should favour elegant, conventional styles. Clothes should not distract from the conversation.

> In business, it is important to pay attention to one's clothes, especially at an interview or presentation. While one should look impressive, it is important not to be overdressed.

In addition, one's clothes should be neither too loose nor too tight. It is important to feel comfortable in one's clothes, particularly in a high-stress situation, such as an interview or presentation. Never try a new set of clothes for such occasions. New clothes may not sit comfortably, and they may distract the wearer from time to time. So, the first rule to follow is the principle of comfort.

Shoes should also be formal and in keeping with the colour of the clothes. Business bags, briefcases, handbags, or portfolios also indicate one's status as a professional. An overstuffed handbag is not as impressive as a sleek briefcase or a smart handbag.

### Personal Space

The personal space between two interacting persons indicates the level of formality, informality, intimacy, or distance between them. Business executives should observe the personal territory that each individual wishes to enjoy. Breaking into someone's personal territory is likely to make him or her feel uncomfortable. When placed under such an intrusion, an important person is bound to show displeasure and signs of withdrawal from the interaction. Thus, it is also important to understand the non-verbal message of displeasure and correct the space-relationship to have a fruitful interaction.

Two interacting parties have a zone of invisible space between them, which is delineated by the nature of their relationship. A public figure for instance, would be used to more space around him or her, whereas one would maintain a smaller distance with a friend or relative.

> Two interacting parties have a zone of invisible space between them, which is delineated by the nature of their relationship.

According to the nature of relationships, there are four distinct zones: (i) the public zone, (ii) the social zone, (iii) the friendly zone, and (iv) the intimate zone.

The *public zone* is the widest territory between the speaker and audience. A public speaker addresses a large gathering of persons. He or she needs to speak from a raised platform at a distance of 10 to 15 feet from the audience. The distance and elevation of the speaker provide visibility and a sense of isolation and superiority for the speaker. An example of the public zone is seen in the armed services, where it is normal practice for army officers to issue commands from a distance of 8 to 10 steps from the troops.

A *social zone* is the space maintained between people who are known to each other in a formal way. All business transactions are to be treated as social interactions. An executive should keep a distance of 4 to 10 feet from his or her audience. This space will ensure the comfort of the listeners, especially if they happen to be seniors, customers, or clients. At this distance, one can observe the body language and facial expressions of the other party closely. The social zone will be applicable for new colleagues at work, new acquaintances, and small group training situations.

The *friendly zone* is the distance observed at business parties, seminars, and other informal business gatherings and get-togethers. In such situations, people remain close to each other, but not close enough to jostle against each other. The gap maintained is nearly 1½ to 4 feet. At this distance, people can comfortably chat, laugh, and joke with each other without invading each other's space.

> The *intimate zone* is the distance between an individual and those he or she loves, such as close relatives and family members. This zone is not appropriate in a professional environment.

The *intimate zone* is the distance between an individual and those he or she loves, such as close relatives and family members. This zone is not appropriate in a professional environment. In this zone, people tend to be near enough to whisper, about 6 to 18 inches. This nearness signals closeness among those involved in the conversation. However, this close distance is possible only when one is sure of the relationship because it is a zone in which one can touch the other person. In all other zones, including the friendly zone, one should not risk touching the other person. Touching can be strongly offensive.

Within the intimate zone, there are, according to the level of intimacy, further zones/bands. They are:

- *Near intimate sphere (up to 6 inches):* The zone for lovers, partners, children, family members
- *Distant intimate sphere (6 inches to 18 inches):* The zone for close friends, close colleagues and relatives

Both these spheres are sensitive. The difficulty lies in knowing how close is too close. When our intimate zone is intruded upon, we may feel embarrassed and, at times, threatened by the unwanted approach. We may have a "flight or fight" response, either confronting the intruder or removing ourselves from the situation. If our friendly zone is violated, we hide our discomfort by smiling or raising questions.

There are times when one cannot help having personal and intimate spaces violated, such as when travelling in a crowded compartment or entering a packed lift. In such situations, people are not usually resentful of others because body language indicates their helplessness. Moreover, to avoid discomfort to anyone, it is best to avoid eye contact with others in such situations and to try to stand straight to avoid physical contact with anyone.

## GESTURES

### Positive Gestures

When a person speaks, his or her hands move freely to indicate the meaning of his or her words. Such gestures are natural. They cannot be avoided. They give strength to the speaker's words. But, gestures should be seen in terms of whether they have a positive or negative message. Although gestures are spontaneous, we can learn to monitor and use positive gestures and minimize, if not avoid, the negative ones.

Positive gestures are body signals that make the communicator look relaxed, confident, and polite. Positive listening gestures include leaning a little towards the other person, tilting the head, making eye contact, and gently nodding as a sign of agreement or understanding. Such gestures encourage the speaker to a great extent. Positive speaking gestures include keeping the hands open and avoiding clutching or folding them across the chest.

Positive gestures are body signals that make the communicator look relaxed, confident, and polite.

When walking, keep your head upright. Hands should swing freely by the sides. Eyes should look straight in front. Steps should be well measured and steady. Many people carry books, files, and documents held against the chest. This makes the person look nervous and defensive. To avoid being perceived as a nervous person, one could carry them on one side. We can use our gestures to politely communicate what we want when we are unable to speak or are interrupting someone. For example, during a serious, formal conversation, if you are offered water or tea, you may politely hold up your palm to ask the other person to wait or to decline if you do not want to interrupt the conversation. Similarly, if you are on the phone and someone asks you something, you can politely request him or her to wait a minute by holding up one finger or some other symbolic gesture. This ensures that you do not ignore the visitor.

3

Recognize different cues and clues given by facial expressions, gestures, postures, body movements, and eye contact.

Gestures can be adequate substitutes for words. We should develop the skill of using them effectively. Equally importantly, we should recognize our negative gestures and learn to hide them.

### Negative Gestures

Negative gestures involve certain body movements, postures, gestures, or non-verbal activities such as shaking, tapping one's feet, looking at the watch, and so on. Putting one's hands in the pockets is also a negative gesture. If you put one hand in your pocket, it usually suggests arrogance. If you put both, it might show nervousness. However, if you want to look confident, but not nervous or arrogant, thrust your hands in your pockets, then keep the thumb out, so that you do not fully insert your hands inside the pockets.

Take note of the clues in Exhibit 5.2.

**Signs of nervousness include the following:**

putting hands in one's pockets, covering the mouth with the hand while speaking, scratching, nail biting, sideways glances, finger-drumming, clearing the throat too often, foot tapping, hand-wringing, crossing arms or legs, a slumped posture, sitting on the edge of the chair, rocking one's legs, looking at the ceiling, straightening one's tie, fixing one's hair, speaking too fast or too haltingly

**The following are the loudest gestures of nervousness:**

adjusting one's glasses, blinking excessively, fidgeting with jewellery, watches, or cufflinks, clicking a pen, frequently sipping water, playing with a paperweight, smoking

**Gestures showing aggression are as follows:**

staring, pointing at someone, showing one's fist, folding both arms, bending over someone

**Gestures showing rudeness include the following:**

shaking hands too firmly or too limply, standing too close, whispering at a social gathering, talking, checking e-mail, or sending text messages on one's cell phone or BlackBerry in meetings or social situations, working while someone is talking, yawning, smirking, glancing at the clock frequently during a conversation, making "tut-tut" sounds, grooming, specially fixing one's hair, when listening or speaking, gathering and folding papers before the meeting is over

**Gestures that show self-importance and should be carefully avoided in situations that demand solutions and negotiated settlements are:**

keeping one's eyes closed while talking, tilting one's head backwards while talking, looking at the tip of one's nose while talking, pursing the mouth, steepling the fingers, peering over the top of one's spectacles, waving a glass or key while talking

**Gestures showing lack of good sense include:**

banging the table instead of laughing at a joke, chewing on the end of a pen, using air quotes and making a "T" in the air when asking for tea, waving one's hands around excessively while talking, wringing one's hands, opening or closing buttons or fidgeting with one's watch strap while talking, wiping one's hands on the face, touching the nose time and again

**Some authority figures, without saying anything, can make one feel subordinate by behaving in the following ways, which display a sense of superiority:**

not responding to or acknowledging the other's greeting, staring, shouting orders, standing too close, leaning or sitting on someone's desk, standing behind someone's seat and watching over his or her shoulder as he or she works, smoking in someone's space, attending to one's cell phone during meetings, making any unwanted or unwarranted physical contact, continuing to work when others address you, having a crushing handshake or holding the other person's hand for too long, reclining in the chair with hands folded behind the head

Creating a feeling of subordination and hierarchy adversely affects good working relationships and makes others uncomfortable. Therefore, executives should avoid such power posturing.

**Exhibit 5.2** Non-verbal Clues

## VOCAL CUES

Body language (how you look) is only one aspect of nonverbal skills. Vocal traits (how you sound) are equally important for establishing credibility. Vocal traits are based on how you say it, not on what you say.

### Intonation

Intonation refers to the modulation, pitch, variation, and inflection in your voice.

- *Do speak* with expression and enthusiasm, sounding natural and interesting, with variety in your pitch.
- *Do not speak* in a dull, robotic, bored-sounding monotone. Watch out for "voice uplift" (ending sentences as if they were questions) that makes you sound tentative and unsure of yourself.

### Volume

Your volume is determined by how loudly or softly you speak. Remember to (1) speak loudly enough to be heard by the people in the back row of the room, (2) vary your volume to add interest, (3) watch out for "volume fade" at the ends of your sentences.

### Rate

Rate is the speed with which you speak. Don't bore your audience with an overly-slow rate or lose them with an overly-fast one. Since you probably cannot judge your own rate, ask a colleague or friend to assess it for you. A good way to slow down your rate is to use more pauses (followed by an in-breath) at the end of your sentences and before or after important points. Remember to slow down especially if you have an unfamiliar accent or if you are speaking to non-native audience members.

### Fillers

Fillers are verbal pauses—like *uh*, *um*, and *y'know*.

- *Try to become comfortable pausing* during your presentation to collect your thoughts. The pause, which may sound interminably long to you, is most likely imperceptible to your audience—so you don't need to fill it up with a sound.
- *Don't obsess* if you notice a few fillers; everybody uses them occasionally. Instead, aim to avoid the distracting, habitual overuse of fillers.

### Enunciation

Enunciation refers to how clearly you articulate your words. Pronounce your words clearly and crisply. Avoid the following, all of which may be perceived as sounding uneducated or sloppy: mumbling, squeezing words together (as is *gonna* or *wanna*), leaving out syllables (as is *guvmint*), and dropping final consonants (as is *thousan*' or *goin*').

## PHYSICAL APPEARANCE AND THE SKILL TO PRESENT YOURSELF

Remember that the first impression is the most important and lasting impression. Hence, present yourself well to make a positive and lasting impression. To do so pay attention to the fact that people form impressions about us by how we look, "over 50 per cent of our personal impact is through our appearance, our body language, and facial expressions," says a research quoted by Steve Smith in 'Be your best' (Kogan Page, 1999, P45).

Here are some practical tips on how to look your best and impress others.

1. *Know your body language:*
    - Develop self-awareness by visualizing yourself as others see you and interpreting your body movements and gestures.
    - Try to develop positive gestures and expressions to present yourself as you wish to be seen by others—as a confident, pleasing, well-meaning team worker.
    - Do not give conflicting non-verbal cues.
    - Convey sincerity through your tone of voice and facial expression.
    - Use symbols, non-verbal cues (gestures, posture, and so on), intonation (volume, pace of delivery, and enunciation), expressions, and so on to reinforce and clarify the meaning of the message.
    - Maintain eye contact with the audience.
    - Smile genuinely.
    - Avoid power posturing.
2. *Know about culture-specific body language:* Though body language is a universal phenomenon, its meaning differs across cultures. Culture, like language, lays down rules for accepted social behaviour of people sharing a set of knowledge, beliefs, practices, and ideas. In present day multi-cultural workplaces, communication between persons of different nations and backgrounds requires an understanding of non-verbal acts, such as eye contact, touch, and the sense of time in different cultures. People attach great significance to what they learn from non-verbal clues in addition to what they hear through words. Non-verbal clues are taken as true indicators of the speaker's subconscious mind. They are, therefore, considered more reliable than words. Be careful not to use non-verbal clues that violate the cultural norms of other countries. Persons who travel and work abroad or in multi-cultural environments must realize that gestures may not mean the same thing they do in their own country. Some of those gestures might even be unwelcome or offensive.

    > Culture, like language, lays down rules for accepted social behaviour of people sharing a set of knowledge, beliefs, practices, and ideas.

3. *Know about touching and its context:* Touching has limited communicative symbolism. It primarily conveys intimacy and closeness and also love. But, its meaning is very closely linked to its context. Take the case of a doctor, who can touch a patient of the opposite sex when medically necessary, without offending the patient. In this context, the doctor's body movements, touching, and so on are instrumental acts, performing certain tasks. They are not communicative body movements that reflect the doctor's state of mind, emotions, or attitude. The context characterizes the nature of a body movement and determines whether it is a communicative or instrumental message.

    > Touching has limited communicative symbolism. It primarily conveys intimacy and closeness and also love. But the act of touching has its meaning in relation to its context.

4. *Watch and read non-verbal clues:*
    - Interpret non-verbal clues in relation to the situation and culture accurately.
    - Be careful about false non-verbal clues deliberately given to deceive you.

- Consider the non-verbal message, along with what the speaker's words say, to know the total message.
- Respond with self-control, but do not react to non-verbal signals.

Among lovers, parents, family members, and very close friends, touching is a normal gesture and goes unnoticed, but between strangers it is at once marked and may be objectionable. Even among those who share the zone of intimacy, only some parts of the body can be touched while communicating.

4

Understand silence as a mode of communication.

Touch usually communicates intimacy. However, which part of the body can be touched by whom and when depends upon the culture of the people involved. In western countries, men and women can walk freely holding each others' hands in public. But in India, Pakistan, and other conservative countries, men and women generally do not do so in public.

To refer to themselves when speaking to someone, Americans may place one hand on their chest, whereas the Japanese may place a finger on their noses. But, some psychologists consider nose touching to be a Freudian symbol of sexuality.

Like other emblematic body movements, eye contact is also culturally decoded in different ways. Eye contact is an important clue of attentive listening. In most western countries, it is considered polite to maintain eye contact when speaking to someone. On the other hand, in Japan and India, subordinates often do not make eye contact when speaking and listening to their supervisors. It is possible that an American may consider a Japanese person to be impolite if he or she keeps his or her eyes lowered during a conversation. In India, this may speak of humility, not shame.

Similarly, silence is communicative, but it may say different things to people of different cultures. For instance, in Japan, one may prefer to remain silent when one does not know much about the matter being discussed. In India, silence may indicate agreement. In the United States, silence may be seen as a sign of withdrawal and non-participation. An American usually looks for involvement and participation through raising questions or doubts.

Silence is communicative, but it may say different things to people of different cultures.

No one can make an exhaustive study of all possible cultural variations of every body movement. However, this is an attempt to highlight the importance of context and cultural differences in the interpretation of body movements and gestures.

Since a face to face interaction is a live act, the speaker's non-verbal cues will influence the listener and vice versa. We have already discussed the power of non-verbal body movements, gestures, and facial expressions in positively or negatively modifying the meaning of the message. For an impressive presentation of oneself at interviews, meetings, public speaking and professional presentations, the following aspects of non-verbal behaviour are particularly relevant:

Since a presentation is a live performance, the speaker's non-verbal cues will influence the audience and vice versa.

- Professional appearance
- Good/positive posture
- Eye contact
- Use of positive gestures and hand movements that reinforce the argument
- vocal cues: intonation, pitch, and clear articulation.
- Smiling and looking relaxed while answering questions

## REVIEW YOUR LEARNING

1. "When you lack confidence in a situation, your body language will shout out to others that you are unsure of yourself." Discuss some of the ways in which body language can betray lack of confidence.
2. Discuss the difference between communicative and instrumental body movements. Give some examples of communicative gestures.
3. What is "leakage" in non-verbal communication?
4. How would you act when a power-posturing superior confronts you?
5. Does our culture influence our interpretation of the behaviour of those from other cultures? Give examples to support your answer.
6. Explain the process of meta-communication as an intentional form of communication.
7. Discuss the main classifications of non-verbal communication.
8. Besides non-verbal gestures and facial expressions, there are lateral gestures, which communicate without using words. Discuss some of these lateral non-verbal gestures with examples.
9. What does personal space signify in interpersonal communication at different levels? Discuss with examples.

## REFLECT ON YOUR LEARNING

1. Reflect on the guidelines for developing communication skills and the extent to which you are able to interpret non-verbal clues accurately.
2. How would you know if your communication with your colleagues is breaking down? Why do communication breakdowns happen?
3. What is "rapport"? How would you establish rapport between yourself and your audience?
4. (a) How would you interpret silence during a discussion between a Japanese businessman and your Indian colleague?

   (b) If a worker requests his supervisor for an increase in his salary and the supervisor remains silent, what should the worker gauge from his silence?
5. Consider the modifying influence of culture on non-verbal modes of communicating feelings and relationships in similar social contexts.

# 6 Listening

*Upon completion of this chapter, you should be able to:*

1. Understand how listening is an essential component of communication and management.
2. Know the internal and external causes of poor listening.
3. Know some guidelines for improving listening skills.
4. Understand how to craft reflective and clarifying responses that demonstrate good listening skills.

## WHAT IS LISTENING?

To listen is to pay thoughtful attention to what someone is saying. It is a deliberate act of attentively hearing a person speak. It is the mental process of paying undivided attention to what is heard. Listening is more than hearing, which is just the physical act of senses receiving sounds. Hearing involves the ears, but listening involves the ears, eyes, heart, and mind. It is rightly said that listening is an essential component of communication. Without this element, fruitful communication is not possible. Listening occurs when the receiver of the message wishes to learn, or be influence or changed by the message. When someone is interested in actively hearing, they are listening. Exhibit 6.1 shows the importance of listening in our daily lives.

> 1
> Understand how listening is an essential component of communication and management.

> Listening is more than hearing, which is just the physical act of our senses receiving sounds. Hearing involves our ears, but listening involves our ears, eyes, heart, and mind.

### How Do We Listen?

Listening is not passive. It is a deliberate act of concentrating on sound waves that the auditory nerve sends to the brain. As a first step in the listening process, the listener focuses his or her attention on what is essential in the communication. At the same time, he or she tries to understand, interpret, and register what is received. It is not easy to pay undivided attention to a speaker, and without giving proper attention to developing listening skills, many people remain poor listeners.

Studies conducted since the 1930s reveal that 70 per cent of our waking time goes into communication. The pie chart below illustrates the activities that take up various portions of this 70 per cent:

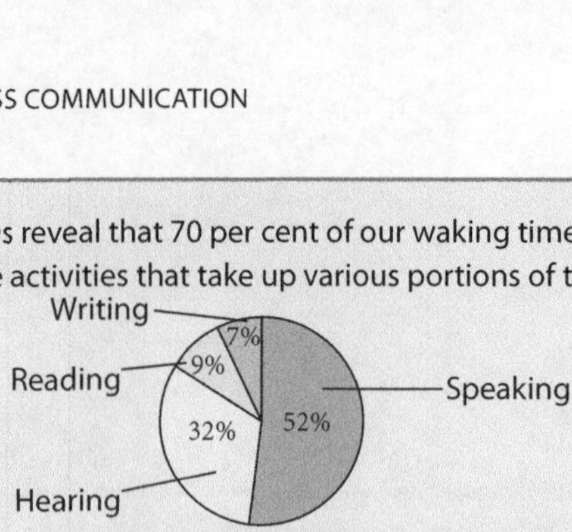


Note that this break-up reflects the norms. The figures would differ from group to group. For example, for a group of young students, "speaking" would be lower than "hearing" (or listening), and their "reading" and "writing" figures will also be higher. For a group of teachers, "speaking" would be high.

**Exhibit 6.1** The Importance of Listening

An Indian saying draws attention to the natural fact that we have two ears but one tongue. Hence, we should listen twice as much as we speak.

Listening, like speaking, reading, and writing, is a skill that can be dramatically improved through training. In this chapter therefore, we will discuss some basic things about listening, such as the complete process from hearing to conceptualizing, causes for poor listening, and some techniques of improving listening as a voluntary behaviour.

## Listening As a Management Tool

The *Longman Dictionary of Contemporary English* defines listening "considering what someone says and accepting their advice". In this sense, far-sighted business heads and senior executives use careful listening to benefit from the valuable views, perceptions, and experiences of junior and middle level workers of the company. They often owe many an initiative or cost-cutting measure to suggestions given by juniors in informal sessions. By listening to what others say about a specific situation, that is by considering and accepting the advice of others, the company succeeds in taking the best possible decision and effectively implementing it.

An example of successful "Management by Listening" is the case of Maruti Udyog, which has flourished using former Managing Director Jagdish Khattar's innovative methods of seeking suggestions from employees.[1] Maruti's decision to showcase a concept car at Delhi's annual Auto Expo was born out of an event called "Tea with the MD". Almost every fortnight, Khattar used to get together with a group of young Maruti engineers and managers in an informal meeting that encouraged them to articulate their ideas for the company's growth. Khattar's purpose was to elicit valuable suggestions for Maruti's growth by holding informal tea-sessions with his engineers and managers or by walking around at dealers' conventions, urging his dealers to make suggestions for improving sales and distribution. This was how he hit upon a formula that saved the company nearly INR 4 million.

Realizing that dealers hesitated to express themselves in an open forum, Khattar urged each of them to put down three of their suggestions on a piece of paper. He said, "On the five-hour flight back from Bangkok to Delhi, I went through each and every sheet. Our dealers had made several suggestions on how we could de-bottleneck distribution. I realized that increasing the sales force and opening small dealership extensions in rural and semi-urban areas could easily cut down on investments."

Khattar would routinely talk with and listen to youngsters before walking into his office. His example demonstrates how providing opportunities to others to express valuable suggestions holds the key to the successful management of problems.

## PRINCIPLES OF EFFECTIVE LISTENING

Listening is an integrated process, which consists of the following phases: undivided attention, hearing, understanding, interpreting, evaluating, empathizing and conceptualizing.

An explanation of these aspects of the process of listening would be helpful before proceeding. These phases do not occur in succession, but instead operate concurrently and in tandem. All aspects of oral or verbal communication require one to focus on what is being said, understand it, and register it as part of one's body of knowledge and experience.

- *Undivided attention:* Effective listening requires a certain frame of mind. The process of listening is rooted in attentively hearing the message. Undivided attention admits no distractions and no intrusive thoughts or ideas that are unrelated to the message. To concentrate on what is being said, an earnest listener would focus on the message and not let other things compete for his or her attention. The listener in this phase discriminates between thoughts, ideas, or images that belong in his or her focus of attention and those that float on its margin and must be kept from entering into conscious consideration.
- *Hearing:* Listening involves hearing distinct sounds and perceiving fine modulations in tone. The receiver recognizes the shape of words and intonation patterns. Familiarity with the sound of words and the spoken rhythm of speech contributes to the attentiveness of the listener. Pitch, voice modulations, and the quality of sound are equally important for hearing with the right attention.
- *Understanding:* A listener can hear words, but must listen to know their intended meaning. Perfect communication is when the full meaning of what is said has been understood. This includes words, tone, and body talk. A good listener hears words, observes body movements, gestures, facial expressions, and eye movements, and notices variations in tone and pitch of voice. If the listener attends only to words without paying close attention to how they are said, he or she may be missing the real, intended meaning of those words.
- *Interpreting:* Understanding and interpretation follow the phase of hearing. The listener attempts to comprehend what is heard. Understanding the language may not be enough for fully comprehending the message and successfully participating in the act of communication. It should be accompanied by the ability to interpret what is communicated, which occurs when the listener takes account of his or her own knowledge and experience.
- *Evaluating:* Communication requires that the listener has the critical ability to see for himself or herself the value of what is being discussed or heard. It is only then that the listener can closely follow the argument. The evaluation of content is closely related to the listener's own interest in what is being communicated.
- *Empathizing:* A sympathetic listener sees the speaker's point of view. He or she may not agree with what is said, yet such a listener allows the other person to say what he or she wants to say.
- *Conceptualizing:* Conceptualization occurs when the listener finally assimilates what has been heard in the context of his or her own knowledge and experiences. This is why listening is not only important, but also indispensable for perfect communication.

## PROBLEMS IN EFFECTIVE LISTENING

Listening is a voluntary behaviour that can be easily affected by internal or external factors that can act as barriers to good listening.

### Lack of Concentration

Many times listeners are not able to concentrate on what is being heard. There may be several reasons for this. There could be external factors responsible for the inability to listen properly. For example, there may be noise inside the room or loud music being played nearby. This external noise can be shut off in several ways. But, the internal factors within the listener's mind that interfere with concentration are more serious and difficult to avoid or manage. These can be overcome through practice once the listener is made aware that they are problematic.

> Know the internal and external causes of poor listening.

Reasons for not concentrating include:

- *Hearing faster than speaking:* Humans normally talk at nearly 120 to 125 words per minute, but the brain is capable of receiving 500 to 600 words per minute. The listener's brain, therefore, must deal with gaps between words, and this gap tends to be filled by other thoughts and images. This phenomenon interferes with concentration. For example, some political leaders or religious preachers deliver t heir speeches with prolonged pauses every few words or sentences. They may be using the pauses as a rhetorical device to emphasize their point. However, these pauses may instead break the listener's attentiveness by letting him or her mentally wander away from the topic to thoughts about the speaker's fluency or halting speech, or altogether unrelated issues, such as what he or she ate for breakfast. In such situations, there may not be much a listener can do to remain attentive. However, if he or she keeps looking at the speaker with steadfast eyes, the mind's tendency to wander could be significantly controlled.
- *Paying attention to the speaker and not the speech:* Many times listeners fail to listen properly because they are distracted by the speaker's face or dress or manner of delivery, just as if a dancer is very beautiful, we may be distracted by his or her beauty and miss the beauty of the dance. Thus, it is important to pay attention to the speech and its contents rather than focus on external factors that are not relevant.
- *Listening too closely:* The purpose of listening is to get the full meaning of what is said. The speaker's point is understood by looking for the central idea underlying individual words and non-verbal signs and signals. So when the listener tries not to miss a single word or detail of what the speaker is saying, he or she may get lost in the details and may miss the point.

### Unequal Statuses

In organizations, there are formal and informal status levels that affect the effectiveness of face-to-face oral communication. A subordinate would generally listen more and speak less while interacting with his or her superior. The exchange of ideas is blocked by diffidence on the part of the subordinate because of the superior position of the speaker. Upward oral communication is not very frequent in organizations. Fear of the speaker's superior status prevents free upward flow of information. This limits free and fair exchange of ideas.

### The Halo Effect

The awe in which a speaker is held by the listener affects the act of listening. If the speaker is greatly trusted and held in high esteem as an honest person, his or her statements are readily taken as true. Oral communication is thus conditioned by the impressions of the listener about the eminence of the speaker. The listener's impressions and not the intrinsic worth of the message determine the effectiveness of such communication. For instance,

> Oral communication is conditioned by the impressions of the listener about the eminence of the speaker. The listener's impressions and not the intrinsic worth of the message determine the effectiveness of such communication.

**Left-sided Listening in Men**

Our brains are divided into four parts, and each part performs different functions and has different abilities. The *right frontal* part is best at creative tasks and ideas; the *right basal* part is responsible for feelings, intuition, compassion, and interest for others. Logic and reasoning are governed by the *left frontal* part, which is responsible for abilities, such as problem solving, strategic vision, leadership, and decision-making skills. The *left basal* part is best at organizing the world; sorting, arranging and filing, and keeping order and maintaining routine.

Each of us possesses the abilities governed by the four parts of the brain to some extent, but there are differences in *how much* we use each part. About 95 per cent of us use some part of the brain more than others (only 5 per cent of us use all the parts equally). Studies show that men tend to use more of the left part of their brain while women usually use more of the right.

Studies also suggest differences in listening in men and women. According to some research studies, men listen with only one side of their brains while women use both. Researchers have compared the brain scans of men and women and found that men mostly use the left side of their brains, the part long believed to control listening and understanding.

The question is: which is normal? Maybe the normal for men is different from the normal for women. Could this be the reason why men don't like to listen to what doesn't interest them, and listen repeatedly to something they like?

**Listening in Left-handed People**

Right-handed people are many more in number than left-handed people on earth. But, when it comes to processing language, a higher proportion of left-handed people process language effectively, as compared to right-handed people.

Normally, people use both sides of the brain to process language. The dominant hemisphere deals with articulation and calculation, and the non-dominant part is used for abstract thinking. According to the findings of the American Academy of Neurology in Philadelphia, the United States, left-handed people may use a (dominant) part of the brain to process language which differs from their right-handed counterparts. As a result, left-handed people could have different types of intelligence. For example, a person could be the CEO of an organization and yet not have good road sense.

*Sources:* Information from "Men Do Hear—But Differently Than Women, Brain Images Show," *ScienceDaily*, 29 November 2000, http://www.sciencedaily.com/releases/2000/11/001129075326.htm, accessed October 2010; and Steve Smith (ed.), "Be Your Best! Readymade Tools for Personal Development", 1st South Asian edition (Cogan-Page India Ltd, 1999).

**Exhibit 6.2** Differences in the Listening Process

due to the halo effect, buyers may go by a trusted seller's view rather than by their own judgment of a product's quality.

## Complexes

Lack of confidence or a sense of superiority may prevent proper interaction between persons in different positions. Sometimes an individual may suffer from a sense of inferiority and therefore, fail to take the initiative or involve himself or herself in conversation, dialogue, or other forms of oral communication. Similarly, some persons consider themselves too important to condescend to talk with others. Often, these are misplaced notions of self-worth, but they do block oral communication.

## A Closed Mind

Listening, to a large extent, depends on one's curiosity to know things. Some individuals believe that they know everything in a field or subject. Their minds refuse to receive information from other sources. In addition, some persons feel too satisfied with their way of doing things to change or even discuss new ideas. A closed state of mind acts as a barrier to oral communication, which demands a readiness and willingness on the part of the listener to enter into dialogue.

> Listening, to a large extent, depends on one's curiosity to know things.

## Poor Retention

In dialogue or two-way oral communication, a logical sequence of thoughts is essential for successful communication. To speak coherently and comprehend completely, one has to understand the sequence of ideas. The structure of thoughts must be received and retained by the listener to understand arguments. The cues that signal the transition from one set of ideas to another must be retained by the listener to be able to grasp the full sense of the message. In case of poor retention, the listener fails to relate what he or she hears with what he or she had heard earlier. Moreover, if the listener fails to remember previous discussions, the whole conversation is likely to be lost in the absence of any written record.

> The cues that signal the transition from one set of ideas to another must be retained by the listener to be able to grasp the full sense of the message. In case of poor retention, the listener fails to relate what he or he hears with what he or she had heard earlier.

## Premature Evaluation and Hurried Conclusions

Listening patiently until the speaker completes his or her argument is necessary for correct interpretation of an oral message. The listener can distort the intended meaning by pre-judging the intentions of the speaker, inferring the final meaning of the message, or giving a different twist to the argument according to his or her own assumptions or by just picking out a few select shreds of information. These mental processes may act as a block to listening, affecting accurate exchange of information.

## Abstracting

*Abstracting* is the mental process of evaluating thoughts in terms of the relative importance of ideas in the context of the total message. This is possible only by listening to the whole message. Abstracting acts as a barrier when a listener approaches a message from a particular point of view and focuses his or her attention on selected aspects of the conversation. This acts as a barrier to a full understanding of whatever is exchanged between two persons.

## Slant

*Slant* is the biased presentation of a matter by the speaker. Instead of straight and honest communication, the speaker may adopt an oblique manner that could verge on telling a lie. When a matter is expressed with a particular slant, important aspects of the message are suppressed, left out, or only indirectly hinted at. Well-informed listeners usually do suspect the cover-up/slant. But, uninformed listeners may accept the slanted message.

## Cognitive Dissonance

At times listeners fail to accept or respond to assumptions deriving from new information as they may be unprepared to change the basis of their beliefs and knowledge. In such a discrepancy between a listener's existing assumptions and the position communicated by the speaker, some listeners try to escape from the dissonance by reinterpreting, restructuring, or mentally ignoring the oral interchange. Cognitive dissonance interferes with the acceptance of new information. It may also lead to several interpretations of a new message or view. In the absence of cognitive dissonance, a listener has the skill, ability, and flexibility of rational thinking, promoting effective oral communication. For business executives, the skill to move from one mental frame to another is essential for efficient oral exchange of ideas, beliefs, and feelings.

Cognitive dissonance interferes with the acceptance of new information.

## INCULCATING LISTENING EFFICIENCY

3

Know some guidelines for improving listening skills.

Effective communication is associated with the power of speaking well, but without good listening, successful communication is not possible. The spoken word fulfils its purpose only when it is carefully heard, understood, interpreted, and registered in the listener's memory.

The effectiveness of communication is the function of both effective speaking and effective listening. To communicate successfully, the speaker's words should be well articulated and, at the same time, they must be well received. The guidelines given here should be helpful in improving one's listening skills.

When two people are talking simultaneously, neither can listen to the other. To have a successful dialogue, it is necessary that when one person wants to speak, the other person keeps quiet and listens. No one can talk and listen at the same time. In classrooms, it is common for teachers to ask students to stop talking to ensure that they are able to listen to the lecture. Similarly, the teacher stops talking when a student wants to say something.

1. *Speak less, listen more:* The purpose of listening is to know what the speaker wants to say or to learn from the speaker. Listening is an act of cooperation in the sense that it takes advantage of others' knowledge and experience. Therefore, devoting time to listening rather than speaking is in our self-interest.
2. *Do not be a sponge:* It is not necessary to concentrate on every word of the speaker. Instead, it is more important to get the main point, theme, or central idea and concentrate on it. Minor details are not as important.
3. *Observe body language:* Effective listeners do not pay attention only to what is being said, but also notice how it is said. They observe the feelings, attitudes, and emotional reactions of the speaker based on his or her body language.
4. *Focus on the speaker:* Facing the speaker and making eye contact make the speaker feel that the listener is interested in what he or she is saying.
5. *Separate the ideas from the speaker:* Good listeners do not allow themselves to be overly awed by the speaker's status, fame, charm, or other physical and personal attributes. They separate the person from his or her ideas. Effective communicators are not conditioned by their personal impressions and prejudices, but are able to focus on the content of what is being spoken.
6. *Listen for what is left unsaid:* Careful attention to what is not said, in addition to what is said, can tell the listener a lot about the speaker's feelings and attitude towards the subject of discussion.
7. *Avoid becoming emotional:* Good listeners remain calm and do not become emotionally charged or excited by the speaker's words. Becoming too angry or excited makes it difficult for the listener to respond or express himself or herself objectively and rationally.

Step1: *Keep quiet*—as much as possible.

Step 2: *Don't lead*—unless you want to hear the opposite of what is being said.

Step 3: *Don't react defensively*—if what you hear bothers you.

Step 4: *Avoid clichés*—to make meaningful statements.

Step 5: *Remain neutral*—no matter what you think of others.

Step 6: *Resist giving advice*—until asked for directly.

*Source:* Based on Michael Purdy and Deborah Borisoff (eds), *Listening in Everyday Life: A personal and Professional Approach* (University Press of America, 1997).

**Exhibit 6.3** Effective Listening—Six Steps Away

8. *Do not jump to hasty conclusions:* Listeners should allow the speaker to conclude his or her point. Only then should they try to interpret and respond to it. Hasty inferences may not represent what the speaker intended to communicate.
9. *Empathize with the speaker:* Effective listeners keep in mind the speaker's point of view by focusing on the big picture, background constraints/limitations, and special needs and the emotional state of the speaker.
10. *Respect the speaker as a person:* It is important to listen with respect for the other person. Do not allow the speaker to feel hurt, ignored, or insulted.

There may be nothing new in these guidelines. However, a reminder of the ways of improving listening, as illustrated in Exhibit 6.3, can be of great value for improving the effectiveness of communication.

## CHARACTERISTICS OF EFFECTIVE AND INEFFECTIVE LISTENERS

To improve our listening skills, we must know the characteristics of effective as well as ineffective listeners and identify our own weaknesses as listeners. Exhibit 6.4 contrasts the characteristics of effective and ineffective listeners.

Good listeners try to encourage the speaker by their body language and expression. They indicate interest and understanding regarding the subject of discussion. Poor listeners, on the other hand,

| *Effective Listeners* | *Ineffective Listeners* |
|---|---|
| Do not interrupt | Take a "Yes, but..." approach |
| Remain patient | Do not give their full attention to the speaker |
| Make eye contact | Look away from the speaker |
| Show interest | Display impatience to talk |
| Look attentive | Are very critical |
| Concentrate | Have poor concentration |
| Ask open questions | Are over-talkative |

**Exhibit 6.4** Characteristics of Effective and Ineffective Listeners

annoy and disturb the speaker. They may have the habit of interrupting or showing little interest in what is being discussed. Unnecessary interjections, such as "yes", "but", and "if" should be avoided when they disturb the speaker.

After knowing how effective and ineffective listeners differ in their listening behaviour, try to recognize your own behaviour and attitude.

## REVIEW YOUR LEARNING

1. "Listening is hearing with thoughtful attention." Discuss.
2. What is the advantage of being a good listener for a business executive?
3. Describe in detail the process of listening.
4. Describe some internal factors that act as barriers to proper listening.
5. "Premature evaluations and hurried conclusions distort listening." Discuss.
6. Describe some methods of improving the listening ability of a person.
7. Explain how a reflective response facilitates listening.
8. Bring out the difference between "clarifying' listeners" and "interpretative" listeners.
9. What do you understand by the term "responsive listening"?

## REFLECT ON YOUR LEARNING

1. Consider the reasons for one's occasional lack of concentration on what is said.
2. How would you evaluate yourself as a listener on the basis of the listening characteristics described in this chapter?
3. In this chapter, there are some guidelines given for improving listening. Which of these would you find suitable for improving your listening?
4. Do you believe that proper training can improve one's listening skills?
5. Do you agree with the view that it is not possible to have appropriate communication between a speaker and a listener?

## ENDNOTE

1. T. R. Vivek, "Strat Talk", *The Economic Times*, April 20, 2007.

# 7 Organizational Communication

*Upon completion of this chapter, you should be able to:*

1 Understand the functional relationship between communication and management.

2 Identify new trends in organizational communication due to technological changes and developments.

3 Know why managers need strong communication skills.

4 Understand the elements that form the structure of an organization's communication network.

5 Understand the formal and informal lines of organizational communication.

6 Know what and how much should be communicated to employees at the workplace.

## SOME IMPORTANT FUNCTIONS OF MANAGEMENT

Exhibit 7.1 shows some important functions of management. The function of communication is to define and support the action involved in each of these functions.

- *Forecasting and planning:* Each function of management depends on effective communication for its success. For example, if the management fails to communicate its objectives, policies, programmes, procedures, and budgetary provisions to the concerned people at the proper time, an organization would fail to run in an organized and targeted manner.
- *Organizing:* Organizing, as a management function, determines the formal and informal relationships within the organization and outside it. These relationships are developed and maintained through interpersonal communication.
- *Instructing:* The function of instructing depends entirely upon effective exchange of information regarding products, processes, and targets.
- *Coordinating:* Coordinating is perhaps the most demanding of all management functions. It requires excellent communication skills to ensure that all efforts are directed towards the achievement of a single organizational goal. To ensure that diverse activities are complementary, a manager should be able to relate with all the people involved, both formally and informally.
- *Controlling:* Finally, in order to control processes, a manager should be able to receive and interpret information and respond quickly.

| | |
|---|---|
| Forecasting | Determines organizational objectives and policies |
| Planning | Prepares programmes, procedures, and budgets |
| Organizing | Sets the organizational structure |
| Instructing | Provides the bedrock of organizational performance |
| Coordinating | Ensures all efforts are directed towards the organization's goals |
| Controlling | Checks the results and receives feedback |

**Exhibit 7.1** Functions of Management

## NEED FOR COMMUNICATION IN MANAGEMENT

### How Communication Is Used by Managers

Management is a unified, organized, and cooperative system committed to the achievement of common goals. Unity of purpose and commitment to a single organizational goal can be developed only through the persuasive power of communication. To do this, a manager needs to have excellent communication skills, including the ability to structure information according to its negative/affirmative nature and use words and tones according to the purpose of the communication. A manager should be able to create the desired relationship with the audience or employees to produce the needed response. Thus, diverse strategies, verbal and non-verbal, of effective communication form an important part of management as a discipline.

> Unity of purpose and commitment to a single organizational goal can be developed only through the persuasive power of communication.

From a small business to a multinational enterprise, every organization today needs an effective communication system to enable it to function and flourish. Communication is a means of:

- Increasing employees' job performance and effectiveness by updating their knowledge
- Promoting employees' sense of belonging and commitment
- Effecting changes smoothly
- Motivating employees and creating a sense of identification with the organization's goals
- Informing and convincing employees about decisions and the reasons behind them
- Helping employees develop a clear understanding of their roles and growth opportunities within the organization
- Empowering employees with information on development and activities

Hence, an active communication system is vital for the good health of an organization. If there is continual sharing of ideas and interactive meetings between the management and employees, an overall atmosphere of understanding and goodwill would prevail in the workplace. When decision-making is transparent, employees understand the reasons behind decisions and accept and implement them, even if those decisions affect them adversely. Thus, communication can help in management in the following ways:

> When decision-making is transparent, employees understand the reasons behind decisions and accept and implement them, even if those decisions affect them adversely.

- *Creating a sense of belonging*: An understanding of their roles and career paths in the organization makes employees feel a part of the whole setup.

- *Resolving disputes:* All disputes in organizations, which lead to huge losses of time, money, and good human relations, are caused by communication failures.
- *Providing a holistic view of the situation:* A great value of effective communication lies in making people not only know, but also perceive and understand the meaning of things happening around them. Through clear communication, employees not only "see" the realities of the business, but also develop a "feel" for it.

In the changing business environment of multinational competition and globalization, communication has become an important component of an organization. Like the functional areas of production, marketing, and finance, communication too is evolving into a distinct discipline in the form of corporate communication.

1

Identify new trends in organizational communication due to technological changes and developments.

Theoretically, corporate communication brings under a single umbrella all communication activities undertaken by different areas, such as marketing and public relations, which are directed at image-building and developing human capital. In this integrated form, communication speaks to the world outside the organization and within it in a single voice that builds the corporate image.

Several changes in the modern technological age of information have made people pay more attention to communication as an important tool in successful management. These changes are:

- *Bigger organizations:* Organizations are getting bigger and bigger, either due to increased levels of production or through multinational collaborations. The large size of organizations today poses problems in communication.

The large size of organizations today poses problems in communication.

- *New developments in information technology:* The modern age, the age of information, is not just an era of new media—telephone, radio, television, communication satellites, computers, and so on; it is also an era of a new attitude towards knowledge and the value of sharing it with others. In fact, communication is now looked upon as a source of empowerment of people. But, the success of these new media depends on the skills of those who use them. It involves a new attitude towards the value and use of good communication.
- *The concept of human capital:* Employees and workers are now considered to be the human component of business and not just the source of labour. Their attitudes, interests, and welfare constitute an important aspect of management. Hence, there has to be a live channel of communication between the employees and the management.
- *Need to learn corporate etiquette:* Top corporate executives are increasingly being sensitized to the importance of conducting meetings, seminars, presentations, and negotiations effectively. They realize that management executives should learn the rules of etiquette if they are not already familiar with them. This includes knowing how to greet others, shake hands, dress for success, exchange business cards, listen, and converse with a diverse variety of clients.

Corporate etiquette training, which is a part of communication skills, focuses on the rules to be observed and practised for success in international and national business ventures. Good business manners speak of the culture of the organization, not just of the individual.

The success of new media depends on the skills of the people who use them.

These contemporary changes suggest that organizations now need not only an effective communication system, but also executives and managers who are well equipped with effective communication skills.

## Communication Concerns of the Manager

In business, a manager spends most of his or her time either speaking or writing to colleagues, supervisors, subordinates, or clients. A manager's success depends largely on his or her ability to communicate what has to be done and why to colleagues.

To be able to do this, the manager has to devote his or her time to:

- Receiving and interpreting information from other managers and departments
- Sending information to other department managers
- Passing on information and suggestions on new plans or projects to senior/top management
- Transmitting information to subordinates
- Developing a positive attitude

To a large extent, the success of an organization requires an atmosphere in which there is a free flow of information—upward, downward, and horizontally. At the workplace, the primary goal is getting things done. For this, instructions, guidelines, supervision, monitoring, and periodic reporting are usually considered enough. But if the company wishes to achieve more than the set task, a real involvement of all employees, from the highest to the lowest levels, is required. This cooperation can only be secured by allowing every level of employee to suggest ideas, express their views, and share their experiences. Such a system of communication can only be established within the organization by the manager. In fact, the manager functions as the point of intersection for all communication channels. One of the most important concerns of the manager is to organize and ensure an effective information system across the organization.

> The success of an organization requires an atmosphere in which there is a free flow of information—upward, downward, and horizontally.

> One of the most important concerns of the manager is to organize and ensure an effective information system across the organization.

As analysed by Henry Mintzberg[1] of the Massachusetts Institute of Technology, managers need effective communication skills to perform in the following interrelated situations:

- Interpersonal
- Informational
- Decisional

> 2 Know why managers need strong communication skills.

These situations, with their descriptions and examples, are clearly described in Mintzberg's book, *The Nature of Managerial Work*.

The interpersonal role refers to situations in which the manager acts as a figurehead, leader, and liaison officer. The informational role is when the manager is a monitor, disseminator, and spokesperson. In the decisional role, the manager functions as an entrepreneur, troubleshooter, resource allocator, and negotiator.

- *Interpersonal role:* It is necessary to ensure the effective operation of the organization's systems and to maintain proper relationships within the organization and with clients, suppliers, and other functionaries. If interpersonal communication is effective, internal systems run smoothly. For example, personnel functions within the organization require managers to inspire confidence, win support, and guide workers. Managers are role models for others and must develop the skill of listening patiently and perceptively in order to understand the needs

> If interpersonal communication is effective, internal systems run smoothly.

of their subordinates. This is essential for creating an atmosphere of mutual understanding and goodwill within the organization and transparent sharing of its objectives, mission, and problems.

- *Informational role*: If the internal information-sharing system of a company is effective, other systems, such as stock control, personnel functions, financial systems, and quality control operate smoothly. Shortcomings and problems can be quickly identified and remedial action taken immediately. Proper maintenance of product and service standards can be ensured through timely monitoring and instructing. Through effective, interactive communication and a strong feedback system, high morale and satisfaction of workers can be secured.
- *Decisional role:* Decision-making is based upon receiving and interpreting all relevant and necessary information. Decisions that are based on guesswork and are made without access to all relevant information may turn out to be unrealistic and harmful. Managers need to possess the skill of receiving relevant and up-to-date information correctly and accurately to be able to take decisions and act rationally, fairly, and to the satisfaction of all concerned.

Decisions that are based on guesswork and are made without access to all relevant information may turn out to be unrealistic and harmful.

All these functions require the manager to handle people and situations with a good knowledge of human needs.

## IMPORTANCE OF COMMUNICATION IN MANAGEMENT

Communication skills constitute an important aspect of effective management. Management is a complex process. In simple terms, it can be described as the organization of capital, labour, and material to achieve production and distribution of particular goods or services.

First, the management determines its objectives—what it must do and how it must do it. Then, there has to be a system through which the production and distribution processes can be guided, coordinated, and controlled to ensure that the management objectives are achieved. Communication is the system by which production and distribution operations are controlled and coordinated and the results correlated to the objectives.

## COMMUNICATION STRUCTURE IN AN ORGANIZATION

In business organizations, the effectiveness of a communication system depends upon the extent to which the necessary information (required for decision-making) reaches the concerned person (the person who needs that information) at the right time (when the information is needed). The network of information should support the overall functioning of management by integrating and coordinating the workforce for achieving organizational objectives.

3

Understand the elements that form the structure of an organization's communication network.

Hence, every organization creates a network (channel) for information to pass through different levels of authority and functional heads and units. The flow of communication follows the structure of the organization. In actual practice, the information passes through the organizational pyramid such as the one shown in Exhibit 7.2.

### Vertical Communication

In organizations, there are well-defined lines or routes for passing on communication. Policy decisions are taken at the boardroom level. From there, information is sent downwards to senior managers or a

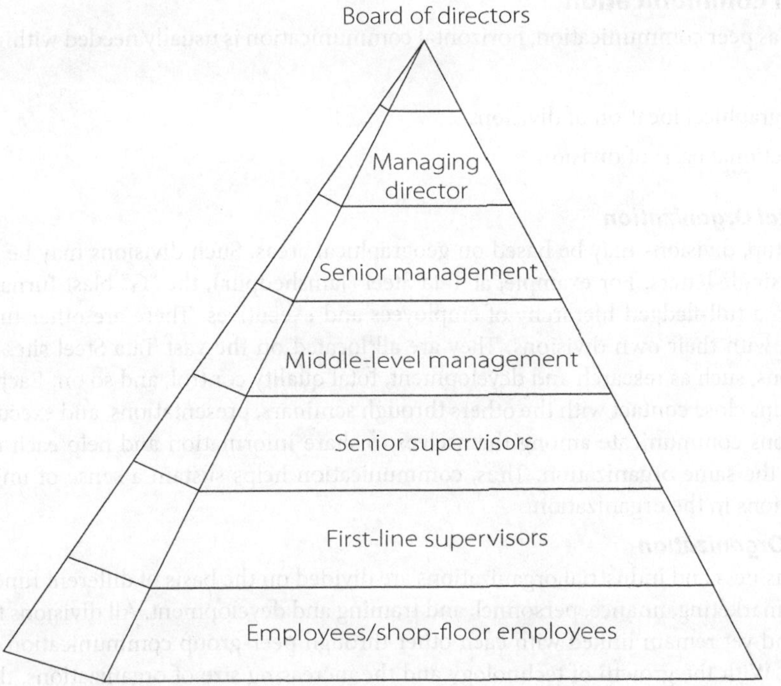


**Exhibit 7.2** Organizational Pyramid

group of senior managers. They ensure that the policy decisions are easily understood, implemented, sustained, monitored, reviewed, and reported. Feedback (performance data or employee experiences or suggestions) is, in turn, sent upwards.

In this system of communication, the key links are the managers and supervisors. They transmit information both upwards and downwards. They are also responsible for following up on ideas and instructions. In all large organizations, the human resource or personnel department manages the circulation of information among employees. Personnel managers are in constant touch with all employees. They are able to identify needs, provide guidance on policy matters, and supervise infrastructural rearrangements.

> When an organization has too many levels of hierarchy, managers may find it difficult to reach ground-level and shop-floor employees.

However, when an organization has too many levels of hierarchy, managers may find it difficult to reach ground-level and shop-floor employees. In such situations, communication tends to be slow in reaching and delayed in being absorbed and acted upon. The cost of this delay, caused by the sheer size of the organization, may sometimes be too high.

Hence, as Peter Drucker holds, large organizations have more recently moved towards a "flatter structure" of information-based management and executives "walk down" the jobs. This is obviously to facilitate information flow downwards and to prevent employees from getting frustrated by their sense of isolation.

### Horizontal Communication

Also known as peer communication, horizontal communication is usually needed within the organization due to:

- The geographical location of divisions
- The functional basis of division

#### *Geographical Organization*

In a large setup, divisions may be based on geographical areas. Such divisions may be known just by numbers or single letters. For example, at Tata Steel (Jamshedpur), the "G" blast furnace has its own division with a full-fledged hierarchy of employees and executives. There are other furnaces known by numbers, with their own divisions. They are all located on the vast Tata Steel site. There are also other divisions, such as research and development, total quality control, and so on. Each of these divisions maintains close contact with the others through seminars, presentations, and executive meetings. These divisions communicate among themselves to share information and help each other as equal members of the same organization. Thus, communication helps sustain a sense of unity among the various divisions in the organization.

#### *Functional Organization*

Normally, business and industrial organizations are divided on the basis of different functions, such as production, marketing, finance, personnel, and training and development. All divisions function independently and yet remain linked with each other through peer-group communication and workflow information. With the growth of technology and the increasing size of organizations, the widespread production of goods and services needs to be coordinated through the channel of horizontal communication. From the stage of selection of raw material to the finished product, numerous processes are involved in completing the given task of production. At each stage of the production process, the job of a workgroup depends upon the timing and form of work received from the preceding workgroup. Any interruption in the workflow adversely affects performance at successive stages of production. The workflow in a company can be steadily managed only through horizontal communication between the sections that are directly linked.

## COMMUNICATION AND THE LINE AND STAFF MANAGEMENT

*Line and staff management (LSM)* is a system of management in large organizations consisting of line managers and staff managers. *Line managers* are responsible for the main activities of the company, such as manufacturing and sales, while *staff managers* control the support and service areas, such as accounting, distribution, and personnel. A network of relationships between those in line (functional) management and staff (support) management is created by means of an effective internal communications system. Without this, an organization can neither function properly nor thrive in the business world. As shown in Exhibit 7.3, the internal communication system can be divided into two categories—formal lines of communication and informal lines of communication.

> A network of relationships between those in line (functional) management and staff (support) management is created by means of an effective internal communications system.

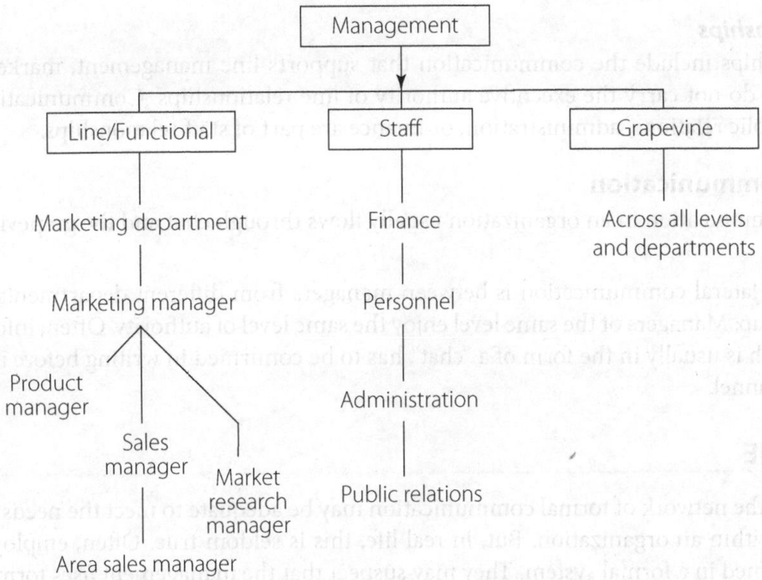


**Exhibit 7.3** Internal Communication System in Organizations

## FORMAL AND INFORMAL COMMUNICATION

### Formal Communication

Formal lines of organizational communication include:

1. Line relationships
2. Functional relationships
3. Staff relationships

> 4 Understand the formal and informal lines of organizational communication.

#### *Line Relationships*

Line relationships refer to the line of authority that sets down the path of communication from supervisors to subordinates and vice versa. All official communications, orders, and instructions move from seniors to subordinates. Similarly, all follow-up actions and compliance and execution information and reports move upwards, from subordinates to supervisors and executives. Usually, all organizations insist on following the normal chain of authority from one position to the next. If the communication is in the form of a letter, this respect for the chain of authority is indicated by writing the phrase "through the proper channels" in the beginning of the letter.

> Usually, all organizations insist on following the normal chain of authority from one position to the next.

If the communication is oral, the message is conveyed to one's immediate supervisor.

#### *Functional Relationships*

Functional relationships are those between departments within an organization. Communication that occurs when departments share information regarding work and related organizational matters with each other is a formal line of organizational communication.

#### *Staff Relationships*

Staff relationships include the communication that supports line management, marketing, and production. They do not carry the executive authority of line relationships. Communications relating to personnel, public relations, administration, or finance are part of staff relationships.

### Informal Communication

Informal communication in an organization usually flows through chat and the grapevine.

#### *Chat*

Horizontal or lateral communication is between managers from different departments or within the same peer group. Managers of the same level enjoy the same level of authority. Often, informal communication, which is usually in the form of a "chat", has to be confirmed in writing before it goes through the official channel.

## GRAPEVINE

Theoretically, the network of formal communication may be adequate to meet the needs of exchanging information within an organization. But, in real life, this is seldom true. Often, employees feel inadequately informed in a formal system. They may suspect that the management uses formal channels to conceal rather than reveal the true message. They may thus, accuse the system of lacking transparency. As a result, employees modify the formal methods of communication by bringing in an informal communication system, the grapevine.

Information obtained via the grapevine is always attributed to "a reliable source". "Learnt through a reliable source", is a common phrase used by the communicator to make the news sound authentic.

> The grapevine may create complications for the information system of organizations.

However, the grapevine may create complications for the information system of organizations.

- The unofficial version of news, irrespective of its basis, is more easily believed by people.
- News through the grapevine spreads like wildfire, quickly and uncontrollably.
- Usually this version of information is somewhat distorted and exaggerated—a result of the vast chain of "filters" used in the process.

> The grapevine exists in all workplaces. It is an informal adjunct or extension of the formal system of organizational communication.

The grapevine exists in all workplaces. It is an informal adjunct or extension of the formal system of organizational communication. In a way, it is a corrective to the management's system of information as it is timely and has a wide reach. It poses a challenge to management's MIS (Management Information System).

The presence of the grapevine shows that the management has missed an opportunity to share information of interest with their employees. The gap in formal communication is filled by informal gossip circulated among employees, who form relationships on the basis of their work or common social factors, such as neighbourhood, language, culture, state, club memberships, and so on These relationships are formed on the basis of friendship and not official status.

Participants in the grapevine are non-official leaders who generally initiate and spread the gossip across the organization. As with formal communication, there is a sender and a receiver.

Normally, the management views the grapevine negatively as it undercuts confidentiality, secrecy, and guarded sharing of information with employees. However, sometimes the management itself may take advantage of the grapevine, for instance to learn in advance the reaction and response of employees to a proposed scheme or change. In such a situation, before officially announcing the change, the managers may deliberately feed the leaders of the grapevine with the concerned message and note employees' feedback and responses.

This managerial practice is not always on the sly. Some management scholars approve of this practice of supplementing formal communication with informal communication. Koontz and O'Donnell observe, "The most effective communication results when managers utilize the informal organization to supplement the communication channels of the formal organization".

When using informal channels of communication, managers have to be very careful about the form of informal communication. For example, it could be very effective to "walk down the job"—move around the office, chat, and informally discuss formal matters. But, the effectiveness of this depends on the personal relationship between the executive and his or her subordinate and the image created by the executive by his or her official behaviour and personal attributes, such as frankness, attitude, and sense of fairness. As Leland Brown says, "In using the grapevine, management must be able to pinpoint the leaders and work through them. It must feed in factual information, listen to the feedback response, and be discerning in not overloading the system and using it inappropriately. It is important that management be sure to follow up the grapevine message with official written messages and statements that will verify the accuracy of data obtained from the grapevine. This helps in building a mutual trust based on open communication followed throughout the organization or business."

### *Merits of Informal Communication*

The chief advantages of informal communication lines are:

- *Uniting force:* The grapevine brings together employees in matters of common interest.
- *Speed:* Informal channels of communication pass on messages speedily.
- *Creation of ideas:* Informal communication, through sharing of ideas and views or by spreading unofficial "grapevine", generates ideas and expectations that often prove of value to decision-makers and planners.
- *Good personal relations:* Public relations fail in organizations because of the lack of good personal relationships. Informal communication that promotes personal relations is, therefore, important for the success of public relations.

Public relations fail in organizations because of the lack of good personal relationships.

Emphasizing the value of informal communication in management, especially via the grapevine, Myers and Myers assert that field research and laboratory experiments indicate that "grapevine communication is fast; predictable in its course, directions, and membership; and also far more accurate than a casual observer might imagine. Grapevine communication is less heavily loaded with task information—how to do the job—than with information about people, attitudes, relationships, interpretation, prediction, values, norms, and needs".

### *Limitations of Informal Communication*

The limitations of informal communication channels are:

- *Rumours:* Sometimes informal communication, especially grapevine, can prove very provocative and disastrous for the relationship between employees and management. By its very nature, grapevine is information that lacks solid evidence. Moreover, there is little accountability in spreading it. By exciting hopes or fears in employees, rumour mongering may result in a negative or misleading situation in the workplace. As a consequence, the management may be confronted with a wave of prejudice, emotions, biases, half-truths, and ambiguity.

By exciting hopes or fears in employees, rumour mongering may result in a negative or misleading situation in the workplace.

- *Inadequacy:* Informal communication can only pertain to certain kinds of organizational information—that is, non-functional issues and matters. Secondary issues regarding staff and management relations are generally the subject of grapevine.
- *Changing interpretations:* When information is allowed to be spread through the grapevine, it tends to result in distortion and dilution of the main issue. The key person, the individual who starts spreading the news, is sometimes surprised by the final form in which that news gets back to him or her. Just as in the game of Chinese Whispers, the distortions are unintentional. Changes in interpretations happen owing to the different perceptions of the persons involved in the chain. The unlimited circulation of a statement can make it lose its original meaning and character. Great caution is, therefore, needed in using informal communication channels as a supplement to formal communication.

Changes in interpretations happen owing to the different perceptions of the persons involved in the whispering chain.

Finally, it is the responsibility of the formal communication system to ensure that opportunities for misinterpretation of information through the grapevine do not occur, by giving full and necessary information to employees in a timely manner. Therefore, besides interactions at the functional level, people should be able to talk to one another about formal matters informally on different occasions.

## CORPORATE COMMUNICATION

In the changing business environment of multinational competition and globalisation, communication tends to become an important component of an organisation. Like the functional areas of production, marketing, and finance, communication too is shaping into a distinct area, in the form of corporate communication.

Theoretically, it is to bring under a single umbrella all communication activities done by different areas, such as marketing, PR/OM, and the like, directed at good image building and developing human capital. In this integrated for, communication is supposed to speak to the world outside the organization and within it in a single voice, what marketing or public relations or quality control speak in different voices, to build the corporate image.

Several changes in the modern, socio-technological age of information have made people pay more attention to communication as an important tool of successful management. These changes are:

***Size of organization*** Big organisations are getting bigger and bigger either through their own increased level of production or through multinational collaborations. The very size of organizations today poses problems for communicating. These problems have got to be looked into for a proper running of the whole project.

***The concept of human capital*** Employees and workers are now considered to be the human component of business and not just the source of labour. Their attitudes, interests, and welfare constitute an important aspect of management. Hence, there has to be a live channel of communication between the employees and the management.

***Need to learn corporate etiquette*** Top corporate executives are increasingly being sensitized about the importance of knowing how to conduct meetings, seminars, presentations, and negotiations. They realize that management executives should learn the rules or etiquette, if not already familiar with them. These include:

1. How to greet
2. How to shake hands
3. How to dress for success
4. How to present cards
5. How to listen
6. How to converse with seniors/ladies/ and clients

The training, which again is a part of communication skills, develops the corporate etiquette to be observed and practised for success in international/ multinational/ or big national ventures. Good business manners speak of the culture of the organization, not of the individual's in particular.

These contemporary changes suggest that organizations not only need an effective communication system; they need to have executives/managers who are well equipped with these skills.

5

Know what and how much should be communicated to employees at the workplace.

## Information to Be Communicated at the Workplace

To reduce the chances of misinterpretation or disinformation being spread by the grapevine, an organization should keep all its employees informed about certain facts regarding it. The content of the information is generally a mixture of facts, opinion, attitudes and interpretation. The purpose is to instruct, persuade, and ensure a routine for one-way transmission of information.

Broadly, all business communication can be divided into five types of information:

1. *Statutory information:* Information regarding terms and conditions of service should be communicated to all employees as a statutory requirement.
2. *Regular work-related information:* Information regarding normal work situations has to be regularly communicated through routine formal briefing sessions or through informal chat sessions between the manager and group members.
3. *Major policy or operational changes:* Any major changes in the organization's policies, which affect everyone or a large number of employees, have to be communicated to all by calling special meetings or by issuing notices.
4. *Information bulletin:* To keep people informed about events and happenings in the organization, periodic information in the form of a newsletter is disseminated to all employees. This helps create a sense of involvement in the working of the organization.
5. *Communication by expectancy:* Information regarding critical changes should be carefully and gradually communicated to those who are going to be directly affected by the decision. Before the decision is implemented, the people concerned must be prepared for it. This process aims at creating expectancy in the receivers, so that they are prepared for upcoming changes.

## REVIEW YOUR LEARNING

1. Discuss how communication is the lifeline of an organization's health.
2. Indicate the new trends in organizational communication due to technological changes and developments.
3. What are the main concerns of a manager? How should he or she fulfil them through effective communication? Discuss.
4. Analyse the corresponding relationship between channels of communication and the structure of an organization.
5. Discuss the formal and informal lines of organizational communication.
6. What is the grapevine? What gives rise to this communication phenomenon in organizations? How can the management prevent it from spreading?
7. Discuss the advantages of informal lines of communication in the workplace.
8. What kinds of information need to be communicated to an employee by the organization?

10. Discuss the responsibility of senior management for establishing and promoting a sound communication system.

## REFLECT ON YOUR LEARNING

1. What are the ways in which organizations encourage or discourage "upward" communication?
2. "A flat organization is a myth". To what extent can an organization function without a structure with levels of authority?
3. How does training promote effective interpersonal behaviour?
4. In an organization, one learns new attitudes towards working with others. How does communication help an individual's learning behaviour?
5. Identify the advantages and disadvantages of having a clearly defined communication policy from a manager's point of view, especially in relation to employees' needs.

## ENDNOTE

1. Henry Mintzberg, *The Nature of Managerial Work* (New York: Harper Collins College Division, 1973).

# 8 Applications

*Upon completion of this chapter, you should be able to:*

1. Use the new forms of electronic media for the communication properly.
2. Learn the culture of telephonic conversation.
3. Develop job-related skills to successfully write CVs , application letters, attend interviews, participate in group discussions, and make effective presentations.
4. Learn business etiquette of meeting and interacting with people for developing goodwill.
5. Learn the strategies of successful negotiations.
6. Develop the art of public speaking.

## NEW MEDIA

In business, the use of telephone, voice mail, phone conferencing, video conferencing, cell phones, and e-mail occurs in accordance with the need and purpose of the communicator. Since the communicators in these situations are not face-to-face, one has to have a high level of oral communication skills to be able to communicate effectively through these methods.

**1** Apply oral communication skills to new communication technologies.

### Phones

In business, for immediate information and response, the handiest mode of communication is the telephone. Though convenient for the caller, it is often viewed by top managers or very senior executives as a source of interruption. Hence, the phone is often received by an administrative assistant. After the caller explains the purpose of the call, he or she is put through to the concerned person.

Most organizations have a standard way of answering phone calls. The normal practice is for the receiver to greet the caller and then state his or her name and department. On picking up the phone, one should never say, "Yes—who is it—what do you want?" Instead, the receiver should sound polite by saying something like "May I know who is calling?" or "May I know in what regard you are calling?"

Nowadays, organizations have automatic exchanges that facilitate direct connections with the desired extension; alternatively, the Interactive Voice Response (IVR) may guide callers to the extension or ask them to wait for the operator. The operator usually begins by stating the organization's name, or by a greeting such as, "Good morning, IMT."

In business, courtesy counts. One doesn't automatically know how important the caller is for the company's business. So, every phone should be received with a standard sequence of phrases. If the intended receiver is not available, courtesy demands that a message be taken. But, for that, one has to be ready and equipped with a pen or pencil and paper. If the call reaches the receiver directly, generally, the response is just the name of the person, for instance, "Vinod".

Business telephone conversations should be only as long as is essential. If the other person starts going off-topic, the receiver may indicate that he or she wants to close the conversation by summarizing and repeating the intended/decided-upon action. The call should end with some expression of good-will, such as "Thanks for calling", "Pleasure talking with you", or "I will get back to you."

## Voice Mail

Voice mail facility is a common feature of an organization's phone system. It is a means of digitally recording voice messages that can be saved and forwarded, or skipped and deleted. It allows executives to attend to calls when they are free. When they are busy with meetings or work outside the office, they can transfer their calls to voice mail and check messages from any location at any time.

The voice mail message should sound as natural as possible and should be courteous. The caller should be able to recognize it as the intended receiver's voice. The recorded message may be something like "This is Pallavi Mehta in the R&D department. Please leave me a message. I shall call you back. Thank you."

## Conference Calls

Telephones and cell phones have a conferencing system that allows several persons to talk with each other at the same time. This technology is now commonly used by companies across the globe.

There can be two types of business calls. The first is a one-way closed circuit communication that allows employees to tune in and hear an announcement; for example, daily/early morning progress reports, plant production reports, or other briefings are simultaneously heard by dozens of widely spread out persons via the phone and/or a public announcement system.

The second type of call is interactive. A number of persons can be on the same conference call. In this system, each participant can listen as well as talk. Through a conference call, different members of a team working on a project together are able to update themselves on the progress, made by the team without conducting meetings face-to-face. Through the interactive conference call system, each team member can interact with others from their own work location. This saves companies' time and transportation costs. Moreover, the interaction is real-time and can happen as and when required.

Conference calls are used by most organizations as a routine communication channel for planning, updating, coordinating, and monitoring activities without requiring employees to travel long distances for a meeting of a few hours.

## Cell Phones

Cellular phones are a popular instrument of communication worldwide. Their utility for business executives has been greatly enhanced by the introduction of General Packet Radio Services (GPRS) technology. GPRS technology allows the radio transmission of small packets of data, especially between mobile phones and the Internet. Mobile handsets enabled with GPRS technology do the work of laptops/computers and voice recorders. They are more convenient than laptops, as they are smaller and easier to transport.

## Video Conferencing

Internet-enabled video conferencing is an electronic version of face-to-face communication. Business meetings, interviews, and other urgent interactions among several distantly located individuals can be effectively conducted without requiring participants to move from their respective places of work. Video conferencing is more complex than talking on the phone. It involves the use of cameras for images and phones for speech and sound communicated back and forth over the Internet. As with face-to-face communication, video conferencing calls for a whole range of oral skills, such as clear and natural speaking, attentive listening, and positive body language. For successful video conferencing, the following points may be kept in mind:

- Choose a quiet place as this will eliminate background noise.
- Set sound/volume to an appropriate level.
- Ensure that the faces of the speakers are visible by checking the lighting in the room.
- Sit comfortably facing the camera. Do not move unnecessarily.
- Wait for the image of the other person and your own image to appear on the screen before beginning the discussion.
- At the beginning of the conversation, introduce yourself and your team to the other party.
- Wait for the transmission to complete before responding. Due to technical issues, there may be pauses between the two speakers.
- Always direct your message or question by specifying the person you are addressing.
- Treat video conferencing as an audio–visual medium of relaxed business and social communication connecting people in different locations.

# TELEPHONIC COMMUNICATION

In telephone conversations, the way we listen, respond, speak, or hang up is often as important as what is communicated.

> **2** Know how to handle telephone and cell phone calls.

## Making a Call

Before initiating a call, be clear about the *why* (purpose) and *what* (content) of the call, how to begin the call, and what to do if the call is cut off.

### *Prepare Before Calling*

For business calls, you must know exactly who you want to speak to and choose the most convenient time to make the call. You should also know whether you are calling to follow up on earlier communication or if it is the first step in the interaction.

- To be brief and concise, jot down the points you want to discuss and think about the order in which to discuss them. Always keep these notes at hand when making the call.
- Keep a notepad and pen ready to write down any information worth recording.
- Consider whether the call is important from your point of view or from the receiver's point of view. In the latter case, structure your information from the receiver's point of interest. Begin first with what is important for the receiver. Talk about your interests later.
- Keep the conversation as short as possible. The other person may not be able to spare much time for your call. During the office hours, call the landline number first, directly or through the assist-

ant, depending on your familiarity with the person. Cell phones should be used in case of urgent matters or when the relationship is of a personal nature.

- Calling a cell phone from a landline number should be avoided as it may give the impression to the receiver that you are taking their availability for granted. In addition, the receiver may not recognize the number if it is not in their cell phone directory.
- Avoid calling a cell phone number through an administrative assistant. It might give an impression of discourtesy.
- Avoid the use of cell phones in movie halls, crowded restaurants, hospitals, fuel stations, and so on. Cell phones should be switched off or kept in the silent mode during meetings and important discussions. People whose calls you have missed in such a situation should be called back later.

### How to Begin or Receive a Call

The first few words spoken by the caller or receiver are important for establishing identities and the purpose of the call. They create the context for further conversation.

> The first few words spoken by the caller or receiver are important for establishing identities and the purpose of the call. They create the context for further conversation.

As a caller, you may not be personally known to the receiver. The receiver may be familiar with your purpose and your company, but may not exactly know you unless you have met in person or spoken to each other earlier. Therefore, begin by introducing yourself—state your name, company, and purpose.

In organizations, calls are generally routed through a receptionist. The usual practice at the reception is to attend to the call within five rings; if you have been kept waiting longer than that, the receptionist will usually greet you with an apology. If your call is not answered even after ten rings, it is advisable to disconnect and try calling later, or try another number, if any.

Greet the receptionist ("Good morning"); tell him or her your name and your organization's name, and then mention whom you want to speak with. When speaking with a personal assistant, use the same introduction and tell him or her the purpose of the call. He or she will connect you to the desired person only after checking whether he or she is free to talk to you at that moment. Remember to be patient and pleasant while dealing with the assistant, who is an important link between the caller and the desired contact person.

> Remember to be patient and pleasant while dealing with the assistant, who is an important link between the caller and the desired contact person.

If the receiver does not know you, you should first introduce yourself, for instance by saying something like "Good morning Mr Chaturvedi, I am Pallavi Mehta, marketing manager of Ferns n Petals. I want to know the details of your company's order for floral decoration…". As a caller, you should use the opportunity to make the receiver feel that the information you want can be acquired only from him or her and that it is required immediately. In other words, involve the receiver in a dialogue, instead of questions that can be answered just by saying "yes" or "no". Suppose you say, "Can I have the details of…", the receiver can respond by saying, "No, not now" and may hang up. Hence, use your conversational skills to establish a good relationship with the other person so that the call ends on a positive note.

In the case of a cell phone conversation, it is always better to check if you are clearly audible. You may be able to hear the other side clearly, but it is possible that the other side is not able to hear you completely because of a poor signal. During official meetings, it is always better to keep the cell phone on silent mode. If you are expecting an important call, you may like to inform the chair about it before the meeting begins and step outside after excusing yourself. It is also necessary to keep all such calls short.

The ring tone expresses a person's style. However, it should be in sync with the environment of the workplace. The volume of the phone's ring should not be too loud. Similarly, the volume of the person should also not be very loud. Sometimes, people discuss even confidential matters so loudly that the entire floor can hear them.

#### *If the Call Is Disconnected*

Sometimes, the call may be suddenly disconnected or dropped. In such situations, courtesy demands that the person who originally initiated the call should redial immediately and say, "Sorry, the call got disconnected". In case the receiver has to suspend the call to attend to some other more important call, it is the duty of the receiver to resume the call and give a satisfactory explanation to ensure that the caller does not feel slighted.

### Common Telephone Courtesies

Always use the interrogative form for making a request, such as "Could I…?" or "May I…?" as Direct categorical statements may seem like an order. "I want to talk to…" is not a polite request. Instead "May I talk to…" is more polite. Even the statement, "I request you to connect me to so and so number/person" is not quite appropriate when ones does not know the other party well. Instead, say, "May I request you to…".

### Telephone Etiquette Observed by Administrative Assistants

In business, telephone calls are mostly received by personal assistants. Sometimes, the assistant has to act quickly to find out whether his or her supervisor is free to talk. So they may say, "Please hold on" while they check. If their supervisor is present but does not want to speak to the caller for some reason, the assistant will choose any one of the following polite excuses:

"Sorry, she is busy in a meeting. May I have your number? She will call you back".

"He is busy with a foreign delegation. May I ask him to call you back as soon as he is free?"

These statements may not necessarily be true. However, they are intended to keep the caller satisfied even when the call is not successful. Personal assistants should never try to overhear the conversation between the caller and the receiver. After putting through the call to their supervisor, they should hang up.

### Telephone Precautions

As a caller you do not know whether the person receiving your call is alone. Therefore, confidential matters should never be discussed over the phone. They can be overheard/tapped in transmission. However, if you have to discuss something personal that you do not want others to know, you should check with the person you are calling in a polite manner. For example, you may say, "Can we talk about the tender for the Golden Highway project?" or simply, "Are you free? Can we talk about the tender?" This would save you from causing any embarrassment to the receiver or risk being overheard.

Communication over the phone requires the use of non-verbal skills, such as pleasant tone, proper intonation, and clear articulation of words. You should be able to convey a large part of the message through your way of speaking rather than the meaning of the words alone.

> Communication over the phone requires the use of non-verbal skills, such as pleasant tone, proper intonation, and clear articulation of words.

## INTERVIEWS

An interview can be defined as an oral tool used to test a candidate's suitability for employment or admission to an institute of learning. As it is an oral test, it calls for the skills of oral and non-verbal communication, which are necessary to impress the interviewers. There are different types of interviews, such as panel interviews, sequential interviews, academic interviews, personality interviews, and so on. Each type requires the careful application of a particular set of communication skills.

3

Learn the art of handling interviews well.

### Types of Interviews

The types of interviews frequently encountered by job applicants are:

- *Panel interviews:* In a panel interview, each member of the panel is closely observing the interviewee. Hence, the interviewee's body language and eye contact are especially important. The interviewee should give the impression of speaking to all the members of the panel, not just a single individual, by making eye contact with all panel members.
- *Telephone interviews:* The interviewee should consider this a face-to-face interview and use proper modulation of voice to reflect his or her thoughts. The interviewee's voice should be clear, steady, and audible.
- *Lunch/dinner interviews:* This type of interview is conducted in an informal environment, but still requires that the interviewee be careful about his or her body language and manners. The interviewee should never drink alcohol at an interview, even if the interviewer does.
- *Preliminary interviews:* As a preliminary interview is a first-stage screening test, the interviewee should pay full attention to it. This stage must be cleared before moving to the final interview. The interviewee's communication skills express his or her confidence and ease.
- *Sequential interviews:* In this form of interview, the interviewee has to report to several people successively. He or she should be very careful about his or her behaviour, speech, and manners in each interview, as each interviewer is a prospective employer.
- *Skill-based interviews:* Such interviews require the interviewee to demonstrate skills that are relevant to the job. For instance, someone seeking to be an actor or a salesperson can be asked to act or read a script or demonstrate his or her pitch and skills of persuasive oral communication.
- *Academic interviews:* An academic interview is conducted in a question-and-answer format. The interviewee should be able to demonstrate attentive listening, eye contact, clarity of ideas, and depth of knowledge.
- *Personality interviews:* This form of interview evaluates the interviewee as an individual in terms of his or her response to certain situations. The emphasis is not on the answers themselves, but on *how* they are delivered. The entire range of non-verbal communication skills are brought into play to demonstrate a "well-rounded personality."

### What Does a Job Interview Assess?

According to the employer's needs, interviewers look for the following attributes in candidates:

- *Clarity:* This refers to the candidate's clarity on academic subjects, his or her career objectives, the reasons for these objectives, long-term goals, national and global issues, and so on.

- *Depth:* Depth of knowledge and understanding across a wide range of subjects and issues, along with clarity, demonstrate the candidate's academic excellence.
- *Personality:* A candidate's attitude, honesty, and professionalism reflect his or her ability to work in an organization and with other people. In addition, the candidate's self-awareness and analysis of personal strengths and weaknesses are important.
- *General awareness:* This refers to the interviewee's level of general awareness about current issues of national and international concern.
- *Application of concepts to real-life problems:* The interviewee's initiative and capacity for independent thought are judged by responses to application-based questions, which assess how far he or she has moved beyond classroom learning.
- *Communication skills:* The candidate's ability to express his or her thoughts clearly and concisely is evaluated along with his or her listening and comprehension skills. In addition, his or her verbal and non-verbal communication and body language exhibit his or her personality as an individual. Assessment of individuals in a job interview is basically an effort to predict their behaviour in a particular job and in the environment of that job.
- *Integrity:* The candidate's integrity is important to prospective employers. Employers look for consistency in what is written in the CV and the interviewee's responses to questions during the interview. Since the résumé is the starting point of the interview, applicants should know their résumés thoroughly and be prepared to discuss and explain anything on them. It is therefore extremely important to be honest when drafting the CV.

Assessment of individuals in a job interview is basically an effort to predict their behaviour in a particular job and in the environment of that job.

Employers look for consistency in what is written in the CV and the interviewee's responses to questions during the interview. It is therefore extremely important to be honest when drafting the CV.

Since the résumé is the starting point of the interview, applicants should know their résumés thoroughly and be prepared to discuss and explain anything on them.

## Focus of Job Interviews

Though each job has its own specific requirements, there are some elements that are common. Most interviews focus on three issues:

- Technical competence
- Motivation
- The candidate's ability to handle situations where he or she does not know the answer

### *Technical Competence*

Technical competence is assessed by examining the candidate's academic background and previous job profiles. For instance, if someone is applying to be a salesperson, his or her knowledge of marketing and sales management and logistics will be tested. The questions asked are related to the candidate's specialization, but are usually of a general nature. They are generally application-based questions.

Suppose you are an applicant for a sales position at Godrej. The interviewers can assess your technical competence by asking questions such as: "What features of our Godrej mini-fridge would you highlight to promote its sale in rural markets?" Your answer would demonstrate your knowledge of the principles of selling in general as well as your ability to apply those principles to a specific, targeted group.

### *Motivation*

All employers want to evaluate a prospective employee's level of interest in a job and how strongly he or she wants to fulfill his or her goals. For instance, in an interview for a sales job, the candidate's motivation can be judged by posing a complex situation (for instance, a transportation strike at the same time as an important meeting with a dealer) and then asking how the candidate would react to it.

Sometimes interviewers may deliberately ask stressful questions, such as "what would you do if you are not selected for this position?". The actual responses to such questions are not as important as how the candidate handles them.

### *Handling Difficult Questions*

When an interviewee does not know the answer to a question, there are several ways to approach it:

- Admit it. He or she can say, "Sorry, I do not know the answer to that."
- Make an educated guess. The candidate can guess and preface the answer with, "I guess/I think/ Perhaps it could mean…".
- The interviewee should not get flustered. Instead, he or should continue to communicate a positive state of mind by making eye contact and using positive facial expressions, tone, and volume of speech.

Interviewees should continuously reflect upon various aspects of their personality and goals in order to respond to different questions at job interviews with clarity and confidence. Since one's style of thinking determines behaviour and personality to a great extent, it helps to consider, in some detail, how one thinks.

## Strategies for Success at Interviews

A candidate's success in converting an interview opportunity into a job offer depends on how well he or she has prepared for the interview. Most candidates falter during an interview only because they do not know enough about themselves, the company they are applying for, or the job profile. The secret of clearing the interview stage lies in preparing a game plan and developing a strategy to target what the specific organization is seeking. First, the candidate's personality traits matter: is he or she motivated, mature, ambitious, and trustworthy? Second, the candidate's level of competence and realism regarding job expectations matter: a candidate can impress prospective employers only when he or she demonstrates solid knowledge of the industry and the job.

As a practical step, job applicants can equip themselves with the following information and knowledge before an interview:

(i) Know yourself
(ii) Know the company
(iii) Know the job profile

### *Know Yourself*

The candidate should ask himself or herself: "Who am I? What are my achievements? What are my skills and strengths? What do I plan to do five years from now?" He or she must be clear about his or her goals and consistent regarding past achievements and future career plans. In addition, he or she should be realistic—if his or her skills, career plans, and

The candidate should ask himself or herself: "Who am I? What are my achievements? What are my skills and strengths? What do I plan to do five years from now?" He or she must be clear about his or her goals and consistent regarding past achievements and future career plans.

objectives align closely with the job's requirements, chances are that he or she will be offered the job. Most interviews begin with a question like "Can you tell us something about yourself?" so it is important to have a clear response ready.

Some ways to know yourself better are to:

- Identify your skills—concentrate on what you can do well.
- Determine what you value—things that are important to you and influence your behaviour.
- Be clear about what motivates you and what you are looking for—whether it is status, security, power, expertise, material rewards, creativity, autonomy.
- Describe your personality—your behaviour and mental characteristics.
- Find out how you think—if you are especially logical, intuitive, or creative, for instance.

An employer does not look for a set of ready-made answers to a volley of questions. Answers do count. But, there is something else that matters a great deal: the personality that accompanies the answers. Employers want to hire a good person, a competent worker, and someone with a well-informed and well-rounded personality.

> Employers want to hire a good person, a competent worker, and someone with a well-informed and well-rounded personality.

***Know the Company***

Job applicants must gather information and research the company they are applying to before the interview. They can learn about the work culture and norms of the company and read up on the company's products and other details through the company's reports and Web site. If possible, they should try to interact with company employees to learn more about the work environment. Then, they should assess the size and systems of the company in accordance with their own ambitions and career plan, and consider how far the company will offer growth opportunities. Reflecting on these aspects of the company prior to the interview will prepare a candidate for the employer's questions.

***Know the Job Profile***

At the interview, one should never be carried away by the salary or designation of the job; rather, the job should be considered in terms of its profile, scope for growth, and one's professional goals and ambitions. This also means that one should not accept a job, however lucrative, in a company that does not suit one's personal goals.

> At the interview, one should never be carried away by the salary or designation of the job; rather, the job should be considered in terms of its profile, scope for growth, and one's professional goals and ambitions.

## Answers to Some Common Interview Questions

Usually, the interviewers move from simple, personal questions to general and then technical questions. The questions put to new graduates focus more on their education and work experiences, current issues, and hobbies. The focus is on education and personality. In the case of candidates with more experience, the focus is on their recent projects, achievements, and what new thing they can do for the organization.

Exhibit 8.1 provides some common questions faced in interviews and explains how a candidate can tackle these questions.

The questions given here are representative of the types of questions you can expect at an interview, though of course the list is not exhaustive. The secret of facing interviews successfully lies in thorough preparation so that one can display a full understanding of content and a well-rounded personality in the interview. Aim at making a good first impression and remember that one has just three to five seconds to do so. Ninety per cent of people form a judgment regarding someone at a job interview in just

**Q: Tell us about yourself.**
(Provide a brief answer describing your educational background and relevant work experience. A sample response follows.)

**A:** I was born in Pilani and completed my education there. After graduating from Birla Public School, I attended Birla Institute of Technology and Science and obtained a dual degree in MMS and Mathematics. I did my summer project at DCM Kota and six months' industry internships at USHA International Delhi in the marketing division, promoting a product line similar to your household durables. I believe I am motivated and capable of doing hard work.

**Q: What are your strengths?**
(Focus on your positive side.)

**A:** I think I am an intelligent, hard-working person who likes to take initiative and shoulder responsibility and complete my assigned tasks to everyone's satisfaction.

**Q: What are your weaknesses?**
(Avoid suggesting anything that could be perceived as detrimental to your working effectively and efficiently. You could talk about a weakness that's not central to the job you are applying for and then indicate how you are working on trying to overcome the weakness.)

***Undesirable response:***

**A:** "My greatest weakness is that I am a workaholic." (Most interviewers would say that this is not really a weakness, and this is probably the most common response they have heard.)

***Desirable response:***

**A:** "I find public speaking stressful, so I have been attending a short course on public speaking for the past three weeks." (Make sure that the job does not require public speaking.)

**Q: Why do you wish to work in our organization?**
(Be objective, realistic, and rational.)

**A:** I know a number of persons working in this organization. I appreciate its work culture and concern for each individual employee. I like the flexibility that allows employees to move from one area to another within the organization.

**Q: Why have you been changing jobs?**
(Discuss how your past experience has helped you in developing skills that will be useful in your new job; it would be better not to answer as follows: "It is generally believed that if you want to grow vertically, you should not work at one position or place for more than four years.)

**Q: Tell us how you can contribute to our company.**
(Without claiming too much, state in specific terms what you are capable of doing for the company.)

**A:** Besides working to improve the sales figures of the division, I would develop the market for mobile editions of our publications.

**Q: If the company could secure the National Highway Golden Triangle Project by bribing the concerned CEO, would you do it?**
(Such questions are asked to judge your sense of morality. Always say no, and give your reasons by praising the organization's reputation for upholding ethical values and moral practices in all spheres.)

**A:** Keeping in view the reputation of the company, one should not even consider it.

**Exhibit 8.1** Model Questions and Answers

**Q: Could you tell us something about your current responsibilities?**
(Describe those areas of work that show your initiative and organizing ability. Be factual, but project your own skills in handling your present duties.)

**A:** Presently, I am the business development manager at Shop-n-Shop. I am responsible for developing the retail business of the company's writing instruments division. This calls for opening company-owned retail outlets in organized setups like malls.

**Q: What are your salary expectations?**
(Justify your expectations in terms of your present package. The challenges of the new job are the reasons for your interest in it, not a better salary alone.)

**A:** My present package is Rs 9.6 lakh per year. Keeping in view my desire to work for a professional organization like this, I would expect the protection of my current salary, at the least, and would like a raise of about 15 to 20 per cent.

**Exhibit 8.1** *Continued*

that time. In 70 per cent of cases, these first impressions prove to be right. Decisive factors in making an impression are body language, clothes, status symbols, scent, and the person's voice.

## GROUP DISCUSSION

The group discussion (GD) tests inter-personal skills. It is most popular with public/private sector undertakings, government departments, commercial firms, and universities and other educational organizations, which use it to screen candidates after a written test. What does a group discussion evaluate? A group discussion primarily evaluates participants' ability to interact in a group that is discussing a given topic. An individual's behaviour in a group means much for his or her success as a manager or an executive responsible for coordinating and organizing activities. The evaluators, therefore, focus on group dynamics rather than the content of each participant's views.

4 Be an effective participant in group discussions.

The group usually consists of 8 to 10 candidates. No one is nominated as a leader, coordinator, or chairman. Normally, 20 to 30 minutes are given to complete the discussion. Each candidate has a roll number by which he or she is to be addressed. For easy recognition, the roll number is prominently displayed on a tag worn by each candidate. The candidates are seated in ascending order of roll numbers, usually in a circle.

### Leadership

As group discussions start without an official leader, the atmosphere allows all participants free and equal opportunity to express their views. During the course of the discussion, a leader often emerges. No candidate should try to dominate the group to become the leader. Such an attempt is self-defeating, because in a group discussion all participants are supposed to be equal. However, a candidate, by his or her initiative, ability to direct the discussion, maturity, clarity of ideas, and understanding of group dynamics, might gradually begin to direct the course of the

In a group discussion, all participants are supposed to be equal. No one is officially chosen as the leader. However, a candidate, by his or her initiative, ability to direct the discussion, maturity, clarity of ideas, and understanding of group dynamics, might gradually begin to direct the course of the discussion and mediate between opposing views to evolve a comprehensive view.

discussion and mediate between opposing views to evolve a comprehensive view. Such a candidate is implicitly recognized by all other candidates as the leader of the discussion group.

## GD Protocol

Group discussions are "formally informal". There are rules of conduct to be observed by the participants. Some of these rules are discussed in Exhibit 8.2.

## Discussion Techniques

A group discussion is not a debate in which each participant either opposes or supports the topic. There are no clear-cut positions or stands required. A group discussion is a continuous discussion,

- Ways of addressing other members of the group:

  "Sir/Madam": too formal

  "Mr/Ms": too colloquial

  "Excuse me": a bit rude

  By their roll numbers: a bit odd

  First name: ideal

  The problem is it may be difficult to remember the names of fellow participants in a short time. In this case, the best way is to address the whole group instead of an individual.
- Do not create sub-groups by referring to individual members. The tendency is to speak to one's neighbour, but this creates sub-groups and acts against the cohesive team spirit of the group.
- Gaining the entire group's attention:
  - To begin, speak to the person sitting diagonally opposite you. Alternatively, address the person who has just finished talking.
  - When you have the group's attention, use the opportunity to take the discussion forward. Do not let an opportunity pass by if you want to participate in the discussion.
  - Make friends by speaking to those who have been left alone by the rest of the group.
  - Do not invite somebody who has been keeping quiet to share his or her views unless you have the formal authority to do so; everyone is equal in a group discussion.
- It is best to use language that is formal, simple, and correct. It should not be colloquial or flowery.
- One should dress formally for a group discussion. Men should wear business suits and women should be in sarees, *salwar kameezes*, or formal trousers and shirts.
- Body language is important:
  - Posture should be formal and must reflect enthusiasm (straight back; hands in front/on the edge of the table).
  - Gestures and body movements should not be threatening or restrictive to other participants.
  - Excessive hand movements should be avoided.
  - Body language should be natural.
  - One should establish eye contact with as many people as possible.
- No one should attempt to be a leader by trying to sum up or conclude when the group has not clearly reached any conclusion.

**Exhibit 8.2** GD Protocol

an ongoing interaction in which participants examine a subject or problem from different angles and viewpoints. Participants may disagree with or support others' points of view, or bring up a new point of view. But, it is essential for all participants to always show respect for others, even if they disagree with each other. Courtesy in discussions indicates a level of politeness and maturity.

Good analytical abilities, critical assessment of arguments, and strong verbal and non-verbal skills of communication can give one a competitive edge over others. Exhibit 8.3 presents some guidelines for GD participants.

A group discussion is not a debate in which each participant either opposes or supports the topic. There are no clear-cut positions or stands required.

- **To join in the discussion, the following phrases can be used:**

  I'd like to raise the subject of …
  What I think is …
  I think it's important to consider the question of …
  If I could say a word about …
  May I make a point about …

- **When supporting what another participant has said, remember that you should not say, "I agree with him/her". Instead, you should say that you support their *views*—not the person.) Phrases that can be used are:**

  I'd like to support Renuka's point about …
  That is what I think too.
  I agree fully with what Rahul has just said.

- **When voicing disagreement, again remember that you are opposed to someone's *ideas* and not the person. You can disagree by using polite expressions instead of saying something curt such as "You are wrong". For instance, you can say:**

  Please allow me to differ.
  I beg to differ.
  I think differently on this issue.
  I do not agree; in my opinion …

- **To emphasize a point, one can say:**

  I am convinced that …
  You can't deny that …
  It is quite clear to me that …

- **To bring the discussion back on track, one can say:**

  That's very interesting, but I don't think it is relevant to the point.
  Perhaps we could go back to …
  Could we stick to the subject please?
  I am afraid we are drifting from the original point.

**Exhibit 8.3** Guidelines for GD Participants

### Listening

In a group discussion, listening too is a participative act. Participants should listen thoughtfully to what others have to say, with the goal of assimilating and analysing rather than contradicting or refuting others. Instead of interrupting others, it is better to try to join the discussion tactfully and use words that demonstrate that you have been listening to others.

## NEGOTIATION SKILLS

5

Explain the negotiation process.

Negotiation is a process of bargaining in which two parties, each of which has something that the other wants, try to reach an agreement on mutually accepted terms.

Negotiation is a process of bargaining in which two parties, each of which has something that the other wants, try to reach an agreement on mutually accepted terms. Everyday examples of negotiation are:

- A brother and a sister debating which movie to watch
- Two friends trying to settle the amount for which one wants to sell his old car to the other
- Two sisters fighting over how a box of chocolates should be divided between them
- An employee making a suggestion to her manager regarding her salary
- A salesperson trying to arrange a meeting with a prospective wholesaler/dealer

The *Oxford Dictionary of Business English* defines negotiation as:

(a) "a process of trying to reach an agreement through discussion",

(b) "a meeting where this discussion takes place".

*The Winston Simplified Dictionary* defines negotiation as, "the discussion and bargaining that goes on between parties before a contract is settled or a deal is definitely agreed upon". Alan Fowler defines negotiation as "a process of intervention by which two or more parties who consider that they need to be jointly involved in any outcome, but who initially have different objectives, seek by the use of argument and persuasion to resolve their differences in order to achieve a mutually acceptable solution"1. According to Bill Scott, "A negotiation is a form of meeting between two parties: our party and the other party"[1]. The objective of most negotiations is to reach an agreement in which both parties together move towards an outcome that is mutually beneficial.

### The Nature of Negotiation

The following points make the nature of negotiation quite clear:

1. Negotiation takes place between two parties. Both the parties are equally interested in finding a satisfactory result.
2. Negotiation leads to agreement through discussion, not instructions, orders, or power/influence/authority.

When a manager deals with other managers or customers and suppliers over whom he or she has no authority, he or she tries to reach an agreement through discussion, persuasion, and argument. In other words, the manager must negotiate with the other party.

Suppose you are a manager in the marketing department of a company. You need the help of an analyst from another department to complete an urgent project report. The other department may not be willing to spare the services of the analyst you badly need. You would need to discuss the matter with your colleagues and make your case using convincing arguments, by negotiating with the analyst and the other department. Reaching an agreement is the objective of negotiation.

> Reaching an agreement is the objective of negotiation.

Consider the following situation, which shows how negotiations work.

Mr and Mrs Rai wanted to sell their house. They had approached many property dealers in their area. Several agents had seen their property and knew their intentions, including the minimum price they would be willing to accept. The Rais quickly realized that in their area, nearly every property agent had come to know of their desire to sell the house as early as possible. This worked against them, and every time they were made an offer, it was lower than the previous one. They became desperate and began to believe that it would not be possible to sell their house for a reasonable price because they made the mistake of disclosing their keenness to sell. One day, they happened to mention this to one of their friends. He gave them the contact information of a very prominent builder, Mr Devraj, from another part of the city. Mr Devraj answered the Rais' call and immediately enquired about the location of the plot and the built-up area. Next, he asked them their asking price. He paused, and then said, "Think about the price again". This made the Rais feel a bit shaky. They had told him the price they wanted, not the prices the property dealers had offered them thus far. Not wanting to lose the chance of selling their house, they reduced their asking price by Rs 5 lakh. Mr Devraj promptly asked, "Is that final?" With some trepidation, they said, "Yes". In a businesslike tone, he said, "Done" and promised to send them Rs 10 lakh as an advance the next day. He also remarked that he would have the remaining amount sent within a week. The Rais wanted him to see the house, but he said, "There is no need for that; I am familiar with the sector".

At the time of the full and final payment, the Rais learnt that they were not able to get the desired price for the house from other, smaller property dealers because the house had an old-fashioned design and would need to be demolished. What these property dealers were offering was the price of the land only. However, Mr Devraj, being a builder, would be able to use the basic architecture and give the house a new look.

## The Need for Negotiation

The need to negotiate is defined by the situation. Some situations require negotiating, others don't.

### *Situations Requiring Negotiation*

Negotiation is necessary when an issue involves more than one person and the problem cannot be resolved by a single person. Whenever two or more persons or parties are involved, they are bound to have different views or aims regarding the outcome. The way to overcome disagreement is by negotiating.

Negotiation can take place only when both concerned parties are willing to meet and discuss the issue at hand. That is, they both must want to reach a decision by discussion, not force or authority.

There are formal and informal situations in negotiation.

### *Formal Negotiations*

- There is a prearranged meeting of the two parties.
- The agenda is already fixed, and both parties know what is going to be discussed.
- Generally, more than two persons are involved in the discussion.
- In formal negotiations, there is time to prepare and assign roles for each person in each party. For instance, one person can put forth their side's reasons and suggestions, another can explain the

side's points more thoroughly, and the third can closely follow the flow of the discussion and point out anything that has been missed.

- A formal negotiation is simpler to handle than unannounced meetings. There is time to study the entire situation and find out the strengths and weaknesses of the other party.

A formal negotiation is simpler to handle than unannounced meetings.

Generally, a formal negotiation is for settling a dispute or a conflict between two warring parties, such as for a labour or workers' strike. Negotiations in such situations are formal; the meeting between the two parties is fixed beforehand and both parties have time to prepare their bargaining points.

***Informal Negotiations*** Informal negotiations are unannounced and casual meetings, such as when a staff member drops by a colleague's office and discusses a problem, which they attempt to resolve. This is an informal negotiation because:

- It is unannounced.
- It involves just two persons.
- It appears casual (although the colleague who initiated the discussion might have planned this approach deliberately).
- It does not give one time to prepare for the discussion, so one cannot study the strengths or weaknesses of the other side.
- Its friendly and informal approach is meant to influence the outcome.

***Situations Not Requiring Negotiation***

The following types of situations will not require negotiation:

- When one of the two parties/persons immediately accepts or agrees to what the other is suggesting. In such a situation, there is no need for negotiating. The desired result is already achieved.
- Whenever one of the two parties refuses even to consider or discuss the suggestion or proposal. For example, suppose a supplier or a dealer completely refuses to reduce the price or consider any suggestion of partial payments, there is no possibility for negotiation.

However, people often encounter situations in which there is neither direct acceptance nor complete refusal at the outset. In such cases, the two persons deal with each other by discussing the possibility of reaching a mutually acceptable end.

## Factors Affecting Negotiation

6

Understand the factors affecting negotiation.

The factors discussed in this section usually affect the outcomes of negotiations.

***Location***

The location of a negotiation can influence the level of confidence of one party. When the location is one party's office, for instance, that party has several advantages. They are on home ground, an area of strength. They can access whatever information or material is needed during the course of the negotiation. They can also extend social courtesies as a token of goodwill; this could move the negotiation towards agreement.

***Timing***

- The choice of time for holding discussions and the length of the discussion should be fixed according to mutual convenience.

- There should be adequate time for the smooth exchange of ideas through different stages of negotiation. The preparation time and the timeframe for implementing the agreement afterwards should also be carefully fixed.
- To be effective, negotiations should be timely. That means they should be carried out before it is too late to reach an agreement.

### *Subjective Factors*

7 Know about the subjective factors that affect negotiation outcomes.

Often the outcome of a discussion does not depend wholly on objective factors, such as logic and the facts of the matter under consideration. The final outcome may also be determined by subjective factors relating to influence and persuasion.

1. *Individual relationships:* The conduct of negotiations is influenced not only by the real situation of the matter, but also by the relationship and rapport between the two persons/parties involved in the process of discussion.
2. *Fear of authority:* Often one side's bargaining power is conditioned by fear of authority, higher connections, and the other party's capacity to hurt their professional future.
3. *Future and practical considerations:* When personal relationships are at stake, the negotiators may not wish to win the argument at the cost of the relationship. Moreover, the fear of losing business in the future is a strong factor in bargaining/negotiation positions, as is the effect on the participants' reputations.
4. *Mutual obligations:* The memories of past favours by the other party may also influence the negotiation.
5. *Personal considerations:* Self-questioning helps the negotiator identify the factors influencing his or her bargaining position and strengths. Both, formal and informal negotiations, are influenced by questions, such as:
   - "How does my position on this proposal/issue take into account the likely effect on our future working relationship?"
   - "Am I allowing myself to be unduly influenced by a sense of obligation? Am I hoping to achieve too much by emphasizing past obligations?"
   - "What are my goals for this negotiation?"

### *Persuasive Skills and the Use of You-attitude*

Persuasion includes a range of skills for convincing other people of the need to accept or agree to a course of action.

Persuasion includes a range of skills for convincing other people of the need to accept or agree to a course of action. It is an essential element of effective business communication. It helps in resolving issues on which there is a difference of opinion, but that need solutions that are in the interest of all. In negotiations, people are gradually persuaded to accept the other party's view to some extent.

As you must have seen yourself, persuasion is not one single thing. It is a mixture of skills—attitude, psychology, language, tone, body language, and so on—used to convince the other party to accept one's view despite their objections or alternate proposals.

"You attitude" is an essential aspect of negotiations. Nothing convinces more than facts. But, in order to persuade people, the facts should be discussed from the other party's point of view. A skilled negotiator should be able to highlight how the other person stands to gain from his or her suggestions. He or she must understand the other party's needs and be able to reconcile what would be a good result for him or her with the needs of the other party. This allows persuasion to end negotiations and discussions with a satisfying conclusion for both sides (creating a win–win situation).

> Persuasion is not just one single thing. It is a mixture of skills—attitude, psychology, language, tone, body language, and so on—used to convince the other party to accept one's view despite their objections or alternate proposals.

The range of persuasive skills can be classified under the following broad headings:

- Style: Being collaborative rather than confrontational
- You attitude: considering the other person's viewpoint
- Talking and listening
- Probing and questioning
- Taking breaks when necessary
- Concessions and compromises
- Summarizing
- Reaching an agreement

> A skilled negotiator must understand the other party's needs and be able to reconcile what would be a good result for him or her with the needs of the other party.

At the end of the discussion, both sides should be sure that the final agreement covers all necessary points and they are clearly expressed and understood.

## Stages in the Negotiation Process

> 8
> Understand the stages in the negotiation process.

Generally, the process of negotiation moves from the stage of "offer" to that of "agreement" via the stages of "counter-offer", "concession", and "compromise". All discussions that progress successfully from opening differences to a final, mutually acceptable outcome/conclusion usually move through the same general sequence. During informal discussions, this sequence may not always be obvious, yet it is there with respect to the most important aspects of negotiations.

According to Alan Fowler, the stages of an effective discussion are:

- Preparing and planning
- Exchanging initial views
- Exploring possible compromises
- Searching for common ground
- Securing an agreement
- Implementing the agreement

> At the end of the discussion, both sides should be sure that the final agreement covers all necessary points and they are clearly expressed and understood.

These six stages can be grouped into three basic phases:

- A preparation phase before the negotiation begins
- The actual negotiating process—the interaction that leads to the final agreement and an outcome
- The implementation of the agreement

> Negotiation implies that both parties accept that an agreement between them is needed (required or desirable) before any decision is to be implemented.

Negotiation implies that both parties accept that an agreement between them is needed (required or desirable) before any decision is to be implemented. The direction of the discussion is towards that desired agreement. Hence, it requires careful preparation and handling.

### *The Preparation Phase*

Like all effective communication/discussion, negotiations have to be planned. Tim Hindle, in his book *Negotiating Skills*, says, "Bear in mind that it is almost impossible for a negotiator to do too much preparation".[2]

There are two respects in which the negotiator has to be prepared before the negotiation:

- Assessing the relative strength of the two parties
- Setting negotiating objectives. At this stage, the negotiator should try to answer the following two questions:
    - What are the real issues?
    - Which parties should be involved?

Knowing the real issues at hand helps the negotiator feel confident and fully prepared about two things:

- That he/she knows the subject matter well and is not likely to be surprised by the other party introducing unexpected facts or figures
- That he/she is clear about the desired goal of the discussion

Negotiators should be realistic about their objectives. If they fail to persuade the other side to accept their ideal solution, they should be prepared to lower their expectations. If the ideal is not achievable, they should be very clear and firm about the lowest outcome acceptable to them. It is important for the negotiators to know what points they are willing to concede and what their limits are.

In the preparation stage, negotiators should also plan the best way of arguing their case, considering particularly the other person's likely viewpoint and objectives. They should assess the strength of each party's bargaining position. To be well prepared before the actual negotiating process begins, negotiators should:

- Be sure that they know enough about the subject matter to be discussed
- Decide their objectives and limits
- Plan how best to argue their case

### *The Negotiation Phase*

Most effective negotiations follow a set sequence:

- The parties begin by defining the issues at hand. They ascertain the scope of the negotiation.
- Each side then puts forward what it is seeking. First, the party that is making a claim presents its case, and then the other party gives an initial response—thus, both the parties define their initial positions.
- After that comes a more open phase in which the initial positions are tested through argument.
- The parties then move to discussing a possible solution that could result in a resolution.
- Firm proposals in more specific terms are then discussed and modified before both parties accept them.
- Finally, an agreement is spelled out and a conclusion is reached.

### *The Implementation Phase*

Some scholars do not consider the stages of preparation and implementation to be parts of negotiation. But, they constitute two basic phases of the actual process of negotiation—one before initiating the negotiation process and the other after concluding discussions.

Some scholars do not consider preparation and implementation to be parts of negotiation.

- The purpose of negotiation is to achieve a decision; the purpose of an agreement is to implement the agreed-upon decision/outcome.
- If due attention is not paid to the implementation of a negotiation, then the negotiation fails.

Three steps to prevent failure of implementation are:

- In all formal negotiations, confirm in writing all that has been agreed upon.
- As far as possible, mention an implementation programme in the agreement. This includes mentioning who is supposed to do what and by when. This matter, if left undefined, may become the subject of disagreement later.
- Ensure that every concerned person, not only those involved in the discussion, is told about the agreement, its implications, and the actions that are to follow.

## Negotiation Strategies

Some of the elements listed as part of the negotiation process are strategic in nature. They are discussed here as strategies to be used at different stages of negotiation.

9

Identify different skills of initiating, discussing, and concluding the process of bargaining.

### *Initial Strategies*

Before the negotiation, the negotiators must plan their strategies.

- A successful negotiation should plan the discussion according to the psychological needs of the other party and use appropriate strategies to maximize his or her advantage and gain information about the objectives of the other party.
- He or she should focus on the need to reach a mutually satisfactory conclusion by joint problem-solving.
- The negotiator should sell "sunny-side up". He or she should think about how the other person will see the proposal and should try to identify and "sell" the benefits of his or her case.
- The negotiator should be able to alter his or her position (within planned limits) if needed to achieve this approach.
- Instead of talking compulsively, a good negotiator allows the other party to say what they wish and develops a dialogue with them.

Instead of talking compulsively, a good negotiator allows the other party to say what they wish and develops a dialogue with them.

One can start the discussion with language such as: "The general point of our discussion is…, which I think has come up because of…. But, before I go into details, it would be helpful if you first outline your view".

### *During the Discussion*

The following are some strategies that should be used during the course of the negotiation:

- Neither side should state its entire case in the beginning of the discussion; this should develop as the discussion proceeds. If one side puts forth everything at the beginning, it leaves itself no chance to change position in light of the other side's arguments.

- It is important to listen carefully to the other speakers' arguments and notice their facial expressions, gestures, and body movements, in addition to the words. Non-verbal clues and cues will tell the listener how the other side feels—confident or nervous, irritated or calm.
- Neither side should interrupt the other. Interruptions annoy instead of encouraging cooperation.
- Good negotiators put forth searching questions to verify the correctness of facts offered by the other party, such as dates, figures, and so on, or of their logic. If a negotiator doubts the accuracy of the other side's information, he or she should not directly challenge them by saying, "You are wrong". Instead, the negotiator may ask further, probing questions, such as "Could you explain the connection between that point and what you said earlier about X?" or "I have not understood the logic of that. Could you put it in a different way?"
- One should not take on a confrontational tone. The strategy should be to allow the discussion to move towards agreement. To do this, one must psychologically encourage cooperation throughout the discussion.

The strategy should be to allow the discussion to move towards agreement. To do this, one must psychologically encourage cooperation throughout the discussion.

- Both parties should use impersonal terminology to point out corrections, rather than making personal criticisms.

Both parties should use impersonal terminology to point out corrections, rather than making personal criticisms.

- It can be useful to take breaks. During the discussion, a short break of 10 minutes can be useful for two purposes: to have a chance to consider new points or proposals before deciding on final commitments and to change the mood of the discussion, if it has become too emotionally charged.
- Both sides must use concessions and compromises. At times, it may be impossible to move further without making some concessions. Strategy is concerned partly with timing and partly with the way possible concessions are introduced into the discussion. When the participants realize that attitudes are hardening and the same points are being repeated without a resolution, the discussion could be changed to an exploratory phase.
- Participants can use conditional compromises, such as by saying things like, "Since we now know each other's initial views, could you tell me what your response would be if I accepted this part of X, which you have suggested?", "Would you do X if I agreed to do Y?", and "Would you be able to agree to X if I am able to postpone taking action on Y?"
- It helps to emphasize what the other person stands to benefit from the compromise. The other side should not feel that he/she is losing by accepting the concession or compromise. Some tips include:
    - Commending and thanking the other party for a good suggestion.
    - Not allowing the discussion to go on for too long without bringing in concessions/compromises necessary for reaching agreement.
    - Introducing concessions/compromises on a non-commitment basis.
    - Seeing that the concessions made by each side match.

***Reaching an Agreement***

Tips for reaching a final agreement are:

- After a long and difficult discussion, "final" should be taken as final. No further concessions or compromises should be allowed.

- Negotiators should be tactful and persuasive to ensure that the final outcome is seen as beneficial by the other party.
- The key strategy in any negotiation is persuasion.
- Negotiators should emphasize the other party's benefits and should be enthusiastic about the other party's cooperation and suggestions.

Be tactful and persuasive to ensure that the final outcome, which is of advantage to you, is also seen by the other party as a benefit to them.

### *Summarizing*

It helps to summarize the agreements and conclusions at the end of the discussion.

- The negotiators can suggest something, such as, "I think it would be helpful if we could summarize all that we have discussed to reach this agreement".
- Alternatively, one party might suggest: "Let's note it down so that no point is later missed by anyone". It is a good strategy to use written summaries at the end of discussions. This leaves no scope for disagreement later about what has or has not been agreed upon.

### *Deadlocks*

Reaching a mutually satisfactory end is the basic objective of any negotiation. If there is no final agreement reached, even after a prolonged discussion, the strategy should be to:

10 Know how to handle deadlocks.

- Instead of going round in circles on a contentious point, move on to the next point on the agenda.
- Point out that no further concessions can be made regarding the point of contention, as they would be of no benefit to either party.
- Explain and emphasize the consequences that would result from a deadlock, such as the need to refer the matter to those with greater authority or eventually to external arbitration or third-party mediation.
- Use the ethical aspect of agreement, such as upholding the organization's values, the greatest good of the largest number of people, and so on.
- Even in the situation of a deadlock, remain positive and hopeful of reaching a mutually agreeable solution.
- Finally, point out that third-party intervention in the form of legal arbitration or conciliation may not benefit either of the parties, for whom it is best to decide the matter through mutual understanding.

## BUSINESS ETIQUETTE

Etiquette refers to conventional rules of social behaviour or professional conduct. These rules are unwritten and act as norms to be observed by all professionals who work as a team in a particular company or department. They help individuals identify what sort of behaviour is appropriate or inappropriate in a business environment.

11 Understand the general rules of business etiquette.

Professional etiquette affects business deals. An intelligent business executive knows that visitors assess the status of a company not just from its balance sheets and inventory books, but also from the manner in which they are received, addressed, taken around, and briefed in the boardroom. In business, as in life, etiquette is a self-rewarding trait.

Successful professionals know how to conduct themselves at company meetings, parties, and dinners.

Successful professionals know how to conduct themselves at company meetings, parties, and dinners. They are aware of their company's culture and etiquette. Further, business etiquette means more than just being nice. It is fundamental to conducting business successfully. Those who ignore norms run the risk of being labelled as "unfriendly" or "inflexible". This may disrupt the smooth working of the team by causing misunderstandings or tension among fellow workers.

Choosing to be habitually late for meetings, ignoring deadlines, indulging in character assassination during coffee breaks, or demanding (as a right) instead of requesting (as a favour) help are examples of ignoring, knowingly or unknowingly, the rules of good professional conduct, behaviour, and etiquette.

Every workplace evolves its own norms of behaviour and attitude. For example, if one were to undertake a survey of banks or hospitals during lunch breaks, one would notice that in some companies everyone resumes working without even a minute's delay after lunch, while in others taking an extra 10 to 15 minutes for lunch may be a general practice. In such cases, the etiquette is not governed by rules written down anywhere.

The business etiquette rules discussed in this chapter relate to the following:

- Introductions
- Telephone/cell phone calls
- Business dining
- Interaction with foreign clients
- Business-to-business etiquette

This chapter describes the behaviour and customs that would be considered appropriate and acceptable in most business organizations in modern, mostly westernized workplaces.

In an organization, the basic concern is to create a comfortable and productive work environment where each person helps others work with ease.

This approach to business etiquette assumes that each business setting has its own business protocols that an employee learns by working in that environment and observing others. But, there are general rules of business etiquette that are based on the fundamental principles of organizational behaviour. In an organization, the basic concern is to create a comfortable and effective work environment where each person helps others work with ease. This is made possible by empathizing with others' concerns and priorities. Identifying with others is the best form of business etiquette.

Learning the rules of business etiquette helps professionals be comfortable in any business setting. Let us, therefore, consider some common situations in business and find out how to act appropriately.

## Introductions

First impressions and meetings play a significant role in facilitating a business relationship. It is important, therefore, to make a positive impression when meeting someone for the first time.

12

Learn ways of introducing yourself and others.

### *Self-introductions*

A confident self-introduction always makes a positive first impression, but many people are reluctant to introduce themselves. This may be because they think it too bold an act or they feel too shy to do so. But, when two people meet for the first time, they are bound to want to know each other's identity, affiliation, and purpose. Even when

As a norm of business etiquette and the first step towards cordial business transactions, people greet each other by stating their full names and positions (in office) at the very outset.

people meet the second or third time after a gap of some weeks, there is no harm in repeating introductions by saying something simple, like, "Good morning, I'm Smita Sharma".

Suppose two applicants are waiting for an interview with the general manager of marketing of a company. They are sitting in the waiting lounge across the corridor leading to the general manager's office. A smart-looking middle-aged executive walks into the corridor moving towards the general manager's office. The candidates are not sure whether he is the person for whom they have been waiting. Now, suppose one of them stands up, walks up to him, and says, "Good morning, I am Reena Seth. I am here for an interview with Mr S. K. Nair". Hopefully, the person would respond, "Good morning! I am Mr Nair. Pleased to meet you. We shall have the interview shortly". Reena Seth's bold introduction to Mr Nair would give her an edge over the other candidate, who remained silent. Most likely, Mr Nair would have a positive and favourable impression of Reena Seth as a confident, assertive, and enterprising young individual.

If there is an advantage in introducing oneself at the first opportunity, why do people shy away from doing so? Some cultures, such as British culture, have a sense of reserve. Americans are more outgoing in general. Indians are traditionally more shy and, generally, would still consider it impolite to go up to someone and say "Hi, I am Amit Misra" (though this is now changing).

Introductions are standard protocol when two or more persons meet formally. Each person should introduce himself or herself in a clear manner, pronouncing their first names and surnames as well as stating their positions, which helps establish the purpose and direction of the conversation. For instance, one should say something like "Prafulla Misra, CEO, Sterling Gold Informatics", instead of just "Misra" or "Prafulla". Americans prefer to introduce themselves by their first names only, like "John" or "William". But, the British use the first name and surname: "WB Yeats" or "Tony Blair". Names, specially foreign or unfamiliar ones, are generally only partially understood unless spoken distinctly. For instance, the name "Kanwal Jeet Singh Sidhu" has to be uttered slowly, so that the other person follows it fully.

During a conversation, one party may have forgotten the other's name or may not remember how to pronounce it. At such moments the other person should help them immediately by politely repeating their name — "I am Irfan Mohammad, I am sorry, I should have told you". Business etiquette seeks to make all concerned parties comfortable. This is why it is polite to apologize for forgetting to introduce oneself. If one simply says, "I am Irfan Mohammad", it suggests that the other person is at fault for forgetting the name.

Here are some rules for making introductions correctly:

1. In the case of a pre-arranged business meeting, if you are an expected visitor, you should introduce yourself by stating your name and the purpose of the visit: "I am Ramesh Bose and I have come here to meet Ms Divya Lahari in the marketing department". Only after introducing yourself should you ask for the name and position of the other party.

2. Do not use honorifics, such as Sri, Mrs, Mr, Ms, or any other titles before your name while introducing or referring to yourself. Others can call you "Mr Chandra", but you should refer to yourself as just "Rajan Chandra", or "Chandra", or "Rajan". If you have a PhD, you may use "doctor" before your name and refer to yourself as "Dr Sharma". Surgeons and physicians usually do not add the salutation before their names when introducing themselves. Saying something like "I am Roopa Salwan, cardiologist from Escorts Heart Institute in New Delhi, India, I am here to attend the International Summit of Cardiologists as an Indian delegate" is a universally appropriate self-

announcement. The point is that others may add titles or professional descriptions (such as "professor"), but the individuals themselves should not.

3. Speak your name slowly and clearly. As mentioned earlier, the listener may not catch an unusual or unfamiliar name. Therefore, articulate your name as distinctly as possible, and if required, help others by spelling it.

> Speak your name slowly and clearly. The listener may not catch an unusual or unfamiliar name. Therefore, articulate your name as distinctly as possible, and if required, help others by spelling it.

In business, one encounters a variety of people, and it may be difficult to recognize or place someone one has previously met in a different context, such as a seminar or conference. Before the other person detects this, you should ask for his or her business card by simply saying, "Could I have your latest business card for your telephone number and e-mail address?"

To be tactful in such situations is also good business etiquette. If you let the other person know that you have forgotten his or her name, it may make the person feel that he or she is not important enough to be remembered. Try to act as if you know the name, but wish to have more details about the person.

### *Introducing Others*

It is common to have to introduce others at business meetings. A clear and complete introduction of each person, both members of the visiting party and the host party, makes everyone feel relaxed and creates a congenial atmosphere for the meeting. In such situations, the person who is making the introductions should know the names and professional statuses of both parties before the meeting. The professional status refers to the role the person plays in the business transaction.

> A clear and complete introduction of each person, both members of the visiting party and the host party, makes everyone feel relaxed and creates a congenial atmosphere for the meeting.

Normally, the senior-most person among the visitors or the host team introduces the other members of his or her group. The practice is that visitors are first introduced to the hosts. Then members of the host group are introduced. Usually a senior is not introduced to a junior, but instead, the lowest-ranked person is introduced to the highest-ranked person. Accordingly, avoid saying to the CEO of a company: "Mr Chopra, may I introduce you to Payal Muttoo? Payal is this year's first position holder and a gold medalist, working in our placement department". Instead, say "Mr Chopra, may I introduce Payal Muttoo to you? Payal is this year's university topper and gold medalist, working in our placement department".

Notice two things here. One, the polite form "May I introduce…" is appropriate and formal when speaking to a superior. But, when introducing someone to others it is okay to just say, "This is Neelam Gulati. Neelam is a senior lecturer in finance". Also note that this introduction repeats the name so that it is duly received and remembered by the other person. To repeat the name naturally, the person who is making the introductions has to create a context by mentioning a significant detail about the person concerned—such as what work they do.

After introducing the junior person to the senior, introduce the senior person to the junior, for instance by saying something like: "Payal, as you know, Mr Chopra is our President. Mr Chopra will discuss our placement status and strategies with you".

Here, it may be important to point out that in India, and perhaps in other Asian countries, it is a usual practice to use *President* or *Chairman* as a title before the name, such as "President G. P. Chopra" or "Chairman Chopra-ji", or even "Chairman Mr Chopra". In the United States and other western cultures, this may sound a little odd. Americans refer to one another just by using "first name, last name", even in the case of very senior persons. However, in Asian countries, people observe social courtesies out of respect for age and position, even in the context of business.

### *Handshakes and Non-verbal Gestures*

Most business meetings begin and end with a handshake. Shake hands after the introduction by extending your right hand and firmly holding the other person's right hand very briefly. In modern business, a handshake is a non-verbal clue of friendliness.

The handshake is so spontaneous that usually both parties simultaneously put forward their right hands to make the gesture. Nowadays, in business, as in society, there is no gender distinction and women shake hands in business situations too. Sometimes, while parting, people shake hands again or put their arm on the back or shoulder of the other person to communicate warmth.

As a winning form of non-verbal communication, handshakes must be accompanied by eye contact and a gentle smile. In some situations, you may express your feelings by saying, "Pleased to meet you". The other party would generally respond by saying, "my pleasure". These words are just pleasantries. They do not mean much as verbal communication.

> As a winning form of non-verbal communication, handshakes must be accompanied by eye contact and a gentle smile.

As already indicated while discussing non-verbal forms of communication, there are, besides handshakes, other gestures that are culture-specific. For instance, even in business situations, Arabs often shake hands, embrace, and also kiss to communicate their warmth and respect for the other person. East Asians often bow to one another.

If you are not sure of the cultural and personal sensitivities of your visitor or host, it is best to shake hands, as this is the general norm across the world. However, in some culture-specific countries, such as India, many senior business heads, executives, and officers still prefer to receive or bid adieu to highly placed guests in the traditional form—with folded hands, slightly bowed head, and eye contact. As a visitor, follow your host's cue and greet accordingly.

## PUBLIC SPEAKING

### The Art of Public Speaking

Speaking in public effectively is an art worth developing. People consider this form of communication to be most effective in spreading one's ideas and influencing other people. Consider how great thinkers, political leaders and social wouliers, such as Swami Vivekanand, Martin Luther king Jr., Winston Churchill, Mahatma Gandhi, made a difference in the life of the people and the destiny of the nations by spreading their ideas and influencing people with the power of their spoken words.

### Goals of Public Speaking

There are three main goals of public speaking: to persuade, to inform, and to delight. These are the very goals of communication as such. As a public speaker you want to persuade people to accept to do or believe what you think is right, or you wish to make them feel better placed by informing them of things you consider important to know. And finally you seek to entertain people with your unit and interesting anecdotes.

### Speech Styles

Speaking has various styles. Some of these are formal, informal, polite, normal, blunt, tentative, and direct.

It is important to choose appropriate ways of saying things according to the situation you are in. In many situations it will be appropriate to use normal or neutral language. In other situations, it is necessary to use language forms that are appropriate to special situations.

- We use ***tentative*** language when we are sincerely unsure of our facts or of how we feel. E.g. It's very kind of you to invite me, but I'm not sure if I can come.

We also use ***tentative*** language when we want to give the impression of being unsure in order to be tactful and diplomatic. For example, if we want to disagree with a superior, it would probably be too strong to say "***I can't agree with you***" and it would be more appropriate to be ***tentative*** and say ***I'm not sure if I'd agree with you***."

- ***Direct language*** is the opposite of *tentative* language; it gives the impression that the speaker is very sure. This impression is appropriate if, for example, we want to agree with someone. But, it can sound rude and inappropriate in many situations like inviting a superior to a party.

For Example i. *No. You are mistaken the statistics just cannot be this high.*
ii. *I see your point. But, we'll have to go ahead with our previous plan.*

- We use ***polite language*** when we want to sound particularly polite without being tentative.

For Example i. *I'm sorry. But, I feel there is a mistake somewhere. According to my calculations, the statistics should not be so high.*
ii. *You definitely have a point. But, I'm afraid this time we'll have to go ahead. Next time onwards, we'll definitely consider these points.*

- ***Formal language*** creates the impression of social distance between people. It occurs mostly in official situations e.g. business meetings, official receptions.

For Example i. *I'd be delighted if you could make it to the party. We'll all look forward to it.*
ii. *Forgive me if I sound curious. But, isn't this the same girl we saw him with yesterday?*

- ***Informal language*** is used basically between friends. It is generally inappropriate to use it with anyone else.

For Example i. *Cut it out' Will you? I've had enough of this.*
ii. *You're coming to the party tonight, aren't you? I just wont take "no" for an answer.*

- ***Strong language*** carries with it a strong sense of conviction. It usually sounds very direct.

For Example i. *This is impossible! How could you ever promise without consulting me?*
ii. *I'm gone without this project. I must get it, come what may.*

- ***Blunt language*** is extremely frank. It should be used with extreme care, as in most cases it will simply sound rude.

For Example i. *I know you're lying. You can't fool me!*
ii. *I must tell you. Your work was not up to the mark and we'll have to review your extension.*

In most cases we use normal and neutral language, but sometimes, depending on the situations we are in and also on the basis of our co-speakers, we use special language. The type of language we use shows our attitude.

Style of public speech: Public speaking requires formal language, jargon, slang and incorrect language have no place in public speeches. The speakers have to raise the level of their language and polish their expressions for creating a favorable impression on the audience. Public speaking requires a forceful and passionate delivery.

## The Public Speaking Process

If you are speaking to inform or to persuade a group of people (regardless of whether in a stand-up presentation, a seated deck-presentation, a videoconference, or a webcast), use these techniques to structure what you say. Since, unlike readers, your listeners can't glance back or skip ahead, you'll need to be repetitive and exceptionally clear by including (1) an opening, (2) a preview of the main points, (3) clearly demarcated main points, and (4) a closing.

### *Use an Effective Opening*

Openings are important in all forms of communication, when you make an oral presentation, however, your opening is even more crucial than it is when you write. Therefore, always use the first minute or so of your presentation for your opening, what many experts call a "grabber" or a "hook."

To decide what to say during your opening, think about the audience: Are they interested? Do they know how the topic relates to them? Do they know you well or not? Given your audience, choose from among the following techniques:

- **Tell them why you're speaking**. What they will learn in a tell presentation or what you hope they will do as a result of a sell presentation—so they can listen with these ideas in mind.

- **Grab their attention.** Why should they listen? Often, your audience will have other things on their minds or will not be especially interested in your topic, so you may need to open with a provocative question, a problem definition, a promise of what your presentation will deliver, a personal story that makes a business point, a vivid image, or a striking example or statistics.

- **Show them "what's in it for them (WIIFT)."** Why should they care? Why should they bother?

- **Build your credibility, if necessary.** If your audience doesn't know about you, introduce yourself and use any of the persuasion techniques to enhance your credibility by establishing a "common ground."

- **Use humor with caution.** Humor can be an effective grabber; however, use it only if it fits your personality and style, if it is appropriate and inoffensive for every member of the audience, and if it relates to the topic or occasion. Never use humor that might make anyone feel, put down, or trivialized.

### *Give a Preview*

Without a doubt, the most important part of your presentation is a preview (also known as an agenda, an outline, or a table of contents) of what you will be covering. Always give an explicit preview at the beginning of your presentation.

Previews help your audience understand and remember what you say. Think again about the contrast between listeners and readers. Your readers can skim a document and read your headings and subheadings before they start reading. Your listeners, in contrast, have no idea what you will be covering unless you tell them.

Typical previews include a list of key points (such as reasons, examples, or recommendations), key questions, or a problem followed by a solution.

*Examples of Previews*

*Longer and more formal:* I will discuss sales in each of our four European regions: the Northern, Southern, Western, and Central.

*Shorter and less formal:* Let's take a look at the sales figures in our four European regions.

### State Your Points Clearly

Your main points need to be organized and easy to follow, much more so than in writing. Readers can look over, slow down, and reread when they wish; listeners, of course, cannot. Therefore, remember these three guidelines when you're speaking.

***Limit Your Main Points*** Experiments in cognitive psychology show that people cannot easily comprehend more than five to seven main points, so do not exceed that number when you're speaking. That means grouping all of your points in any section or subsection into no more than seven major areas.

***Use Strong Transitions*** When you are speaking, you need longer, more explicit transitions between major sections and subsections than you do when you are writing. Listeners do not stay oriented as easily as readers do; they may not even remember what it is that you are listing unless you use these longer transitions.

*Ineffective short transition*

Second, . . .

*Effective longer transitions*

The second recommendation is . . .

Let's move on to the second recommendation.

***Use Repetitive Transitions*** In addition to stronger, more explicit transitions, you also need to use more repetitive transitions when you're speaking, because listeners may not remember information they hear only once. Although you may feel as if you're being too repetitive, your listeners will appreciate detailed reminders that reinforce your structure. Therefore, between each major section and subsection, use a backward look/forward look transition. The backward look refers to recapping what you just covered, and the-forward look provides a smooth transition to the upcoming part of your talk.

*Effective backward look/forward look transition*

Example: Now that we have looked at the three elements of the marketing plan **(backward look)**, let's turn to the financial implications of the plan **(forward look)**.

***Keep the Audience's Interest High*** Remember that your listeners' attention will decrease in the middle of your speech. Hence, consider the following techniques to keep up their interest, involve them, add variety, and wake them up:

- *Include stories*, case illustrations, analogies, and examples—not just numbers.
- *Incorporate their names* (e.g., "Pat in accounting and Wahid in human resources" instead of "people from different departments").
- *Change your personal energy* (e.g., your tone, pauses, or nonverbal dynamism),
- *Ask rhetorical questions* that relate to audience benefits (e.g., "So what does this mean for your business?").

- *Ask for a show of hands* (e.g., "How many of you think our current policy is effective?").
- *Tell them you'll be asking* for their input after the presentation.

### *Close Effectively*

The Audience Memory Curve also shows that your listeners are likely to remember your last words. Therefore, your closing should be more than a mere "thank you" or the all-too-common "dribble" closing like "I guess that's about it."

Instead, use a strong, obvious transitional phrase—such as "to summarize" or "in conclusion"—to introduce your closing remarks. Here are some options for effective closings:

- **Give a summary.** Summarize your main points. Your audience will appreciate the wrap up.
- **End with the action steps.** Based on your communication objective. You might remind the audience "what's in it for them", if they take these action steps.
- **Refer to the opening.** A third kind of closing is to refer to the rhetorical question, promise, image, or story you used in your opening.
- **If you end with Q and A,** add a second closing, similar to your first one, so you get the last word.

## Guidelines for Developing Public Speaking Skills

Nervousness and stage fright is natural for all beginners before a large audience. However, this feeling is gradually overcome by knowing that everyone who stands before an audiance feels like you. Remember the techniques discussed by Stephen E Lucas in his book, "the art of public speaking" (1989) to develop self confidence and skills of public speaking.

1. The importance of developing Courage and Self-Confidence.

   Courage to speak is the first requisite for a public speaker. One who has stage-fright cannot face the public. He cannot have confidence in himself/herself. And one who has no confidence is bound to fumble. But, the fact is that at the beginning every renowned speaker had stage-fright. Born speakers are rare. George Bernard Shaw was a spell-binder. But, at the beginning his legs trembled and his voice faltered when he rose to speak. Stage-fright can be conquered. One can acquire perfect self confidence. Only one must do certain things.

   (i) **Desire:** One who wants to become a good public speaker must have a strong desire to speak well and must have enthusiasm for speaking. And he can get desire and enthusiasm only if he remembers the benefits he can reap by becoming a good speaker. A good speaker can do well in interviews, selling his goods, influenceing the people and their leader. If one remembers all this, their desire will be whetted, their fear will gradually vanish, and they will acquire confidence.

   (ii) **Mastery of the subject:** One cannot have confidence unless one knows one's subject well. Hence, one must prepare the topic thoroughly, one must read some books, analyse the ideas, and take down points.

   (iii) **Act confidently:** A speaker must put on the appearance of boldness. He/she must dress well. He/she must not have any feelings of inferiority. He/she must always think that they are masters of their subject. And this will surely be able to impress the audience. This auto-suggestion will remove their nervousness and give them self-confidence.

   (iv) **Practice:** Practice is most important in overcoming stage-fright and getting self-confidence. A speaker must prepare his speech beforehand. He must read it several times. Then he must stand before a mirror and speak, as if before an audience.

2. Develop self-confidence through preparation.

   There are very few who can speak extempore. Most of the famous speakers of the world prepared their speeches in advance. Unless you go prepared, you can't have confidence in youself. And without self-confidence you are sure to feel nervous. And ultimately you may cut a sorry figure. Hence, one must prepare one's speech thoroughly. But, how to prepare a speech? A few points for preparing a speech are briefly given below.

   (i) **Thinking over the speech:** In preparing a speech external help is not enough. The speaker must think over the topic day and night. He must even dream of the speech. Gradually many points will evolve automatically. Gradually the logical order of speech will emerge. At this stage the speaker should make necessary changes in the rough draft. Then he should prepare a final draft.

   (ii) **Discussion with friends:** Reading the speech again and again helps to memorize it. But, a quicker method to memorize the speech is to discuss it with friends. So discuss the points of your speech whenever you get an opportunity. Make the speech a topic of conversation with friends. All this will help you to remember what you are going to speak.

   (iii) **Taking down points:** A speaker must take down the important points of his speech on a piece of paper. He can carry it in his pocket. If need be, he may consult it while speaking.

   (iv) **Rehearsal:** Before going to speak, one must confine himself in a room and deliver this speech, as if before an audience. He must practise it until all the falterings disappear.

3. Improvement of memory.

   To deliver a speech one has to remember a lot of things. Hence, for a speaker, good memory is an asset. But, very few possess good memory. And even those who have good memory cannot always depend on it. Memory is treacherous. It often plays tricks on its possessors. But, memory can be cultivated. By following certain methods, memory can be improved. There are three natural laws of remembering-impression, repetition, and association.

   (i) **Impression:** You must have a deep impression of the thing you want to remember. And you can have a deep impression by concentrating on the thing, by observing it closely, and by associating it with something similar. Also, if possible get the impression through more than one sensory organ. For example, you can see and picture and hear about it.

   (ii) **Repetition:** Repetition of a thing helps to remember it. It engraves the thing on the memory. But, do not repeat the thing continuously for hours together. Repeat at intervals. And before leaving home for delivering the speech go through it,

   (iii) **Association:** Associate the thing you want to remember with something similar. Create a picture of the thing in your mind. For example, if you want to remember the name of a person, associate it with the special features of his face or associate the name with his business or profession.

   One more thing, besides these three natural laws, is to be done. Arrange the points of the address in the logical order so that one point naturally leads to the next.

4. Hold the audience attention.

   The aim of the speaker is to leave a deep impression on the minds of the audience. The audience must go deeply impressed and highly satisfied, but it is very difficult to achieve this end. The speaker must be able to captivate the attention of the audience. But, very few are born with this capacity. It has to be developed by following certain methods. Some of the methods are pointed out here.

(i) **Enthusiasm:** The response of the audience largely depends on the enthusiasm with which the speaker speaks. If the speaker is lukewarm, the response of the audience will be lukewarm. If he is mild and dull, the audience will remain unaffected. A gloomy speech can never get en enthusiastic applause. On the other hand, an enthusiastic speaker catches the attention of the audience at once. Enthusiasm is one of the most important factors in delivery. A speaker must speak from conviction. Every word must have the warmth of the heart. He must be sincere in what he says. He must say what he really wants to say. No beating about the bush. Say earnestly what you believe to be right. Be frank, honest, and straightforward, and the audience is captivated by you. Whatever you say, must be said with intensity. Enthusiasm, sincerity, frankness, conviction, and intensity go together. If you possess these qualities, you are sure to exercise a magnetic influence over the audience.

(ii) **Physical movements:** The speaker must be at ease. He must be calm and quiet and appear undisturbed. He must stand erect and look the audience in the face. Occasionally, he must use emphatic gestures. He must speak vigorously. His voice must be loud enough to reach the last row of audience. All this will deeply influence the audience. They will feel that the speaker has a good command of the subject. And they will listen to him attentively.

(iii) **Avoidance of "weasel" word:** A speaker must speak with conviction. He must use emphatic words. And he must avoid using "weasal words", such as "I think", "it seems to me", "in my humble opinion", "perhaps". For such expressions give the impression that the speaker lacks conviction. And the audience pays no attention to a man with no convictions.

(iv) **Love of the audience:** The speaker must have keen interest in the audience He must love them. He must have sympathy for them. Then only the audience will take interest in what he says. Abraham Lincoln won the heart of the audience by his sympathy and goodness to a great extent. One famous actress rightly said, "The secret of my success is absolute devotion to the audience. I love my audience."

5. Essential elements of public speaking.

Public speaking is an art. But, very few are born with this art. Like other arts, it has to be acquired by following certain essentials. There are many methods to acquire it. A few of them are pointed out here,

(i) **Patience and perseverance:** Almost every speaker has stage-fear at the beginning. He often cuts a sorry figure. He feels that he can never become a public speaker. And he wants to give up speaking in public. This attitude is wrong. He must have patience. However great his failure, he must not lose heart. He must try again and again. And he is sure to win at last. Indeed, failures are the pillars of success. Success does not come at once. It has many obstacles to overcome. Nervousness, fear, shock are some of the obstacles. But, do not give up hope. Have patience and Perseverance. Keep on practising. And you are sure to progress. And at last you are sure to become a good speaker. John Brig at Gladstone, Wilier-force had such experiences of failure. But, they had patience. They persevered. And they became world famous speakers. Do not give up even if you cut a sorry figure a hundred times.

(ii) **Will and determination:** Will and determination play a very important role in making one a good public speaker. You must will, and will strongly to become a speaker. You must have determination to become a speaker. A man becomes what he wills to become, if you are resolutely determined you are sure to become a good speaker. Will and determination can overcome all difficulties. Nepoleon rightly said. "Victory is will." An army's will enables it to win a war. A speaker's will and determination are sure to crown him with success. Fight and fight even when hope is out of sight.

It is easy to give up, but the glory is in keeping on. You need dogged determination. Those who keep on arrive at destination.

(iii) **Picturing success:** If you want to become a good public speaker, you must picture yourself to be one. You must visualize that you are on the platform. You must visualize that you are applauded by the audience. This visualization will work miracle psychologically. It will give you confidence and fill your mind with hope.

(iv) **Enthusiasm:** Deliver your speech with enthusiasm. The applause of the audience will be in proportion to the enthusiasm with which you speak. You must speak with confidence. Every word you utter must have the spark of enthusiasm.

(v) **Four Gs:** In art of public speaking and influencing in business, Dale Carnegie says that essentials for success in public speaking are four Gs. He means four words beginning with "G"—grace, gumption, grit, and guts. Grace is the quality of being pleasing and attractive in your appearance, movement, and delivery. Gumption means common sense and initiative. Grit is the quality of courage and endurance. And guts is courage and determination.

6. The Element of Delivery. In public speaking delivery matters most. A speaker, therefore, must take care of his delivery. He must know the qualities of a good delivery. Some of these qualities are: Three things matter in a speech—the speaker, manner of delivery, and matter. Of these, the manner of delivery is the most important. Edmund Burke's speeches contained admirable logic and reasoning. But, as an orator he was a failure, because he did not know how to deliver his gems.

(i) **A sense of communication:** When you speak the audience must feel that you are delivering a message to them. That is the first essential of good talking. To give the audience a sense of communication, you must speak to them intimately. You must look at the audience and talk as if they are familiar to you. You must not look over them at the wall and utter the words mechanically. That is soliloquy, not talk. Talk to the audience directly as if you are engaged in a conversation with them. Your tone must be natural, enlarged a bit. You must not imitate others. You must be your natural self. You must have individuality. As a speaker that is your most precious possession. Thus only, a sense of communication can be established. And once the sense of communication is established, you gain the confidence of the audience and you make a deep impression on them.

(ii) **Sincerity and enthusiasm:** Enthusiasm is one of the most important features of good delivery. The speaker must be honest, sincere, and straightforward. He must speak with conviction. In other words, he must put his heart in his talks. Every word must have the warmth of the heart. If his heart is in his work, his delivery is sure to be effective. A thing said with conviction and said enthusiastically is sure to deeply impress one and all.

(iii) **Stressing important words:** The speaker must put more stress on some significant words and hurry over the others. This is what we do in our daily conversation. Emphasis on the important words will convey your ideas vividly to the audience.

(iv) **Change of pitch:** The speaker's voice must not be monotonous. The pitch of his voice should flow up and down, Then only the effect will be pleasing. On the other hand, if the speaker's voice is always on the same level, it will become monotonous. And monotony will bore and even disgust the audience.

(v) **Variation of the rate of speaking:** The speaker must vary his rate of speaking This is a good method of driving a point home. Speak several words with great rapidity, and when you come to the words you wish to emphasize, let the voice linger. And then again rush to the end of the sentence like lightning. This method arrests the attention. It is natural. It is emphatic. Above all, it is pleasing.

(vi) **Pause before and after important ideas:** Pausing before and after an important idea attracts the attention of the audience.

This was Lincoln's method. He often paused in his speaking. This sudden silence has the same effect as a sudden noise. But, the speaker must practise this method. He must pause naturally. If pauses are judiciously used, they produce a tremendous effect on the audience. Silence becomes more eloquent than eloquence itself.

7. The importance of personality. Personality of the speaker has a lot to do with his success. But, personality is an intangible and elusive thing. It cannot be clearly defined. And it is difficult to say how it can be developed. But, by following some suggestions the speaker can appear at his best. His dress and his behaviour on the platform etc count. By paying proper attention to this, one can favourably impress the audience.

(i) **Rest and food:** Before going to talk, you must take sufficient rest. Take light food. For, a heavy meal makes one uneasy. Do not do anything that dulls your energy. You must look fresh and energetic. Vitality has a magnetic power. It impresses the people around.

(ii) **Dress:** Dress neatly and attractively. You must appear cheerful. Never look gloomy. Good dress has a great psychological effect on the mind. It heightens one's, self-respect and increases self-confidence. Such is the effect of dress on the wearer. It also leaves a good impression on the audience. Shabby dress, on the other hand, makes one feel ill at ease. And the audience generally forms an unfavourable impression about a shabbily dressed person.

(iii) **Arrangements in the hall:** Surroundings count. The hall where you are going to speak should be spacious, well ventilated and well lighted. The audience should sit together, it is difficult to influence an audience that is scattered. Empty chairs between the audience dampen and have a chilling effect on the enthusiasm of the speaker.

(iv) **How to stand:** Stand erect. Do not hide yourself behind *a* table. Let the light fall on your face. Let there be no useless things on the table. Let there be no attractive things behind or on either side of you. There should be as few people on the stage as possible. The speaker's hands should not play with his clothes. Nor should they make any nervous movements. For, all these distract the attention of the audience. The speaker should stand still and control himself physically.

(v) **Gestures:** For gestures, no fixed rules can be laid down. For, if you follow rules for making gestures, the gestures become mechanical and repulsive. Gestures must be born on the spur of the moment. They must be the spontaneous results of your enthusiasm and impulses. Imitated gestures are like imitated smiles, which are not smites but grimaces. Gestures should be as pleasing as a spontaneous smile. In short, make only those gestures that come natural.

8. How to open a talk to capture the audience?

The manner of opening a talk is of great importance. The audience forms the first impression from it. And the first impression counts very much. But, the opening of a talk is difficult. It has to be carefully worked out in advance. Some hints as to how to open a talk are given here:

(i) **Introduction:** The introduction should be short and precise—a sentence or two. Go straight to the heart of the subject. Do not waste much time on introduction.

(ii) **Apology:** It is unwise to begin a talk with apologies. Do not be too modest. Do not emphasize that you are unprepared or that you are not a fit person to speak on the subject. Do not praise the chairman and other dignitaries too much.

(iii) **Humorous story:** It is bad to begin a talk with a humorous story. Very few can tell a humorous story interestingly. Such a story at the beginning of a talk embarrasses instead of entertaining the audience. It is difficult to excite laughter. If your story fails to generate laughter, the effect is tragic rather than comic.

(iv) **Curiosity:** You should begin your talk in such a manner that it can arouse curiosity. You can begin with a personal experience, a specfic illustration, or by asking a question.

(v) **Exhibit:** The easiest way to arouse curiosity is to show an exhibit. By holding up an exhibit you can at once draw the attention of the audience towards it.

(vi) **Question:** You can begin your talk by asking a question. By a question you make the audience co-operate with you. You take them into confidence. And they form a good impression about you.

(vii) **Quotation:** You can begin with *a* quotation from a famous man. It draws the attention of the audience at once to you. For, everybody is interested in what famous people say.

(viii) **Shocking facts:** Shocking facts easily capture the attention of the audience. Hence, it is good to open a talk with them. But, you must tell them the sources of these secrets. Otherwise they may not believe your statement.

(ix) **On-the-spot remark:** One can open *a* talk with an on-the-spot remark. That is to say, begin with a casual remark that is relevant in the circumstances. For example, you may refer to what the earlier speaker said. Or, you may refer to an incident that happened in the course of the function.

(x) **Capture the audience:** You aim is to capture the audience. Hence, open a talk with a statement with which everyone will agree. If you can do so, you get the audience on your side at the very outset.

9. How should one close a talk?

The manner of closing a speech is as important as the manner of opening a speech. Perhaps the close is more important. For, it is likely to be remembered longer! Hence, it must be planned, prepared, and carefully mastered in advance. Rehearse it, learn it by heart so that you can deliver it enthusiastically and convincingly. Famous orators like Webster, Bright, and Gladstone did it.

(i) **No sudden ending:** Do not end your talk abruptly. It should be natural. It should be closely connected with what you have discussed. You can end by summarizing the points you have talked about.

(ii) **Appeal for action:** If you want the audience to do something, end your talk with an appeal. The appeal should be emotional. You must touch the very depth of their feelings.

(iii) **Compliments to the audience:** You must pay sincere compliments to the audience. You want the audience to admire you. Naturally, you should please them. But, you must guard yourself against flattery and extravagance. Your compliment must be sincere. Then only they will be effective. If the audience think that you are false, the effect will be just the reverse.

(iv) **Quotation:** You can close your talk with a quotation from some authority. Quotations from religious books or poets have great appeal.

(v) **Climax:** A popular way of closing a talk is the climax. It is difficult to construct a climax, But, when well done, it produces a tremendous effect on the audience.

10. How to make your meaning clear?

Whatever you say must be clearly understood by the audience. Every word, every sentence must convey what you intend to say. Otherwise your talks will fall flat on the ears of the audience. Your efforts to win their hearts will be futile. Therefore, take care of the language you use. Also take care of the ideas you want to convey to the audience. Some hints as to how you can make the meaning clear are given here

(i) **Simple language:** The audience is generally composed of all kinds of people. Take care that your talk does not go over their heads. Always use simple language. In speech simple and direct language has great impact on the audience. The language of the Bible is simple, emotional and emphatic. Read the Bible as often as you can. Famous creators like, John Bright often read the Bible. Avoid technical language when you are addressing a lay audience. Abraham Lincoln always put his ideas into a language which could be understood even by a boy,

(ii) **Appeal to the sense of sight:** One can understand a thing more clearly by seeing it than by hearing about it. Eyes are better carriers of ideas than ears. Hence, you can use charts, maps, diagrams, etc.

(iii) **Repetition:** Important ideas can be repeated. But, do not repeat the ideas in the same language. Vary the sentences. Repetition in different language will make the ideas clear.

(iv) **Illustrations:** It is very difficult for the common people to grasp abstract ideas. So, whenever you deal with abstract ideas, give illustrations. Better refer to specific instances and concrete cases.

**Limited points:** Do not try to cover many points. Refer to only a few points. But, develop each point fully.

(vi) **Summary:** Give a brief summary of what you have dealt with.

11. How can the speaker create interest in the audience?

To impress and convince the audience is your aim. But, how to do it? It is an uphill task. But, if you cannot do it, you are a failure as a speaker. Follow the suggestions given here. You are sure to succeed.

(i) **Convince yourself:** If you want to convince others, you yourself must be convinced first. You must have a mastery of the ideas you are dealing with. And then deliver them with enthusiasm. The audience is bound to be convinced of what you say. And they will be interested in your talk.

(ii) **Common ground:** If you have something new to say, do not attack the beliefs and ideas of the audience. If you attack, the audience will become antagonistic. On the contrary, you should say that your ideas are similar to something they already believe. This will disarm their opposition. They will be impressed. And they will be interested in the talk.

(iii) **Restatement:** If the audience is not impressed by your ideas, repeat them several times. Daniel O'Conneil said that a political truth is taken up and adopted by the audience only if it is repeated again and again. Incessant repetition is required to impress truths upon the minds of the people. But, for repetition of the same thing one must have a command of the language. Language of restatement must vary,

(iv) **General illustrations and concrete instances:** General illustrations and concrete instances can impress the audience. They help to prevent the audience from putting forth opposite ideas. General illustrations and concrete instances make the ideas clear. Hence, they impress the people.

(v) **Quote authorities:** If you quote from any author, you must quote the exact words. Also you must tell from whom you are quoting. The sources should be authoritative. Quote a popular man. Quote a local man. Quote one who is accepted as authority by all.

(vi) **Extraordinary facts:** People are always interested in extraordinary facts about ordinary things. So consult as many books as you can and dig out some unusual facts about the things you are dealing with. The audience will at once be impressed and take interest in your talk.

(vii) **Audience's interests:** Talk about things in which the audience are interested. Refer to the local people and local incidents. The audience will be keenly interested in such a talk.

(viii) **Mental pictures:** Use words which conjure pictures before your mind's eye. Such pictures are deeply impressed on the mind. Sprinkle them through your talks.

(ix) **Contrast:** Use of balanced contrasts creates interest. Good contrasts are the brick and mortar of a good speech. Macaulay used them often. One example—"The rules are meant to be observed in the spirit, not in the letter-for the comfort, not the discomfort of the passengers".

12. How can the speaker improve his diction?

Language is the medium through which we express our ideas. As the vehicle of ideas, it is the most Important element in public speaking. Without having a good degree of command of the language, one cannot hope to have success as a public speaker. On the other hand, one who is master of the language can command the audience. The manner is more important than the matter. But, how to acquire command over the language. There are several methods.

(i) **Company of great masters:** Your language will be largely a reflection of the company you keep. Therefore, keep company with the masters of literature. Devote several hours every day to reading Shakespeare and other poets and prose-writes. Gradually and unconsciously your mind will be enriched and your diction will have the stamp of these masters. This is what Lincoln did. This is what Jefferson did. Read the newspapers hurriedly. And devote the time thus saved to reading enduring books the Holy Bible is an excellent book. John Bright read it daily. Read it whenever you get time.

(ii) **Dictionary:** Make a dictionary your constant companion. Look up the familiar word: Find out its real significance. Find out how it is used.

(iii) **Derivation:** Study the derivation of the words you use. The histories and developments of words are not at all dull and dry; they are very interesting. Indeed, they are replete with romance. Enjoy the romance of words.

(iv) **Worn out words:** Do not use threadbare words. Take care to use words which express the meaning precisely. Do not beat about the bush. Say firmly what you want to say by using the appropriate words. If need be consult a dictionary or Roger's "Treasury of Words". Do not use the words that have become hackneyed by constant use. For example, use 'elegant' for 'beautiful'. Use adjectives sparingly and appropriately. An adjective is the enemy of a noun.

(v) **Trite comparisons:** Do not use trite comparisons, such as "cool as cucumber". Use fresh comparisons. Use the language boldly. Have the courage to create similes of your own.

## PRESENTATION SKILLS

A presentation is a live mode of sharing information with a select audience. It is a form of oral communication in which a person shares factual information with a particular audience. To get a clear idea of presenting as a distinct communicative activity—different from lecturing or training—it is possible to define a presentation as an oral activity that uses a visual medium (such as, LCD projectors or PowerPoint slides) to discuss new ideas and information with a specific audience in a persuasive and convincing manner.

### Preparing a Presentation

Presentations have three major elements:

- The presenter
- The audience
- The specific content and definite objective to be achieved

A trained presenter approaches a presentation with an awareness of all its elements and a fully planned strategy. He or she knows that just standing up and speaking to an audience for a given amount of time to show how much he or she knows on the topic does not imply that the presentation is good. A presentation is a particular mode of communicating with a group of people and conveying a message. It involves prior preparation and planning.

> A trained presenter approaches a presentation with an awareness of all its elements and a fully planned strategy. A good presentation involves prior preparation and planning.

A presenter should undertake the following steps to prepare for the presentation:

- Identify the purpose and goal of the presentation
- Analyze the audience and their needs
- Collate the relevant information
- Design and organize the information
- Time the presentation
- Decide on the medium of presentation and visual aids
- Become familiar with the location of the presentation

#### *Identify the Purpose of the Presentation*

The presenter should ask himself or herself: *Why am I giving this presentation?* He or she may be giving the presentation to:

- Sell something or persuade people to follow a course of action that they may not be inclined towards.
- Inform people about an idea or describe a business opportunity to gain support for some course of action or to suggest a likely course of action for the future.
- Gather people's views on new plans, products, or proposals to introduce changes.
- Put across a problem to seek a solution or to minimize people's reaction to it.
- Create awareness by sharing information, without requiring any action or response.
- Motivate, educate, or impart training to promote a more productive work culture.

After identifying his or her objective, the presenter should outline it in a single sentence. For example, assume the dean of the BITS Distance Learning Programme (DLP) has to put forward a proposal to the board of governors to expand the institute's Distance Learning Programme by creating off-campus centres in Gulf cities, such as Dubai or Muscat. He is required to make a presentation before the board members to justify the proposal. He knows exactly why he is giving the presentation; the purpose can be written in a single sentence that outlines the structure of his ideas: "To convince the board members of the viability and desirability of creating overseas (off-campus) learning centres in Gulf countries, in view of the growing demand for BITS courses abroad". This precise formulation of the objective will help him organize his ideas in a logical manner that will convince the board.

### *Analyze the Audience and Identify Their Needs*

Before making a presentation, the presenter must know the audience he or she is going to address. The presenter should have an idea of the number, nature, needs, level of knowledge, and likely attitude of those who are going to receive the message. These factors will determine the language of delivery and selection of inputs. Understanding the audience's needs will help the presenter focus the presentation on issues that would be of interest to his or her listeners. In addition, knowing about the likely attitude of the audience in advance would make the presenter feel more confident. All members of a group will not have a similar attitude and as individuals they are bound to respond differently. Also, presenters should keep in mind that different persons attending the presentation may be looking for different information based on their own interests or needs. Therefore, the presenter must define the focus and scope of the presentation at the very outset. Most importantly, the speaker must never consider the audience to be a hostile group. They may be opposed to one's ideas or message, but they are not the speaker's enemies.

> Before making a presentation, the presenter must know the audience he or she is going to address. The presenter should have an idea of the number, nature, needs, level of knowledge, and likely attitude of those who are going to receive the message.

Guidelines for analyzing an audience include finding answers for the following questions:

- Who is the audience?
- Why are they attending the presentation? What are their needs?
- What is their background and level of knowledge, in relation to the subject of presentation?
- How many persons will there be?
- What is their attitude towards the subject and the speaker expected to be?
- What does the audience expect will be the outcome of the presentation?

The last question is the most important and needs to be clearly understood and answered. The answer to it will clarify and define the speaker's purpose. It will help the presenter understand the audience's expectations. For instance, in the presentation on creating overseas BITS DLP centres in the Gulf, the expected outcome will be: "After listening to the presentation, the board members will agree to approve, in principle, initiating overseas DLP centres and setting up a committee to work out the feasibility of opening two centres, one each in Dubai and Muscat". The presenter can visualize the audience's response as if the presentation has already happened. Positive expectations will give the speaker added confidence. In addition, if the speaker has too many ideas or too much information on the topic at hand, knowing the audience's needs and expectations will help him or her determine what information is most relevant and interesting.

The needs of the audience vary from category to category. For example, a student's content will change depending on whether he or she is making a presentation before fellow students, professors, local business people, or friends. In some cases, one would expect that the audience already has a high level of information, while in other cases, there will be little information known. The speaker should consider the audience's needs and tell them what they need to know without talking about everything.

### *Design and Organize the Information*

By this point, the speaker has done two essential things to give shape to the presentation: he or she is aware of the purpose of the presentation and the audience's needs. These will guide him or her in gathering and systematically arranging the information to be presented. The speaker should structure and design the delivery to be effective, with the goal that the audience will ultimately accept his or her ideas.

> **13** Learn how to design a presentation.

Considerable thought should be given to how to start the presentation. What should be said first? This does not refer to how to greet the audience but, rather, to what main point the speaker should begin with. The normal order of any exposition is to first list the main ideas and then elaborate on each of them. This is the pattern that all written reports follow too. The sequence and timing of each part in a 30-minute presentation should be:

> The normal order of any exposition is to first list the main ideas and then elaborate on each of them.

- *Introduction:* 3 minutes
- *Main body:* 15 minutes
- *Conclusion:* 2 minutes
- *Question–answer session:* 10 minutes

The presentation should be designed in such a way that it is logical, clear, and complete in the 30 minutes allotted to it. Let's use the BITS DLP proposal example to see how this can be done.

***Introduction (3 minutes)*** The introduction indicates the main idea of the presentation. It does only that, without giving details of what is to follow. This helps the audience know the subject and focus of the presentation. For instance, the objective in this situation is: "We propose that BITS should open Distance Learning Centres in two Gulf cities, Dubai and Muscat". Next, the presentation should explain why it is proposing overseas BITS centres by speaking about how popular BITS' educational programmes are nationally and internationally. This background provides the launching pad for more detailed information, which is covered in the main body of the presentation.

***Main Body (15 minutes)*** The main part of the presentation is devoted to informing the audience about the advantages of the proposal, both for BITS and the concerned countries in the Gulf (see Exhibit 8.4).

**Benefits to BITS**

- Will help the faculty develop new teaching strategies to promote BITS' academic rigour and excellence in a different climate where there is economic affluence, but limited opportunities for higher education, specially in technology, science, and management.
- Will support BITS programmes in general and add opportunities for summer training and placements.
- Will increase financial benefits and foreign exchange earnings.

**Benefits to DLP-associated Countries**

- Will create good opportunities for Arab and non-resident Indian students to study engineering, science, or management at an international level.
- Will help Gulf countries use the research capabilities of BITS' faculty and postgraduate students to promote their technical know-how in the areas of construction, plant management, and human relations development.
- Will enable developing countries to learn new ways of social and intellectual growth through interaction and contact with India.

**Viability: How Will BITS Centres Abroad Work?**

An MOU can be signed between BITS and the partner countries. The BITS centre will be recognized as a centre for higher learning and education, duly approved by the Sultanate of Oman and the Emirate of Dubai.

- All physical facilities, such as land, building, furniture, laboratories, and library are to be provided by the host country free of rent and cost for five years. Subsequently, rent and costs will be fixed through mutual agreement.
- Faculty provision: The teaching faculty and administration will be provided by BITS, Pilani (India).
- Syllabus and exams: The courses and evaluation systems used abroad will be the same as those used in BITS Pilani, India.
- Admissions system and fees: Admissions will be made on the basis of merit and will be determined through normalization of the marks of applicants (mostly NRIs).

**Exhibit 8.4** The Main Body of the Presentation

This section would include findings of a survey and analysis of the data. This section of the presentation should generally be divided into sub-sections. As a general rule, the speaker should avoid having more than three sub-sections under the main point.

Generally, a presentation is delivered in an analytical and logical manner: the introduction leads to the main content, which in turn leads to the conclusions and recommendations. To integrate these parts into a continuous whole, there should be proper transitions from one section to the next and from one stage to another. The speaker should summarize what has been said in the previous section or stage before explaining how the next point is related. An example is: "So, you have seen how BITS overseas centres are feasible and viable. Now let's discuss some of the potential problems that we may face".

***Conclusion (2 minutes)*** The conclusion (see Exhibit 8.5) summarizes the speaker's main arguments and connects them to the objectives stated in the introduction and the larger picture.

- BITS' experience of running three DLP centres in India has built confidence and expertise regarding its abilities to do so abroad, negating distance as a factor for excellence in education.
- The faculty is committed and ready to take advantage of this opportunity.
- There is a lot of faith in the promised support from the Gulf nations.

**Exhibit 8.5** The Conclusion

To end the presentation, the speaker should do the following:

- Repeat the main idea of the presentation.
- Restate the most important points with supporting information.
- Thank the audience and invite questions.

***Question–Answer Session (10 minutes)*** This is an important opportunity for audience interaction. The speaker should encourage questions and answer each question seriously and with honesty. The speaker should not try to bluff; if he or she does not know the answer to a question, it is best to be frank and admit this.

## VISUAL AIDS AND ELEMENTS

A presentation can be made more vivid by the use of statistical data, figures, diagrams, and so on, which can be displayed via transparencies or PowerPoint slides. Through visual display of ideas, the presenter can make the audience see what they hear. Graphics tend to garner and hold attention more easily than spoken words, so they also help keep the audience fully absorbed. Having visual projection of the message also enables the speaker to keep to the structure of the presentation. Moreover, often a greater amount of information can be communicated with a visual than lengthy verbal explanations. This saves time.

14

Select the proper medium of presentation and visual aids.

A presentation can be made more vivid by the use of statistical data charts, figures, diagrams, and so on, which can be displayed via transparencies or PowerPoint slides.

Often, a greater amount of information can be communicated with a visual than lengthy verbal explanations. This saves time.

### When to Use Visual Aids

Visual aids should be used to:

- Present numerical and statistical data.
- Present topics related to art, design, or any subject that is visual in nature.
- Present comparative statements of facts and figures, specially graphic and diagrammatic forms. Visual presentation of comparisons always helps comprehension. For instance, if the presenter wants to demonstrate the comparison of two structures, the point of comparison can be better appreciated when shown rather than described.
- Present new interpretations of old data. If the speaker has discovered or noticed something new as a fresh interpretation of an existing phenomenon, showing it makes the information look more concrete. By projecting the old information side-by-side with the new, the speaker can demonstrate how he or she has gone beyond the old data.

## How to Use Visual Aids

Here are some guidelines regarding how to use visual aids:

- One should not use too many images as this will lessen their impact.
- The speaker should plan the graphics according to the main points and make one graphic for each point.
- It is best to use bold, clear letters that can be seen from the other end of the room.
- The speaker should not fill a slide with too many words. As far as possible, one should write single words or short phrases to summarize concepts. See Exhibit 8.6 for an example.
- Different colours can help to distinguish different points.
- The presenter should reveal only one point at a time. This can be done by progressively exposing the hidden portion of the slide.

> **Functions of a Finance Manager**
>
> The finance manager of an organization is involved in:
> - forecasting and predicting the short- and long-term requirement of money by the business
> - analyzing the costs and benefits associated with long-term investments
> - Coordinating and controlling the various organizational activities are to ensure cost effectiveness and maximum efficiency in terms of value generation
> - eliminating, reducing, and avoiding the risks the business faces
> - evaluating the performance of his/her firm

A word-heavy, ineffective slide; the audience may find it hard to grasp the main points in a short time.

An effective slide that captures the main points in brief. If required, the presenter should explain these points in detail.

> **Functions of a Finance Manager**
>
> - Forecasting and planning
> - Analyzing and evaluating the investment activities
> - Coordination and control
> - Risk management
> - Performance measurement

**Exhibit 8.6** An Effective and an Ineffective Slide

- The slides should be numbered and the presentation should be rehearsed with the slides. This ensures that the words match the visuals.
- The speaker should explain the purpose and content of each slide when it is shown. It should be displayed for sufficient time to allow the audience to read it and, if required, make notes from it.

## Different Mediums of Presentation

Some common mediums of presentation are boards (black or white), flip charts, overhead projectors and transparencies, and Microsoft PowerPoint slides.

### *Boards*

A board is a primary aid used in classrooms and can be black or white. The use of a board helps listeners concentrate, as it is used to note important words and concepts, or to do calculations. It is better to divide the board into different parts for noting down points, doing calculations, and drawing figures. Bold, clear letters should be used so that words are visible at a distance.

### *Flip charts*

A flip chart is a large pad of paper set on a stand. It is used for presenting information to a small group of 15 to 20 persons. The advantage of using flip charts is that they can be readily generated and added to during the talk. They can also be prepared in advance for presenting complex diagrams, bar charts, and graphs. The speaker can sketch outlines of a diagram in the presence of the audience. He or she can also use them for prompting and for creating and presenting the audience's feedback, suggestions, comments, or any other observations at the end of the talk. Flip charts that can be written over in water-soluble ink can be reused.

### *Overhead projectors and transparencies*

A frequently used medium of presentation is an overhead projector (OHP). Overhead projectors allow the presenter to speak while looking at the audience and also have a prepared transparency projected on the screen. An OHP can have typed or handwritten matter, but the best impact is made when the content is neatly and clearly typed. Tips on preparing transparencies and using OHPs are given in Exhibit 8.7.

### *PowerPoint presentations*

Computer-based Microsoft PowerPoint presentations have now become more widespread than transparencies and slides. These are projected with the help of multimedia projectors. Usually, a computer screen displays the information to a large audience. Pictures and photographs are all displayed as part of the presentation. The entire presentation is saved on a laptop (with a backup on CD, if possible). The laptop is then connected to the projection equipment so that the laptop screen is cloned on the projector. The whole operation is automatic and simple. The visual impact is impressive and absorbing.

## Time the Presentation

The total presentation, including the question–answer session at the end, should be covered within the time allotted to it. In actual practice, while speaking, many people tend to ignore the fact that the audience's interest and attention are affected by the time factor. An effective presentation is one that has a smart beginning and logically arrives at a conclusion without wandering off-topic or rambling, while providing sufficient explanation for tricky or controversial points. The speaker should not repeat his or her points excessively. In addition, he or should learn to change the pacing of the presentation in response to the non-verbal cues received from the audience's body language.

> The total presentation, including the question–answer session at the end, should be covered within the time allotted to it.

- Make your transparencies/slides clear and visible to everyone in the audience.
- Put only one main point on each transparency/slide.
- Do not crowd the transparency/slide with too much information. Place information at the centre, and do not crowd the margins.
- Avoid having more than eight lines on each transparency/slide, and use about six words in each line. Thus, try to limit each transparency to about 48 words.
- Mark sections and sub-sections with clarity to make the organization of information clear.
- Check before the presentation that the projector is working. In the case of PowerPoint presentations, ensure that the laptop is not low on battery and that it is connected to the projector.
- Clean the projector lens and surface if needed.
- Adjust the focus and projector position to obtain the brightest and largest image possible.
- Switch off the machine between visuals. In the case of OHPs, run the fan inside the projector when showing visuals.
- The projection screen should be clean. If the projection is made on a whiteboard or wall, ensure that there is nothing written or marked on the board/wall.
- Use a pointer to point to parts of the transparency and emphasize specific points.
- Show the points one by one. In the case of an OHP, one may hide the matter that has not yet been discussed with tracing paper. In the case of PowerPoint slides, this can be done by clicking on **Slide Show** on the tool bar, selecting **Animation,** and selecting the required effect (*fade in one by one, appear and dim*, etc.) from the right-hand side panel, as follows:

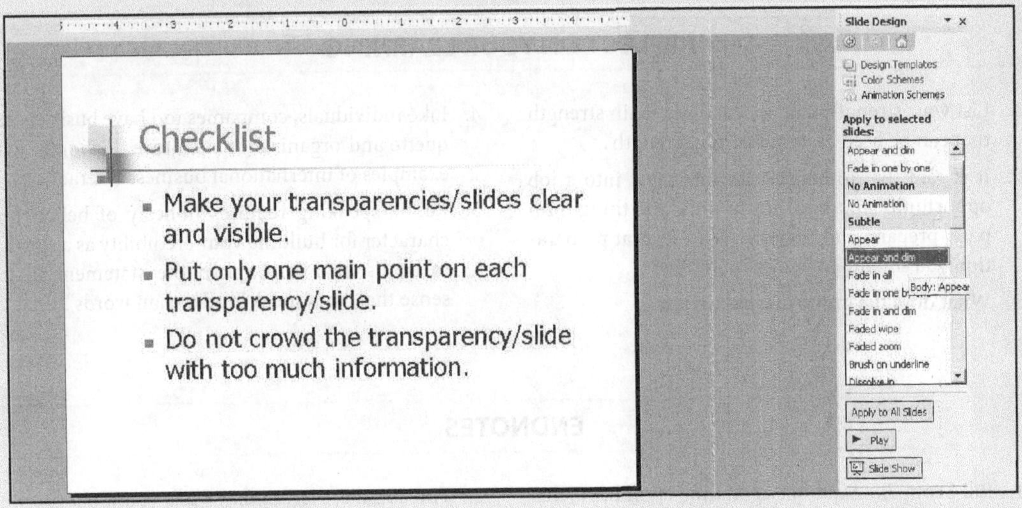


- Finally, one should remember that slides and transparencies are aids in presentations, and not a substitute for one's own words and explanations. So, it is important to face the audience while speaking and to make eye contact with them.

**Exhibit 8.7** Tips for Preparing Transparencies and PowerPoint Slides

### Become Familiar with the Location of the Presentation

Before presenting, the speaker should check the size, ventilation, and seating arrangement of the room. This helps position the screen according to the number of persons and the size of the room, ensuring it will be visible to everyone. The presenter should keep enough space between himself or herself and the screen so that he or she can refer to points on the screen with a pointer.

## REVIEW YOUR LEARNING

1. Discuss at least three characteristics of a good CV.
2. What qualities are evaluated by the interviewers for the job of a management trainee?
3. Comment on the importance of body language for success in an interview.
4. How does someone become a natural leader in a group discussion?
5. Why are good manners necessary for a good business? Discuss.
6. "In telephonic conversations, the way we listen, respond, speak or hang up is often as important as what is communicated". Discuss.
7. Describe the factors affecting the success of negotiations.
8. Discuss public speaking as an effective form of persuasive communication with an appeal for action.
9. Discuss the importance of visual aids in presentations.
10. "Video conferencing is more complex than talking on the phone". Elaborate.

## REFLECT ON YOUR LEARNING

1. List your strengths and discuss one main strength that can be used as your "selling strength".
2. It is said that to convert an interview into a job opportunity you need to do only one thing: prepare, prepare, and prepare. What is that preparation you should do before interview?
3. What does the group discussion test?
4. Like individuals, companies too have business etiquette and organizational culture. Elaborate with examples of international business interactions.
5. Public speaking requires honesty of beliefs and character for building your credibility as a speaker to be listened to. Explain the statement in the sense that "acts speak louder than words".

## ENDNOTES


1. Bill Scott, *The Skills of Negotiating* (Bombay: Jaico Publishing House, 1995), p. 3.
2. Tim Hindle, *Negotiating Skills* (London: Dorling Kindersley, 1998), p. 6.

# 9 Grammar

*Upon completion of this chapter, you should be able to:*

1. Learn how to write correct sentences.
2. Know the use of appropriate words.
3. Learn to punctuate sentences for clarity.
4. Know foreign words and phrases.
5. Use correct tone for better communication.

## AVOIDING SUBSTANDARD LANGUAGE

### Language, Tone, and Level of Formality

To ensure that a piece of writing is understood by the target audience, it is essential to use language that is commonly understood. The tone used should also reflect the appropriate level of formality for a particular context.

1 Develop an effective tone in written communication.

#### *Standard English*

"Standard English" includes the most commonly used and accepted words. It is considered "standard" because it follows the norms laid down by the rules of grammar, sentence construction, punctuation, spelling, paragraph construction, and so on. It is the language used in formal writing, such as books, magazines, newspapers, letters, memos, reports, and other forms of academic writing. For example, *ain't*, a contraction of "I am not", "is not" or "has not", is usually considered unacceptable in written (and also spoken) English. It can, however, appear as slang or in informal writing.

#### *Tone*

After determining the purpose and audience of a piece of writing, one has to then choose the appropriate tone in terms of formality. Tone refers to feelings created by words used to communicate a message. The tone of a piece of writing basically depends on the relationship between the writer and those who receive the message. As discussed earlier, communications in an organization can be classified as upward, downward, or horizontal. It requires skill and competence on the part of the writer to use the appropriate tone based on the status of the reader or receiver. It is obvious that something

Tone refers to feelings created by words used to communicate a message.

written for one's superiors will have a formal tone, whereas something written for one's peers will be more informal.

According to Muriel Harris, "The level of formality is the tone in writing and reflects the attitude of the writer toward the subject and audience".[1]

The tone can be:

- Informal
- Semi-formal
- Strictly formal

**2**

Use appropriate words and language for writing correctly and effectively.

***Informal Tone*** A writer uses an informal tone for social or personal communication and for informal writing. Deviations from standard English change the tone of writing from formal to informal or very formal. The informal tone includes the use of slang, colloquialisms, and regional words. The writer may also include contractions and incomplete sentences. An example of informal tone is: "The guy was damn annoyed because he couldn't get a hang of the mumbo-jumbo."

- **Colloquialisms**: Colloquialisms are casual words or phrases used in informal writing. Some examples of colloquialisms are "guy" for a person; "ain't" for *am not*, *is not*, or *are not*; "kids" for *children*; "hubby" for *husband*; "flunk" instead of *fail*; "wannnabe" for an avid fan who tries to emulate the person he or she admires; "whopping" for *huge* (for example, "a whopping success").
- **Slang**: Slang consists of informal words, phrases, or meanings that are not regarded as standard and are often used by a specific profession, class, and so on. Slang words, like colloquial words, are non-conventional. They are used in some special sense, but they exclude jargon and dialect-specific words. If a slang word acquires greater respectability, it moves into the category of colloquialism and may even reach the acceptability of standard English. For instance, "whodunit" is a colloquial word that appears in the critical writing of Northrop Frye, an eminent contemporary critic. It is gradually acquiring acceptability and is used to refer to modern murder mysteries. Some slang words and phrases are shown in Exhibit 9.1.

Slang consists of informal words, phrases, or meanings that are not regarded as standard and are often used by a specific profession, class, and so on.

The richness of English lies in its openness to words from other areas and countries.

- **Regional words**: Regional words, as the term suggests, are used primarily in a particular geographic area. The richness of English lies in its openness to words from other areas and countries. Words such as "porch", "verandah", "portico", "gherao", "hartal", "bazaar", "bag", "sack", "tote", or "phone" form part of spoken and written English, sometimes as standard usage.

Words such as *hype* and *ad* are gaining wider acceptability among professionals and writers.

Slang and regional words constitute the texture of language and give colour and tone to communication. In the world of business, the main concern is to communicate with sincerity, courtesy, and a sense of mutual respect. The aim is to write or speak in simple and clear English using the language of everyday speech. The aim of business writing is to earn the goodwill of the reader. The writing should

| *Slang* | *Meaning* |
|---|---|
| Pot | Marijuana |
| Get one's act together | Prepare/properly organize |
| Hip | Trendy/stylish |
| Pie-eyed | Drunk |
| Pig | Derogatory use for a police officer |
| Pig out | Eat (food) greedily |
| Brass | Money |
| Brass tacks | Essential details |
| Hype | Extravagant or intensive promotion of a product |
| Ad | Advertisement (contraction) |

**Exhibit 9.1** Examples of Slang

sound friendly and cooperative. For this purpose, special care should be taken to create a friendly and pleasant tone in business writing (letters/memos) by avoiding harsh and rude words.

***Semi-formal Tone*** The semi-formal tone lies somewhere between informal and academic. It is expressed mostly through standard English and is written according to the accepted rules of grammar, punctuation, sentence construction, and spelling, with a few contractions that add a sense of informality. The following sentence also has a semi-formal tone: "Much to their embarrassment and Mammachi's dismay, Chacko forced the pretty women to sit at the table with him and drink tea."

***Strictly Formal Tone*** The strictly formal tone is scholarly and uses words that are long and not frequently spoken in everyday conversation. The construction of the sentence and paragraph is also academic and literary in its tone.

The strictly formal tone is scholarly and uses words that are long and not frequently spoken in everyday conversation.

***Positive Language***

Business letters and memos should accentuate positive thoughts and expressions while stemming negative ones. Some tips to do so are:

- Avoid using words that underline the negative aspects of the situation.
- Write with a cool frame of mind. Do not write out of anger of excitement.
- Do not allow anger or harshness to creep into the writing.
- Focus on the positive when possible.

The following are examples of how, by substituting positive-sounding words and phrases for negative ones, the general tone (effect/impact) of each sentence can be changed without changing the message.

Negative: We have received your complaint.

Positive: We have received your letter.

(We receive letters. No one can mail a complaint.)

Negative: Your faulty fan motor will be replaced.

Positive: We are sending you a new fan motor with a one-year guarantee.

Negative: The delay in dispatching your order because of our oversight will not be longer than a week.

Positive: Your complete order will reach you by July 24.

To eliminate the accusing and insulting tone of the original sentence, substitute neutral words for words that are insulting or make the reader feel dishonest or unintelligent.

Insulting: Don't allow your carelessness to cause accidents in the blast furnace.

Neutral: Be careful when you are working in the blast furnace.

Insulting: Because you failed to inform the members of the board about the agenda in time, the meeting had to be postponed.

Neutral: The meeting had to be postponed as the board members did not receive the agenda in time.

Remember that negative language regarding the situation is bound to distance the reader. To win the reader's cooperation, one must emphasize solutions instead of criticizing the situation.

### *You-attitude*

In all writing, the author has a point of view. *You-attitude* is the reader's point of view. In good business writing, especially letters, the author should write from the reader's point of view, by viewing things as readers would. He or she should be able to see and present the situation as the reader would see it. Writers should try to convey an understanding of the reader's position and present the information by visualizing how it will affect the feelings of readers.

> In all writing, the author has a point of view. You-attitude refers to the reader's point of view.

In the following examples, the focus is shifted from the author's point of view to the reader's point of view by emphasizing the benefits and interests of the reader in the given situation.

Author's emphasis: I congratulate you on successfully completing the task.

Reader's emphasis: Congratulations on successfully completing the task.

Author's emphasis: To reduce office work and save time, we are introducing a new system of registration for you.

Reader's emphasis: To facilitate the registration process, we are changing our system of registration.

Author's emphasis: We are sending out interview calls next Monday.

Receiver's emphasis: You should receive the interview letter by Thursday, August 12.

The change of emphasis in these examples is psychological. By giving importance to the reader's concerns (his or her point of view) and benefits, one can develop a friendly tone.

Some guidelines for reflecting the "you" point of view in business correspondence are:

1. Empathize with the reader. Place yourself in his or her position.
2. Highlight the benefits to the reader in the situation.
3. Adopt a pleasant tone as far as possible.
4. Avoid negative words and images. Do not use words that insult or accuse the reader.
5. Offer helpful suggestions if possible.
6. Use words that are familiar, clear, and natural. Avoid old-fashioned expressions or jargon.

### *Natural Language*

Letters and memos should be written in the language of everyday speech. They should avoid using clichés and hackneyed expressions. Archaic expressions will make the message dull and uninteresting for the reader. Exhibit 9.2 lists some examples of phrases that should be rewritten.

Consider the naturalness of the following sentence. Do we normally talk like this?

> As per your request, we beg to inform you that we have booked a single room for you at our lodge for 4 days from 18 July to 21 July, 2003.

This sentence lacks the spontaneity and liveliness of a natural response. It should be revised as:

> As you desired, we have booked a room for you from 18 July to 21 July, 2003.

The message should be brief. The specification of the room, single or double, need not be given here. Simply confirming the dates is sufficient.

### *Active Voice*

There are two parts of a sentence—the subject and the predicate. The subject is that about which something is said; the predicate is whatever is said about the subject. In a sentence, the subject is the main focus, the doer of an action. It is frequently positioned at the opening of a sentence.

> Choose the active voice to help the reader understand the main message at the very beginning of the sentence.

Choose the active voice to help the reader understand the main message at the very beginning of the sentence. Passive voice is long-drawn because the "to be" form of verb

| *Hackneyed Language* | *Natural Language* |
|---|---|
| The undersigned | I/We |
| We beg to advise | We can say |
| Prior to receipt of | Before we/I received |
| As per your request | As you requested |
| Attached herewith | Attached is |
| Pursuant to | In accordance with |
| Hoping for the favour of your kind reply | We/I hope to |
| Yours to hand of 20th | Received your letter of July 20 |

**Exhibit 9.2** Old-fashioned Expressions

is used with the preposition "by" and is then followed by the doer of the action. In passive voice, the main focus of the sentence, the subject (in the writer's mind), is mentioned at the end of the sentence—by then the reader may become impatient and lose focus. For example, read the following sentences closely:

Active: Packaging often describes the product's look and feel to the buyer.

Passive: The product's look and feel are often described to the buyer by its packaging.

Read both the forms of the sentence together. You will find that the passive sentence reads slowly and moves heavily. It tells you about "packaging" only at the end of the sentence. It first speaks about the product's look and feel. Technically, the two sentences are talking about two different things. The passive-voice sentence tells the reader about a product's look and feel and how they are described for the buyer through packaging. It indirectly talks about packaging. The active-voice sentence speaks more directly about packaging and its functions of describing a product's look and feel to the buyer. The sentence is short and it grips the reader's attention. Readers therefore, usually prefer active voice for its directness, faster pace, and clarity.

Here are a few problems readers often face because of the use of passive voice:

- *Passive voice in issuing instructions:* Instructions should be clear, direct, and complete because passive voice may confuse the reader. The instruction may omit the "by" preposition phrase and thereby leave the question "who should do it" unclear. The doer of the action is left implied and is not clearly stated.

  Unclear: The strike should be called off. [By whom? Not stated]

  Clear: The strike should be called off by the union.

- *Dropping the "by" phrase:* Often, the writer attempts to shorten the length of the passive-voice sentence by leaving out the "by" phrase after the verb. This makes it difficult for the reader to understand the full process of the action as the sentence does not offer complete information.

  Incomplete: To make these allocations, marketing managers use sales response functions that show how sales and profits would be affected.

  Complete: To make these allocations, marketing managers use sales response functions that show how sales and profits would be affected by the amount of money spent in each application.

- *Confusing use of dangling modifiers*: The reader is often confused by the misplaced modifier in the passive construction. Therefore, avoid this form of passive construction and write in active form.

  Unclear: Besides saving on mailing expenses, a double-digit response will be achieved by a customer database system.

  Clear: Besides saving on mailing expenses, a customer database system will achieve a double-digit response.

### *Sexist Language*

Sexist expressions and ideas should be avoided in business communication. Sexist language consists of words or phrases that show bias against the competence or importance of women. In today's gender-sensitive age, business writing should scrupulously leave out all words that question women's dignity, competence, or status.

Often the use of sexist language is unconscious—one may fail to realize that a certain phrase or word is an unfavourable reference to the abilities of women. However, such expressions are not acceptable to modern readers.

Often the use of sexist language is unconscious—one may fail to realize that a certain phrase or word is an unfavourable reference to the abilities of women.

Consider the following guidelines to avoid sexist words and phrases:

1. Do not use "he" as a generic pronoun. In the past, it has been customary to refer to people in general, or a group of persons, as male. "He" is grammatically correct, but should be avoided in generic situations, especially job descriptions.

   Sexist: A manager writes to his peers in an informal or semi-formal tone.

   Revised: Managers write to their peers in an informal or semi-formal tone.

   In this example, the number of the subject has been changed from singular to plural, and "their" has been used as the pronoun, thus avoiding any hint of sexism.

2. In job descriptions, do not use words which suggest that all employees are of the same gender.

   Sexist: An experienced professor is needed. He should…

   Revised: An experienced professor is needed. He or she should…

   Or

   An experienced professor is needed. The person should be…

   Sexist: The policeman should listen to the common man's complaints.

   Revised: The police officer should listen to the common man's complaints.

   Sexist: The stewardess explained the safety measures before take-off.

   Revised: The flight attendant explained the safety measures before take-off.

3. Do not use words that lower the dignity and status of women. Also never use slang words to refer to women.

   Do not use words that lower the dignity and status of women. Also never use slang words to refer to women.

   Sexist: The girls in the central office will endorse these papers.

   Revised: The office assistants in the central office will endorse these papers.

   Sexist: Do bring the little woman (*slang for one's wife*) to the party.

   Revised: Do bring your spouse to the party.

4. Always refer to women and men in the same way.

   Sexist: Denise Samrat, Dr Ian Campbell, and Dr Philip Kotler were members of the CRM panel.

   Revised: Ms Denise Samrat, Dr Ian Campbell, and Dr Philip Kotler were members of the CRM panel.

Sexist: Women of this sector were represented by two doctors and one lady lawyer.

Revised: Women of this sector were represented by two doctors and one lawyer.

Finally, writing business letters clearly and accurately requires that the following points be kept in mind:

- A sentence is the smallest unit of a complete thought.
- Each sentence should have only one thought.
- Sentences and paragraphs should be constructed according to the principles of unity and coherence.

For instance, consider this sentence: "This activity makes no attempt to be a comprehensive test of accurate writing, but offers a valuable chance for you to test your own skill and identify areas of weakness." This sentence talks about only one topic—"a test of accurate writing". Other ideas are related to the main subject.

In contrast, examine the following sentence: "I hasten to inform you that your complete order has been shipped on April 10, the invoice will reach you with the goods." This sentence is not correctly constructed. It has two separate thoughts, which should be expressed in separate sentences. A better version would be: "I hasten to inform you that your complete order has been shipped on 10 April. The invoice will reach you with the goods."

## ENGLISH USAGE

In this section, we shall discuss some common pitfalls that need to be avoided in order to write correct and complete sentences.

### Dangling Modifiers

Incorrect: Expecting a large crowd, extra chairs were provided by the management. (This is a dangling modifier because the modifier does not logically and sensibly refer to the subject of the main clause. It is not the "extra chairs" (subject) that are "expecting a large crowd".)

Correct: Expecting a large crowd, the management provided extra chairs.

Correct: Since a large crowd was expected, extra chairs were provided by the management.

### Vague References of *This, That,* and *Which*

Incorrect: He wants to begin immediately and to make his first sale before the end of the year. As a result of this, he will probably become a successful salesman.

Correct: He wants to begin immediately and to make his first sale before the end of the year. As a result of this attitude, he will probably become a successful salesman. (*This* must not refer to a cause, sentence, or idea; it must refer to one specific word.)

### Lack of Parallel Construction

Incorrect: The man liked meeting and to talk to people. (*And* joins one gerund and one infinitive construction here.)

Correct: The man liked to meet and talk to people. (*And* joins parallel infinitive constructions here.)

Correct: The man liked meeting and talking to people. (*And* joins parallel gerund constructions that express ideas of equal importance.)

Note that parallel construction is equally important in the enumeration of points in lists, as shown by the following example:

Incorrect:

1. The company should increase the price of all products.
2. Increase the variety of products.
3. Provide more services.
4. They should review their advertising programme.

Correct:

The company should:

1. increase the price of all products.
2. increase the variety of products.
3. provide more services.
4. review their advertising programme.

## Inconsistent Use of Verb Tenses

**The verb tense should be consistent within the sentence (as in the example below) and from sentence to sentence within the paragraph.**

Incorrect: He usually makes sensible decisions although he frequently changed his mind. (Tense shifts from present tense in the main clause to past tense in the subordinate clause.)

Correct: He usually makes sensible decisions although he frequently changes his mind.

## Choosing the Mood

**Generally speaking, the imperative mood should be avoided in report writing. The imperative expresses a command or a strong request; a report should suggest or recommend rather than command.**

Incorrect: Do this work carefully; you should also do it slowly. (Verb shifts from imperative to indicative mood.)

Correct: You should do this carefully; you should also do it slowly.

Correct: Do this work carefully; also, do it slowly.

### Separation of Related Sentence Elements

Incorrect: I, hoping very much to find Mrs Singh at home and to sell her one of our new products, knocked at the door. (Separation of subject, *I*, and verb, *knocked*, is not necessary.)

Correct: Hoping very much to find Mrs Singh at home and to sell her one of our new products, I knocked at the door.

Incorrect: I only telephoned those men. (Separation of adverb *only* and *those men*, which *only* modifies, is not necessary.)

Correct: I telephoned only those men.

### Lack of Subject–Verb Agreement

Incorrect: The price of the new products were reasonable.

Correct: The price of the new products was reasonable. (A singular verb is used to agree with the singular subject, even though a plural word intervenes.)

Incorrect: The advantage of Product A and Product B are the profits.

Correct: The advantage of Product A and Product B is the profits.

Incorrect: There are a man and some women waiting to see me.

Correct: There is a man and some women waiting to see me. (When a sentence begins with 'there', the verb agrees with the subject that immediately follows it.)

Incorrect: Everyone on the top three floors work for one company.

Correct: Everyone on the top three floors works for one company (A singular verb is used to agree with a singular subject, especially when the subject is "everyone" or "each".)

Incorrect: Only one of the girls who play the sitar came today.

Correct: Only one of the girls who plays the sitar came today. (A singular verb is used to agree with *one*, the singular word to which the subject *who* refers. This is important when the subject of the verb is *who, which*, or *that*.)

Incorrect: Neither the report nor its appendix were published.

Correct: Neither the report nor its appendix was published. (A singular verb is used to agree with singular subjects joined by *or* or *nor*.)

Note that if one subject is singular and one is plural, the verb agrees with the nearest subject. For example, it is correct to say, "Neither the report nor the books were published". Also, note that the plural subject is kept after *or* or *nor*, near the verb.

### Lack of Pronoun Agreement

Incorrect: Everyone brought lunch to work.

Correct: Everyone brought his lunch to work. (One must use a singular pronoun to agree with *everyone*, the singular word to which the pronoun refers.)

Incorrect: He does not usually make those kind of errors.

Correct: He does not usually make that kind of error. (Singular pronoun is used to agree with *kind*, the singular noun that the pronoun modifies. This is important when *this, that, these*, or *those* modify *kind* or *sort*.)

Correct: He does not usually make these kinds or errors. (Here, a plural pronoun modifies the plural noun.)

Incorrect: Neither the manager nor his favourite employee could do their work alone.

Correct: Neither the manager nor his favourite employee could do his work alone. (A singular pronoun is used to agree with the singular words, which are joined by *nor* and to which the pronoun refers.)

If *or* or *nor* joins one singular word and one plural word, the pronoun agrees with the one nearest to it.

Neither the manager nor the workers were aware of their error.

## Confusing Adjectives and Adverbs

The words *hard, hardly, late, lately, most*, and *mostly* need to be used carefully. As adjectives, *hard, late*, and *most* have two adverb forms, which should be clearly understood.

*Hard*, when used as an adverb means "strenuously" or "diligently". It is normally placed after the verb and is an adverb of manner.

I worked hard yesterday. (not *hardly*)

She worked hard to pass the examination. (not *hardly*)

Sometimes, for emphasis, *hard* can be used at the beginning of a sentence. However, this usage is relatively rare.

Hard as she tried, she could not get through.

*Hardly*, an adverb, means "not much" or "scarcely". It is an adverb of degree and is used before the verb. If the verb is used with an auxiliary, the adverb is placed between the auxiliary and the next part of the verb.

He sang so softly that the audience could hardly hear him.

He was so shrunken that I hardly recognized him.

This pen has hardly been used.

Hardly had he gone when his wife reached here.

The adverb *late* means two things:

(i) "after the expected time" or "after the time by which something should have happened or been done".

Every Sunday morning they wake up late.

Three times this week he has come to office late.

(ii) "towards the end of a specified period of time"

Doctors refuse to visit patients late at night.

I called her late in the afternoon.

She did not have a child until quite late in life.

*Lately* means "recently".

Have you seen any good movies lately?

Have you met your brother lately?

*Most,* as an adverb, means "to the greatest extent".

The thing that I admire most is simplicity. (not *mostly*)

He who boasts most is often one who does least.

*Mostly* means "for the most part".

The lecture mostly covered recent trends in politics.

The paper consisted mostly of old questions.

Complete the following sentences with one of the words given in parentheses:

1. The student could ________ get passing marks. (hardly, hard)
2. She could ________ raise her arms. (hard, hardly)
3. The child can ________ lift the school bag. (hardly, hard)
4. It has rained ________ this year. (hardly, hard)
5. He had ________ entered the road when he was injured. (hard, hardly)
6. She studies ________ into the night. (lately, late)
7. The train arrived ten minutes ________. (late, lately)
8. The examinations will be held ________ in April this time. (late, lately)
9. I reached home very ________ last night. (late, lately)
10. We have not heard anything from them ________. (late, lately)
11. The great singers have been ________ women. (mostly, most)
12. Join the course that will help you ________. (mostly most)
13. I have books that are ________ novels. (mostly, most)
14. It was ________ my elder brother who guided me to this position. (most, mostly)
15. In this computer course, the students are ________ girls from a renowned school. (mostly, most)

**Exercise E.1** Usage of Adverbs

### *Adverbs Ending in –ly*

Consider the adverbs formed by adding *ly* to an adjective: *gladly, slowly, foolishly, wisely, nicely.*

These adverbs are usually adverbs of manner. But, if an adjective itself ends with *ly*, it cannot normally be changed into an adverb. Such words can act as both adjectives and/or adverbs.

> If an adjective itself ends with *ly*, it cannot normally be changed into an adverb. Such words can act both as adjectives and/or adverbs.

1. Words that act both as adjectives and adverbs, without any modification, include *cowardly, daily, early, fortnightly, hourly, surely, nightly, only, weekly,* and *yearly.*

She has arrived via an early flight. (adjective)

She has come early. (adverb)

There is an hourly change of classes. (adjective)

The classes change hourly. (adverb)

*The Statesman* is a daily newspaper. (adjective)

*The Statesman* is published daily. (adverb)

2. Words ending in *ly* that are used only as adjectives include *brotherly, fatherly, motherly, friendly, gentlemanly, godly, goodly, homely, likely, lovely, manly, seemly, unseemly*, and *womanly*. These can be changed into adverbs by using a phrase, such as "in a brotherly manner" or "in a lovely fashion", or "in a manly way".

He is a very friendly boss. (adjective)

She received us in a very friendly manner. (adverb)

Note that the word *kind* (an adjective) has *kindly* as its adverb. But, *kindly* is also an adjective.

My father had a kindly nature. (adjective)

My father always talked to us in a very kindly manner. (adjective)

In each of the following pairs of sentences, complete the second sentence by using an adverb or an adverbial phrase having the same meaning as the adjective in the first sentence:

1. She is an early bird. She rises ______.
2. From here, there is an hourly bus service to Delhi. The buses to Delhi run ______.
3. That was a cowardly action. That was acting ______.
4. I have hired this car on a monthly basis. I pay the car charges ______.
5. The tutor held daily classes. The tutor holds classes ______.
6. Most magazines are monthly publications. Most magazines are published ______.
7. She is a very gentle person. She always behaves ______.
8. He gave us friendly advice. He advised us ______.
9. My friend noticed my fatherly smile at the child. My friend noticed my smiling at the child ______.
10. He is a very gentlemanly person. He always behaves ______.

**Exercise E.2** Words Used as Both Adjectives and Adverbs

***Errors in the Use of Adjectives and Adverbs***

Adjectival complements

1. Study the following sentences:

The sky became bright. (not *brightly*)

This year good apples are rare. (not *rarely)*

She got angry. (not *angrily*)

The tea became bitter. (not *bitterly*)

The job is difficult though it appears easy. (not *easily*)

The price seems to be low. (not *lowly*)

In these sentences, the verbs *to be, to seem, to become*, and so on (*appear, feel, look, grow, turn*) need an adjective and not an adverb to act as a complement that qualifies the subject to complete the meaning of the sentence. No adverb is required to modify the verb. Note that when the verbs *turn, grow*, and *appear* are used in a different sense, they are followed by an adverb, not an adjective.

The ship appeared suddenly on the horizon.

These plants have grown quickly.

She turned and left unexpectedly.

In these sentences, *appear* means "come into sight", *grow* means "increase in size", and *turn* means "move in a particular direction".

On the other hand, an adjective, not an adverb, is used after verbs, such as *feel, sound, taste*, and *smell*, to show a quality experienced by one of the physical senses.

This cloth feels smooth.

These pipes sound nice.

This orange tastes sour.

That rose smells sweet.

Fill in the sentences below using the adjective or adverb given in parentheses.

1. It feels very ______ in this room. (cold, coldly)
2. The weather has turned ______. (hot, hotly)
3. At her call, I turned around ______. (sudden, suddenly)
4. He seems very ______ at this result. (sad, sadly)
5. Some trees grow very ______. (slow, slowly)
6. She looks ______ in this dress. (pretty, prettily)
7. His story is to appear very ______. (short, shortly)
8. Her signature does not appear to be ______. (genuinely, genuine)
9. If you feel ______, remove the shirt. (warm, warmly)
10. The director congratulated the award winners ______. (warm, warmly)
11. The girl was very ______ to catch the robber by herself. (brave, bravely)
12. The audience became ______ when the winners of the Best Film award came on stage. (excited, excitedly)
13. Her room smells ______ of sandalwood. (strong, strongly)
14. Our new teacher seems very ______. (strict, strictly)
15. This food smells very ______. (appetizing, appetizingly)

**Exercise E.3** Usage of Adverbs and Adjectives

## PUNCTUATION

Of all punctuation symbols, the four discussed below are the ones most commonly misused.

### The Comma

A comma is used to:

(i) Set off main clauses joined by *and*, *but*, *or*, *nor*, and *for*.

The first alternative certainly offered the company many advantages, but the second was probably more economical.

However, if the clauses are short, the comma separation is unnecessary.

She bought him a nice shirt but lost it.

(ii) Separate long introductory elements from the rest of the sentence.

When all the proposals had been fully investigated and discussed, we were able to make the final decision.

However, when the introductory element is particularly short, a comma is not required.

On Friday we were able to make the final decision.

(iii) Separate words in a series of three or more. The last comma in the series is optional and depends on the writer's preference.

The controller of accounts, vice-president and president took part in the investigation.

The last comma in the series may be required in some cases, for clarity.

The controller of accounts, vice-president and general manager, and the president took part in the investigation. (The second comma in this sentence indicates that one person holds the dual position of vice-president and general manager.)

(iv) Set off parenthetical expressions from the rest of the sentence.

A parenthetical expression is one that is inserted into a sentence; therefore, the latter must be grammatically complete without it. Unless it begins or ends a sentence, a parenthetical expression should be set off by two commas.

Ram, unlike his brother, was a good salesman.

Sometimes, if the expression does not cause an abrupt interruption, the comma separation is unnecessary (especially with the words *also*, *too*, *indeed*, *at least*, *perhaps*, and *likewise*).

Ram's personality was indeed more pleasing than his brother's.

When a parenthetical expression (particularly a lengthy one) causes an abrupt interruption, dashes or parentheses may be used instead of commas. Like the comma, dashes and parentheses must be used in pairs. However, they should be used much less frequently than commas.

Ram was a good salesman—he sold more than anyone else in the company—and had a pleasing personality. (emphatic.)

Ram was a good salesman (he sold more than anyone else in the company) and had a pleasing personality. (less emphatic.)

(v) Set off non-restrictive elements

Non-restrictive elements are parenthetical (see iv above) and are not essential to the meaning of the sentence. They must be set off by two commas.

Ram, who sold more than anyone else in the company, was awarded the salesmen's trophy.

(vi) Set off a direct quotation from the rest of the sentence.

The foreman replied, "I have done all I can" and left the room.

A comma is not used to:

(i) Separate the subject and the verb or the verb and the object.

Incorrect: The company with the best reputation in this area, was awarded the contract. (subject–verb separation)

Correct: The company with the best reputation in this area was awarded the contract.

Incorrect: The company knew last week, that it had been awarded the contract. (verb–object separation)

Correct: The company knew last week that it had been awarded the contract.

**If words requiring punctuation (see points (d) and (e) above) intervene between the subject and the verb or between the verb and the object, the comma is then necessary.**

ABC Company, which has a good reputation in this area, was awarded the contract. (Non-restrictive phrase intervenes between the verb and object.)

The company knew last week, probably by Wednesday, that it had been awarded the contract. (Non-restrictive phrase intervenes between the verb and the object.)

(ii) Join two main clauses unless *and, but, or, nor,* or *for* comes between them.

Incorrect: The salesman displayed his goods, then he talked about the newest product.

Correct: The salesman displayed his goods. Then he talked about the newest product.

Correct: The salesman displayed his goods, and then he talked about the newest product.

(iii) Separate two words or phrases joined by *and, but, or, nor,* or *for.*

Incorrect: I cannot remember whether the head office is in Calcutta, or in Bombay.

Correct: I cannot remember whether the head office is in Calcutta or in Bombay.

(iv) Separate an adjective from the noun it modifies.

Incorrect: We should choose an economical, flexible, plan.

Correct: We should choose an economical, flexible plan.

(v) Separate parentheses from the rest of the sentence.

Incorrect: Several miscellaneous items are included in the total expense.

Correct: Several miscellaneous items are included in the total expense.

Incorrect: Although several miscellaneous items are included in the total expense, they are not important.

Correct: Although several miscellaneous items are included in the total expense (see Exhibit I), they are not important. (Second comma is necessary to set off the introductory element.)

### *The colon*

A colon is used to:

**(i) Introduce a list (often preceded by "the following" or "as follows").**

The following men were nominated for the top honour: Singh, Jain, Basu, and Jha.

**(ii) Separate two main clauses where the second clause explains the first.**

The purpose of his speech was obvious: he wanted to present a concise outline of company policy.

### *The Semi-colon*

A semi-colon is used to:

**(i) Separate two main clauses that are not joined by the conjunctions *and, but, or, nor* or *for*.**

At this time last year, Mr Singh was the company's general manager; he is now the president. (A full stop could be substituted for the semi-colon, but the latter is preferable when the clauses are short and closely related in thought).

**(ii) Separate two main clauses joined by *however, therefore, moreover, consequently, also, furthermore, nevertheless, then, thus,* or *likewise*.**

We thought that Ram would be the new president; however, his brother was chosen instead.

**(iii) Separate two independent clauses when the second clause is preceded by "for example", "that is", or "namely".**

We do not like the attitude of the new manager; that is, we resent his air of superiority.

**(iv) Separate items in a series when the items within the series contain commas.**

We called on Mr Singh, the president; Mr Jain, the vice-president and general manager; Mr Basu, the controller of accounts; and Mr Jha, the secretary.

We chose these people because they held responsible positions, both within the company and in organizations outside; because they had valuable experience; because they had the ability to work well with others; and because they all had the time for outside work.

**A semi-colon should not be used to separate a main clause from a subordinate clause.**

Incorrect: Mr Singh was named honorary president; because of his long association with the firm.

Correct: Mr Singh was named honorary president because of his long association with the firm.

**Except in cases where it separates items in a series, the semi-colon always separates one main clause from another main clause.**

***The Apostrophe***

The apostrophe is used to show possession in the following instances:

(i) For possessive singular nouns, such as "manager's salary" and "man's character" (an *s* is added to the noun).

(ii) For possessive plurals of nouns, such as "managers' salaries" (only the apostrophe is used if the plural form of the word ends in *s*) and "men's salaries (where an *s* is added after the apostrophe as the plural does not end in *s*).

(iii) For the possessive form of the pronouns *one, someone, somebody, everyone, everybody, anyone, anybody, none,* and *nobody*. An example is *anyone's*, in which an *s* is added to the pronoun.

An apostrophe should not be used for the pronouns *his, hers, ours, yours, theirs,* or *whose* because they are already possessive.

Incorrect: It's meaning was clear ("It's" means "it is")

Correct: Its meaning was clear

## ENRICHING VOCABULARY

**Accept, Except.** *Accept*, a verb, means to agree to something, to believe, or to receive. *Except* means "not including" or "other than".

**Advice, Advise.** *Advice* is a noun, and *advise* is a verb.

**Affect, Effect.** Most frequently, *affect*, which means to influence, is used as a verb, and *effect*, which means a result is used as a noun.

**Ain't.** This is a non-standard way of saying "am not", "has not", "have not", and so on.

**All Right, Alright.** The phrase *all right* has two words, not one. *Alright* is an incorrect form.

**All Together, Altogether.** *All together* means in a group, and *altogether* means entirely or totally.

**Alot, A lot.** *Alot* is an incorrect form of *a lot*.

**Among, Between.** *Among* is used to refer to three or more nouns and *between* is used for two nouns.

**Amount, Number.** *Amount* is used for things or ideas that are general or abstract and cannot be counted. *Number* is used for things that can be counted.

**Anyone, Any One.** *Anyone* means any person at all. *Any one* refers to a specific person or things in a group.

**As, As If, Like.** *As* is used in a comparison when there is an equality intended; *as if* is used when a supposed situation is there; and *like* is used when similarity is intended. **Assure, Ensure, Insure.** *Assure* means to declare or promise; *ensure* means to make safe or certain; and *insure* means to protect with a contract of insurance.

**Awful, Awfully.** *Awful* is an adjective meaning "extremely unpleasant". *Awfully* is an adverb used in informal writing to say "very". It should be avoided in formal writing.

**Beside, Besides.** *Beside* is a preposition meaning "at the side of", "compared with", or "having nothing to do with". *Besides* is a preposition meaning "in addition to" or "other than".

**Breath, Breathe.** *Breath* is a noun, and *breathe* is a verb.

**Choose, Chose.** *Choose* is the present tense of the verb, and *chose* is the past tense.

**Compared to, Compared with.** Use *compared to* to point out similarities between dissimilar items. Use *compared with* to show similarities and differences between similar items.

**Data.** This is the plural form of *datum*. In informal usage, *data* is used as a singular noun.

**Different from, Different than.** *Different from* is always correct, but some writers also use *different than* when a clause following this phrase. (For example, "This book is *different from* the others." and "That is a *different* outcome *than* they expected.")

**Farther, Further.** While some writers use these words interchangeably, dictionary definitions differentiate between them. *Farther* is used when actual distance is involved, and *further* is used to mean "to a greater extent" or "more".

**Fewer, Less.** *Fewer* is used for things that are countable (for example: fewer trains, fewer trees, fewer students). *Less* is used for ideas, abstractions, or things that are thought of collectively, not separately (for example: less gain, less furniture), and things that are measured by amount not number (for example: less tea, less money).

**Good, Well.** *Good* is an adjective and therefore, describes only nouns. *Well* is an adverb and describes adjectives, other adverbs, and verbs.

**Got, Have.** *Got* is the past tense of "get" and should not be used in place of *have*. Similarly, "got to" should not be used as a substitute for "must". "Have got to" is an informal substitute for *must*.

**Imply, Infer.** Sometimes these two words are used interchangeably. However, *imply* means to suggest without stating directly. *Infer* means to reach an opinion from facts or reasoning.

**Its, It's.** *Its* is a personal pronoun in the possessive case. *It's* is a contraction for "it is".

**Kind, Sort.** These two forms are singular and should be used with the words "this" or "that". Their plurals, *kinds* and *sorts* should be used with the words "these" or "those".

**Lay, Lie.** *Lay* is a verb that needs an object and should not be used in place of *lie*, a verb that takes no direct object.

**OK, Okay.** These can be used interchangeably in informal writing, but should not be used in formal or academic writing.

**Such.** This is an often overused word in place of "very" or "extremely". It should be avoided.

**Sure.** The use of *sure* as an adverb is informal. In formal writing, the adverb "surely" is used.

**That, Which.** Use *that* for essential clauses and *which* for non-essential clauses.

**Their, There, They're.** *Their* is a possessive pronoun; *there* means "in", "at", or "at that place"; *they're* is the contraction for "they are".

**Theirself, Theirselves.** These are incorrect forms that are sometimes used in place of "themselves".

**Use to.** This is incorrect; "used to" should be used instead.

**Who, Whom.** *Who* is used for the subject case; *whom* is used for the object case.

**Who's, Whose.** *Who's* is a contraction for "who is"; *whose* is a possessive pronoun.

**Your, You're.** *Your* is a possessive pronoun; *you're* is a contraction for "you are". (*Your* feet are cold. *You're* a great writer.)

**Yours, Your's.** *Yours* is the correct possessive form; *your's* is an incorrect version of "yours".

## IDIOMS AND PROVERBS

Oxford dictionary defines an idiom as a group of words whose implied meaning is different from the meaning of the individual words. We can see that *an apple of one's eye* is a group of words whose meaning has nothing to do with that of the individual words. Idioms are an indispensable part of English. An idiomatic language is always better equipped to communicate as it lends charm and expression to a routine language. Idioms and phrases are language specific and also vary from culture to culture. However, excessive use of idioms may not be advisable as it makes the language showy and may give an impression that the speaker wants to impress the listener.

## FOREIGN WORDS AND PHRASES

*adieu:* farewell; good-bye

*aide-de-camp:* an army officer acting as assistant to a general

*aide-mémoire:* an aid to memory

*à la:* after the fashion of. We use it colloquially in such contexts as: "If you think you can dictate to me, *à la* Hitler, you're very much mistaken!"

*à la carte:* by the bill of fare, with a stated price for each dish, the customer pays for such dishes as he chooses. See *table d'hôte* below.

*à la mode:* in the fashion; fashionable

*amour:* love; *amours,* love affairs

*amour-propre:* self-esteem; conceit

*ancien régime:* the old order of things

*à propos:* to the purpose

*arrière-pensée:* not an afterthought, but a mental reservation, a thought not put into words

*attaché:* a member of the staff of an ambassador. An attaché case is a small leather case

*au fait:* well acquainted with a matter

*au revoir:* until we meet again

*à votre santé:* to your health

*beau monde:* the people of fashion

*belles-lettres:* polite literature

*bête noire:* "black beast"; a bugbear; a pet aversion

*bêtise:* stupidity; a stupid thing; a silly act

*billet-doux:* a love-letter

*blasé:* bored; sick of pleasure

*bonhomie:* good nature

*bon mot:* a clever remark

*bonne bouche:* a tasty morsel; a titbit

*bon ton:* good taste; good style

*bon vivant:* one fond of luxury and good food

*bon voyage:* a good voyage or journey, e.g. "I went down to the docks to wish him *bon voyage* when he left for the Far East."

*bric-à-brac:* odds and ends

*café:* coffee; a coffee-house or tea-shop; *café au lait:* coffee with milk; *café noir:* black coffee (i.e. without milk)

*carte blanche:* full power; a free hand, e.g. "I gave the builder *carte blanche* to do whatever repairs he thought necessary."

*chaperon:* a married or elderly woman who accompanies a girl on social occasions

*chargé d'affaires:* an official who acts as deputy to an ambassador; an ambassador at a minor court

*chauffeur:* a fireman or stoker. In modern usage a driver of a car who is paid for his services

*chef-d'œuvre:* a masterpiece. Michelangelo's *chef-d'œuvre* is the painting on the ceiling of the Sistine Chapel, Rome

*chic:* literally, a knack (*Il a du chic,* "He is skilful, a dab hand"), but used today in the sense of "stylish", e.g."She wore a chic little hat",

*cliché:* hackneyed phrase

*comme il faut:* as it should be

*confrère:* a fellow member; a colleague

*contretemps:* an unfortunate happening

*coup de grâce:* the finishing stroke; merciful killing, e.g. "The poor creature had broken its back, so I gave it the *coup de grâce* with a bullet from my rifle." The phrase is used figuratively in such contexts as: "In the third game Mr Jones administered the *coup de grâce* with the ace of trumps."

*coup d'état:* a change of government by sudden and violent means, e.g. "By this swift *coup d'état,* the army gained control of the whole country."

*crème de la crème:* "cream of the cream"; the very best

*cuisine:* Literarlly "kitchen", but also used in the sense of the style in which food is cooked or prepared, e.g. "This little restaurant is famous for its cuisine."

*cul-de-sac:* "bottom of the bag"; a blind alley, open at one end only

*débris* (usually without the accent in English). scattered fragments; piles of rubbish, e.g. "The mass of debris resulting from the collision greatly hampered rescue work."

*début:* a first appearance, e.g. "Sir John Gielgud made his *début* at the Old Vic in 1921, when he played the part of the herald in *Henry V.*" The accent is sometimes omitted in English

*déjeuner:* breakfast; sometimes also luncheon

*demi-monde:* "half world"; a class of women on the outskirts of society and of doubtful respectability

*dénouement:* "unknotting", the final solution of a play, novel, etc., e.g. "In the exciting *dénouement,* the most unlikely character turns out to be the murderer." The accent is sometimes omitted in English.

*de rigueur:* required by etiquette or custom, e.g. "White flannels are *de rigueur* in cricket and tennis."

*de trop:* too much; not wanted; in the way, e.g. "Feeling that I was *de trop* I quietly withdrew and left the young couple alone in the room."

*Dieu et mon droit:* "God and my right", the motto of Richard I, meaning that he held his right from God alone. Since then, it has been inscribed on the royal standard of English kings and queens.

*double entendre:* a double meaning; words that can be taken two ways, one of them indelicate or vulgar; the kind of remark that caused the child at the pantomime to ask: "Mummy, what's Daddy laughing at?"

*doyen:* senior; oldest member, e.g. "With the death of Mr Wallace, the doyen of the association is now Mr Green, who is eighty-six."

*éclair:* a finger-shaped puff of pastry filled with cream

*élite* (or *elite):* the best people; the *crème de la crème*

*embarras de choix:* embarrassment of choice; too many from which to choose

*embarras de richesse:* embarrassment of wealth; having so much money that one does not know what to do with it

*en bloc:* in a lump; in bulk; wholesale, e.g. "The ship's cargo was bought *en bloc* by a trading company as soon as she reached port."

*encore:* again, once more; a demand for the repetition of a song, dance, etc., e.g. "After deafening shouts of 'Encore!' from all parts of the theatre, the final chorus was repeated by the whole company." Oddly enough, the French themselves do not cry "Encore!" but "Bis!", which means "Twice!"

*en famille:* at home; with one's own family, e.g. "After a week of public engagements, he delighted in spending Sunday *en famille.*"

*enfant terrible:* a terrible child, one who asks awkward questions at the wrong moment, or repeats remarks he has overheard, e.g.: "What's a wolf in sheep's clothing, Mr Johnson?" "Why do you ask, Tommy?" "Because that's what Dad says you are."

*en masse:* in a mass; all together, e.g. "On the approach of the enemy, the inhabitants fled from the city *en masse.*"

*ennui:* tedium; boredom

*en passant:* in passing; by the way

*en rapport:* in sympathy with

*en route:* on the way; bound for

*entente cordiale:* a friendly understanding or agreement

*entourage: a* retinue; a group of advisers, attendants, friends, etc., e.g. "The crown prince and his entourage went riding in the royal park."

*entrée:* right of admittance; freedom of entry; also a dish served between the fish course and the main course at dinner

*entre nous:* between ourselves, e.g. "I don't think she will make him a good wife, but that's *entre nous:* Don't tell them I said so!"

*esprit de corps:* the spirit of loyalty and comradeship among the members of a group, regiment, etc.

*etiquette:* the rules of behaviour in polite society. Professional etiquette governs the conduct of those in certain walks of life—medical, legal, etc.

*fait accompli:* an accomplished fact; a thing done and no longer worth making a fuss about

*faute de mieux:* for want of better

*faux pas:* a false step; an indiscretion; an error of judgment

*fiancé* (feminine *fiancée):* one who is engaged to be married

*force majeure:* superior force; greater strength, e.g. 'It's no use reasoning with those people. The only argument they understand is *force majeure.*'

*gourmand. gourmet:* The first eats greedily; the second with discrimination

*habitué:* a frequenter; a regular customer

*Honi soit qui mal y pense:* This is the Old French for "Shame be to him who thinks evil". It is the motto of the Order of the Garter

*hors de combat:* Once translated by an English schoolboy as "war-horse", this means literally 'out of the fight'; disabled

*hors-d'œuvre:* a side dish served as a relish at the beginning of a meal

*idée fixe,* a fixed idea. one that no persuasion or argument can alter

*impasse:* a blind alley; a deadlock

*laisser-faire:* the principle of non-interference, especially by the Government in commercial matters

*mal à propos* (Anglicized malapropos). out of place; inopportune. See under MALAPROPISM

*matinée:* an afternoon performance, either theatrical or musical

*mauvais quart d'heure:* "a bad quarter of an hour"; a short but unpleasant experience or interview

*mauvais sujet:* a worthless fellow; a scoundrel; a black sheep

*menu:* a bill of fare in a restaurant

*messieurs:* gentlemen, the plural of *monsieur:* Used in English in the abbreviated form *Messrs* (no full stop) when addressing a letter to more than one person, e.g. "Messrs Taylor & Lawson".

*mise en scène:* the scenery and general setting of a play. Figuratively, the surroundings of an event

*naïve* (usually without the diaeresis in English), artless, natural, ingenuous

*née:* born

*négligé* (sometimes spelt *negligee* in English). informal dress; a woman's loose gown

*noblesse oblige,* meaning that if one is of noble rank, one is obliged to behave accordingly

*nom de guerre,* literally a "war-name", but used figuratively for an assumed name under which one follows a calling or profession, e.g. "When George Edward Wade began his long career as a music-hall comedian he adopted George Robey as his *nom de guerre.*"

*nom de plume:* a pen name. See under PSEUDONYM

*nonpareil:* without equal; matchless

*outré:* exaggerated; extravagant

*panache:* literally a tuft or plume worn in a helmet; figuratively it means "display; swagger; bounce"

*papier mâché:* "chewed paper"; paper pulp moulded into shape and used for various purposes, such as *egg* boxes

*par excellence:* pre-eminently; above all

*parole:* a military word meaning a promise not to escape

*parvenu:* a newcomer; an upstart

*pâté de foie gras:* a paste or a patty made with the livers of geese fattened for that purpose

*patois:* dialect

*pièce de résistance:* the main dish of a meal. It is also used figuratively in such contexts as: "The *pike de résistance* of the evening was a magnificent firework display."

*pied-à-terre:* a temporary lodging

*poste restante:* till called for

*pourboire:* "drink money"; a tip

*précis:* an abstract or summary

*protégé:* a person under the protection of another

*purée:* a thick soup made by pressing peas, beans, etc. through a sieve

*qui s' excuse s' accuse:* he who excuses himself accuses himself

*qui vive:* To be on the *qui vive* is to keep a sharp look-out

*Répondez, s'il vous plaît* (abbreviated R.S.V.P.). "Reply, if you please", printed on invitations to dinners, parties, etc.

*résumé:* a summary

*Revenons à nos moutons:* "Let us return to our sheep." Figuratively, "Let us return to our subject", said when the conversation has drifted away from the main topic. The quotation is from *Patelin,* by the French dramatist, Pierre Blanchet *(c.* 1459-1519)

*riposte:* a smart retort

*roué:* a rake; a profligate

*sabotage:* deliberate damage to railways, factories, machinery, etc. by discontented employees. In World War II it was used extensively to impede the enemy in the occupied countries

*sang-froid:* "cold blood"; coolness; composure

*sauve-qui-peut:* "save who can"; "every man for himself"; a general panic; a headlong flight

*savoir-faire:* tact; knowing the right thing to do; presence of mind

*soupçon:* suspicion; a taste; a small quantity, e.g. "Pink gin requires only a *soupçon* of angostura bitters."

*souvenir:* a keepsake

*table d'hôte:* "the host's table"; a set meal served at a set time and at a fixed price, unlike *à la carte* (see above), where the customer chooses his meal from the menu and pays for each dish

*tête-à-tête:* "head to head"; a private conversation or interview between two persons, e.g. "I waited outside the office while my wife had a *tête-à-tête* with the manageress."

*tour de force:* a feat of strength; a striking exhibition of power or skill

*tout ensemble:* "all together"; in costume and the arts, the general effect of anything considered as a whole, without regard to details

*trousseau:* a bride's outfit of clothing, etc.

*voilà tout:* that is all

*vol-au-vent:* "flight on the wind"; a pastry case of light puff paste with a filling of chicken, prawn, lobster, mushroom, etc.

*volte-face:* a turning round; a change of front in an argument or in politics

## Latin Words and Phrases

Hundreds of these are in common use in English. Below is a selected list. Those asterisked are treated more fully under their own headings in the body of the book.

*ad hoc:* for this

*ad infinitum:* to infinity; endless

*ad libitum:* at pleasure

*ad nauseam:* to a disgusting extent, e.g. "He repeated *ad nauseam* all the details of his many ailments."

*ad valorem:* according to value

*a fortiori:* all the more; for a still stronger reason

*Alma Mater:* "the bounteous mother", a name used by ex-students for their school or university

*Anno Domini:* the year of our Lord. Abbreviated A.D. *(q.v.)*

*ante meridiem:* before noon. Abbreviated *a.m.*, e.g. 10.30 a.m. =half past ten in the morning

*bona fides:* good faith, sincerity, genuineness, e.g. "Assured of his *bona fides,* I handed him the keys of the house."

*caveat emptor:* let the buyer beware

*circa:* about. Abbreviated c. (*q.v.*)

*compos mentis:* sound mind, e.g. "The lawyer pleaded that his client had not been in *compos mentis* at the time of the accident."

*contra:* against. It is found in words such as *contradict* (speak against), *contravene* (come against), also in compound words such as *contra-regulations* (against regulations), and from it derives *counter,* e.g. *counteract,* to act against

*cum:* with. It is found in place names, e.g. Chorlton-cum-Hardy, and in such combinations as gardener-cum-chauffeur, a man who performs the double duties of gardener and chauffeur, and *shop-cum-garage,* where one can buy a pound of butter or a gallon of petrol

*cum grano salis:* with a grain of salt, used figuratively in the sense of not entirely believing a thing, e.g. 'I take all he says *cum grano salis.*'

*de facto:* in fact; existing, whether legal or not; the opposite of *de jure*

*Dei gratia:* by God's grace

*de jure:* by right; according to law. For example, a *de jure* government is one that has legal standing, whilst a *de facto* government is one that is in control, whether legally or not

*Deo volente:* God willing. Abbreviated D.V. "I shall see you again next year, D.V."

*deus ex machina:* a god from the machine

*dramatis personae:* a list of the characters in a play, often with the names of the actors taking the parts

*Eheu fugaces... labuntur anni:* This is a quotation from the Roman poet, Horace. It means "Alas, the fleeting years glide past." It is our custom to use only the first two words, implying the rest, as if with a shrug of our shoulders

*errare est humanum:* to err is human

*et cetera:* and the rest

*et sequitur:* and the following. Abbreviated *et seq.*

*exempli gratia:* for example. Abbreviated *e.g.* and treated under that heading

*exit* (plural *exeunt):* a stage direction meaning "he goes off". The word is also used as a noun, e.g. "They have their exits and their entrances."

*ex libris:* from the library (of); printed at the head of a slip pasted inside the cover of a book and giving the owner's name

*ex officio:* because of one's office. The chairman of a main committee is an ex-officio member of all sub-committees that may be formed

*felo de se:* "felon of self", one who takes his own life, e.g. "The jury returned a verdict *of felo de se.*"

*Festina lente:* "Hasten slowly", a paradox attributed to the Roman emperor Augustus

*fidus Achates:* a faithful follower

*finis:* the end, sometimes printed below the text on the last page of a book

*flagrante delicto.* in the very act. Its literal meaning is "while the crime is blazing". "A policeman arrived suddenly and caught the thief in *flagrante delicto.*"

*hic jacet:* "here lies", often found on tombstones

*ibidem:* in the same place

*idem est:* that is. Abbreviated *i.e. (q.v.)*

*in camera:* In Latin *camera* means "a vault". The term *in camera* is a legal one, e.g. "The evidence was heard *in camera.*" That is to say, it was heard in the private chamber of the judge, not in open court

*infra dignitatem:* beneath one's dignity. Abbreviated *infra dig {q.v.),* usually without a full stop

*inter alia:* among other things, e.g. "This book contains, *inter alia,* a list of Latin words and phrases."

*lapsus linguae:* a slip of the tongue

*lapsus memoriae:* a slip of memory

*laudator temporis acti:* one who praises past times—"the good old days"

*locum tenens:* "holding the place"; a deputy, especially for a clergyman or a doctor. It is often abbreviated, e.g. "Dr Harrison is acting as locum for Dr Brown, who is on holiday."

*magnum opus:* great work; the chief production of an artist or a writer. See OPUS

*mater:* mother

*mea culpa:* by my own fault

*mens sana in corpore sano:* a healthy mind in a healthy body

*meum et tuum:* mine and thine (yours). We use the term euphemistically in "He doesn't know the difference between *meum* and *tuum*", which is another way of saying that we think he is a thief

*mirabile dictu:* wonderful to relate, e.g. "*Mirabile dictu,* the weather was fine."

*modus operandi:* a way of working, particularly doing the same thing in the same way every time, e.g. "The house had been entered through a skylight, which the police recognized as the *modus operandi* of a thief known to be in the neighbourhood."

*multum in parvo:* much in little

*mutatis mutandis:* with any necessary change of detail, e.g. "The new agreement shall be on the same terms, *mutatis mutandis,* as the existing agreement."

*nemine contradicente:* Usually abbreviated *nem. con.*, this means "no one speaking against", e.g. "Mr Jones's proposal that the clubhouse should be redecorated was carried *nem. con.*"

*ne plus ultra:* "not more beyond"; the utmost limit, e.g. "In dress and appearance he was the *ne plus ultra* of good taste."

*non sequitur:* "it does not follow"

*nota bene:* "note well". Abbreviated N.B., this is used to draw particular attention to what follows, e.g. "The annual general meeting will be held on 25th October next. N.B. Subscriptions are now due."

*obiit:* "he died". Abbreviated *ob.*, this is used as follows: "Gilbert Harding *(ob.* 16th Nov. 1960) was the most controversial broadcaster of his day."

*opus:* work

*pater:* father; hence *paternoster* (our father), the Lord's Prayer in Latin *paterfamilias:* head of a family. Generally used facetiously or to end a letter published in a newspaper, e.g. "Dear Sir, Referring to recent correspondence in your columns, my belief is that school terms should be longer and holidays shorter. Yours faithfully, Paterfamilias."

*Peccavi:* "I have sinned"

*per annum:* by the year

*per aspera ad astra:* "to the stars by rough ways"

*per capita:* per head, i.e. for each person

*per centum:* per hundred. Abbreviated *per cent* or %

*per diem:* per day

*per mensem:* per month

*per procuriationem:* by proxy; by the agency of. Abbreviated *per pro* or *p.p.* See *per pro* under ABREVIATION

*post meridiem:* after noon. Abbreviated *p.m.*, e.g. 4.15 p.m. - quarter past four in the afternoon

*post mortem:* after death. A post mortem examination of a body is made to find out the cause of death

*post scriptum:* written afterwards. See POSTSCRIPT

*prima facie:* first impression, e.g. "The *prima facie* evidence suggested that he had met with a fatal accident, but further investigations proved that he had committed suicide."

*pro patria:* for one's country. It is to be found in Horace's *Dulce et decorum est pro patria mori,* "It is sweet and glorious to die for one's country"

*pro rata:* in proportion; proportionately

*pro tempore:* for the time being. Abbreviated *pro tern,* it is used in such contexts as: "We hope to move into our new house at the end of the month and are living in a caravan pro tern."

*Quod erat demonstrandum:* that which was to be proved. In its abbreviated form Q.E.D. it is used at the end of Euclid's theorems. Q.E.F. (*Quod erat faciendum,* that which was to be done) is used at the end of his problems

*quod vide:* which see

*rara avis:* rare bird. It is used figuratively in such contexts as: "The visitor to this little secluded village is a *rara avis* indeed."

*sic:* thus

*sine die:* "without a day"; put off until some unspecified date in the future, e.g. "It was considered too early to make a final decision, so the matter was deferred *sine die.*"

*sine qua non:* "without which not"; an indispensable condition or qualification; something essential, e.g. "In the art of public speaking, clear diction is a *sine qua non.*"

*sotto voce:* in an undertone

*status quo:* the existing state of affairs; the way things are now. To maintain the *status quo* is to ensure that things remain unchanged. To restore the *status quo* is to re-establish a former state of affairs

*stet:* let it stand

*terra fama:* "firm earth"; dry land, e.g. "After a rough crossing of the Straits of Dover, we were relieved to be back on *terra fama.*"

*ubique:* everywhere. From it derives the adjective *ubiquitous,* e.g. "All over the world the ubiquitous Englishman is to be found."

*ultima Thule:* the utmost limit. *Thule* was the name given by the Romans to the most northerly country known to them, which may have been Iceland, Norway or the Shetland islands. We use it in such contexts as: "During my convalescence, when walking quickly tired me, my *ultima Thule* was the tobacconist's at the end of the road."

*ultra vires:* beyond one's power or authority, e.g. "The magistrates decided that the local council had acted *ultra vires* by closing this footpath to the public."

*vade mecum:* "go with me". We use the term for anything we carry about with us because we may need it at any time, particularly a handbook for ready reference, e.g. a tourist's vade mecum, an angler's vade mecum, a typist's vade mecum.

*Vae victis:* "Woe to the conquered!"

*vale* (plural *valete):* farewell. The plural form is often used in school magazines to head a list of those leaving at the end of the term

*verbum sapienti:* The full phrase is *verbum sat sapienti,* meaning "a word to the wise is enough", but we usually omit *sat* (enough) and abbreviate the rest to *verb. sap.* in such contexts as: "Verb. sap.," he said when she tried to explain. "I can guess the rest."

*versus:* against. It is frequently abbreviated *v.* in sporting fixtures, e.g. England *v.* Scotland, Manchester City *v.* Tottenham Hotspurs, and in legal cases, e.g. Andrews *v.* Director of Public Prosecutions

*via:* "way; road". We use it in the sense of *by way of,* e.g. "He flew from London to Australia *via* Singapore."

*via media:* sometimes *media via,* a middle way or road. We use it figuratively with the meaning of "a middle course", which is safer than venturing too far to one side or the other, e.g. "My doctor recommended me to take a month's holiday. I could not afford to be away so long from my business, so chose the *via media* and spent a fortnight at the seaside."

*vice:* in the place of. A vice-president takes over the duties of the president when the latter is unable to attend. Also vice-admiral, vice-chairman, vice-captain (in cricket, football, etc.) and others. A viceroy is one who rules territory as the deputy of the sovereign. Lord Curzon was Viceroy of India from 1898 to 1905

*vice versa:* conversely; the other way round, e.g. "After the collision the motorist blamed the driver of the lorry, and vice versa." That is, they blamed each other

*videlicet:* "one may see". It is abbreviated *viz* and is treated under that heading

*Vita brevis, ars longa:* "Life is short, art is long". An alternative version is *Ars longa, vita brevis*

*viva voce:* "with the living voice"; oral or orally, e.g. "In the French examination, I passed the written test, but failed in the *viva voce* because my accent wasn't good enough."

## Some English Idioms

1. A bed of roses: A comfortable position.
2. A bed of thorns: An uncomfortable position.
3. A bird in the hand is worth two in the bush: Having something that is certain is much better than taking a risk for more.
4. A bird's eye view: A brief general view.
5. A blessing in disguise: Something good that isn't recognized at first.
6. A bolt from the blue: Any calamity that overtakes somebody suddenly.
7. A chicken-hearted fellow: A timid person.
8. Achilles heel: A point of vulnerability.
9. A doubting Thomas: A skeptic who needs physical or personal evidence to believe something.
10. A drop in the bucket: A very small part of something.
11. A fair weather friend: One who betrays in difficulty.
12. A fish out of water: A person in uncomfortable surroundings.

13. A fool and his money are easily parted: It is easy for a foolish person to lose his/her money.
14. A hen-pecked husband: A person servile to his wife.
15. A leopard can't change his spots: You cannot change what you are.
16. A penny saved is a penny earned: Saving money little by little.
17. A picture paints a thousand words: A visual presentation is far more descriptive than words.
18. A piece of cake: A task that can be accomplished very easily.
19. A red letter day: An important day.
20. A slap on the wrist: A very mild punishment.
21. A snake in grass: A deceitful person.
22. A taste of your own medicine: When you are ill-treated the same way you ill-treat others.
23. At loggerheads: Engaged in a head-on dispute.
24. Actions speak louder than words: It's better to do something in reality than just talk about it.
25. Add fuel to the fire: To do something to make a bad situation even worse than it is.
26. Against the clock: To do something fast to finish it before a particular time.
27. All bark and no bite: Someone is threatening or aggressive but not willing to engage in a fight.
28. All Greek to me: Meaningless and incomprehensible like someone who cannot read, speak, or understand any of the Greek languages.
29. All in the same boat: When everyone is facing the same challenges.
30. An axe to grind: To have a dispute with someone.
31. An apple of someone's eye: Someone who is cherished above all others.
32. As high as a kite: Anything that is high up in the sky.
33. At the drop of a hat: Willing to do something immediately.
34. Back-seat driver: People who criticize from the sidelines, much like someone giving unwanted advice from the back seat of a vehicle to the driver.
35. Back to square one: Having to start all over again.
36. Beat a dead horse: To force an issue that has already ended.
37. Beating about the bush: Avoiding the main topic. Not speaking directly about the issue.
38. Between a rock and a hard place: Stuck between two very bad options.
39. Bite off more than you can chew: To take on a task that is way too big.
40. Bite your tongue: To avoid talking.
41. Black sheep: A person who is considered a disgrace to a family.
42. Blood is thicker than water: The family bond is closer than anything else.
43. Blow one's own horn: To praise your own abilities and achievements.
44. Blue moon: A rare event or occurrence.
45. Break the ice: To remove the tension, hesitation at the first meeting or at the opening of a party, etc.
46. Burn the midnight oil: To stay awake late at night to work or to study.
47. By hook or by crook: By whatever means possible, fair or unfair.
48. Carry a torch: To be infatuated with.
49. Chew someone out: To scold someone verbally.

50. Chip on his shoulder: Angry today about something that occurred in the past.
51. Chip off the old block: People who closely resemble their parents in some way or the other.
52. Clean slate: To make a new start by clearing records.
53. Cock and bull story: An unbelievable tale.
54. Crocodile tears: Pretending to be sad, in an attempt to manipulate the situation.
55. Cross your fingers: To hope that something happens the way you want it to.
56. Cry over spilt milk: When you complain about a loss from the past.
57. Cry wolf: Intentionally raise a false alarm.
58. Curiosity killed the cat: Being inquisitive can lead you into a dangerous situation.
59. Dark horse: One who was previously unknown and is now prominent.
60. Devil's advocate: Someone who takes a position for the sake of argument without believing in that particular side of the argument.
61. Don't count your chickens before they hatch: Don't rely on something until you are sure of it.
62. Don't put all your eggs in one basket: Do not put all your resources in one possibility.
63. Drastic times call for drastic measures: When you are extremely desperate you need to take extremely desperate actions.
64. Draw the line: To set a limit, as of accepted behaviour.
65. Drink like a fish: To drink very heavily.
66. Drive someone up the wall: To irritate and/or annoy very much.
67. Dropping like flies: A large number of people either falling ill or dying.
68. Every cloud has a silver lining: Be optimistic, even difficult times will lead to better days.
69. Everything but the kitchen sinks: Almost everything and anything has been included.
70. Eye for eye: Revenge.
71. Feather in one's hat: An accomplishment a person can be proud of.
72. Field day: An enjoyable day or circumstance.
73. Finding your feet: To become more comfortable in whatever you are doing.
74. Fixed in your ways: Not willing to change from your normal way of doing something.
75. Flash in the pan: Something that looks promising in the beginning but fails to deliver anything in the end.
76. Flesh and blood: Material of which people are made of, or it can refer to someone's family.
77. Fools' gold: A worthless rock that resembles real gold.
78. From pillar to post: From one place or thing to another.
79. From rags to riches: To go from being very poor to being very wealthy.
80. Fuddy-duddy: An old-fashioned and foolish type of person.
81. Get over it: To move beyond something that is bothering you.
82. Get up on the wrong side of the bed: Someone who has a horrible day.
83. Give him the slip: To get away from, to escape.
84. Go down like a lead balloon: To be received badly by an audience.
85. Go out on a limb: Put yourself in a tough position to support someone/something.
86. Go the extra mile: Making extra efforts for the task at hand.

87. Good Samaritan: Someone who helps others when they are in need with no thought of a reward.
88. Great minds think alike: Intelligent people think like each other.
89. Green room: The waiting room, especially for those who are about to go on stage, a TV, or radio.
90. Gut feeling: A personal intuition that something may not be right.
91. Haste makes waste: Quickly doing things results in a poor ending.
92. Hat trick: Three scores made continuously without break in a sport, such as three wickets in cricket or three soccer goals.
93. Have a finger in every pie: To be involved in a lot of different activities and have influence over them.
94. He lost his head: Angry and overcome by emotions.
95. Head over heels: Very excited and/or joyful, especially when in love.
96. Hell in a hand basket: Deteriorating and headed for complete disaster.
97. Hit below the belt: An unfair or cruel remark.
98. Hit the books: To study, especially for a test or exam.
99. Hit the nail on the head: Do something exactly right or say something exactly right.
100. Hold your horses: Be patient.
101. Icing on the cake: Something extra that is added to an already good situation.
102. Idle hands are the devil's tools: You are more likely to get into trouble if you have nothing to do.
103. If it's not one thing, it's another: When one thing goes wrong, then another, and another.
104. In the heat of the moment: Overwhelmed by what is happening in the moment.
105. It takes two to tango: A two-person conflict where both people are at fault.
106. It's a small world: You frequently see the same people in different places.
107. It's anyone's call: A competition where the outcome is difficult to judge or predict.
108. Jack of all trades master of none: Someone good at many things but, excellent at nothing.
109. Keep an eye on somebody: You should watch a person carefully.
110. Keep body and soul together: To earn a sufficient amount of money to keep yourself alive.
111. Keep your chin up: To remain joyful in a tough situation.
112. Kitty-corner: Diagonally across, sometimes called Catty-Corner as well.
113. Knee jerk reaction: A quick and automatic response.
114. Knock on wood: Knuckle tapping on wood to avoid some bad luck.
115. Know the ropes: To understand the details.
116. Last but not the least: An introduction phrase to let the audience know that the last person mentioned is no less important than those introduced before him/her.
117. Lend me your ear: To politely ask for someone's full attention.
118. Let bygones be bygones: To forget about a disagreement or argument.
119. Let sleeping dogs lie: To avoid restarting a conflict.
120. Let the cat out of the bag: To share a secret that wasn't supposed to be shared.

121. Level-playing field: A fair competition where no side has an advantage.
122. Like a chicken with its head cut off: To act in a frenzied manner.
123. Liquor someone up: To get someone drunk.
124. Loose cannon: Someone who is unpredictable and can cause damage if not kept in check.
125. Maiden speech: The first speech made by a person.
126. Make no bones about: To state a fact so there are no doubts or objections.
127. Mumbo jumbo: Nonsense or meaningless speech.
128. Nest egg: Savings set aside for future use.
129. Never bite the hand that feeds you: Don't hurt anyone who helps you.
130. New kid on the block: Someone new to the group or area.
131. No dice: Not to accept a proposition.
132. No room to swing a cat: An unusually small or confined space.
133. Not playing with a full deck: Someone who lacks intelligence.
134. Off on the wrong foot: Getting a bad start on a relationship or task.
135. Off the hook: No longer have to deal with a tough situation.
136. Off the record: Something said in confidence that the one speaking doesn't want attributed to him/her.
137. On pins and needles: Anxious or nervous, especially in anticipation of something.
138. On the fence: Undecided.
139. On the same page: When multiple people agree on the same thing.
140. Out of the blue: Something that suddenly and unexpectedly occurs.
141. Out on a limb: When people put themselves in a risky situation.
142. Out on the town: To enjoy yourself by going out.
143. Over the top: Highly excessive.
144. Pass the buck: Avoid responsibility by giving it to someone else.
145. Pedal to the metal: To go full speed, especially while driving a vehicle.
146. Peeping Tom: Someone who observes people in the nude or sexually active people, mainly for his own gratification.
147. Pick up your ears: To listen very carefully.
148. Pig out: To eat a lot and eat it quickly.
149. Pipe down: To shut up or be quiet.
150. Pour oil on troubled waters: To calm a disturbance.
151. Practice makes perfect: By constantly practicing, you will become better.
152. Pull the plug: To stop something. To bring something to an end.
153. Pulling your leg: Tricking someone as a joke.
154. Put a sock in it: To tell noisy person or a group to be quiet.
155. Queer the pitch: Destroy or ruin a plan.
156. Raining cats and dogs: A very loud and noisy rain storm.
157. Read between the lines: To pay attention to what is implied in writing or speech.

158. Ring fencing: To protect a particular sum of money by putting restrictions on its use.
159. Rise and shine: Time to get out of bed and get ready for work/school.
160. Rome was not built in one day: If you want something to be completed properly, then it is going to take time.
161. Rule of thumb: A rough estimate.
162. Run out of steam: To be completely out of energy.
163. Saved by the bell: Saved at the last possible moment.
164. Scapegoat: Someone else who takes the blame.
165. Show your true colours: To reveal your true intentions, personality or behaviour.
166. Sick as a dog: To be very sick (with the flu or a cold).
167. Sitting shotgun: Riding in the front passenger seat of a car.
168. Sixth sense: Intuition; a special ability to know something without using any of the five senses.
169. Smell a rat: To detect someone in the group who is betraying others.
170. Smell something fishy: Detecting something isn't right and there might be a reason for it.
171. Southpaw: Someone who is left handed.
172. Spitting image: The exact likeness or kind.
173. Start from scratch: To do it all over again from the beginning.
174. Strike while the iron is hot: Act quickly when the opportunity is still available.
175. The ball is in your court: It is your decision this time.
176. The best of both worlds: There are two choices and you have them both.
177. The bigger they are the harder they fall: While the bigger and stronger opponent might be a lot more difficult to beat.
178. The last straw: When one small burden after another creates an unbearable situation, the last straw is the last small burden that one can take.
179. The whole nine yards: Everything.
180. Third times a charm: After no success the first two times, the third try is a lucky one.
181. Tie the knot: To get married.
182. To be in one's good books: To be favoured.
183. To build castles in the air: Imaginary projects.
184. To call a spade a spade: To be plain and outspoken.
185. To carry the day: To be victorious.
186. To eat humble pie: To have to apologize.
187. To pay lip service: To pretend to be faithful.
188. To steal someone's thunder: To take the credit for something someone else did.
189. To the backbone: Thoroughly.
190. Tongue and cheek: Humour, not to be taken seriously.
191. To nip in the bud: To put a stop to a thing in the beginning.
192. Turn a blind eye: Refuse to acknowledge something you know is real or legitimate.
193. Under the weather: Feeling ill or sick.
194. Up a blind alley: Going down a course of action that leads to a bad outcome.

195. Use your loaf: Use your head. Think smart.
196. Variety is the spice of life: The more experiences you try the more exciting life can be.
197. Wag the dog: A diversion away from something of greater importance.
198. Water under the bridge: Anything from the past that isn't significant or important anymore.
199. Wear your heart on your sleeve: To openly and freely express your emotions.
200. When pigs fly: Something that will never ever happen.
201. Wild and woolly: Uncultured and without laws.
202. Wine and dine: When somebody is treated to an expensive meal.
203. Without a doubt: For certain.
204. X marks the spot: A phrase that is said when someone finds something he/she has been looking for.
205. You are what you eat: To stay healthy you must eat healthy food.
206. You can't judge a book by its cover: Decisions shouldn't be made primarily on appearance.
207. Your guess is as good as mine: I have no idea.
208. Young Turk: An insurgent person trying to take control of a situation.
209. Zero tolerance: The policy of applying laws very strictly so that people are punished even for mild offences.

### Phrasal Verbs

Phrasal verbs are verbal compounds with a grammatical structure of *verb + preposition and/ or adverbs.* They form a fixed group of words with an idiomatic meaning. They are expressions (also known as verbal idioms) whose real meaning cannot be detected from that of the constituent words. Like idioms, phrasal verbs are widely used in English and they make our expression rich and fresh. Phrasal verbs are better suited to informal speech. You would complain about your friend who has not kept his/her promise by saying, "He has backed out at the last moment." On the other hand if you are a buyer, you would better express the similar idea formally to a supplier who has not supplied the ordered goods by writing, "we are sorry to say that you have not fulfilled your commitment."

### Some Common Phrasal Verbs

1. Abide by: Respect or obey the law, a decision, a rule
2. Account for: Explain, give a reason
3. Add up: Make sense, seem reasonable
4. Agree with: Have the same opinion as somebody else
5. Allow for: Take advantage of something (an opportunity)
6. Answer back: Reply rudely
7. Apply for: Make a formal request for something ( job, permit, loan, etc.)
8. Avail (oneself) of: Take into consideration, include in a calculation
9. Back away: Move backwards, in fear or dislike
10. Back down: Withdraw, concede defeat
11. Blow up: Explode; be destroyed by an explosion
12. Back up: Give support or encouragement; make a copy of (file, program, etc.)
13. Black out: Faint, lose consciousness

14. Block off: Separate using a barrier
15. Boil down to: Be summarized as
16. Break down: Go out of order, cease to function; lose control of one's emotions
17. Break out: Start suddenly
18. Break into: Enter by force
19. Bump into: Meet by accident or unexpectedly
20. Burn out: Stop (something) working; become exhausted from overworking
21. Butt in (on something): Interrupt impolitely
22. Call back: Return a phone call
23. Call off: Cancel
24. Call on/upon something: Formally invite or request
25. Calm down: Become more relaxed, less angry or upset
26. Carry on: Continue
27. Carry out: Do something as specified (a plan, an order, a threat); perform or conduct (test, experiment)
28. Check in: Register at a hotel or airport
29. Check out: Pay one's bill and leave (a hotel); investigate
30. Clam up: Refuse to speak
31. Close down: Stop operating (company, restaurant, cinema)
32. Come across: Find by chance; appear
33. Come forward: Present oneself
34. Conk out: Stop working; stop or fall asleep from exhaustion
35. Come up against: Be faced with or opposed by
36. Count on: rely or depend on (for help)
37. Cross out: Remove by drawing a line through
38. Cut down on: Reduce in number or size
39. Cut out: Remove using scissors; stop doing something
40. Deal with: Handle, take care of (problem, situation)
41. Die down: Calm down, become less strong
42. Dress up: Wear elegant clothes; disguise oneself
43. Do without: Manage without
44. Drag on: Last longer than expected
45. Draw up: Write (contract, agreement, document)
46. Drop in: Visit, usually on the way somewhere
47. Drop out: Leave school without finishing
48. Drop off: Deliver someone or something; fall asleep
49. Ease off: Reduce, become less severe or slow down (pain, traffic, work)
50. Even out: Eliminate differences of opinion; become level or regular
51. Fall through: Fail; doesn't happen

52. Figure out: Understand, find the answer
53. Fill out: Complete (a form/an application)
54. Find out: Discover or obtain information
55. Focus on: Understand; find a solution
56. Figure out: Concentrate on something
57. Get at: Imply
58. Get away: Escape
59. Get back at: To get revenge on somebody
60. Get in: Enter
61. Get into (+noun): Manage to cope or to survive
62. Get off: Leave (bus, train, plane); remove
63. Get on: Board (bus, train, plane)
64. Get on with (something): Continue to do; make progress
65. Get out: Leave
66. Get on (well) with (somebody): Have a good relationship with
67. Get out of: Avoid doing something
68. Get over: Recover from (illness, disappointment)
69. Give up: Stop doing something
70. Get rid of: Eliminate
71. Get together: Meet each other
72. Get up: Rise, leave bed
73. Go through: Experience
74. Grow up: Spend one's childhood; develop; become an adult
75. Hand in: Distribute
76. Hand out: Submit (report, homework)
77. Hang out: Spend time in a particular place, or with a group of friends
78. Hang up: End a phone conversation
79. Hit at: Aim a blow at
80. Hit back: Retaliate; reply to an attack
81. Hit on/upon: Find unexpectedly or by inspiration
82. Hold on: Wait; grip tightly
83. Hurry up: Be quick, act speedily
84. Iron out: Resolve by discussion, eliminate differences
85. Join in: Participate
86. Join up: Engage in, become a member of, meet and unite with
87. Jot down: Take quick notes
88. Keep on: Continue doing something
89. Keep up with: Stay at the same level as someone or something
90. Kick off: Begin, start

91. Leave out: Omit, not mention
92. Let down: Disappoint
93. Look after: Take care of
94. Look ahead: Think of the future
95. Look down on: Consider as inferior
96. Look on: Be a spectator at an event
97. Look for: Try to find something
98. Look forward to: Await or anticipate with pleasure
99. Look up to: Admire
100. Make fun of: Laugh at/ make jokes about
101. Make up: Invent (excuse, story)
102. Mix up: Mistake one thing or person for another
103. Move in: Arrive in a new home or office
104. Move out: Leave your home/office for another one.
105. Nod off: Fall asleep
106. Note down: Write something
107. Opt out: Leave a system or decide not to participate
108. Own up: Admit or confess something
109. Pass away: Die
110. Pass out: Faint
111. Pay back: Reimburse
112. Put off: Postpone, arrange at a later date
113. Put on: Turn on, switch on
114. Put out: Extinguish
115. Put up: Accommodate, give somebody a bed
116. Pick up: Collect somebody
117. Point out: Indicate/direct attention to something
118. Rely on: Count on, depend on, trust
119. Rule out: Eliminate
120. Run away: Escape from a place or suddenly leave
121. Run into: Meet by accident or unexpectedly (also: bump into)
122. Run out of: Have no more of something.
123. Set off: Start a journey
124. Set up: Start a business
125. Shop around: Compare prices
126. Show off: Brag or want to be admired
127. Show up: Appear/arrive
128. Stick up for: Defend
129. Take after: Resemble, in appearance or character

130. Take care of: Look after
131. Take off: Leave the ground
132. Take on: Hire or engage staff
133. Tell off: Reprimand/criticize severely
134. Think over: Consider
135. Try on: Wear something to see if it suits or fits
136. Turn down: Refuse
137. Use up: Finish a product (so that there's none left)
138. Vouch for: Express confidence in, or guarantee something
139. Watch out: Be careful
140. Wear out: (1) Become unusable (2) Become very tired
141. Work out: (1) Do physical exercise (2) Find a solution or calculate something
142. Wipe off: Clean (board, table)

## REVIEW YOUR LEARNING

1. Discuss the characteristics of standard English.
2. Define mood. Give examples.
3. What is meant by positive language. Give some examples of positive and negative expressions.
4. Discuss the effectiveness of active voice in making the main message clear and focused. Give some examples.
5. Explain the phrase 'Dangling Modifier'. Show how it causes difficulty in understanding the correct meaning of a sentence.
6. What is meant by the rule of concord? Discuss.
7. Differentiate between a clause and sentences of different kinds.
8. Which is the most commonly used and misused punctuation mark? Why?

## REFLECT ON YOUR LEARNING

In the following sentences, point out the error in simple terms, e.g., meaning not clear, spelling mistake, grammatical error of concord, change of tense, incorrect punctuation mark or any other kind of error. Also, rewrite them correctly.

1. It's important to keep improving your reading skills.
2. He is one of the professors who is teaching communication.
3. For sale, 2011 Mercedes as new, lovingly maintained by a senior army officer with two litre engine.
4. There is a ten minute interval between each act of the play.
5. She says she was too busy to go to the airport last night.
6. Neither the director nor the deputy director are present.
7. Divided into two sections, the department she teaches the students more effectively.
8. Between you and I, Rita is not as popular as she thinks she is.
9. The chief guests lecture was so long, its actual message was completely lost.
10. Having eaten our lunch, the train departed.

## ENDNOTE

1. Muriel Harris, *Guide to Grammar and Usage* (New Jersey: Prentice Hall, 2002).

# Index